T0212211

More information about this series at http://www.springer.com/series/7412

Lecture Notes in Computer Science 11994

Joel Janek Dabrowski · Ashfaqur Rahman ·
Manoranjan Paul (Eds.)

Image and Video Technology

PSIVT 2019 International Workshops
Sydney, NSW, Australia, November 18–22, 2019
Revised Selected Papers

 Springer

Editors
Joel Janek Dabrowski
CSIRO
St. Lucia, QLD, Australia

Ashfaqur Rahman
CSIRO
Sandy Bay, TAS, Australia

Manoranjan Paul
Charles Sturt University
Bathurst, NSW, Australia

ISSN 0302-9743   ISSN 1611-3349   (electronic)
Lecture Notes in Computer Science
ISBN 978-3-030-39769-2   ISBN 978-3-030-39770-8   (eBook)
https://doi.org/10.1007/978-3-030-39770-8

LNCS Sublibrary: SL6 – Image Processing, Computer Vision, Pattern Recognition, and Graphics

This Springer imprint is published by the registered company Springer Nature Switzerland AG
The registered company address is: Gewerbestrasse 11, 6330 Cham, Switzerland

Preface

We welcome you to the 9th Pacific-Rim Symposium on Image and Video Technology (PSIVT 2019) Workshops. PSIVT is a premier level biennial series of symposiums that aim at providing a forum for researchers and practitioners who are involved in, or contributing to, theoretical advances or practical implementations for image and video technology. Following the editions held at Hsinchu, Taiwan (2006), Santiago, Chile (2007), Tokyo, Japan (2009), Gwangju, South Korea (2011), Singapore (2010), Guanajuato, Mexico (2013), Auckland, New Zealand (2015), and Wuhan, China (2017), this year, PSIVT was held in Sydney, Australia, during November 18–22, 2019. The following four workshops were held at PSIVT 2019:

Vision-Tech: A Workshop on Challenges, Technology, and Solutions in the Areas of Computer Vision: vision technology and their applications have evolved significantly over the past decades. Along with new technology and applications, there has been a rise in new challenges. In this workshop, we bring together the new challenges, technology, and potential solutions to those challenges in the areas of computer vision.

Passive and Active Electro-Optical Sensors for Aerial and Space Imaging: advances in the miniaturization, performance, and low cost sensors, has allowed researchers access to camera technology for wide-ranging applications. Developments in sensor fusion and the proliferation of platforms offers researchers opportunities to extend the range of devices available. However, there is still a need to provide quality assurance of sensors, such as calibration, to minimize artefacts and bias in the data received and facilitate high-quality processing. The workshop will focus on new and improved methods, techniques, and applications of (electro-optical) sensors on airborne and space platforms. The aim of this workshop was to bring together engineers and scientists from academia, industry, and government to exchange results and ideas for future applications of electro-optical remote sensing.

International Workshop on Deep Learning and Image Processing Techniques for Medical Images: the recent advancements in deep learning algorithms and image processing techniques have provided a wealth of opportunities in the field of medical image analysis. This workshop aims to gather high quality research papers on novel work and start-of-the-art approaches that advance this field. These include papers that use approaches such as image processing, artificial intelligence, computer vision, traditional machine learning, and deep learning to analyze medical images such as retinal images, ultrasound images, brain images, and breast cancer scans.

International Workshop on Deep Learning for Video and Image Analysis: there has been a surge of opportunities for the development of deep learning algorithms and platforms for advanced vision systems. This has been boosted by the availability of large amounts of visual data (i.e., big data) and high performance computing systems. These systems will reduce the expensive costs associated with elder's health and home care expenses, and enhance competitiveness in agriculture and marine economies.

This workshop aims to gather high quality research papers on state-of-the-art deep learning techniques for video and image analysis.

Over all workshops, a total of 26 papers were received and underwent a full double-blind review process. Of these 26 papers, 16 have been published in this proceedings. Each workshop arranged its own set of reviewers and reviews were conducted independently of other workshops.

We hope that you found the workshops at PSIVT 2019 enjoyable, enlightening, and thought provoking. We hope you had a very memorable PSIVT.

November 2019   Joel Dabrowski
                                                                         Ashfaqur Rahman
                                                                         Manoranjan Paul

PSIVT 2019 Workshops Organization

General Chair

Manoranjan Paul   Charles Sturt University, Australia

General Workshop Chairs

Mark Pickering   University of New South Wales, Australia
Yanyan Xu   Massachusetts Institute of Technology, USA
Anwaar Ulhaq   Charles Sturt University, Australia
D. M. Motiur Rahaman   Charles Sturt University, Australia

Proceeding Chairs

Joel Dabrowski   CSIRO, Australia
Ashfaqur Rahman   CSIRO, Australia

International Workshop on Deep Learning for Video and Image Analysis

Organizers

Syed Afaq Shah   Murdoch University, Australia
Abdul Bais   Univesity of Regina, Canada
Fady Al-Najjar   United Arab Emirates University, UAE
Touseef Ahmed Qureshi   Cedars-Sinai Medical Center, USA

Program Committee

Debiao Li   UCLA, USA
Sofiane Yous   Intel Corporation, Ireland
Usman Qayyum   NESCOM, Pakistan
Hossein Rahmani   Lancaster University, UK
Hasan Firdaus   IIU, Malaysia
Syed Zulqarnain Gilani   ECU, Australia
Naveed Mufti   UET Mardan, Pakistan
Muhammad Farooq   Phyn, USA
Muhammad Asif Manzoor   University of Regina, Canada
Munkhjargal Gochoo   UAE University, UAE
Tariq Bashir   COMSATS University Islamabad, Pakistan
Muhammad Sarfraz   Kuwait University, Kuwait
Ali Mahmood   KPK EZDM, Pakistan
Adel Al-Jumaily   University of Technology Sydney, Australia

Nor Shahida	PSU, Saudi Arabia
Omar Mubin	Western Sydney University, Australia
Rehan Ullah Khan	Qassim University, Saudi Arabia
Abdullah Al Mahmud	Swinburne University of Technology, Australia
Hany Alashwal	UAE University, UAE
Ghulam Mubashar Hassan	UWA, Australia
Zia Ur Rehman	JCU, Australia
Asif Khan	20face Enschede, The Netherlands
Muhammad Uzair	UniSA, Australia
Ammar Mahmood	AES, Australia
Habib Ullah	University of Hail, Saudi Arabia
Monji Kheralla	University of Sfax, Tunisia
Hamidah Ibrahim	UPM, Malaysia
Avinash Sharma	MMU, India
El-Kaber Hachem	MIU, Morocco

Passive and Active Electro-Optical Sensors for Aerial and Space Imaging

Organizers

Ralf Reulke	Humboldt-Universität zu Berlin, Germany
Petra Helmholz	Curtin University and Western Australian School of Mines, Australia

Program Committee

Bin Luo	Wuhan University, China
Byron Smiley	Planet Labs, USA
Andreas Brunn	Planet Labs, USA
Andreas Eckardt	DLR Berlin Adlershof, Germany
Clive Fraser	University of Melbourne, Australia
Norbert Haala	University of Stuttgart, Germany
Peter Reinartz	DLR Oberpfaffenhofen, Germany
Mark R. Shortis	RMIT Melbourne, Australia
Ruediger Hohn	Airbus DS, Germany
Dominik Rueß	HU-Berlin, Germany
Jens Kremer	IGImbH Kreuztal, Germany
Uwe Sörgel	University of Stuttgart, Germany
Jakub Kolecki	AGH University Kracow, Poland
Christian Fischer	DLR Berlin Adlershof, Germany
Heinz-Wilhelm Hübers	DLR Berlin Adlershof, Germany
Petra Helmholz	Curtin University, Australia
Krzysztof Bakuła	Warsaw University of Technology, Poland

Vision-Tech: A Workshop on Challenges, Technology, and Solutions in the Areas of Computer Vision

Organizers

Subrata Chakraborty	University of Technology Sydney, Australia
Tanmoy Debnath	Charles Sturt University, Australia
Gnana Bharathy	University of Technology Sydney, Australia
Pallab K. Podder	Pabna University of Science and Technology, Bangladesh
D. M. Motiur Rahman	Charles Sturt University, Australia

Program Committee

Mohammad Zavid Parvez	Brac University, Bangladesh
Arash Mahboubi	Charles Sturt University, Australia
Ken Eustace	Charles Sturt University, Australia
Abdul Hafeez-Baig	USQ, Australia
Sophie Cockcroft	USQ, Australia
K. C. Chan	USQ, Australia
Ashek Ahmmed	Charles Sturt University, Australia
Mustafa Ally	USQ, Australia
Juan Castilla Rho	UTS, Australia
Toufique Soomro	Quaid-e-Awam Engineering, Science and Technology, Pakistan
Prema Sankaran	FIREBIRD INSTITUTE OF RESEARCH IN MANAGEMENT, India
Nader H. Aldeeb	Technische Universität Berlin, Germany
Munsif Jatoi	Universiti Teknologi PETRONAS, Malaysia
Olaf Hellwich	Technische Universität Berlin, Germany
Gulsher Ali Baloch	Sukkur IBA University, Pakistan

International Workshop on Deep Learning and Image Processing Techniques for Medical Images

Organizers

Toufique Ahmed Soomro	Charles Sturt University, Australia, and Quaid-e-Awam Engineering, Science and Technology, Pakistan
Junbin Gao	The University of Sydney, Australia
Manoranjan Paul	Charles Sturt University, Australia
Lihong Zheng	Charles Sturt University, Australia

Program Committee

Tariq M. Khan	COMSATS University Islamabad and IIT, Pakistan
Mohammad A. U. Khan	Effat University Jeddah, Saudi Arabi
Ahmed J. Afifi	Technische Universität Berlin, Germany

Shafiullah Soomro	Chung-Ang University, South Korea
Ahmed Ali Shah	Sukkur IBA University, Pakistan
Ming Yin	Guangdong University of Technology, China
Safeeullah Soomro	AMA International University, Bahrain
Norashikin Yahya	Universiti Teknologi PETRONAS, Malaysia
Ibrahima Faye	Universiti Teknologi PETRONAS, Malaysia
Ahmed Ali Shah	Sukkur IBA University, Pakistan
Faezeh Karimi	UTS, Australia
Kaveh Khalilpour	UTS, Australia
Nagesh Shukla	UTS, Australia
Osama Sohaib	UTS, Australia
Ravindra Bagia	UTS, Australia
Prema Sankaran	FIREBIRD INSTITUTE OF RESEARCH IN MANAGEMENT, India

Contents

International Workshop on Deep Learning for Video and Image Analysis

Vision-Tech: A Workshop on Challenges, Technology, and Solutions in the Areas of Computer Vision

Rain Streak Removal with Well-Recovered Moving Objects from Video Sequences Using Photometric Correlation

Muhammad Rafiqul Islam$^{(\boxtimes)}$ ⓘ, Manoranjan Paul ⓘ, and Michael Antolovich ⓘ

School of Computing and Mathematics, Charles Sturt University, Bathurst, NSW, Australia
{muislam,mpaul,mantolovich}@csu.edu.au

Abstract. The main challenge in a rain removal algorithm is to differentiate rain streak from moving objects. This paper addresses this problem using the spatiotemporal appearance technique (STA). Although the STA-based technique can significantly remove rain from video, in some cases it cannot properly retain all the moving object regions. The photometric feature of rain streak was used to solve this issue. In this paper, a new algorithm combining STA and the photometric correlation between rain streak and background is proposed. Rain streak and moving objects were successfully detected and separated by combining both techniques, then fused to obtain well-recovered moving objects with rain-free video. The experimental results reveal that the proposed algorithm significantly outperforms the state-of-the-art methods for both real and synthetic rain streak.

Keywords: Rain removal · Photometric correlation · Spatiotemporal appearance · Video cleaning

1 Introduction

In an outdoor computer vision system like a surveillance video system, several atmospheric interferences such as rain streak, snow, etc. affect the video contents and features[1, 2]. In challenging weather, these unwanted interferences degrade the performance of video content analysis (VCA) algorithm such as scene analysis [3], event detection [4], object detection [5] and tracking [6] of various computer vision system [7]. Rain streak removal in the video (RSRV) has lots of importance in several computer vision applications i.e. driverless car, surveillance camera, traffic surveillance, and other relevant applications.

The RSRV has recently got lots of attention in the computer vision research area due to its new challenging applications. Various numeric methods have been proposed to remove rain streaks in a video sequence to increase the visibility of video content [8–10]. Garg *et al.* [8] initially introduced to an RSRV technique with a comprehensive analysis of the visual characteristic of the rain streak in a video sequence. Since then many techniques have been proposed for the RSRV tasks and achieved good results in various rain conditions. An extensive summarization of video-based rain streak removal is included in [9]. Chen *et al.* [10] have been proposed an RSRV technique for the highly

© Springer Nature Switzerland AG 2020
J. J. Dabrowski et al. (Eds.): PSIVT 2019 Workshops, LNCS 11994, pp. 3–13, 2020.
https://doi.org/10.1007/978-3-030-39770-8_1

dynamic scenes. Considering the directional properties of rain streak, a tensor-based rain streak removal method has been proposed in [11]. In Wei *et al.* [12], authors have modelled the rain streak stochastically using a mixture of Gaussian technique while Li *et al.* [13] proposed multiscale convolutional filters to separate different size of rain streaks.

In recent time, a technique using spatiotemporal appearance (STA) properties of rain streak has been proposed to remove rain streak in a video sequence [14]. The method counts moving objects including rain appearances at the pixel level for a number of frames and assumes that if the counts of the appearance of moving objects are within a mid-range then the pixel is identified as a rain pixel, otherwise, the pixel is identified as a background or foreground object (not rain). Normally, the pixel is a part of the background if the count is zero or the pixel is a part of the foreground object if the count is very high. This method is very successful to remove rain streak but it loses some parts of the moving object especially the short appearance part of the foreground. In this technique, authors have assumed that the appearance of moving object in a pixel exists for several frames. Sometimes, the appearance of moving objects in some pixels exists for a very short time only e.g. one or two frames and these pixels are excluded by the STA technique as a moving object. Figure 1(a) shows the generated mask of frame 72 of a video sequence "Traffic" by applying the STA properties of the rain streak. In this figure, the yellow marked pixels of moving object are missed by this method. The appearance of moving objects in these pixels exist for current few frames only. The corresponding original frame is given in Fig. 1(b).

(a) Moving objects mask for the 72nd frame   (b) The original 72nd frame of the
       of the video sequence "Traffic"   video sequence "Traffic"

Fig. 1. Moving objects mask generated by STA and Photometric Correlation

In this paper, we address this problem and proposed a new method which uses the photometric correlation properties of rain streak in a video sequence. Photometric features already introduced in Garg *et al.* [8], based on their observation that a rain streak appears brighter than the background they have been proposed two photometric constraints. Here they consider the background as stationary, the candidate pixels which may include a rain streak should comply with the equation below

$$\Delta I = I_n - I_{n-1} = I_n - I_{n+1} > c, c = 3 \tag{1}$$

where I_n is the current frame image, I_{n-1} and I_{n+1} are the adjacent previous and next frame respectively. C is a threshold which indicates the minimum intensity change due to rain streak. In Eq. (1) authours have used a future frame, that is not possible for real-time application. The second photometric constraint proposed in Garg $et\ al.$ [8] is

$$\Delta I = -\beta I_b + \alpha,\ \beta = \frac{\tau}{T},\ \alpha = \tau \overline{E}_d \tag{2}$$

where authors consider $I_b = I_{n-1}$, and photometric constraint β is calculated as $(0 < \beta < 0.039)$. Since the maximum value of $\alpha = 3.5 \times 10^{-3}$, where $\overline{E}_d$ is the average irradiance. β involved with camera exposure time T and time τ that a drop projects onto a pixel. τ depends on the physical properties of the rain. τ can vary with the various size of rain streak. The range of τ obtained as $0 < \tau < 1.18$. Camera exposure time T also can vary in different video sequence captured by a different camera. In this paper, we propose a novel algorithm by combining the STA properties of rain streak and the photometric correlation of rain streak with the background to improve the recovered moving objects in rain-free videos.

We have applied the proposed algorithm on four different video sequences including real and synthetic rain streak to observe the performance and compare them with the state-of-the-art methods. The overall performance of the proposed algorithm is significantly better than the state-of-the-art methods for both real and synthetic rain streaks.

2 Proposed Method

This section will describe the details of the proposed methodology. We divide our methodology into four sections and describe separately. This method has been proposed by combining the photometric features of rain streak with the STA property of rain streak. In this method, firstly we have applied background modelling to separate background and foreground including the rain of a video frame. The STA properties of rain streak are used to separate moving objects and rain streaks from the foreground of the video frame. In parallel, we have applied the photometric correlation of rain streak to separate the moving objects and rain streaks from the rainy frame. Then, we have fused the output results of both different features of the rain streak and generated a rain-free frame of the video sequence.

2.1 GMM Background Modelling and Foreground Generation

GMM is a well-known algorithm in the field of computer vision. We use this algorithm to generate the background of every frame and subtract the background to find the foreground of the frame. Generally, the GMM technique is used in video processing to detect moving objects. Here, all moving substances (including rain streak) in a video has been considered as moving objects and separated from the frame to generate background. In this technique, each pixel is modelled independently by a mixture of K Gaussian distributions (usual setting $K = 3$) [15, 16]. In our proposed technique, we assume that at time t, the value of kth Gaussian intensity $= \eta_{k,t}$, mean $= \mu_{k,t}$, variance $= \sigma_{k,t}^2$, and weight in the mixture $= \omega_{k,t}$, so that $\sum_{k=1}^{K} \omega_{k,t} = 1$. In the first step of our experiment, the parameters are initialized as follows: standard deviation $(\sigma_k) = 2.5$, weight $(\omega_k) = 0.001$ and learning rate, $\alpha = 0.1$. α is used for balancing the contribution between current and previous values and the value is $0 < \alpha < 1$ [17].

In the second step, after initializing the parameters, the current pixels are used to match with k^{th} Gaussian for every new observation if the condition $|X_t - \mu_{k,t}| \leq 2.5\sigma_{k,t}$ is satisfied against existing models, where X_t is the new pixel intensity at time t. If a model matches, the Gaussian model will be updated as follows:

$$\mu_{k,t} \leftarrow (1 - \alpha)\mu_{k,t-1} + \alpha X_t \tag{3}$$

$$\sigma_{k,t}^2 \leftarrow (1 - \alpha)\sigma_{k,t-1}^2 + \alpha(X_t - \mu_{k,t})^T(X_t - \mu_{k,t}); \tag{4}$$

$$\omega_{k,t} \leftarrow (1 - \alpha)\omega_{k,t-1} + \alpha, \tag{5}$$

and the weights of other Gaussians models are updated as

$$\omega_{k,t} \leftarrow (1 - \alpha)\omega_{k,t-1} \tag{6}$$

In the third step, the values of weights are normalized among all models in such a way that $\sum_{k=1}^{K} \omega_{k,t} = 1$. On the other hand, if a model fails to match, then a new model is introduced with initial parameter values. If it has already crossed the maximum allowable number of models, based on the value of weight/standard deviation, a new model substitutes the existing model. At each frame, we generate a background frame using the mean value of the stable model. The model is considered stable if the ratio of weight and the standard deviation is the minimum compared to other models of the pixel. We use the background frame to find rain streak and other foregrounds and as well to generate the rain-free video in the proposed method.

Initially, we have generated foreground by subtracting the background from the input frame,

$$F_n = |I_n - B| \tag{7}$$

where F is foreground image of the nth frame and I is the original image of the nth frame. This image contains rain streak and moving objects.

2.2 STA Properties of Rain

The rain streak appearance is temporary in a frame. This temporary appearance property has been used to separate rain streak and moving objects from the foreground in [14]. To apply this property, authors first apply an intensity threshold 20 [15, 18, 19] to generate a binary image of foreground contains rain streak and moving objects. To separate rain streak and moving objects, a mask has been generated using STA properties of rain streak.

$$M_n = \sum_{i=n}^{n-m} F_i; (i = n, n-1, n-2, \ldots n-m) \tag{8}$$

Where M is the mask for n^{th} frame generated by summing the binary foreground images F of m number adjacent frame. The mask contains value 0 to m for every pixel and this value represents the appearance value of moving objects and rain in a pixel. If an appearance value in a pixel is more than 20% of the maximum value m, this pixel is considered as moving object. Using this phenomenon, moving objects and rain streak can be separated in a frame.

2.3 Photometric Correlation

The rain streaks produce a positive fluctuation of the intensities in the pixels of a frame. The rain streak intensity depends on the brightness of the drop as well as the background scene radiance [8]. The fluctuation of positive intensity for rain streaks is not very high, because the rain streak intensity includes the background radiance. On the other hand, the moving object intensity does not depend on the background radiance. Thus, the moving objects can produce a high-intensity fluctuation in the pixels of a frame. Here we have applied this different photometric property of the rain streak and moving objects to separate them. We observe that moving objects produce intensity fluctuation significantly high in most of the scenario. Here we used an intensity correlation for each pixel which is obtained between background B and separated foreground F.

$$\gamma = \frac{F(i, j)}{B(i, j)} \tag{9}$$

Where γ is photometric correlation constraint. The candidate pixels which may contain the moving objects should comply with the condition $\gamma > 1$. Otherwise, it will consider as rain streak or background.

2.4 Rain Free Video Generation

Here we have fused the output of both features and generate an object mask for the processing frame. To generate rain-free video we have used a background image and input image of the processing frame. The moving objects have been generated from the input image and the other part of the frame have been generated from the background image of the processing frame.

3 Experimental Results

We have applied the proposed algorithm on four different video sequences including two synthetic rain streak and two real rain streak. For synthetic rain streak dataset, we have compared results in objectively and subjectively as ground truth is known in these cases while the results of the real rain streak datasets have been compared in subjectively only. Here we have compared the performance of the proposed method with two other methods [12, 14]. We have obtained the results of these methods by implementing their software on the datasets. The software of Wei *et al.* [12] has been downloaded from their website [20] whereas we have collected the software of [14] by personal communication.

3.1 Results on Videos with Synthetic Rain Streaks

To evaluate the performance of the proposed method on video sequences with synthetic rain streak, we have used two video sequences with heavy rain and dense rain respectively. The first video sequence named "truck" has been downloaded from CDNET dataset [21] which contains a moving truck and externally added heavy rain streak. Figure 2 shows the visual performance comparison of the state-of-the-art methods with the proposed method in one of the important frame (Frame 65) of the video sequence. In Fig. 2, the red circle indicates the rain streak removal performance by all methods respectively. The proposed method outperforms Wei *et al's* method [12] whereas the method in [14] performs better than the proposed method by a small number of rain streaks. However, the method in [14] losses more part of the moving object than the proposed method. The rectangle indicates the loss of moving objects in the frame.

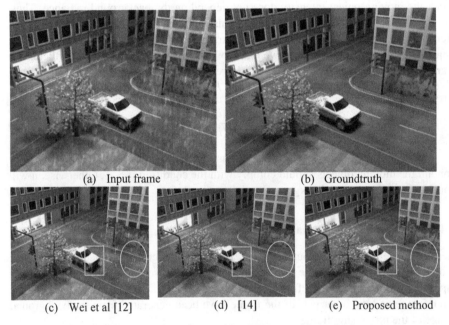

(a) Input frame   (b) Groundtruth

(c) Wei et al [12]   (d) [14]   (e) Proposed method

Fig. 2. Rain removal results on video sequence with synthetic rain.

Figure 3 shows the performance comparison in objectively. The calculated PSNR value of every frame of the video sequence "truck" for all methods are shown in the graph. The PSNR graph in Fig. 3 shows that Wei *et al.* [12] perform better than the proposed method for the first few frames. The proposed method outperforms all other methods after the first 30 frames. The proposed algorithm processes input video frames as it comes in, typically without storing input frames of the video and the learning process is also real-time. Thus, the proposed algorithm needs the first few frames to learn and then delivers a better result for the rest. That is the main reason why the proposed method struggles for the first few frames. The advantage of this algorithm is that it can serve in a real-time application with the consideration of required processing time.

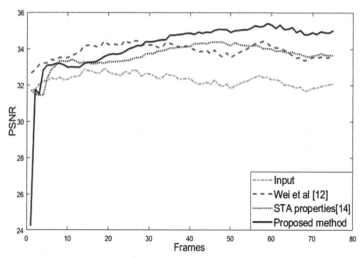

Fig. 3. Comparison graph of PSNR calculated against ground truth of full video sequence with synthetic rain streak in frame level.

Fig. 4. Rain removal results on video sequence with synthetic rain.

Figure 4 shows the subjective performance comparison of the state-of-the-art methods with the proposed method for the video sequence "Highway". This video sequence includes a moving car and externally added dense rain streaks. The proposed method shows better performance in subjective comparison. The circle indicates the rain streaks those are removed by the proposed method and [14] but missed by Wei *et al's* method

[12]. The rectangle marked area shows the distortion of moving objects by the RSRV process. The method in [14] provides the maximum distortion of the moving objects.

The objective performance of the synthetic video sequence is listed in Table 1. Table 1 represents the PSNR and SSIM value of the frame that is shown in Figs. 2 and 4 for visual comparison. Thus, we can evaluate the methods in terms of objective and subjective in the same manner. For the frame shown in Fig. 2, the proposed method outperforms the state-of-the-art method. On Fig. 4, the method in [14] and the proposed method shows almost the same PSNR value which is higher than Wei *et al.* [12]. In terms of SSIM, the proposed method outperform all the state-of-the-art methods.

Table 1. Performance comparison of the different methods on video with synthetic rain in terms of PSNR and SSIM against ground truth

	Fig. 2		Fig. 4	
	PSNR	SSIM	PSNR	SSIM
Original Input frames with rain	31.94	0.8845	27.09	0.9257
Wei et al. [12]	33.65	0.9265	26.96	0.9481
STA Properties [14]	33.83	0.9381	**28.40**	0.9542
Proposed Method	**35.18**	**0.9523**	**28.40**	**0.9557**

3.2 Results on Videos with Natural Rain Streaks

To observe the performance on a video sequence with natural rain streaks, we show the experiments on two different video sequences. One of them includes moving objects and the other does not have any moving object. The rain streaks are varied from moderate to dense in these different video sequences.

In Fig. 5, we represent the experimental results of the video sequence denoted as 'traffic' [22] by implementing both methods. Input video includes two moving objects, one moving car and one pedestrian with dense rain. The subjective comparison of the proposed method shows better performance compared to the state-of-the-art methods. The proposed method outperforms Wei *et al.* [12] and [14] by removing rain streak and maintaining moving objects in a better way.

Figure 6 clearly shows the performance comparison of all methods on the video sequence denoted as 'wall' [22] of size $288 \times 368 \times 171$ in terms of subject quality. The video sequence 'wall' consists of a regular pattern in the background. The input frame represents moderate rain streaks. The proposed method and [14] both outperform Wei *et al.*'s method [12] for almost complete rain streak removal.

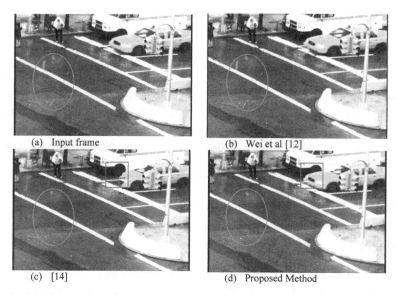

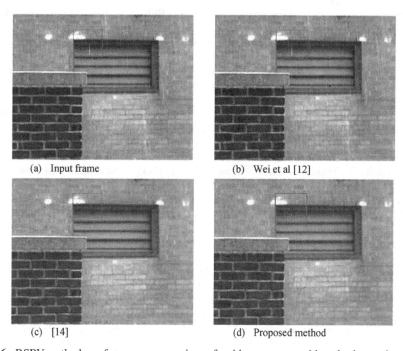

Fig. 5. RSRV methods performance comparison of a video sequence with real rain streaks.

Fig. 6. RSRV methods performance comparison of a video sequence with real rain streaks where no moving objects exist.

4 Conclusion

This paper proposed a new algorithm combining STA properties of rain streak and photometric features to remove rain streak in videos. This method uses photometric correlation of rain streak with background intensity as a photometric feature. This method can separate moving objects and rain streak from the foreground of the video frame. This method successfully exploits the duration trend of the rain and the moving objects through the STA features and the amount of pixel intensity variations of the rain and moving objects and then combines them to separate rain and other moving regions for better performance. The results on real and synthetic rains in videos reveal that the proposed method outperforms the state-of-the-art methods by removing rain and keeping other moving objects in better quality. In future, we will investigate a wider range of moving objects and rains.

References

1. Li, Y., Tan, R.T., Guo, X., Lu, J., Brown, M.S.: Rain streak removal using layer priors. In: Proceedings of the IEEE Conference on Computer Vision and Pattern Recognition, pp. 2736–2744 (2016)
2. Liu, R., Fan, X., Hou, M., Jiang, Z., Luo, Z., Zhang, L.: Learning aggregated transmission propagation networks for haze removal and beyond. IEEE Trans. Neural Netw. Learn. Syst. **99**, 1–14 (2018)
3. Itti, L., Koch, C., Niebur, E.: A model of saliency-based visual attention for rapid scene analysis. IEEE Trans. Pattern Anal. Mach. Intell. **11**, 1254–1259 (1998)
4. Shehata, M.S., et al.: Video-based automatic incident detection for smart roads: The outdoor environmental challenges regarding false alarms. IEEE Trans. Intell. Transp. Syst. **9**(2), 349–360 (2008)
5. Zhang, X., Zhu, C., Wang, S., Liu, Y., Ye, M.: A Bayesian approach to camouflaged moving object detection. IEEE Trans. Circuits Syst. Video Technol. **27**(9), 2001–2013 (2016)
6. Ma, C., Miao, Z., Zhang, X.-P., Li, M.: A saliency prior context model for real-time object tracking. IEEE Trans. Multimedia **19**(11), 2415–2424 (2017)
7. Bouwmans, T.: Traditional and recent approaches in background modeling for foreground detection: an overview. Comput. Sci. Rev. **11**, 31–66 (2014)
8. Garg, K., Nayar, S.K.: Detection and removal of rain from videos. In: Proceedings of the 2004 IEEE Computer Society Conference on Computer Vision and Pattern Recognition (CVPR 2004), vol. 1, p. I. IEEE (2004)
9. Tripathi, A.K., Mukhopadhyay, S.: Removal of rain from videos: a review. SIViP **8**(8), 1421–1430 (2014)
10. Chen, J., Chau, L.-P.: A rain pixel recovery algorithm for videos with highly dynamic scenes. IEEE Trans. Image Process. **23**(3), 1097–1104 (2013)
11. Jiang, T.-X., Huang, T.-Z., Zhao, X.-L., Deng, L.-J., Wang, Y.: A novel tensor-based video rain streaks removal approach via utilizing discriminatively intrinsic priors. In: Proceedings of the IEEE Conference on Computer Vision and Pattern Recognition, pp. 4057–4066 (2017)
12. Wei, W., Yi, L., Xie, Q., Zhao, Q., Meng, D., Xu, Z.: Should we encode rain streaks in video as deterministic or stochastic?. In: Proceedings of the IEEE International Conference on Computer Vision, pp. 2516–2525 (2017)
13. Li, M.:et al.: Video rain streak removal by multiscale convolutional sparse coding. In: Proceedings of the IEEE Conference on Computer Vision and Pattern Recognition, pp. 6644–6653 (2018)

14. Islam, M.R., Paul, M.: Rain streak removal from video sequence using spatiotemporal appearance. In: International Conference on Digital Image Computing: Techniques and Applications (DICTA), pp. 1–7. IEEE (2019)

15. Haque, M., Murshed, M., Paul, M.: Improved Gaussian mixtures for robust object detection by adaptive multi-background generation. In: 2008 19th International Conference on Pattern Recognition, pp. 1–4. IEEE (2008)

16. Lee, D.-S.: Effective Gaussian mixture learning for video background subtraction. IEEE Trans. Pattern Anal. Mach. Intell. **5**, 827–832 (2005)

17. Rahaman, D.M., Paul, M.: Virtual view synthesis for free viewpoint video and multiview video compression using Gaussian mixture modelling. IEEE Trans. Image Process. **27**(3), 1190–1201 (2017)

18. Haque, M., Murshed, M., Paul, M.: A hybrid object detection technique from dynamic background using Gaussian mixture models. In: 2008 IEEE 10th Workshop on Multimedia Signal Processing, pp. 915–920. IEEE (2008)

19. Haque, M., Murshed, M. Paul, M.: On stable dynamic background generation technique using Gaussian mixture models for robust object detection. In: 2008 IEEE Fifth International Conference on Advanced Video and Signal Based Surveillance, pp. 41–48. IEEE (2008)

20. (10 May, 2019). Available: https://github.com/wwzjer/RainRemoval_ICCV2017

21. Goyette, N., Jodoin, P.-M., Porikli, F., Konrad, J., Ishwar, P.: Changedetection. net: a new change detection benchmark dataset. In: 2012 IEEE Computer Society Conference on Computer Vision and Pattern Recognition Workshops, pp. 1–8. IEEE (2012)

22. (10 May, 2019). Available: http://www.cs.columbia.edu/CAVE/projects/camerarain/

Face Analysis: State of the Art and Ethical Challenges

Domingo Mery[✉]

Department of Computer Science, Pontificia Universidad Catolica de Chile,
Santiago, Chile
domingo.mery@uc.cl
http://domingomery.ing.uc.cl

Abstract. In face analysis, the task is to identify a subject appearing in an image as a unique individual and to extract facial attributes like age, gender, and expressions from the face image. Over the last years, we have witnessed tremendous improvements in face analysis algorithms developed by the industry and by academia as well. Some applications, that might have been considered science fiction in the past, have become reality now. We can observe that nowadays tools are far from perfect, however, they can deal with very challenging images such as pictures taken in an unconstrained environment. In this paper, we show how easy is to build very effective applications with open source tools. For instance, it is possible to analyze the facial expressions of a public figure and his/her interactions in the last 24 h by processing images from Twitter given a hashtag. Obviously, the same analysis can be performed using images from a surveillance camera or from a family photo album. The recognition rate is now comparable to human vision, but computer vision can process thousands of images in a couple of hours. For these applications, it is not necessary to train complex deep learning networks, because they are already trained and available in public repositories. In our work, we show that anyone with certain computer skills can use (or misuse) this technology. The increased performance of facial analysis and its easy implementation have enormous potential for good, and –unfortunately– for ill too. For these reasons, we believe that our community should discuss the scope and limitations of this technology in terms of ethical issues such as definition of good practices, standards, and restrictions when using and teaching facial analysis.

Keywords: Face analysis · Social networks · Social and ethical challenges

1 Introduction

Nowadays, it is very easy to download thousands of images from social networks and build a database with information extracted from all faces that are present in the images as illustrated in Fig. 1. Thus, we can build a relational database of

J. J. Dabrowski et al. (Eds.): PSIVT 2019 Workshops, LNCS 11994, pp. 14–29, 2020.
https://doi.org/10.1007/978-3-030-39770-8_2

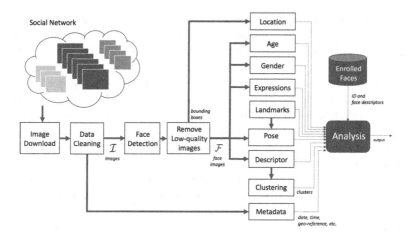

Fig. 1. Proposed approach for facial analysis in social networks.

the images with their faces and facial attributes. In this database, we can store for all detected faces: the bounding box, size, quality, location, age, gender, expressions, landmarks, pose, face descriptor and face cluster. With a simple query on this database, we can retrieve very useful and accurate information. Having this powerful database and a query image of a person, for example from a woman called Emily, some questions could naturally arise:

1. Is it possible to find Emily in the majority of the images (even in unconstrained environments with different poses, expressions and some degree of occlusion)?
2. Is it possible to extract the age, gender and facial expressions of Emily?
3. Using metadata of the pictures of the database, is it possible to establish when and where Emily was present (or absent)?
4. Is it possible to analyze the gender, age, and expressions of James and Louise that appears in the same picture with Emily?
5. Is it possible to search in the whole database those pictures in which Emily appears with other persons and select the person that most frequently co-occurred with Emily? And can we add a constraint to this person (it must be a man, or a woman, or a boy, or a girl, etc.)?
6. Is it possible to use the head poses of Emily and Gabriel (present in the same picture) and find if they are looking to each other?
7. Is it possible to build a graph of connections of Emily with other subjects that co-occurred in the pictures of the database?
8. Is it possible to determine from the face of James if he is criminal? or part of the LGTBQ community?

This is the wrong paper, if the reader is looking for the answer of the last question[1], however, for the remaining questions (#1 to #7), the answer is: yes, it

---

[1] We hope that our community will not research on fields related to question #8.

is possible. Over the last decade, the focus of face recognition algorithms shifted to deal with unconstrained conditions. In recent years, we have witnessed tremendous improvements in face recognition by using complex deep neural network architectures trained with millions of face images (see for example advances in face recognition [4,9,13] and in face detection [19,21]), and in many cases, algorithms are better at recognizing faces than human beings. In addition, there are very impressive advances in face clustering [12,18], and in the recognition of age [16], gender [20], (FER) facial expressions [2] and facial landmarks [23].

In this field, many works deal with applications that can be developed using the face analysis tools. Here, some examples, just to cite a few. In [15], social networks are built by detecting and tracking faces in news videos, the idea is to establish how much and with whom a politician appears on TV news. In [3], for example, facial behavior analysis is presented. The method can extract expressions and action units (facial movements such as 'inner portion of the brows is raised' or 'lips are relaxed and closed'), that could be used to build interactive applications. In [22], 'social relations' (defined as the association like warm, friendliness and dominance, between two or more persons) are detected in face images in the wild. In [7], face-based group-level emotion recognition is proposed to study the behavior of people participating in social events. Similar advances have been made in video analysis using the information of the location and actions of people in videos. See for example [6], where a 'context aware' configuration model is proposed for detecting groups of persons and their interactions (*e.g.*, handshake, hug, etc.) in TV material. Nowadays, some applications, that might have been considered science fiction in the past, have become reality now. Nevertheless, it is worthwhile to note that we are able to develop applications for a 'good cause' (*e.g.*, personal applications like searching the happiest faces in a family photo album; applications for history research like searching people in old archives of pictures; forensic applications like detection of pornographic material with children, etc.) and applications for a 'bad cause' (*e.g.*, security applications that collect privacy-sensitive information about the persons that appears in a surveillance video) as well.

In this paper, our main contribution is to show that anyone with certain computer skills can use (or misuse) this technology. The open-source tools are available on public repositories, and it is not necessary to train complex deep learning networks, because they are already trained. We will show that the state of the art is able now to do very accurate facial analysis in very complex scenarios (like mentioned in the first seven questions) with outstanding results as shown in Figs. 3, 4, 5, 6, 7, 8, 9. We believe that these two results, accurate and easy implementation of facial analysis, should challenge us to discuss possible restrictions and good practices. For this reason, in this paper, we give some ethical principles that can be considered when using this technology.

2 Open Source Tools

2.1 Tools for Social Networks

1. Image download: Images from social networks can be downloaded in a very simple way by using Application Program Interfaces (API's) or dedicated software. For example, there are API's for Twitter[2], Instagram[3] and Flickr[4]. For YouTube, there are some websites that offer the download service in an easy way. On the other hand, GitHub is a repository for code and datasets in which the datasets can be downloaded directly.

2. Data cleaning: Data cleaning is very relevant in these kind of problems. In our experiments, it has been mandatory to eliminate duplicated images when dealing with images that have been downloaded from twitter with a common hashtag (because there are many retweeted or copied images). In order to eliminate the duplicate images, we follow a simple strategy with very good results as follows: For a set of K images, $\{\mathbf{I}_k\}$, for $k = 1 \cdots K$, we convert each image $\mathbf{I}_k$ to a grayscale image $\mathbf{Y}_k$ and we resize it to a 64×64-pixel image $\mathbf{Z}_k$ using bicubic interpolation [5]. In addition, the gray values of the resized image is linearly scaled from 0 to 255. The resulting image is converted into a column vector $\mathbf{z}_k$ of $64^2 = 4096$ elements with uni-norm. Thus, we remove from the set of images those duplicated images that have a dot product $\mathbf{z}_i^\mathsf{T}\mathbf{z}_j > 0.999$ for all $i \neq j$. In our experiments, from 1/4 to 1/3 of the images were eliminated because they were duplicated. This method removes efficiently and quickly those duplicated images that have been scaled, however, this method does not remove those rotated or translated images (approx. $1 \sim 2\%$ of the images). In case it is necessary to remove rotated or translated images, a strategy using SIFT points can be used [10].

3. Metadata extraction: Usually, the downloaded images have associated metadata, *e.g.*, date and time of capture, or date and time of the tweet, or GPS information that can be used as geo-reference. In many images, the metadata information is stored in the same image file as EXIF data (Exchangeable Image File Format).

2.2 Computer Vision Tools

1. Face Detection: Face detection identifies faces in an image. In our work, the goal is to detect all faces that are present in an image independent on the expression, pose and size. For this end, we use the method called Multi-task Cascaded Convolutional Networks (MTCNN) [21][5] that has been demonstrated to be very robust in unconstrained environments against poses, illuminations, expressions and occlusions. The output of the face detection function (h) of a

---

[2] https://developer.twitter.com.
[3] https://www.instagram.com/developer/.
[4] https://www.flickr.com/services/api/ or software Bulkr.
[5] https://github.com/kpzhang93/MTCNN_face_detection_alignment.

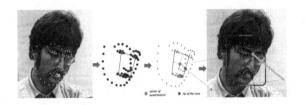

Fig. 2. Landmarks of a face and estimation of its pose vector.

given image $\mathbf{I}$ is bounding box $\mathbf{B}$ which defines a rectangle that contains the face:

$$\{\mathbf{B}_k\}_{k=1}^{N} = h(\mathbf{I}). \tag{1}$$

For N faces detected in image $\mathbf{I}$, we define the founding box $\mathbf{B}_k = (x_1, y_1, x_2, y_2)_k$, where $(x_1, y_1)_k$ are the coordinates of the top-left corner and $(x_2, y_2)_k$ the coordinates of the bottom-right corner of detected face image k. From these coordinates, it is possible to extract face image $\mathbf{F}_k$, *i.e.*, the rectangular window of $\mathbf{I}$ defined by the mentioned two corners.

2. Face Location and size: From the bounding box of the face detected in previous step, it is possible to establish the location and the size of the face image. Typically, the center of mass of the bounding box is used: $\bar{\mathbf{m}}_k = (\bar{x}_k, \bar{y}_k)$, with $\bar{x}_k = (x_1 + x_2)_k/2$ and $\bar{y}_k = (y_1 + y_2)_k/2$. This information can be used to establish the closeness between two faces i and j as $d_{ij} = ||(\mathbf{m}_i - \mathbf{m}_j)||$. In addition, the size of an image can be computed as the geometric mean of the length of the sides of the rectangle: $s_k = \sqrt{(x_2 - x_1)_k(y_2 - y_1)_k}$.

3. Quality: Typically, face images that are smaller than 25×25 pixels, *i.e.*, $s_k < 25$, are not so confident because of the low quality and low resolution. In addition, for the measurement of quality of a face image, we use a score based on the ratio between the high-frequency coefficients and the low-frequency coefficients of the wavelet transform of the image [14]. We call this quality measurement q_k for face image k. Low score values indicate low quality. For this end, we resized all face images to 64×64 pixels before the blurriness score is computed. It is recommended to remove those face images that are too small or too blur.

4. Age, gender, expressions: The age, gender and facial expressions of a person can be estimated from the face image. Many models based on convolutional neural networks have been trained in the last years with promising results. The library py-agender[6] offers very good results for age and gender estimation. The age, given in years, is estimated as a real number and can be stored in variable a_k for face k. On the other hand, the gender is estimated as a real number between 0 and 1 (greater than 0.5 means female, otherwise male). The gender value for face k can be stored in variable g_k. Finally, the facial expressions are

---

[6] https://pypi.org/project/py-agender/.

typically defined as a vector of seven probabilities for the seven main expressions [2]: angry, disgust, scared, happy, sad, surprised, and neutral. Thus, $\mathbf{e}_k$ can be defined as the 7-element vector of expression for face k. It can be established, for example, that if the fourth element of vector $\mathbf{e}_k$ is maximal, then face image k shows a smily face.

5. Face Landmarks: In the same way, using a large dataset of face images with different poses, models have been trained to extract landmarks in a face image. Typically, 68 facial landmarks can be extracted from a face image. They give the coordinates (x, y) of the eyebrows (left and right), eyes (left and right), nose, mouth and jawline. For each of them several salient points are given (see Fig. 2). For this end, we use the library Dlib[7] with very good results. The landmarks of image k are stored in the 68-element vector $\mathbf{l}_k$.

6. Face Pose: We use a simple and fast method to establish the pose of the face given its 68 landmarks as follows (see Fig. 2): we define a quadrilateral with the four corners defined by the center of mass of each eye and the extrema points of the mouth, we compute the center of this quadrilateral and we define the vector that starts at this central points and goes through the point of the tip of the nose. The vector is shifted and located between the eyes. We call this vector $\mathbf{v}_k$ for face image k. The direction of the vector indicates approximately the direction the face is looking to.

7. Face Descriptor: Face recognition by using complex deep neural network architectures trained with millions of face images has achieved a tremendous improvement in the last years. The models have been trained with thousands of identities, and each of them with thousands of face images. The idea is to use these models and extract the descriptor embedded in one of the last layers. These kind of descriptors are very discriminative for faces that have not been used in the training. That means descriptors extracted from face images of same/different subjects are similar/different. Thus, the idea is to extract a descriptor $\mathbf{x}$, a column vector of d elements, for every face image:

$$\mathbf{x}_k = f(\mathbf{F}_k) \tag{2}$$

We use descriptor with uni-norm, *i.e.*, $\|\mathbf{x}_k\| = 1$. In our experiments, we used many trained models (like VGG [13], FaceNet [17], OpenFace [1], Dlib [8] and ArcFace [4]). Our conclusion is that ArcFace, that computes an embedding of $d = 512$ elements, has achieved outstanding results comparing its performance to human vision in many complex scenarios. Thus, we can establish that for face images i and j of the same person the dot product $\mathbf{x}_i^\mathsf{T}\mathbf{x}_j$ is greater than a threshold. For ArcFace, in our experiments we set the threshold to 0.4.

8. Face Clustering: The idea of face clustering is to build subsets (clusters) of faces that belong to the same identity. Typically, face clustering works using a similarity metric of the face descriptors, because face images of the same identity

---

[7] http://dlib.net/face_landmark_detection.py.html.

should have similar face descriptors. Thus, the task is to assign –in an unsupervised way– all similar face faces to one cluster considering that different faces must belong to different clusters. For a set of m face images, in which face image $\mathbf{F}_k$ has a face descriptor $\mathbf{x}_k$ computed by (2), face clustering assigns each descriptor $\mathbf{x}_k$ to a cluster c_k, for $i = 1 \cdots m$. Thus, face images of the same identity have the same cluster number ($e.g.$, if face images 10, 35 and 221 are from the same subject, then $c_{10} = c_{35} = c_{221}$). For this end, we use an agglomerative hierarchical clustering [12]. Since our descriptors has unit norm, we use cosine similarity as metric, the closer to one is the dot product $\mathbf{x}_k^\mathsf{T} \mathbf{x}_j$, the more similar are the faces $\mathbf{F}_k$ and $\mathbf{F}_j$. The algorithms of face clustering is as follows: (i) each face image starts in its own cluster, (ii) we merge cluster i with cluster j if the maximal cosine similarity of all combinations of members of both clusters is maximal for all $i \neq j$ and $i < j$, (iii) last step is repeated until the maximal cosine similarity is below to a threshold.

2.3   Facial Analysis

In this section, we present our proposed facial analysis. We assume that the images have been downloaded from the social network, the duplicated images have been removed and the existing metadata has been stored as explained in Sect. 2.1. Before we perform the analysis, it is necessary to do some preliminary computations as explained in Sect. 2.2 to generate a relational database of two tables, one for the images and one for the faces. For each face image of all images we have following information, bounding box, size, quality, location, age, gender, expressions, landmarks, pose, face descriptor and face cluster.

0. Preliminary Computations: The idea of our approach is to analyze a set $\mathcal{I}$ of n images $\{\mathbf{I}_i\}$, for $i = 1 \cdots n$. The images of set $\mathcal{I}$ should not be duplicated. It is recommended to follow the procedure explained in sub-section 2.1.2 for images downloaded from Twitter to avoid duplicate ones. We detect all faces of $\mathcal{I}$ using function h of (1) explained in sub-section 2.2.1. All detected faces are stored as set $\mathcal{F}$ of m face images $\{\mathbf{F}_k\}$, for $k = 1 \cdots m$. In addition, we store in vector $\mathbf{z}$ of m elements the image index of the detected face image, $i.e.$, $z_k = i$, if face image $\mathbf{F}_k$ was detected in image $\mathbf{I}_i$. Furthermore, the m bounding boxes of the detected faces are stored in matrix $\mathbf{B}$ of $m \times 4$ elements with coordinates $\mathbf{b}_k = (x_1, y_1, x_2, y_2)_k$ for face image k.

After face detection is performed, for each face image k, we compute the size (s_k) and the quality (q_k) as explained in sub-sections 2.2.2 and 2.2.3. It is highly recommended to remove from $\mathcal{F}$ those images that are too small of too blur. Afterwards, we compute for the remaining face images the age (a_k), the gender (g_k), the seven expressions ($\mathbf{e}_k$), the 68 landmarks ($\mathbf{l}_k$), the pose vector ($\mathbf{v}_k$) the face descriptor of d elements ($\mathbf{x}_k$) as explained in sub-sections from 2.2.4 to 2.2.7. It is very useful to define matrix $\mathbf{X}$ as a matrix of $d \times m$ elements (one column per face descriptor), in which column k stores descriptor $\mathbf{x}_k$. Finally, we compute the cluster of each face image (c_k) following the face clustering algorithm explained in sub-section 2.2.8.

1. Search for subjects (recognition): There are two typical ways to search a person in the set of m face images (with m face descriptors stored in matrix $\mathbf{X}$ of $d \times m$ elements). The first one is using an enrolled picture $\mathbf{E}$ and its corresponding descriptor computed by (2) as $\mathbf{x}_e = f(\mathbf{E})$. The second one is using a detected face of the group of images. For instance, we find a face in an image of the set and we want to know where is this person in the rest of images. In this case, we define $\mathbf{x}_e = \mathbf{x}_j$, where j is the number of the detected face in the group, and we delete this face from the gallery by setting column j of $\mathbf{X}$ to zero. There are three main approaches that can be used to find the enrolled person in the images of set $\mathcal{I}$. (a) Similar faces: It is necessary to compute the similarity between 'enrolled image' and 'gallery images' as $\mathbf{y} = \mathbf{X}^{\mathsf{T}}\mathbf{x}_e$. Thus, we find all elements $y_k > \theta$, that means, images $\mathbf{F}_k$, that are located in bounding box $\mathbf{B}_k$ in image $\mathbf{I}_{z_k}$. (b) Clustered face images: using last approach (a), we look for the most similar face image in the gallery as $k = \mathrm{argmax}(y_k)$ and we find all face images that belong to the cluster of face image k, that means the subset of images that have cluster number $c_i = c_k$ for $i = 1 \cdots m$. c) Refine: In addition, we could find those face images that are similar enough to those already selected face images in previous steps (a) or (b). The output is a list $\mathbf{k} = (k_1 \cdots k_p)$ of the indices of p face images that belong to the person being searched.

2. Analysis of expressions: From list $\mathbf{k}$ of face images (that belong to the same person) we could analyze the expression of each face image of the list. There are two simple ways to analyze them: a) Average: we compute the average of the expressions: $\bar{\mathbf{e}} = (\mathbf{e}_{k_1} + \cdots \mathbf{e}_{k_p})/p$. An histogram of $\bar{\mathbf{e}}$ show the distribution of expressions across the p face images. b) Predominant expression: we can define vector $\hat{\mathbf{e}}$, in which the element j of this vector is the ratio of face images of $\mathbf{k}$ that have the expression j maximal. For instance, if we have $p = 20$ face images, and in 5 of them the expression 'happy' (the fourth expression) is maximal, then $\hat{e}_4 = 5/20 = 25\%$. Obviously, we could find the *happiest picture*, by looking for the face image that have the maximal value in the fourth element of vector $\mathbf{e}$.

3. Analysis of age: Similarly to the analysis of expression, we can compute the average of the age, we can select the *oldest* one, or we can sort the face image according to the estimated ages.

4. Co-occurrences: Using the clustering information we could analyze the other faces that are present in the images where the person being searched appears. It is easy to count the number of co-occurrences. For instance, if the person being searched belongs to cluster c_i, it is easy to count the number of images in which faces from cluster c_i and faces from cluster c_j are present. We can find the pair (c_i, c_j) that has the maximal co-occurrence. In our experiments in family albums, this pair corresponds typically to couples. In addition, it is very simple to add some constraints to person c_j in the co-occurrence, for example the gender of c_j must be female or male, or the age must be older or younger than a certain age, or we can select the happiest pictures of persons c_i and c_j. Moreover, we can select co-occurrence pairs of face images that are very close to each other, *e.g.*, $\|\bar{\mathbf{m}}_i - \bar{\mathbf{m}}_j\| < 3(s_i + s_j)/2$, and in order to avoid perspective problem, both face images should have similar size, *e.g.*, $|1 - s_i/s_j| < 0.15$.

5. Connections: We can use the pose information in a picture as follows: if we have a picture with two faces (face i and face j), it is possible to analyze the face poses (vectors $\mathbf{v}_i$ and $\mathbf{v}_i$) by estimating if the intersection of both vectors are between of in front of the faces. The distance of the intersection point to the faces can be used to determine how connected are to each other. In addition, if the vectors are parallel to each other it can be established that both persons are looking at the same direction.

6. Attendance: If we have pictures of the same place in different days, and we have the metadata of the date of the images, it is easy to establish if a person was present across the days. This is very typical in a student attendance system.

3   Experimental Results

In this section, we report the experiments that we used to validate the proposed approaches. For this end, we used sets of images download from Twitter, YouTube, Flickr and GitHub. On these sets of images, we tested the following facial analysis techniques: recognition, expressions, ages, co-occurrences, connections and attendance.

3.1   Datasets

In order to test our algorithms, we used the following datasets:

1. Twitter - The Beatles: On July 9th, 2019, we downloaded images from Twitter given the hashtags `#TheBeatles` and `#Beatles`, and from the accounts `@TheBeatles` and `@BeatleHeadlines`. In these images, we can observe many pictures of the famous English rock band 'The Beatles' and its members (Paul McCartney, John Lennon, George Harrison and Ringo Starr) in many poses, facial expressions and with different ages. This dataset has 1266 images, 452 were removed because they were duplicated, and 2228 faces were detected.

2. Twitter - Donald Trump: On July 19th, 2019, we downloaded images from Twitter given the hashtags `#Trump` and `#DonaldTrump`. In those days, Trump suggested on Twitter that the legislators that "originally came from countries whose governments are a complete and total catastrophe" should "go back" to those "totally broken and crime infested places"[8]. In the downloaded images, we can observe many reactions for and against the four mentioned Democratic congresswomen. This dataset has 494 images, 126 were removed because they were duplicated, and 677 faces were detected.

3. Flickr - Family Album: On July 18th, 2019, we downloaded from Flickr twelve different family albums of pictures taken by Sandra Donoso (username sandrli)[9]. The pictures are licensed under a Creative Commons "Attribution-NonCommercial-NoDerivs 2.0 Generic". In these pictures, we can observe the

---

[8] https://time.com/5630316/trump-tweets-ilhan-omar-racist-conspiracies/.

[9] https://www.flickr.com/photos/sandreli/albums.

members of the family in celebrations and visiting vacation places in the last 5 years. This dataset has 1478 images, and 2838 faces were detected.

4. Flickr - Volleyball Game: On July 2nd, 2019, we downloaded from Flickr the album "VBVBA RVC 2 2010" of pictures taken by Bruce A Stockwell (username bas68)[10]. The pictures are licensed under a Creative Commons "Attribution-NonCommercial-NoDerivs 2.0 Generic". In these pictures, we observe pictures of different volleyball games played on April 2010 by teenage players. This dataset has 1131 images, and 4550 faces were detected.

5. YouTube - Films of the 90s: We downloaded the summaries done by WatchMojo.com of the "Top 10 Most Memorable Movies of 199" and the"Top 10 Movies of the 1990s" (12 min each)[11] and took one frame per second to build the set of images. In these images, we can observe movies like 'Matrix', 'Schindler List', 'Pulp Fiction', 'Ghost',etc. This dataset has 1492 images, and 1449 faces were detected.

6. GitHub - Classroom: A dataset for student attendance system in crowded classrooms was built in [11] with pictures taken in 25 sessions. The dataset contains pictures of a classroom with around 70 students[12]. In each dataset, approx. 6 pictures have been taken per session. Very useful for this dataset is the metadata of the dates on which each picture was taken. With this information, it is possible to establish the attendance record of each student previously enrolled (an enrolled face image is available for all students). This dataset has 153 images, and 5805 faces were detected.

3.2 Experiments

For all datasets mentioned in previous section, we performed the preliminary computations of section 2.3.0. For each analysis mentioned in Sect. 2.3, we show in this section at least one example.

1. Search for subjects: Given a face image of a volleyball player, in this example we show how this person was searched in all images of dataset 'Flickr-Volleyball Game'. The person was found in 170 images, twelve of them are shown in Fig. 3. We can see that the person was perfectly found in very complex scenarios with different facial expressions, poses and occlusion. The reader can check the effectiveness of the method by recognizing the number '15' in her T-shirt.

2. Analysis of expression: Given a face image of Paul McCartney, in this example we show how he was searched in all images of dataset 'Twitter-The Beatles', his facial expressions were analyzed and the happiest pictures was displayed. 100 face images were sorted in a descending way from more to less happy (see Fig. 4). We can see that after this analysis, in 21% of the pictures in which he appears, the expression 'Happy' was maximal.

---

[10] https://www.flickr.com/photos/bas68/albums/72157624234584197.

[11] https://youtu.be/5GvBPtlb-Ms and https://youtu.be/dA-KcQ5BzUw.

[12] https://github.com/mackenney/attendance-system-wacv19.

3. Analysis of age: Given a face image of each member of The Beatles, in this example we show how they were searched in all images of dataset 'Twitter-The Beatles', their ages were analyzed and 100 face images of each one were sorted in ascending way from younger to older (see Fig. 5). We can see that the method is able to recognize and sort face images of Ringo Starr and Paul McCartney when they were very young (around 20 years old) and how they are now (older than 75 years old).

4. Co-occurrence: Given a face image of a young man, in this example, we search pictures in which he appears with other persons in all images of dataset 'Flickr-Family Album'. We select from them the most present woman and show the pictures in which he and she appears together. The result is shown in Fig. 6. It is very impressive to see that the pictures correspond to a couple in different moments of its life.

5. Connections: Given pictures extracted from dataset 'YouTube - Films of the 90s', it is possible to analyze the pose vectors of the faces as shown in Fig. 7. In another experiment, given a face of Donald Trump, in this example we show how he was searched in all images of dataset 'Twitter-Trump'. We select one picture and we analyze the connections, that means which persons are close to each other, and which pairs are looking to each other (see Fig. 8). In addition, we can cluster them by closeness and compute a graph of connections: 'A → B' means person A is looking to person B, 'A - - - B' means the intersection of pose vectors of A and B is close to the faces of A and B. Moreover, the expressions of each person can be estimated.

6. Student Attendance: Given pictures of enrolled students, we can establish the attendance record of each student in dataset 'GitHub-Classroom'. In this

Fig. 3. Searching a volleyball player in dataset 'Flickr-Volleyball'.

Fig. 4. The happiest pictures of Paul McCartney, and his expression analysis.

Fig. 5. 100 face images of each member of The Beatles sorted from younger to older.

Fig. 6. Female co-occurrences of young man in dataset 'Flickr-Family Album'.

Fig. 7. Connections in face images of dataset 'YouTube - Films of the 90s'.

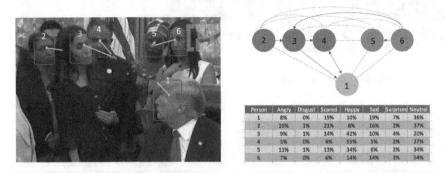

Person	Angry	Disgust	Scared	Happy	Sad	Surprised	Neutral
1	8%	0%	19%	10%	19%	7%	36%
2	16%	1%	21%	8%	16%	2%	37%
3	9%	1%	14%	42%	10%	4%	20%
4	5%	0%	6%	55%	5%	2%	27%
5	11%	1%	13%	34%	6%	2%	34%
6	7%	0%	6%	14%	14%	3%	54%

Fig. 8. Connections and expressions in a picture of dataset 'Twitter-Trump' (see text).

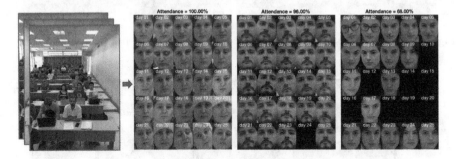

Fig. 9. Student attendance record of three students in 25 sessions.

example, we search three students in 25 sessions. The results are shown in Fig. 9, in which the attendance was 100%, 96% and 68%. It is very easy to see when students 2 and 3 were absent.

4   Final Discussion

In this paper, we presented how easy is to develop very effective applications with open source tools. From a group of pictures (downloaded for example from social networks), we can build a relational database of the images with their faces and facial attributes. With a simple query on this database we can retrieve very accurate information, *e.g.*, we can search very quickly a person, extract age, gender, and facial expressions, find the person that most frequently co-occurred with him/her, the connections and the other persons that he/she is watching, etc. Surprisingly, no training is necessary, because the required deep learning models are already trained and available in public repositories. Thus, anyone with certain computer skills can use (or misuse) this technology.

Face analysis has been assimilating into our society with surprising speed. However, privacy concerns and false identification problems in facial recognition software have gathered an anti-surveillance movement[13]. The city of San Francisco, for example, recently banned facial recognition technology by the police and other agencies[14]. We think that the warnings are clear and it is time to discuss the social and ethical challenges in facial analysis technologies. In this way, we can reduce errors that have severe social and personal consequences.

In this direction, some ethical principles that can be considered when using and teaching a technology based on facial analysis are the following:

- It must respect human and civil rights such as privacy and non-discrimination.
- It must not decide autonomously in cases that require human analysis/criteria.
- It must be developed and implemented as a trustworthy system[15].
- Its pros and cons, such as recognition rates and false matching rates, must be rigorously evaluated before operational use.
- It must be lawful, that means capturing, processing, analyzing and storing of images must be regulated and accepted by the individuals.

Since there is no clear regulation in this field, we believe that our community should discuss the scope and limitations of this technology in terms of the definition of good practices, standards, and restrictions when using facial analysis. It is time to deepen our understanding of the ethical impact of facial analysis systems, in order to regulate and audit these processes.

Acknowledgments. This work was supported by Fondecyt Grant No. 1191131 from CONICYT, Chile.

---

[13] https://www.biometricsinstitute.org/facial-recognition-systems-and-error-rates-is-this-a-concern/.

[14] https://edition.cnn.com/2019/07/17/tech/cities-ban-facial-recognition.

[15] https://ec.europa.eu/digital-single-market/en/news/ethics-guidelines-trustworthy-ai.

References

1. Amos, B., Ludwiczuk, B., Satyanarayanan, M.: Openface: A general-purpose face recognition library with mobile applications. Tech. rep., CMU-CS-16-118, CMU School of Computer Science (2016)
2. Arriaga, O., Valdenegro-Toro, M., Plöger, P.: Real-time convolutional neural networks for emotion and gender classification. arXiv preprint arXiv:1710.07557 (2017)
3. Baltrusaitis, T., Zadeh, A., Lim, Y.C., Morency, L.P.: Openface 2.0: facial behavior analysis toolkit. In: 2018 13th IEEE International Conference on Automatic Face & Gesture Recognition (FG 2018), pp. 59–66. IEEE (2018)
4. Deng, J., Guo, J., Xue, N., Zafeiriou, S.: Arcface: additive angular margin loss for deep face recognition. In: Proceedings of the IEEE Conference on Computer Vision and Pattern Recognition, pp. 4690–4699 (2019)
5. Gonzalez, R., Woods, R.: Digital Image Processing. Prentice Hall, third edn, Pearson (2008)
6. Hoai, M., Zisserman, A.: Talking heads: Detecting humans and recognizing their interactions. In: Computer Vision and Pattern Recognition (CVPR), pp. 875–882 (2014)
7. Huang, X., Dhall, A., Goecke, R., Pietikäinen, M., Zhao, G.: Multimodal framework for analyzing the affect of a group of people. IEEE Trans. Multimedia $20(10)$, 2706–2721 (2018)
8. King, D.E.: Dlib-ml: A machine learning toolkit. J. Mach. Learn. Res. 10, 1755–1758 (2009)
9. Li, P., Prieto, L., Mery, D., Flynn, P.J.: On low-resolution face recognition in the wild: comparisons and new techniques. IEEE Trans. Inf. Forensics Secur. $14(8)$, 2000–2012 (2019)
10. Lowe, D.G.: Distinctive image features from scale-invariant keypoints. Int. J. Comput. Vis. $60(2)$, 91–110 (2004)
11. Mery, D., Mackenney, I., Villalobos, E.: Student attendance system in crowded classrooms using a smartphone camera. In: 2019 IEEE Winter Conference on Applications of Computer Vision (WACV), pp. 857–866. IEEE (2019)
12. Otto, C., Wang, D., Jain, A.K.: Clustering millions of faces by identity. IEEE Trans. Pattern Anal. Mach. Intell. $40(2)$, 289–303 (2017)
13. Parkhi, O.M., Vedaldi, A., Zisserman, A.: Deep face recognition. In: British Machine Vision Conference (BMVC2015). vol. 1, p. 6 (2015)
14. Pertuz, S., Puig, D., Garcia, M.: Analysis of focus measure operators for shape-from-focus. Pattern Recogn. $46(5)$, 1415–1432 (2013)
15. Renoust, B., Kobayashi, T., Ngo, T.D., Le, D.D., Satoh, S.: When face-tracking meets social networks: a story of politics in news videos. Appl. Netw. Sci. $1(1)$, 4 (2016)
16. Rothe, R., Timofte, R., Van Gool, L.: Deep expectation of real and apparent age from a single image without facial landmarks. Int. J. Comput. Vis. $126(2\text{–}4)$, 144–157 (2018)
17. Schroff, F., Kalenichenko, D., Philbin, J.: FaceNet: a unified embedding for face recognition and clustering. In: IEEE Conference on Computer Vision and Pattern Recognition (CVPR), pp. 815–823 (2015)
18. Shi, Y., Otto, C., Jain, A.K.: Face clustering: representation and pairwise constraints. IEEE Trans. Inf. Forensics Secur. $13(7)$, 1626–1640 (2018)

19. Sun, X., Wu, P., Hoi, S.C.: Face detection using deep learning: An improved faster rcnn approach. Neurocomputing **299**, 42–50 (2018)
20. Zavan, F.H.D.B., Bellon, O.R., Silva, L., Medioni, G.G.: Benchmarking parts based face processing in-the-wild for gender recognition and head pose estimation. Pattern Recogn. **123**, 104–110 (2019)
21. Zhang, K., Zhang, Z., Li, Z., Qiao, Y.: Joint face detection and alignment using multitask cascaded convolutional networks. IEEE Signal Process. Lett. **23**(10), 1499–1503 (2016)
22. Zhang, Z., Luo, P., Loy, C.C., Tang, X.: Learning social relation traits from face images. In: Proceedings of the IEEE International Conference on Computer Vision, pp. 3631–3639 (2015)
23. Zhu, M., Shi, D., Zheng, M., Sadiq, M.: Robust facial landmark detection via occlusion-adaptive deep networks. In: Proceedings of the IEEE Conference on Computer Vision and Pattern Recognition, pp. 3486–3496 (2019)

Location Analysis Based Waiting Time Optimisation

Hami Aksu[1], Wolfgang Dorner[2], and Lihong Zheng[1(✉)]

[1] Charles Sturt University, Wagga Wagga, Australia
HamiAksu@gmx.de, lzheng@csu.edu.au
[2] Technische Hochschule Deggendorf, Deggendorf, Germany
wolfgang.dorner@th-deg.de

Abstract. Customer satisfaction is very important to keep customer retention for any food and retail stores. Waiting time has been found is one of the most important factors to influence customers' shopping experience and purchase termination rate and customers' perceptions of retailer service offerings. Increasing customer retention can be achieved by avoiding long waiting time queuing at the checkouts. This paper investigates the current different types of sensor-based technologies in location detection to capture the customers' behavior and then provides a fundamental optimization mechanism to avoid the long waiting time economically. Various approaches to identify a person's location are compared in terms of principle and operation. Each makes its contribution to controlling the resources in a better way depending on the expected number of customers at checkout. Through an experiment on a supermarket, this paper contributes value to the improvement of operational resource planning, overcapacity avoiding while not increasing or reducing queues and waiting time of customers. The recommendation that waiting time is perceived by customers as a factor of lower service quality to business managers is given finally.

Keywords: Customer satisfaction · Sensor · Location detection · Waiting time optimisation

1 Introduction

Food and retail stores have been aware that increasing customer retention would also increase customer satisfaction [1]. Waiting time is critical to influence customers' shopping experience and purchase termination rate and more generally customers' perceptions of retailer service offerings [2]. Paper [3] found that the psychological factors at the checkout area may influence perception, called the irritation of waiting. To increase customer retention can be achieved by avoiding waiting queues at the checkouts [4].

A custom-designed optimum is required to avoid waiting queues of customers at checkouts, also required to attend to them as economically as possible. Obviously, cost-effectiveness increases when the customers experience reduced waiting and dwell times, and when this is achieved with an optimal attend capacity.

© Springer Nature Switzerland AG 2020
J. J. Dabrowski et al. (Eds.): PSIVT 2019 Workshops, LNCS 11994, pp. 30–41, 2020.
https://doi.org/10.1007/978-3-030-39770-8_3

Apparently, optimization of waiting time and the needed resources at the checkouts requires a forecast of the customers' inflow into the checkout area. A various sensor-based technologies have been developed to get more dynamic customers' information for better business decision-making. For this reason, the supermarket can be divided into shopping and a checkout area. The inflow into both areas is measured to get the number of customers separated. This paper investigates the current different sensor technologies applied in location prediction systems to provide fundamental data for further customer satisfaction optimization.

The paper is organized as follows. Section 2 introduces various sensor platforms. Section 3 discusses the location prediction methods developed so far. Section 4 summaries their applications for the retail environment. Then experimental results are presented in Sect. 4. Finally, we conclude in Sect. 5.

2   Sensor Technologies

A variety of sensor technologies is available for collecting dynamic information about customers' numbers in the supermarket or other community areas. Mechanical systems were the first generation of counting systems. For example, a turnstile counts the customers when passing. Because of the separation of the customers, these counting systems have high accuracy. But it is not possible to pass the entrance simultaneously. Later on, electronic counting systems appeared. The electronic counting systems are divided into categories: Those mounted at floor or ceiling and "active" or "passive" sensors. In the following, we give a short introduction of these technologies in terms of the principle of operation and measurement, operational conditions and features of each type.

2.1   Photoelectric Sensor Systems

Photoelectric sensor systems are used in a pair of transmitter and receiver. The transmitter sends a horizontal linear light beam to a photosensitive sensor element - the receiver. When a person breaks this light beam a signal is sent to the electronic device and interprets this as counting an object. Photoelectric sensor systems are "passive" systems. In retail stores or supermarkets the transmitter and the receiver can be installed directly at the entrance. Customers have to cross the light beam of the photoelectric counting system. To avoid miss detection, multiple paired need to be used in an unobstructed detection zone. This system is cheap, but its light beam limited by distance, and blind spots. Accuracy of detection decreases depending on the width of entrances.

2.2   Radar and Laser Systems

Radar and Laser systems are "active" systems. The sensor sends an active signal and this signal is interpreted by reflecting the environment. In the case of radar systems, the signals are electromagnetic waves (radar beam). Laser systems use a focused light beam (laser beam). The respective environment of the object generates a specific reflective characteristic which can be interpreted as an entry of a person. The field of view is diversified by using a rotating mirror inside the laser system. If two or more parallel laser beams are used, grid flooring is applied to the area, in which case the direction of motion can be determined. Radar systems determine the direction of motion by using the Doppler Effect. It is the change in frequency of a radar wave for an observer moving relative to its source. Both sensor types can be installed at ceiling height. The accuracy of these systems depends on the surface texture of the environment or objects.

2.3   Infrared Systems

Infrared systems differ between "active" and "passive". Active infrared systems are similar to radar systems. They send an infrared beam and analyse the reflected beam. An evaluation unit interprets this as an object. These active sensors are called "position sensitive devices" (PSD-sensors). The passive infrared systems detect heat sources by measuring the temperature of the environment. Since the body temperatures of humans have a different temperature compared with the surrounding environment, the sensor can detect people easily.

These systems are typically mounted at the ceiling height of an entrance. They are usually used for door openers or revolving doors. Its advantage is that the passive system will not count objects or anything else that is not human body temperature. But the passive system is affected by sudden temperature and light changes. Furthermore, the passive system is affected by immobile persons because the person becomes part of the background. That means the passive system is affected by changes in the background, especially in quick temperature changes and strong sunlight. But active systems are unaffected by sudden temperature and light changes. Furthermore, they are unaffected by immobile passengers. These active systems are more accurate than passive systems. To cover wide entrances, an array installation can be set up.

2.4   Video-Based Two-Dimensional (2D) Systems

Video-based systems are composed of a video camera and a downstream processing unit. Video-based two dimensional counting systems are mounted at the ceiling height of the entrance.

Fig. 1. Background and head counting (Vitracom AG)

This processing unit provides the images continuously. The counting software evaluates the counting events by a virtual counter line, which is placed in the field of view. Either background counting based or head counting based can be seen in Fig. 1. The counting results are stored at the processing unit and can be fetched for further processing by the network. However, if an object does not move anymore, the object becomes part of the background and will not be detected anymore. The counting system using IP camera can be maintained and validated remotely. The accuracy of such systems is very high, even in crowded situations. Characteristics like shape, colour, velocity and size or kinetics behaviour can separate objects or pets from people. Such video sensors can also evaluate more features such as dwell time of people in certain areas or detection of the walking path in a store of customers. But they are affected by vibrations and changing light conditions, etc. The image quality and the image processing software influences accuracy.

2.5   Video-Based Three Dimensional Systems

One camera can only capture 2-D information. So it faces the difficulty when occlusion happens. 3D systems provide not just punctuate or area information, but 3D distance or height information about the object. 3D sensor systems simulate humans' binocular vision. Two camera lenses that are calibrated with each other have a different perspective of the scene. By triangulating the virtual visual beam, the distance between each pixel can be reconstructed. Figure 2 shows the stereoscopic camera of Hella Aglia. Another possibility of 3D measurement is Photo-Mixing-Devices (PMD). This camera system measures the time of flight of a light signal between the camera and the subject for each point of the image. These "time-of-flight"-cameras use a coordinate infrared beam. The reflection of this infrared beam is measured by an optical sensor chip. Using the time of flight, the distance of the environment point of the image is continuously determined. Video-based three-dimensional counting systems were mounted at the ceiling height of the entrance. More rich information can improve the accuracy of video-based three-dimensional sensor systems who are less affected by vibrations and changing light conditions, etc.

2.6   IoT Based Wireless Sensor Networks

The rapid progress of the Internet of Things (IoT) has accelerated the development of wireless sensor networks dramatically. With the advances in wireless communication, now it is possible to utilise wireless signals to track people who are with a smartphone. Meshlium Scanner [5] is a new product of the Libelium which allows detecting iPhone and Android devices or any device which works with WiFi or Bluetooth interfaces. The devices can be detected without the need of being connected to a specific Access Point, enabling the detection of any smart phone, laptop or hands-free device which comes into the coverage area of Meshlium AP scanner. Thus such a product can be applied in the supermarket

Fig. 2. Video-based three-dimensional system in the supermarket (A stereoscopic camera)

to detect the number of people at a specific time. Hence, the data collected can be used to evaluate and analyse the real traffic of people.

3   Existing Location Detection Methods

Location can be identified later by checking the captured sensors' data. There are several location detection techniques developed: a topological graph-based, grid searching based, Markov Models or Hidden Markov Models, Bayesian Networks, self-organized maps, Neural Network approaches and the state predictor methods. Following we compare and contrast these various methods in details.

A topological graph-based method [6] requires sensors that relate to the layout of an environments. Topological graphs seem to be robust to the fragility of purely geometrical methods. Due that the topological approach depends on the semantics of the environments, it is more capable than others in managing reactive behaviors, especially in large-scale cases [7]. However, this approach is the coarseness of its representation. Thus these methods may lack the details of an environment. It only provides rough information about the person's location. To overcome its shortcomings, Shi et al. [7] proposed a hybrid map combining topological and the metric paradigm of the grid-based approaches. Their research showed that the positive characteristics of both can be integrated to compensate for the weakness of each single approach. Moreover, Shi et al. [7] combined the topological paradigm with the grid-based paradigm. They used the topological map to represent the building map and the grid-based approach for the localization.

While grid-based approaches [8] can represent arbitrary distributions over the discrete state space. However, the requirement of computational and space complexity to keep the position grid in memory and to update it for predictions. The complexity grows exponentially with the number of dimensions and supposes using a grid-based approach for low-dimensional estimations [6]. They apply the Bayesian Filtering to the Voronoi graph has the advantage that they can represent arbitrary probability densities.

Furthermore, various machine learning-based methods have been integrated into location detection for higher accuracy. Gellert et al. [9] improved accuracy of 84.81% by using the Hidden Markov model. They predicted the next location of person movements. Ashbrook and Starner [10] used in their study a Markov chain model and K-means clustering algorithm to predict future movements. They clustered the GPS data by K-means algorithm to find significant locations at which persons stayed for a long time. They designed a Markov chain model with the historical movements among these locations. They found in their study that changes in routine take longer in their developed model. For that reason, they propose a way of weighting certain updates. Zhou [11] proposed the Markov object location prediction to get the initial position of the object for compressive tracking. This method can locate the object accurately and quickly, and the classifier parameter adaptive updating strategy is given based on the confidence map.

On the other hand, the Bayesian filter can converge to the true posterior probability even in nonlinear dynamic systems. Furthermore, they claim that the Bayesian filtering approach compared with the grid-based (cellular automaton) approaches are more efficient because their focus is on their resources (particles) on regions in state space with high probability. Nevertheless, the efficiency depends on the number of samples used for filtering [6].

The complexity grows exponentially in the dimensions of the state space in all of the presented methods. Furey et al. [8] noticed that a researcher applying these methods has to be careful with high-dimensional estimation problems. This complexity of cellular automaton can be avoided by representing the area in a non-metric way using a topological approach [6]. The researcher claimed that motion models in general use topological approaches and give a discrete or fixed number of probabilities. Furthermore, they notice that the efficiency increases in areas where no sensors are available for measuring people.

Furey et al. [8] compared different filter implementations to measure how well the different approaches can estimate the location of people given appropriate sensors. It seems that cellular automaton or grid-based approaches can reach arbitrary accuracy. High accuracy means on the other handy high computational costs. Using Bayesian Kalman filters means robustness and efficiency regarding computation and memory. Han et al. [12] tried to use a Self-Organising Map based on Ashbrook and Starner [8] for learning without any prior knowledge. Self-Organising Maps overcome the gap of missing prior knowledge of moving patterns. Such Self-Organising Maps are learning neural networks that can preserve the topology of a map as they create it.

Applying it to a Markov chain Han et al. [12] converted GPS data into a significant pattern. Hence the researcher can predict the next location of a person by the output from the Self-Organising Maps. Jiang et al. [13] designed a multi-order Markov Chains to take consideration of users' current location and associated historical mobility data to predict human mobility.

A further way to predict the movement of persons is neural networks. Vintan et al. [9] suggested a prediction technique to anticipate a person's next move by using neural networks. In their study, they used neural predictors of the multi-layer perceptron with backpropagation. Their results show an up to 92%

accuracy of pre-trained cases of next location prediction. Mantyjarvi et al. [14] applied the same multi-layer perceptron classifier to recognize a human's motion by using neural networks.

Assam [15] proposed a robust location predictor for check-in data by using Wavelets and Conditional Random Fields (CRF) with an assumption that check-in generation is governed by the Poisson distribution. In [16] a novel model called Space Time Features-based Recurrent Neural Network (STF-RNN) was proposed for predicting people's next movement based on mobility patterns obtained from GPS devices logs. Through extracting the internal representation of space and time features automatically, this model improves the capability of RNN and shows good performance to discover useful knowledge about people's behavior in a more efficient way.

So, location detection does play a key role in various retail environments. [17,18] processed and characterise queuing data of inflow and outflow through distribution models. [19–22] focused their study about queuing control theory on retail stores. The research [23] calculates a deterministic model dependent on the current in- and outflow also at the shop area and the checkout area. The methods mentioned before present researches that measure just the inflow and outflow of a supermarket [23,24]. The customer's dwell time is estimated from the captured data. Therefore, the system developed should control the operational resources depending on the expected number of customers at the checkout desk in a supermarket. Our proposed approach considers monitoring of inflow and outflow of the service area together with monitoring of queue length and inflow to the checkouts, to better differentiate between dwell time in the shop area and processing in the checkout area.

4   Experiment and Results

4.1   Setup

Based on the video-based counting system, we investigate a supermarket that has the following settings as an example.

The selected sale area is approximately $8000\,m^2$, which includes a mall with a bakery, dry cleaner, post office, bank, a pharmacy and a newspaper kiosk. The building has two main entrances. The supermarket has 12 checkouts and 4 self-scanning checkouts. To reach the entrances of the supermarket area, customers have to pass the mall area first and then use one of the two entrances into the supermarket which are available. The width of each main entrance is 8 m, the width of each entrance into the supermarket is 3.10 m, and the width of the checkout line is approximately 28 m.

The research assumes that the inflow of subjects arrives in an observed time interval with a fixed time lag. One more assumption is that the checkout time during the time interval at the checkout is constant. That means the system is deterministic. The research assumes if the rate of inflow and checkout rate is balanced, the waiting queue length doesn't change. In reality, this is not possible, because with regard to the waiting queue theory the randomized interruptions of events are continuously increasing. According to the state of the waiting queue theory, the present challenge is an interaction between multiple processes which are characterized by non-steady Poisson processes. This is the basis of the waiting queue models which are formally defined in the waiting queue theory.

In this paper, to leave the supermarket, all customers have to pass through one of these checkouts. The selected 3D video technology has to be installed at the point of entering/leaving the main shop (includes the mall) and the point of entering into the supermarket area. Furthermore, the counting sensors should be placed at the checkout area in order to count the customers entering this area, to observe the waiting queue and to count the leaving customers of the checkout area.

4.2   Results and Analysis

To achieve a good and realistic forecast of dwell times, the sample supermarket area has to be divided into the shop area and the checkout area. By the entering of the customers into the checkout area, it can be assumed that the operational resources requested are to be used. If the customers are not in the checkout area and just in the flow field, no staff are requested at the checkouts. Besides the inward counting of customers in the supermarket, this research also counts the inward flow of customers to the checkout area. Furthermore, the length of the waiting queue in front of each checkout is monitored. In our experiment, the inflow, outflow of customers have to be prepared for presentation, analysis and interpretation. To handle the huge amount of data, the average of the queue length of all checkouts during one day will be considered. In addition, to avoid the irregular behavior of customers, a variation of the number of customers, the minimum measured period time is one week (Monday to Saturday) without any holiday.

Table 1 presents the average inflow and outflow values from Monday to Saturday of 12 months monitored. We noticed that Fridays and Saturdays have the most customers. The supermarket has fewer customers on other days. External effects and different situations like public holidays, bridging days, seasons (e.g. Christmas, Easter) influence the behavior of customers. The proposed system treats these as the new situation.

Table 1. Average values of each weekday

	Average inflow	Average outflow
Monday	7923	8134
Tuesday	7353	7445
Wednesday	8007	8169
Thursday	8005	8133
Friday	10026	10174
Saturday	13796	14255

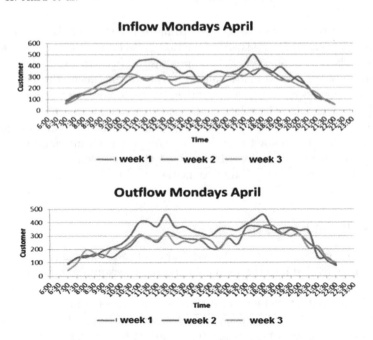

Fig. 3. A sample in- and out- flow trend of customers

Also, Fig. 3 presents the structure of the trend of inflow and outflow during a weekday for three weeks in April. We compared three weeks daily data across different months, we found similar buying behavior of customers. The summary of the system performance is shown in Table 2.

Table 2. Overview of system performance

Terms	Value
Dwell time (mins.)	6–55
Handling rate (seconds)	10–60
Opening hours	7 am–10 pm
Average handling rate (seconds)	21
Conversion rate	81%

According to our proposed counting method, the dwell time is not affected by the purchase process, and can be evaluated separately. In general, considering the desired customer satisfaction which is expressed in the waiting queue length, we set the maximum queue length is 3 customers. We noticed that there is a difference between inflow and outflow. The reason for this was introduced by the counting system. The variance between the inflow and outflow would represent the dwell time. Based on the estimation of the dwell time, the opening and closing of checkouts have been scheduled in a better way. Thus it helps relief the stress of staff. With our current counting system, it is not accurate enough. In the future, people tracking and trolley tracking system can increase the accuracy.

Depending on the captured dynamic process data, a forecasting model has been developed. Process data are the inflows of customers at the entrance, number of customers entering the checkout area, current waiting queue length and the number of available checkouts. With these parameters staffing has to be sufficient in order to keep the waiting queue time short.

The principle of making the decision is to provide additional or less operational resources is a cost-benefit calculation. On one hand, the personnel costs at the checkout area should be as low as possible, and on the other hand, the waiting queues length or respectively the waiting time should not be too long to annoy the customers. For that reason, the optimum value of the number of available resources has to be determined using the following cost function K:

$$\overrightarrow{N_B} : K(\overrightarrow{N_B} = min(K(N_B, j_A, j_O, L, \overrightarrow{Z}) \tag{1}$$

where $(\overrightarrow{N_B})$ is the amount of requested resources, NB the available resources, j_A the inward flow into the checkout area, j_O the outward flow of the shop, L the length of the waiting queue and the vector $\overrightarrow{Z}$ as a combination of boundary conditions. Boundary conditions can be, for instance, a minimum time period for operational resources. This boundary condition is important because an evaluation unit based on the inward flow, the outward flow and the waiting queue length is necessary to cover short-term fluctuations. Otherwise this could result in a very high number of opening and closing of checkouts (as Fig. 4 shows), which would be neither economical nor reasonable for the staff which has to deal with the customer.

To avoid this fluctuation, the controller has to evaluate if it is necessary to change the status in a new state which is persistent for relevant time periods, or transient just for short time periods. If such a trend is not persistent, there is no change in the actual number of open checkouts.

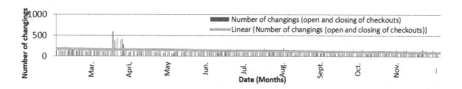

Fig. 4. Long-term-view of the numbers of openings and closings

5   Conclusions

This paper investigates the problem of how to avoid waiting queues of customers at checkouts as economically as possible. We found that cost effectiveness increases when the customers experience reduced waiting and dwell times, and when this is achieved with an optimal attend capacity. Since these requirements conflict, the best optimisation could be achieved through the opening and closing checkouts. Thus, it helps to improve the staff and customers' satisfaction; improve work processes/stress reduction and control waiting time, checkout efficiency and conversion rate. Moreover, similar problems and solutions can be applied to different other fields such as telephone switching systems, computers and communication systems, telecommunication systems, SAN (storage area network) and recovery systems, economy, quality control, transportation systems and much more.

References

1. van Riel, A.C.R., Semeijn, J., Ribbink, D., Bomert Peters, Y.: Waiting for service at the checkout: negative emotional responses store image and overall satisfaction. J. Serv. Manag. **23**(2), 144–169 (2012)
2. Peritz, J.: Retailers who keep score know what their shoppers value. Mark. News **27**(11), 9 (1993)
3. Maister, D.H.: The Psychology of Waiting Lines. Harvard Business School, Boston (1984)
4. Tom, G., Lucey, S.: Waiting time delays and customer satisfaction in supermarkets. J. Serv. Market. **9**(5), 20–29 (1995)
5. Libelium.com: Libelium - Connecting Sensors to the Cloud (2019). http://www.libelium.com. Accessed 7 Sept 2019
6. Fox, D., et al.: Bayesian techniques for location estimation. In: Proceedings of the 2003 Workshop on Location-Aware Computing (2003)
7. Shi, C., Wang, Y., Yang, J.: Online topological map building and qualitative localization in large-scale environment. Rob. Auton. Syst. **58**(5), 488–496 (2010)
8. Furey, E., Curran, K., Mc Kevitt, P.: A Bayesian filter approach to modelling human movement patterns for first responders within indoor locations. In: Third International Conference on Intelligent Networking and Collaborative Systems (INCoS). IEEE (2011)
9. Vintan, L., et al.: Person movement prediction using neural networks (2006)
10. Ashbrook, D., Starner, T.: Learning significant locations and predicting user movement with GPS. In: Proceedings of Sixth International Symposium on Wearable Computers (ISWC 2002). IEEE (2002)
11. Zhou, X., et al.: Adaptive learning compressive tracking based on Markov location prediction. J. Electron. Imaging **26**(2), 023026 (2017)
12. Han, S.-J., Cho, S.-B.: Predicting user's movement with a combination of self-organizing map and Markov model. In: Kollias, S., Stafylopatis, A., Duch, W., Oja, E. (eds.) ICANN 2006. LNCS, vol. 4132, pp. 884–893. Springer, Heidelberg (2006). https://doi.org/10.1007/11840930_92
13. Jiang, J., et al.: Predicting human mobility based on location data modeled by Markov chains. In: Fourth International Conference on Ubiquitous Positioning, Indoor Navigation and Location Based Services (UPINLBS) (2016)
14. Mantyjarvi, J., Himberg, J., Seppanen, T.: Recognizing human motion with multiple acceleration sensors. In: IEEE International Conference on Systems, Man, and Cybernetics. IEEE (2001)

15. Assam, R., Seidl, T.: Check-in location prediction using wavelets and conditional random fields. In: 2014 IEEE International Conference on Data Mining (2014)
16. Al-Molegi, A., Jabreel, M., Ghaleb, B.: STF-RNN: space time features-based recurrent neural network for predicting people next location. In: IEEE Symposium Series on Computational Intelligence (SSCI) (2016)
17. Berman, O., Larson, R.C.: A queueing control model for retail services having back room operations and cross-trained workers. Comput. Oper. Res. **31**(2), 201–222 (2004)
18. Furey, E., Curran, K., Mc Kevitt, P.: Learning indoor movement habits for predictive control. Int. J. Space Based Situated Comput. **1**(4), 222–232 (2011)
19. Lu, F., Serfozo, R.F.: M/M/1 queueing decision processes with monotone hysteretic optimal policies. Oper. Res. **32**(5), 1116–1132 (1984)
20. Zeithaml, V.A., Berry, L.L., Parasuraman, A.: The nature and determinants of customer expectations of service. J. Acad. Mark. Sci. **21**(1), 1–12 (1993)
21. Liu, N., Lovell, B.C.: Gesture classification using hidden Markov models and Viterbi path counting. In: VIIth Digital Image Computing: Techniques and Applications (2003)
22. Shi, C., et al.: Modeling and safety strategy of passenger evacuation in a metro station in China. Saf. Sci. **50**(5), 1319–1332 (2012)
23. Holliday, S.: Automatic self-optimizing queue management system. Google Patents (2010)
24. Frey, R.G., Nelson, J.D.: Checkout lane alert system and method for stores having express checkout lanes. Google Patents (1996)

Passive and Active Electro-Optical Sensors for Aerial and Space Imaging

In-Orbit Geometric Calibration of Firebird's Infrared Line Cameras

Jürgen Wohlfeil[1]([⊠]), Tilman Bucher[1]([⊠]), Anko Börner[1]([⊠]), Christian Fischer[1]([⊠]), Olaf Frauenberger[2]([⊠]), and Björn Piltz[1]([⊠])

[1] Germany German Aerospace Center (DLR), Institute of Optical Systems, Rutherfordstr. 2, 12359 Berlin, Germany
{juergen.wohlfeil,tilman.bucher,anko.boerner,c.fischer, bjoern.piltz}@dlr.de
[2] Germany German Aerospace Center (DLR), German Remote Sensing Data Center, 17235 Neustrelitz, Germany
olaf.frauenberger@dlr.de

Abstract. The German Aerospace Center (DLR) has developed and launched two small satellites (TET-1 and BIROS) as part of the FireBIRD mission. Both are capable to detect and observe fire related high temperature events (HTE) from space with infrared cameras. To enable a quick localization of the fires direct georeferencing of the images is required. Therefore the camera geometry measurements with laboratory set-up on ground have to be verified and validated using real data takes. This is achieved using ground control points (GCPs), identifiable in all spectral bands, allowing the investigations of the whole processing chain used for georeferencing. It is shown how the accuracy of direct georeferencing was significantly improved by means of in-orbit calibration using GCPs and how the workflow for processing and reprocessing was developed.

Keywords: Small satellite · Geometric calibration · Line sensor · Infra-red (IR) · Accuracy assessment · FireBIRD

1 Introduction

Different scientific studies have been made investigating relevant optical sensor system parameter and technical concepts using small satellite systems for mapping high temperature events starting in the early 1990 [1, 2]. In order to detect and observe fire from space, the German Aerospace Center (DLR) developed and launched two small satellites (TET-1, BIROS) in the context of the FireBIRD (Fire Bispectral InfraRed Detector) Mission. The mission aims to significantly improve detection, mapping and analysis of HTE [3] compared to currently existing sensor systems.

The FireBIRD IR sensor systems are based on cooled photodetectors. Various methods for HTE detection and quantification have been developed. While single band methods rely on the robust demarcation of background pixels and higher temperature pixels, considered as being anomalous, the FireBIRD systems facilitate the application of the widely used bi-spectral algorithm approach introduced by Dozier [4], using the

© Springer Nature Switzerland AG 2020
J. J. Dabrowski et al. (Eds.): PSIVT 2019 Workshops, LNCS 11994, pp. 45–58, 2020.
https://doi.org/10.1007/978-3-030-39770-8_4

mid-infrared (MWIR) and longwave-infrared (LWIR) channels. While this meanwhile proven concept has shown its capabilities successfully in various case studies [5–8], multi-channel data processing approaches require an accurate co-registration of the data (Fig. 1).

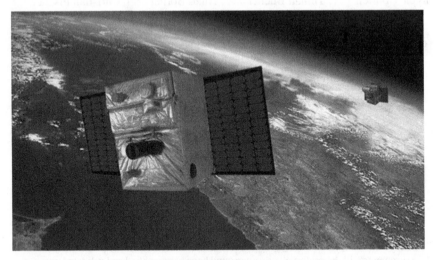

Fig. 1. TET-BIROS constellation (animated)

Each of the highly agile satellites with up to 30° off-nadir pointing is equipped with three line cameras, one in the visible and near-infrared (VIS/NIR) spectral range with high spatial resolution, used to detect sun glint; one in the MWIR range to measure high temperatures and one in the LWIR to derive the background temperature with high precision (Fig. 2).

Fig. 2. Camera sub-assembly. Left: MWIR, center: VIS, right: LWIR, parameters see Table 1

The main camera parameters are shown in Table 1.

Table 1. The main parameters of the three line cameras

	VIS/NIR (three CCD lines FPA)	2 IR cameras (different spectral ranges)
Center wavelengths	0.51, 0.65, 0.86 μm (green, red, NIR)	MWIR: 3.8 μm LWIR: 8.9 μm
Focal length	90.9 mm	46.39 mm
Field of view	19.6°	19°
Detector type	CCD array	HgCdTe array
No of pixels	3 × 5164	2 × 512, staggered
Quantization	14 bit	14 bit
Pixel width	42.4 m	356 m
Sample width	42.4 m	178 m (staggered)
Swath width	211 km	178 km

This configuration and the corresponding radiometric calibration and processing allow fire to be detected reliably directly after downlink. Additionally, to be able to inform the relevant authorities about a detected fire, it is necessary to determine the location of the fire accurately and quickly. To that end, the FireBIRD satellites have the capability of directly georeferencing their images. This relies on the position and (exterior) orientation of the satellite, provided by the Attitude and Orbit Control System (AOCS), as well as the geometric camera calibration (interior orientation). The AOCS data are mainly based on GPS (position) and a system of star-trackers and Inertial-Measurement Units (IMU) for the orientation.

Although the cameras' interior geometries have already been measured in a laboratory set-up on ground, verification and in this case re-calibration in orbit was necessary. This was necessitated by the occurrence of small changes in the cameras viewing geometry, possibly caused by the structural loads during launch.

A usual setup for in-flight calibration of a (push-broom) line camera is a set of strips (line images) of a test field scanned in different directions with ground control points (GCPs) [9–11]. For a satellite based camera the flight direction cannot be changed significantly, resulting in a less constrained geometry for calibration. Fortunately the required accuracy for georeferencing is an order of magnitude lower than the accuracy of the GPS, allowing us to take the position as given. Also the lever arm between the satellite's origin and the cameras' centers of projections is negligible compared to the much larger ground sampling distance.

What remains to be determined is the boresight alignment of each camera as well as the refined interior orientations.

A special case in terms of line geometry are the MWIR and LWIR cameras, which enhance the spatial resolution using two staggered lines as shown in Fig. 3 and discussed in Sect. 2.

For geometric calibration only scenes with highly accurate exterior orientation were selected. The georeferencing chain was verified using GCPs. The so-called boresight of each camera (angular misalignment relative to the satellite coordinate system used by the AOCS) was determined and improved via bundle adjustment. The new boresights were introduced into the processing configuration and the scenes were reprocessed.

The issue and the proposed solution described in this paper are of special importance for small, micro and nano satellites. Satellites of these classes have small mass budgets implying higher sensitivities and instabilities with respect to thermal and structural loads. Approaches for in-orbit re-calibrations are a precondition for such satellite systems.

In the following chapter the in-orbit calibration procedure used for both satellites is described. The results are shown in Sect. 3 and the lessons learned in Sect. 4. Conclusions and an outlook are given in Sect. 5.

2   Calibration

For every detector array of every camera a set of geometric calibration parameters is defined. These are based on the definition of the pointing view of each individual pixel, with respect to (i) the camera coordinate system, known due to laboratory measurements, (ii) definition of the mounting position of the camera system. With these parameters and the calculation specification (described below) it is possible to calculate the line of sight in satellite coordinates for each physical pixel. Using the absolute satellite position and orientation obtained by the AOCS and the time to synchronize them with the imagery, the line of sight can be transformed into a global coordinate system, e.g. WGS84 or a local space rectangular coordinate system, thus allowing direct georeferencing of the imagery.

In the following the special geometry of FireBIRD's line cameras are explained. The parameters of the interior orientation and distortion were not optimized during the in-orbit calibration because they did not contribute significantly to the achieved accuracy. However, for the understanding of the geometry of rather unusual focal plane arrays with staggered lines the following paragraphs may be helpful.

The IR-detector consists of a pair of adjacent lines with 512 imaging pixel each, where the second line is shifted by a half pixel in line direction (Fig. 3). In combination with a doubled temporal sampling rate the ground sampling distance is half the size of the pixel size.

Each of the two staggered line detectors is regarded as one single detector with a special geometry. It is described by the following calibration parameters (see Figs. 3 and 4).

- FocalLength c
- FirstPixelX $x0$ *(along track)* and FirstPixelY $y0$ *(across track)*: Position of the first active pixel of the swath in the detector line coordinate system
- StaggeringOffsetX sx and StaggeringOffsetY sy: Offset of the shifted detector line with respect to the position in the ideal (non-staggered) case

- PixelPitch *si*: Distance between pixel mid-points along the detector line
- LineAngle α: Angle of rotation of the detector line with respect to the image plane
- Distortion *k1, k2, k3*: Radial symmetric distortion parameters
- AlignmentAngles q_R: Rotation of the camera with respect to the satellite coordinate system (AOCS).

For the VIS/NIR camera the same set of parameters is used with neutral staggering offsets.

Geometric Calculation: The input for the calculation is the pixel index *i*, starting with the value 0 for the first pixel of the swath running over all subsequent pixels in line direction. For staggered lines, *i* alternates between the pixels of the two detector lines. The pixel index refers to the order of pixels within the detector array. This means that in case of subsampled images, the appropriate scale factors between the image pixel and the physical pixel have to be applied in order to get the correct position.

Interior Orientation: The position *(x, y)* of a pixel *i* on the detector line coordinate system is calculated as follows:

$$r = i \bmod 2$$
$$x = x_0 + r\, s_x$$
$$y = y_0 + s_i + s_y$$

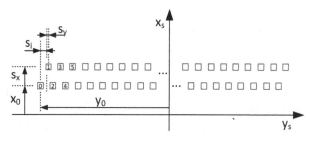

Fig. 3. Parameters of the detector line coordinate system (x_s, y_s) (Color figure online)

Some pixel indices are denoted in the corresponding symbols for the pixels (blue boxes). For cameras with multiple detector lines on the focal plane (e.g. VIS), the rotation of the detector line around the optical axis is expressed by the parameter α. The position of the pixel on the image plane *(x', y')* is then

$$x' = x\cos(\alpha) - y\sin(\alpha)$$
$$y' = x\sin(\alpha) + y\cos(\alpha)$$

Image Distortion: The radial symmetric distortion of the image is modeled according to Brown's distortion model [12] with the three radial symmetric parameters *k1, k2* and *k3*. The distorted pixel coordinate *(x'', y'')* is calculated in the following way from the undistorted coordinate in the image coordinates *(x', y')*.

$$\begin{matrix} x'' \\ y'' \end{matrix} = \begin{matrix} x' \\ y' \end{matrix} + \frac{x'}{y'}\left(k_1 r^2 + k_2 r^4 + k_3 r^6\right) \quad with \quad r^2 = x'^2 + y'^2$$

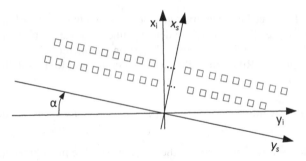

Fig. 4. Rotation of the detector line coordinate system (x_s, y_s) with respect to the image plane coordinate system (x_i, y_i)

Camera Coordinates: The corresponding camera coordinate (X', Y', Z') of the distorted pixel coordinate (x'', y'') is defined to be

$$\begin{pmatrix} X' \\ Y' \\ Z' \end{pmatrix} = \begin{pmatrix} x'' \\ y'' \\ -c \end{pmatrix},$$

where c is the focal length of the camera. As the focal plane is at a negative z-coordinate of the camera coordinate system, it is located at the negative z-coordinate $-c$.

Sensor Alignment: The next step is the transformation of the camera coordinate to the satellite coordinate system. This is performed in two steps. First, the sensor alignment is corrected and second, the resulting coordinates are flipped into the satellite coordinate system.

The camera coordinate system is intended to be almost identical to the flipped satellite coordinate system, but they are translated and rotated anyway. Whereas the translation is assumed to be negligible, the rotation is determined during the geometric calibration procedure. It is a three-dimensional rotation q_R.

The satellite coordinates (X, Y, Z) of the camera coordinates vector (X', Y', Z') can be determined by rotating it with the inverse rotation q_R^{-1}.

Exterior Orientation: Finally, the exterior orientation of the satellite is necessary to define the geometric relation between the camera and the world (Fig. 5). The exterior orientation is provided by the AOCS (attitude and orbiting control system), measuring the satellites position and orientation mainly with a GPS-receiver, two star trackers and an IMU. While the position is already given in earth centered, earth fixed (ECEF) coordinates, the orientation has to be transformed from the stellar coordinate system to the moving earth. This complex system is an elementary part of the georeferencing chain and was investigated in-depth in the context of the geometric calibration and is beyond the scope of this paper.

The vector (X, Y, Z) is now given in satellite coordinates and is defined as pointing in the direction of the pixel i, corresponding to the line of sight.

Using the exterior orientation the vector (X, Y, Z), as well as the center of projection, can be transformed into the earth centered and earth fixed WGS84 coordinate system.

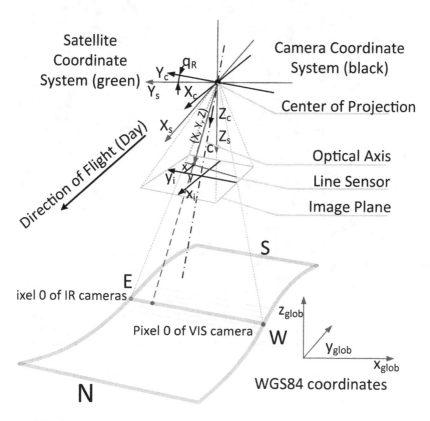

Fig. 5. Image and camera coordinates with respect to the satellite coordinate system

The exterior orientation is obtained from the AOCS and is already transformed into WGS84 coordinates.

Test Field: For almost every part of the world well georeferenced satellite imagery is available with a much higher ground resolution than the resolution of the cameras of TET-1/BIROS. So the ground control points can be arbitrary stationary points where the height is available via SRTM. The challenge is to find points that are clearly visible in all spectral bands.

For GCP selection the images are mapped on to a reference plane at average terrain height with the nominal camera parameters to obtain unstaggered and roughly undistorted images (Fig. 6).

Points on waterlines make for good GCPs, as water and land differ in the visual spectral range as well as having different temperatures and hence a good contrast in the infrared range. The disadvantage is that water lines can change over time, so care must be taken to (visually) ensure that the water level was similar at the time when the reference images were taken.

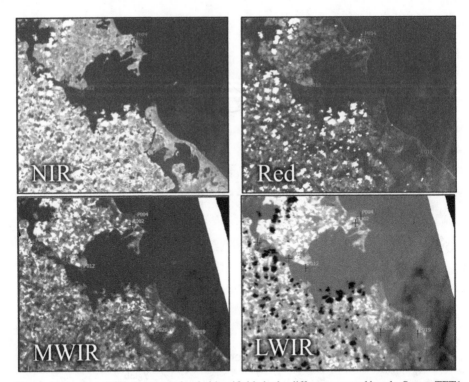

Fig. 6. Exemplary GCPs (crosses) clearly identifiable in the different spectral bands. Scene: TET1 Demmin, 1.8.2014 (Table 2). The displayed part shows the Baltic coast line around Stralsund and Greifswald

Bundle Adjustment: Given the camera model; the exterior orientation and the GCPs, a bundle adjustment was performed to determine the unknown boresight alignments and camera model parameters [13].

Relevant Calibration Parameters: During the calibration of TET-1 it became clear that just determining the boresight of each individual camera clearly improves georeferencing accuracy (as expected). However, no significant gain could be achieved by simultaneously determining the other camera parameters defined in the beginning of this section. An explanation for this is that the nominal camera parameters are accurate enough for the rather low resolution and/or that they are highly correlated with the boresight (e.g. x_0, y_0, and α). This was confirmed at the calibration of BIROS.

Geometric Processing: For the generation of the final data products a geometric processing chain was established following the radiometric correction. It uses the exterior orientation from the AOCS and the interior orientation obtained by the in-orbit calibration. The interior orientation if the cameras shall remain constant under normal circumstances. However, these can vary throughout the life time of the satellite. Therefore it is essential to keep the optical parameter configurable for data processing, in order to allow re-adjusting these parameters to the real state of the sensor at a time. For monitoring

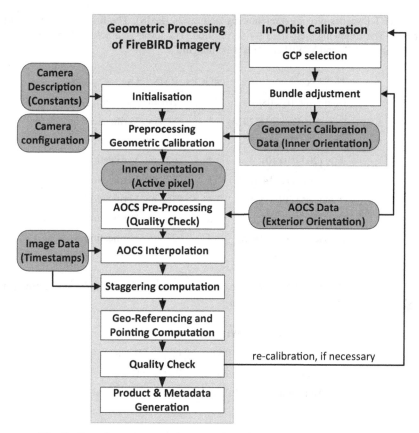

Fig. 7. Overview of geometric processing of TET-1 and BIROS imagery

and especially for maintenance it is crucial to transfer some of the original and derived parameters used as well as meta information to the final product, e.g. selection parameter and versioning or simply ground sampling distance. During processing additional plausibility checks are involved and derived dynamic parameters are provided, e.g. ground track etc. On demand additional geometric data can be generated. Standard metadata are produced in XML files allowing for simple tools to derive information either to generate statistics or to look for specific constellations. Such parameters are AOCS state, sensor state, illumination conditions, or geolocation and orbit parameter, e.g. orbit direction, roll angle (Fig. 7).

3 Results

TET-1

The calibration of TET-1 was performed on a test field around Demmin, Germany on 1.8.2014 during day time. Mostly on the coast to the Baltic Sea, 23 GCPs were manually selected and used for the bundle adjustment (top row of Table 2).

Table 2. TET-1 scenes direct georeferencing accuracies (RMS). The first scene was used for calibration. The following were used for verification. The lower four scenes were night scenes where only the LWIR and MWIR cameras were imaging

TET-1 scene	#GCPs	RMS	Use
Demmin (2014/08/01)	23	201 m	Calibration
Dominic. Rep. (8.8.2014)	3	545 m	Verification
Demmin (2014/09/09)	4	437 m	Verification
Italy (2014/10/10)	3	622 m	Verification
Kazakhstan (2014/10/23)	11	278 m	Verification
Indonesia (2014/10/0)	4	756 m	Verification
Darwin (2014/10/22)	3	609 m	Verification
Indonesia (2014/10/23)	4	230 m	Verification

Table 3. Determined boresight for day scenes with rotation expressed as Euler angles around the axes X (flight direction), Y (right) and Z (up)

TET-1 camera	LWIR	MWIR	VIS/NIR
Boresight r_x	$-0.157°$	$0.026°$	$0.348°$
Boresight r_y	$-1.268°$	$-1.242°$	$-1.253°$
Boresight r_z	$2.142°$	$-0.222°$	$0.253°$

The following lines show the accuracy reached with the above calibration at other scenes. The GCPs were only used as check points for the accuracy of direct georeferencing. In Table 3 the corresponding boresight alignment angles are listed.

BIROS
Consequently, the same approach was used for calibration and verification of the geometric status and accuracy of BIROS images. A set of 140 BIROS scenes was used to determine the on-board calibration values of the MWIR and LWIR sensors onboard of the BIROS satellite and to evaluate the influences of possible error sources on the direct georeferencing, which had not previously been investigated in detail for the TET data sets. The scenes were divided into two sets depending on the availability of star tracker information which serves as highly precise input for the exterior orientation of the system. This separation revealed that the set with at least one star tracker available produced a far more consistent set of boresight angles in comparison to scenes with no contemporaneous star tracker information available. To further reduce complexity of the data takes and a possible error source, scenes with off-nadir pointing angles larger than 10° were removed, which further reduced the RMS. By clustering the remaining boresight angles, two distinct sets of angles differing by 0.8° in pitch direction (r_y) became evident, which cannot be explained by changes in the boresight. This difference can be resolved by a positional error along track of 7.8 km. By analyzing the timing events

and the metadata an irregularly occurring timing error of 1 s in the metadata could be identified and removed, so the two clusters could be merged into one consistent set of boresight angles, which is given in Table 4.

Table 4. Determined boresight for BIROS, rotation expressed as Euler angles around the axes X (flight direction), Y (right) and Z (up)

BIROS camera	LWIR	MWIR
Boresight r_x	$-0.151°$	$-0.260°$
Boresight r_y	$-3.204°$	$-3.824°$
Boresight r_z	$-1.089°$	$1.068°$

Using scenes with highest quality exterior orientation (at least one star tracker available) and exact timing, a direct georeferencing mean accuracy of 419.2 m was achieved for 32 selected scenes; the best scenes showing an RMS with sub-pixel accuracy. This solution allows for a significant improvement of the geometric accuracy of the individual data sets during reprocessing and an automatic mosaicking of the scenes, as observed by [14] (Table 5).

Table 5. Statistics for direct georeferencing using the determined boresight angles and timing correction for 32 BIROS scenes with star trackers, MWIR and LWIR

Source	#GCPs	RMS	Use
Mean 32 scenes	4	419 m	
Median 32 scenes	4	397 m	Calibration
Persian Gulf (2019/05/24), showing minimum RMS	4	156 m	Verification
Chile (2018/06/22) showing maximum RMS	5	792 m	Verification

4 Lessons Learned

The experiences with real space missions show that even obvious issues and challenges are often underestimated, e.g. providing a common time base for different subsystems or defining coordinate systems and their transition matrices. Additionally, the complexity of an entire system is often underestimated. Companies or research institutes focus on single units, the overall view goes short, and e.g. the positioning of a star tracker should be optimized knowing mission operation conditions to maximize star-fix of the trackers. System simulators can help to overcome this issue. The investigations show the important role of image quality (IQ) assessment as an integral part of a mission, as the image reveals the behavior and status of the sensor system (satellite) directly. This begins with simulation of representative images before launch, the definition of requirements for the processing software, including updates during the mission and ends with validation of images taken during the mission.

For calibration of optical sensors for small satellites a few notes shall summarize the lessons learned:

- Be aware of the limitations of the on ground calibration processes.
- Include specialists for system design, calibration and data processing into a calibration team from the very beginning.
- Design an optical system in a way that it can be calibrated in-flight.
- A validation procedure must be an inherent part of the design.

5 Conclusions

Direct georeferencing involves a whole chain of satellite subsystems, such as star trackers, IMU, time synchronization, camera, read out electronics, on-board data processing, and the camera with its subcomponents. A complete verification of the functionality and performance can only be made under flight conditions. Even though all subsystems were tested before launch it turned out, that additional work hat do be done to reach the desired performance (Fig. 8).

Based on detailed investigations, these existing problems, the interior geometry as well the timing regime could have been detected, analyzed. The described solution was developed to solve these problems to reach an operational state of both satellites, TET-1 and BIROS, including direct georeferencing. Using high quality AOCS data, subpixel accuracy can be reached with direct georeferencing,

The presented investigations show the necessity to consider and implement validation procedures as an integral part of the data processing chain. These tasks in combination with data quality assessment procedures are the prerequisite for standardized product development activities within further mission activities.

Fig. 8. Mosaic of two BIROS scenes from Kuwait (MWIR, 2018.05.13 and 2018.08.29) processed using direct georeferencing with optimized boresight angles (Table 4)

References

1. Jahn, H., Brieß, K., Ginati, A.: FIRES - a small satellite mission for fire detection. In: Proceedings of IAA Symposium on Small Satellites for Earth Observation, Berlin, November 1996, pp. 301–304 (1996)
2. Oertel, D., et al.: FOCUS: environmental disaster recognition system. In: First Symposium on the Utilization of the International Space Station, 30 September–2 October 1996, Darmstadt (1996)
3. https://activations.zki.dlr.de/en/activations/items/ACT139.html. Accessed 09 Oct 2019
4. Dozier, J.: A method for satellite identification of surface temperature fields of subpixel resolution. Remote Sens. Environ. **11**, 221–229 (1981)
5. Zhukov, B., Lorenz, E., Oertel, D.: Experiences of detection and quantitative characterization of fires during the experimental small satellite mission BIRD. DLR-FB 2005-04, 96 p. (2005). ISSN 1434-8454

6. Zhukov, B., Lorenz, E., Oertel, D., Wooster, M., Roberts, G.: Spaceborne detection and characterization of fires during the bi-spectral infrared detection (BIRD) experimental small satellite mission (2001–2004). Remote Sens. Environ. **100**(1), 29–51 (2006)
7. Wooster, M., Zhukov, B., Oertel, D.: Fire radiative energy release for quantitative study of biomass burning: derivation from BIRD experimental satellite and comparison to MODIS fire products. Remote Sens. Environ. **86**, 83–107 (2003)
8. Fischer, C., et al.: Data validation and case studies using the TET-1 thermal infrared satellite system. Int. Arch. Photogram. Remote Sens. Spat. Inf. Sci. (ISPRS) **XL-7/W3**, 1177–1182 (2003). 36th International Symposium on Remote Sensing of Environment, 11–15 May 2015 Berlin
9. Cramer, M., Stallmann, D.: System calibration for direct georeferencing. Int. Arch. Photogram. Remote Sens. Spat. Inf. Sci. **34** (2001)
10. Honkavaara, E.: In-flight calibration for direct georeferencing. Int. Arch. Photogram. Remote Sens. Spat. Inf. Sci. **35**, 166–172 (2004)
11. Hieronymus, J.: Comparison of methods for geometric camera calibration. Int. Arch. Photogram. Remote Sens. Spat. Inf. Sci. **XXXIX-B5**, 595–599 (2012)
12. Brown, D.C.: Close-range camera calibration. Photogram. Eng. **37**(8), 855–866 (1971)
13. Wohlfeil, J.: Completely optical orientation determination for an unstabilized aerial three-line camera. In: Proceedings of SPIE 7826, Sensors, Systems, and Next-Generation Satellites, 13 October 2010, vol. XIV, p. 78261F (2010). https://doi.org/10.1117/12.865050
14. Wang, M., Yang, B., Hu, F., Zang, X.: On-orbit geometric calibration model and its applications for high-resolution optical satellite imagery. Remote Sens. **6**(5), 4391–4408 (2014)

Evaluation of Structures and Methods for Resolution Determination of Remote Sensing Sensors

Henry Meißner[1]([⊠]) [iD], Michael Cramer[2][iD], and Ralf Reulke[3][iD]

[1] Institute of Optical Sensor Systems, German Aerospace Center,
12489 Berlin, Germany
henry.meissner@dlr.de
[2] Institute for Photogrammetry (ifp), University of Stuttgart,
70174 Stuttgart, Germany
michael.cramer@ifp.uni-stuttgart.de
[3] Humboldt-University, 12489 Berlin, Germany
ralf.reulke@hu-berlin.de

Abstract. Effective image resolution is an important image quality factor for remote sensing sensors and significantly affects photogrammetric processing tool chains. Tie points, mandatory for forming the block geometry, fully rely on feature points (i.e. SIFT, SURF) and quality of these points however is significantly correlated to image resolution. Spatial resolution can be determined in different ways. Utilizing bar test charts (e.g. USAF51), slanted edges (ISO 12233) and Siemens-Stars are widely accepted techniques. The paper describes these approaches and compares all in one joint experiment. Moreover, Slanted-Edge and Siemens-Star method is evaluated using (close to) ideal images convolved with known parameters. It will be shown that both techniques deliver conclusive and expected results.

Keywords: Resolving power · Image quality · Siemens-Star · Slanted-Edge · USAF51 test-chart

1 Introduction

Ground resolved distance (GRD) or true ground sample distance (tGSD) is an essential parameter of imaging systems [4,9], as it defines the detail of information in any image taken by remote sensing sensors. The effective geometric resolution significantly affects photogrammetric processing tool chains. Tie points, mandatory for forming the block geometry, fully rely on feature points (SIFT, SURF, etc.) and the quality parameters of these points however are significantly correlated to image resolution [7]. This is why resolution determination is of such importance to quantify the potential of a sensor-lens-combination.

Although acquisition of resolving power is a well-studied field of research, there are still some scientific questions to be answered when it comes to a standardized (eventually absolute) determination. This is also research object of a

© Springer Nature Switzerland AG 2020
J. J. Dabrowski et al. (Eds.): PSIVT 2019 Workshops, LNCS 11994, pp. 59–69, 2020.
https://doi.org/10.1007/978-3-030-39770-8_5

committee of the "German Institute for Standardization" and the given contribution outlines the current state of investigation concerning remote sensing sensors.

Orych [9] provided a description of calibration targets used for high-resolution remote sensing imaging equipment and concluded: "Based on a preliminary analysis, three types of test patterns were selected as possible choices for evaluating the quality of imagery acquired by UAV sensors: bar target, Slanted Edge Test and Siemens Star." Extending the perspective from UAV-context to a general remote sensing perspective all three approaches must deliver similar or ideally the exact same results for identical images and image regions.

Furthermore, implementations of Slanted-Edge and Siemens-Star method can be tested for validity by using known (model) parameters for a Gaussian-kernel and subsequent convolution with (close to ideal) images. Then it must be possible to extract (resp. measure) the predefined parameters with both approaches.

Therefore, all techniques (USAF51, Slanted-Edge, Siemens-Star) will be described with mathematical detail in Sect. 2 followed by introducing a model-based approach to simulate distinct image resolution in Sect. 3. Related experiment description and obtained results are given in Sect. 4.

2   Structures and Techniques

Sharpness as an image property is characterized by the modulation transfer function (MTF) which is the spatial frequency response of an imaging system to a given illumination. "High spatial frequencies correspond to fine image detail. The more extended the response, the finer the detail - the sharper the image." [8]. Inverse Fourier-transforming MTF, directly delivers the point spread function (PSF) [10]. The parameter σ (standard deviation) of the PSF (assumed Gaussian-shape function) is one criterion. It directly relates to image space and can be seen as objective measure to compare different camera performances. Another criterion is the spatial frequency where the MTF reaches a certain (minimal-) value (i.e. 10%, MTF10). The reciprocal of that frequency is the approximation for size of the smallest line per pixel. The width of PSF at half the height of the maximum is another criterion (full width half maximum - FWHM) and is related to σ of PSF as follows [14]. Starting by assuming a Gaussian-shape function (Eq. 1).

$$H(x) = \frac{1}{\sigma\sqrt{2\pi}} \cdot e^{-\frac{(x-\mu)^2}{2\cdot\sigma^2}} \tag{1}$$

The constant scaling factor $\frac{1}{\sigma\sqrt{2\pi}}$ can be ignored. Applying $H(x) = 0.5$ leads to Eq. (2):

$$e^{-\frac{x_0-\mu}{2\cdot\sigma^2}} = 2^{-1} \tag{2}$$

Solving Eq. (2) and assuming function value $H(x_{max})$ occurs at $\mu = 0$ half-maximum points x_0 are found (Eq. 3):

$$x_0 = \pm\sigma\sqrt{2\ln 2} \tag{3}$$

The full width at half maximum is then given by:

$$FWHM = x_+ - x_- = 2\sqrt{2\ln 2}\sigma \approx 2.3548\sigma \tag{4}$$

A similar measure exists in frequency domain. The effective instantaneous field-of-view (EIFOV) for MTF at 50% contrast level [3]. Assuming a Gaussian-shape function for PSF (Eq. 1) the Fourier-transformed $\tilde{H}(\nu)$ (MTF, Eq. 5) is formulated as follows [5]. Again, the constant scaling factor can be ignored.

$$\tilde{H}(\nu) = e^{-2\cdot\pi^2\cdot\sigma^2\cdot\nu^2} = 0.5 \tag{5}$$

By setting $\tilde{H}(\nu)$ equal to $= 0.5$ Eq. (5) can be written as:

$$2\cdot\pi^2\cdot\sigma^2\cdot\nu^2 = -\log(0.5) \tag{6}$$

Subsequent transposing then gives:

$$\nu = \sqrt{\frac{-\log(0.5)}{2\cdot\pi^2\cdot\sigma^2}} = \frac{\sqrt{-\log(0.5)/2}}{\pi\cdot\sigma} \tag{7}$$

Substituting with C

$$C = \frac{\sqrt{-\log(0.5)/2}}{\pi} \tag{8}$$

gives the formula for ν_δ (Eq. 9) similar to Eq. (3) and x_0.

$$\nu\cdot\delta = \nu_\delta = \frac{C}{\sigma^\delta} \tag{9}$$

Finally EIFOV can be calculated with the following equation:

$$\text{EIFOV} = \frac{\sigma^\delta}{2C} = 2.67\cdot\sigma^\delta \tag{10}$$

By comparing Eqs. (4) and (10) it is noticeable that both image quality parameters (FWHM & EIFOV) depend in their related domain (image- or frequency-domain) only on parameter σ (PSF or MTF) and a similar constant factor.

Aforementioned image quality parameters can be determined with different structures of patterns and different techniques and will be described in the following sub sections.

2.1 Bar Target

A classic approach is to use defined test targets (e.g. USAF resolution test chart, see Fig. 1, left) with groups of bars [12]. "The resolving power target used on all tests shall be as follows: The target shall consist of a series of patterns decreasing in size as the $\sqrt{2}$, $\sqrt[3]{2}$, $\sqrt[6]{2}$, with a range sufficient to cover the requirements [...]. The standard target element shall consist of two patterns (two sets of lines) at right angles to each other. Each pattern shall consist of three lines separated by spaces of equal width. Each line shall be five times as long as it is wide."

Images of test targets fulfilling these requirements are directly linked to object space metric resolution (see Fig. 1, right). There, the identified resolution corresponds to the distance between bars of the least discriminable group. The decision whether a group still is discriminable or not strongly relies on viewers' perception. To diminish subjective influence statistically the number of viewers n is chosen to be significant (e.g. $n \geq 10$) and the resulting resolution G_r (GRD, tGSD) is calculated (11) as mean of all independent observations G_i.

$$G_r = \frac{1}{n} \sum_{i=1}^{n} G_i \tag{11}$$

With knowledge about interior camera parameters (focal length f, pixel size s) and distance between camera system and test target d the theoretical resolution G_t is calculated as:

$$G_t = \frac{s}{f}\, d \tag{12}$$

While G_r is equivalent to GRD or tGSD, the quotient G_q according to Eq. (13) provides another measure for image resolving power.

$$G_q = \frac{G_r}{G_t} \tag{13}$$

Usually values for G_q greater than 1 are expected to be calculated. In this case theoretical resolution G_t is better than ultimately determined resolution G_r. Values $G_q \leq 1$ either result due to loss-less transition from object space to image space or indicate image enhancement (e.g. edge-sharpening, color refinement or super resolution).

Besides the disadvantage of subjective influence included in this acquisition method values for resolving power are discrete instead of continuous.

2.2   Slanted-Edge

The presented approach uses an edge-step technique [1,6]. It evaluates the transition between a very homogeneous dark area to a very homogeneous bright area along an extremely sharp, straight edge within the image. The most challenging part of the algorithm is to identify suitable horizontal and vertical edges [6] and to make sure that their position is known to sub-pixel accuracy [1]. Identification of the edges is done automatically either by using a line segment detector [13] or by using a Canny edge detector followed by a Hough transform. Each edge is refined to match the actual transition in the current image as closely as possible, using a custom-built refinement procedure.

After the edges have been located and confirmed to meet the quality standards, their complete profile, spanning their entire length, has to be derived. For each point on the edge, moving along the edge pixel by pixel, the profile following the image's pixel grid is extracted and projected onto the perpendicular to the edge. An alternative approach is to scan and combine multiple perpendicular lines by applying bi-cubic or bi-linear interpolations methods [11].

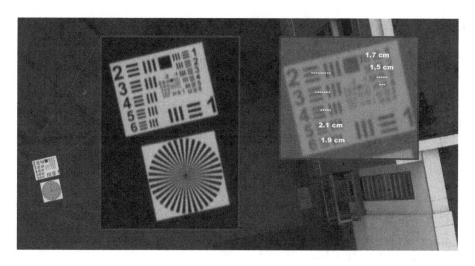

Fig. 1. Aerial image of USAF bar test target (left), corresponding ground resolution [cm] in object space (right)

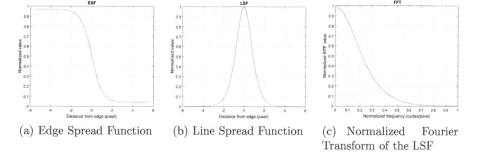

(a) Edge Spread Function (b) Line Spread Function (c) Normalized Fourier Transform of the LSF

Fig. 2. ESF, LSF and normalized FFT of an edge.

The thus obtained projected edge profile is cleaned from blunders, filtered and approximated with a Sigmoid function. The resulting Edge Spread Function (ESF), i.e. the response of the system to this edge [1,6], is shown in Fig. 2(a). The numerical derivative of the ESF yields the Line Spread Function (LSF), the response of the system to a line target [1,6], an example of which is displayed in Fig. 2(b). Finally, a Fast Fourier Transform (FFT) is applied to the LSF (Fig. 2(c)) and the normalized magnitude of the result evaluated at the Nyquist frequency (0.5 cycles per pixel) yields the MTF.

2.3 Siemens-Star

Using a priori knowledge of the original scene (well-known Siemens-Star target) contrast transfer function CTF, MTF and PSF are approximated by a Gaussian shape function [7]. Coordinate axis X for CTF and MTF is the spatial frequency

f (Eq. 14) and is calculated as target frequency f_s divided by current scan radius r multiplied by π. Target frequency f_s is constant and equivalent to the number of black-white segments of the well-known Siemens-Star.

$$f = \frac{f_s}{\pi r} \tag{14}$$

Related (initially discrete) values for contrast transfer function $C_d\left(f\right)$ are derived using intensity maxima I_{max} and minima I_{min} for every scanned circle (Eq. 15). Simultaneously the function value is normalized to contrast level C_0 at spatial frequency equal to 0 (infinite radius).

$$C_d\left(f\right) = \frac{I_{max}\left(f\right) - I_{min}\left(f\right)}{I_{max}\left(f\right) + I_{min}\left(f\right)} * \frac{1}{C_0} \tag{15}$$

Continuous function values C are derived by fitting a Gaussian function into discrete input data (Eq. 16).

$$C = \frac{1}{\sigma\sqrt{2\pi}} e^{-\frac{1}{2}\left(\frac{x-\mu}{\sigma}\right)^2} \tag{16}$$

According to [2] the obtained CTF describes the system response to a square wave input while MTF is the system response to a sine wave input. The proposed solution is a normalization with $\frac{\pi}{4}$ followed by series expansion using odd frequency multiples (Eq. 17).

$$MTF\left(f\right) = \frac{\pi}{4}\left[C\left(f\right) + \frac{C\left(3f\right)}{3} + \frac{C\left(5f\right)}{5} + \dots\right] \tag{17}$$

MTF describes the effective resolving power in frequency domain while PSF is the image domain equivalent. For this reason both functions are linked directly by fourier transform (Eq. 18).

$$PSF \quad \circ\!\!-\!\!\bullet \quad MTF \tag{18}$$

3   Model-Based PSF and MTF

A conclusive validation of Slanted-Edge (Sect. 2.2) and Siemens-Star technique (Sect. 2.3) is to apply predefined modulation (MTF) or spread parameters (PSF) to an ideal representation of resolving patterns (see Fig. 3). This can be done in both domains. In image-domain it can be done by forming a convolution of mathematical-ideal image-intensity values of an image (I), a Gaussian-shape model PSF (H_m) and a mathematical-ideal sensor PSF (H_s). Simulated PSF (H_{sim}) then can be formulated as follows:

$$H_{sim}(\rho) = I(\rho) * H_m(\rho) * H_s(\rho) \tag{19}$$

In frequency-domain calculation gets simpler, only the product of image spectrum ($\tilde{I}$) with a predefined model-based MTF ($\tilde{H}_M$) and (mathematical-ideal)

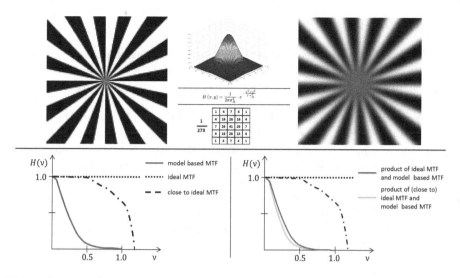

Fig. 3. Original image (upper left) continuous and discrete Gaussian PSF convolution kernel (upper mid) and convolution result (upper right), ideal MTF, close to ideal MTF and model-based MTF (lower left), related products in frequency domain (lower right)

sensor MTF ($\tilde{H}_S$) has to be calculated. Therefore, simulated-image MTF ($\tilde{H}_{Sim}$) can be formulated as follows:

$$\tilde{H}_{Sim}(\nu) = \tilde{I}(\nu) \cdot \tilde{H}_M(\nu) \cdot \tilde{H}_S(\nu) \tag{20}$$

The derived hypothesis is, if both algorithms (Slanted-Edge and Siemens-Star) described in Sect. 2 provide measurements of absolute value then model-MTF ($\tilde{H}_M$) respectively model-PSF (H_m) must directly be confirmed by measurement of simulated-image MTF ($\tilde{H}_{Sim}$) respectively PSF (H_{sim}).

Mathematical-ideal sensor-MTF $\tilde{H}_S(\nu)$ with $\nu \in \mathbb{R}$ is characterized as being equal to 1 for all frequencies (see Fig. 3, dotted line). However, when an ideal pattern is rendered to a pixel grid the resulting (Nyquist-limited) sensor-PSF and sensor-MTF unavoidably will differ from ideal shape. An example of (close to) ideal sensor-MTF can be seen in Fig. 3 (dashed-dotted line) with Nyquist-limit 1.0 line per pixel.

As a result, obtained MTF values ($\tilde{H}_{Sim}$) measure the product of (close to) ideal sensor-MTF ($\tilde{H}_S$) and model-MTF (H_M) and therefore are expected to be smaller than the product of ideal sensor-MTF ($\tilde{H}_S(\nu) = 1$, $\nu \in \mathbb{R}$) and model-MTF (H_M) (see Fig. 3, magenta and cyan line).

Considering that, PSF and MTF are directly linked by (inverse) Fourier transformation (Eq. 18), it can be assumed that for increasing values σ_m (H_s) respectively for decreasing values σ_M ($\tilde{H}_S$) simulated images and corresponding measured quality parameter σ_{SLE} and σ_{Star} of H_{sim} will be continuously less affected by the difference of ideal and (close to) ideal sensor- PSF or MTF. This assumption can be verified (empirically) by an experiment in Sect. 4.2.

4   Experiments

Algorithms for standardized (eventually absolute) determination of resolving power under consideration for norm-description (e.g. by a committee of the "German Institute for Standardization") need to be validated with respect to conditions described in Sects. 2 and 3.

Every method to determine effective resolving power of remote sensing sensors described in Sect. 2 for itself has individual advantages. Slanted-Edge is a well studied approach and has been transferred to a norm-description (ISO 12233, [15]). Bar charts (e.g. USAF51) are very intuitive and responsive. Slanted-Edge uses the first derivative of ESF between intensity maxima and minima, in contrast the Siemens-Star approach uses exact those maxima and minima and calculates CTF (Eq. 14) and MTF. Empirical observations indicate that due to this difference measurements of the Siemens-Star approach are more robust against influence of widely used sharpening filters.

4.1   Simultaneous Resolving Power Determination

Given the variety of approaches and techniques it is consistently necessary to compare their respective results and answer the question if used techniques do or do not perform equivalently and what are reasons for particular observations. Therefore, all described approaches have been applied simultaneously for identical images and image regions (example Fig. 4). Used image quality parameter is ground resolved distance (GRD in cm). For USAF51 bar chart GRD is calculated according to Eq. (11) with number of observers $n \geq 10$. Reciprocal of MTF10 is the approximation for size of the smallest line per pixel. Multiplying reciprocal of MTF10-values from Slanted-Edge and Siemens-Star measurement with calculated ground sample distance (GSD, Eq. 12) delivers GRD for both algorithms. Seven images (example see Fig. 4), showing bar chart and Siemens-Star simultaneously and GSD between 1.24 cm and 1.27 cm, have been taken to obtain following results (Table 1):

The fourth column (Δ SLE-Star) shows the absolute difference between Slanted-Edge and Siemens-Star approach in percent. Except for one outlier, both techniques seem to measure very similar at an overall mean difference of 3.3%.

Values obtained by independent human observers and USAF51 tend to be more static compared to the other methods. This effect could be caused by huge resolution steps between groups of bars. Rearranging the target, including more groups with finer descent, may weaken the effect.

Even when comparing all three approaches at once (Δ Min-Max) the overall mean difference of 7.1% still can be considered very low.

4.2   Measurement of Model-Based MTF and PSF

As described in Sect. 3, a conclusive validation of Slanted-Edge and Siemens-Star technique is to apply predefined modulation (MTF) or spread parameters (PSF).

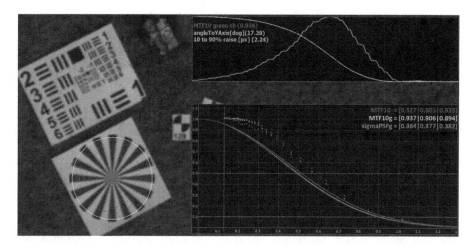

Fig. 4. Simultaneous determination of ground resolved distance (GRD) for USAF51 (left), Slanted-Edge (upper right) and Siemens-Star (lower right)

Table 1. Simultaneous determination of ground resolved distance (GRD) for USAF51, Slanted-Edge and Siemens-Star

	Bar chart	Slanted E.	SiemStar	Δ SLE-Star [%]	Δ Min-Max [%]
Image Nr. 1	1.45	1.49	1.52	2.0	4.6
Image Nr. 2	1.48	1.51	1.52	0.7	2.6
Image Nr. 3	1.55	1.45	1.45	0.0	6.5
Image Nr. 4	1.39	1.32	1.34	1.5	5.0
Image Nr. 5	1.43	1.38	1.30	5.8	9.1
Image Nr. 6	1.45	1.24	1.39	10.8	14.5
Image Nr. 7	1.42	1.50	1.53	2.0	7.2

Then, the used model parameters σ_m must be reproduced by both methods during measurement (σ_{SLE} and σ_{Star} of H_{sim}). For this reason, an image showing a Siemens-Star including (close to) ideal sensor PSF (H_s) has been convolved with different σ_m starting at 0.500 and rising to 1.750. Subsequently, σ of H_{sim} has been calculated with both Slanted-Egde and Siemens-Star approach. Obtained results can be found in following table (Table 2):

Values in column ΔA show the difference between model parameter σ_m and measured parameter σ_{SLE} in absolute percentage [%]. Values of column ΔB provide results for difference between σ_m and measured σ_{Star}. Similar to the comparison of both techniques in preceding experiment Sect. 4.1 column ΔC reflects the absolute difference between σ_{SLE} and σ_{Star} in absolute percentage [%].

Table 2. Model-PSF compared to measured PSF of Slanted-Edge and Siemens-Star

σ_m of (H_m)	σ Slanted Edge	σ Siemens Star	ΔA [%]	ΔB [%]	ΔC [%]
0.500	0.609	0.598	17.8	16.4	1.7
0.750	0.894	0.856	16.1	12.4	4.2
1.000	1.093	1.076	8.5	7.1	1.6
1.250	1.301	1.306	3.9	4.3	0.4
1.500	1.546	1.532	3.0	2.1	0.9
1.750	1.739	1.748	0.7	0.1	0.5

Two observations can be emphasized. First, the difference between Slanted-Edge and Siemens-Star technique again is small. In contrast to experiment Sect. 4.1 overall mean difference of 1.6% here is even smaller and measurements deliver no outliers. Second observation regards constructed hypothesis in Sect. 3: "...it can be assumed that for increasing values σ_m (PSF) ... simulated images and corresponding quality parameter ... will be continuously less affected by the difference of ideal and (close to) ideal sensor- PSF". Columns ΔA and ΔB indicate that this hypothesis is true. With rising σ_m the absolute difference of both methods tend to approach zero.

5   Conclusion and Outlook

Mathematically detailed descriptions of three different techniques for determination of resolving power were presented. A model-based approach and its underlying theory has been introduced to verify two acquisition methods (Slanted-Edge and Siemens-Star). Moreover, two experiments have been conducted to verify similar and correct measurements of all techniques. It can be concluded that all methods deliver expected, similar and mathematical predictable results. In particular, experimental results for difference of Slanted-Edge (ISO 12233) and Siemens-Star deliver very similar output and thus both approaches can be considered for further evaluation regarding standardized norm-description. Presented results highly indicate that both methods can be seen complementary to each other.

Previous work [7] already described influence of used de-mosaicing methods on resolving power and related measurements. Future work and final contribution is going to conclude the investigation and thoroughly clarify further open issues as support to research of the "German Institute for Standardization".

These open issues are: Siemens-Star center position (determination and associated confidence), normalization of contrast magnitude and related requirements of the test pattern layout, exposure time dependency, influence of motion blur, influence of used interpolation methods during signal-scan (e.g. nearest-neighbour, bi-linear, bi-cubic), different mathematical models for PSF/MTF

(Gaussian-shape, polynomial-shape, piece-wise linear) and influence of test target inclination during acquisition.

References

1. Choi, T., Helder, D.L.: Generic sensor modeling for modulation transfer function (MTF) estimation. Global Priorities in Land Remote Sensing, South Dakota (2005)
2. Coltman, J.W.: The specification of imaging properties by response to a sine wave input. J. Opt. Soc. Am. **44**, 468–471 (1954)
3. Goddard Space Flight Center: Advanced scanners and imaging systems for earth observations. NASA SP-335, Scientific and Technical Information Office, National Aeronautics and Space Administration, Washington (1973)
4. Honkavaara, E., Jaakkola, J., Markelin, L., Becker, S.: Evaluation of resolving power and MTF of DMC. Int. Arch. Photogramm. Remote Sens. Spat. Inf. Sci. **36**(6), 1–6 (2006)
5. Jahn, H., Reulke, R.: Systemtheoretische Grundlagen optoelektronischer Sensoren. Wiley, Hoboken (2009)
6. Kohm, K.: Modulation transfer function measurement method and results for the Orbview-3 high resolution imaging satellite. In: Proceedings of ISPRS, pp. 12–23 (2004)
7. Meißner, H., Cramer, M., Reulke, R.: Towards standardized evaluation of image quality for airborne camera systems. ISPRS-Int. Arch. Photogramm. Remote Sens. Spat. Inf. Sci. **XLII-1**, 295–300 (2018). https://doi.org/10.5194/isprs-archives-XLII-1-295-2018. https://www.int-arch-photogramm-remote-sens-spatial-inf-sci.net/XLII-1/295/2018/
8. Mix, P.E.: Introduction to Nondestructive Testing: A Training Guide. Wiley, Hoboken (2005)
9. Orych, A.: Review of methods for determining the spatial resolution of UAV sensors. ISPRS-Int. Arch. Photogramm. Remote Sens. Spat. Inf. Sci. **XL-1/W4** (2015). https://doi.org/10.5194/isprsarchives-XL-1-W4-391-2015
10. Reulke, R., Becker, S., Haala, N., Tempelmann, U.: Determination and improvement of spatial resolution of the CCD-line-scanner system ADS40. ISPRS J. Photogramm. Remote Sens. **60**(2), 81–90 (2006)
11. Russell, W.S.: Polynomial interpolation schemes for internal derivative distributions on structured grids. Appl. Numer. Math. **17**(2), 129–171 (1995)
12. USAF: Military standard photographic lenses, mIL-STD-150A, May 1959
13. Von Gioi, R.G., Jakubowicz, J., Morel, J.M., Randall, G.: LSD: a line segment detector. Image Process. On Line **2**, 35–55 (2012)
14. Weisstein, E.W.: Gaussian function, July 2019. http://mathworld.wolfram.com/GaussianFunction.html
15. Williams, D.: Benchmarking of the ISO 12233 slanted-edge spatial frequency response plug-in. In: PICS, pp. 133–136 (1998)

International Workshop on Deep Learning and Image Processing Techniques for Medical Images

3D Image Reconstruction
from Multi-focus Microscopic Images

Takahiro Yamaguchi[1], Hajime Nagahara[2], Ken'ichi Morooka[1(✉)],
Yuta Nakashima[2], Yuki Uranishi[2], Shoko Miyauchi[1], and Ryo Kurazume[1]

[1] Graduate School of Information Science and Electrical Engineering,
Kyushu University, Fukuoka 819-0395, Japan
t_yamaguchi@irvs.ait.kyushu-u.ac.jp, morooka@ait.kyushu-u.ac.jp
[2] Institute for Datability Science, Osaka University, Osaka 565-0871, Japan
nagahara@ids.osaka-u.ac.jp

Abstract. This paper presents a method for reconstructing 3D image
from multi-focus microscopic images captured with different focuses. We
model the multi-focus imaging by a microscopy and produce the 3D
image of a target object based on the model. The 3D image reconstruction is done by minimizing the difference between the observed images
and the simulated images generated by the imaging model. Simulation
and experimental result shows that the proposed method can generate
the 3D image of a transparent object efficiently and reliably.

Keywords: 3D imaging · Microscopy · Multi-focus images ·
Transparent object

1 Introduction

Cell observation by optical microscopy is widely used in biology, medicine, and
so on. For example, cytodiagnosis and iPS cells culture are based on the cell
observation. A regular microscopy acquires a 2D image of a target cell with
a 3D structure. However, only a part of slices of the 3D cell structure can be
observed as a focused image because the depth of field of the general microscope
is narrow. Under such circumstances, various applications can be expected for
the measurement technology of 3D cell structure. As specific examples of the
applications, there are accurate diagnosis by stereoscopic observation of cells
and improvement of cell identification performance by machine learning using
3D shape information.

A simple way to get the 3D structure using a microscopy is to stack multiple slice images with different focuses. Various methodologies [1] have been
proposed to measure the multi-focus images. However, the simple stacked multi-
focus images include many unclear regions because of reflections of front and

Supported by JST CREST Grant Number JPMJCR1786 and JSPS KAKENHI Grant
Number JP19H04139, Japan.

J. J. Dabrowski et al. (Eds.): PSIVT 2019 Workshops, LNCS 11994, pp. 73–85, 2020.
https://doi.org/10.1007/978-3-030-39770-8_6

backside of the focus. To solve this problem, a confocal microscope is often used. In a confocal microscope, a pinhole in front of a light detector cuts off light that is out of focus while allowing only the fluorescence light from the in-focus spot to enter the light detector. Thus, a confocal microscope is a useful and powerful tool to obtain clear images of only in-focus regions.

In computer vision, there are Depth from Focus (DFF) [2] and Depth from Defocus (DFD) [3,4] as methods for estimating the 3D shape from a multi-focus images. DFF specifies the most focused image from the multi-focus images, and the depth of the object from the position on focused image. DFD estimates the depth of a target object from two images which have different blur. Moreover, a method for estimating the depth of the object from a single image using DFD has also been proposed [5]. These DFF and DFD generally estimate the surface shape of an opaque object. Therefore, even if these methods are directly applied to a transparent object, the 3D shape of the object is not measured well under the influence from the texture information of slices before and after the focused slice.

Another approach for imaging the 3D object structure is a computed tomography (CT) [6]. In CT scanning, when X-rays is irradiated to a target object, an X-ray detector on opposite sides of the object detects the X-ray passing through the object. Here, it is assumed that X-ray is absorbed and attenuated by the object in the irradiation. On the assumption, many intensities of X-ray are measured by rotating a pair of X-ray source and detector around the object. When a target object is represented with a set of voxels, the measured intensities are used to estimate the attenuation coefficient of each voxel.

Similar to X-ray CT, optical projection tomography (OPT) [7] has been proposed for a microscopic 3D imaging. Using a regular light, lens optics and a silicon image sensor, OPT estimates the light attenuation of each voxel. However, since the imaging systems of X-ray and OPT require rotation mechanisms, the methodology of X-ray CT and OPT is directly inapplicable to regular microscopes with no rotation mechanism.

In this paper, we propose a method for reconstructing 3D image from multi-focus microscopic images obtained with different focuses. We model an imaging system for acquiring the multi-focus microscopic images with different focuses. In the imaging system, the microscopic images are produced by the light emitted from its light source. When the light passes through the transparent object, the light is attenuated depending on the transmittance of the object material. This means that each pixel in the microscopic image is related to these attenuated light. Considering this, we reconstruct the 3D image of the object by minimizing the difference between the observed images and the simulated images generated by the imaging model.

Similar with our method, there are two approaches for 3D imaging using multi-focus images. The first is the reconstruction of 3D image which contains appearance of inner slices of transparent objects [8]. The 3D image is generated by simply piling these discrete slices acquired by CCD cameras. The second approach is to reconstruct 3D image of a target object's luminescence

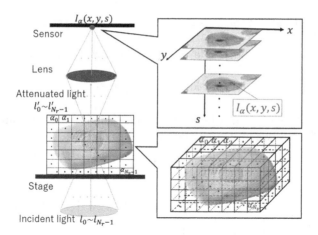

Fig. 1. Imaging system model

from multi-focus images obtained by a fluorescence microscope [9]. Unlike the two approaches, we aim to reconstruct the 3D image as a set of voxels having transmittance values from multi-focus images obtained by a general bright field microscopy.

The contribution of the proposed method is two folded. The proposed method estimates from only multi-focus microscopic images with no special equipments or measurement methods. Therefore, the proposed method is applicable to various applications using microscopic images. In addition, although the target is a cell in this paper, this method can also be applied to general translucent objects other than cells.

2   3D Image Reconstruction from Multi-focus Images

2.1   Imaging Model for Multi-focus Microscopic Images

Figure 1 shows how the pixel intensity is observed by a microscopy. We denote as $I_\alpha(x, y, s)$ an intensity value of an arbitrary pixel (x, y) in the s-th image in the sequence of the multi-focus microscopic images. Here, it is assumed that a target space including one or more than cells is represented by a set of voxels. 3D image is estimated as transmittances of the voxels α_i $(i = 0, 1, \cdots, N_v - 1)$ as shown in Fig. 1.

An incident light is emitted from a light source under a stage. The incident light is discretized as a set of N_r discrete rays. The intensity l_j of the j-th $(j = 0, 1, \cdots, N_r - 1)$ ray is attenuated every time the ray passes through each voxel. The attenuation is affected by the transmittance of the voxel and the length of the ray through the voxel. Hence, we model the relationship between l_j and the attenuated ray l'_j by

$$l'_j = l_j \times \prod_i \alpha_i^{d_{ji}}, \tag{1}$$

where d_{ji} is the length of the j-th ray in the i-th voxel if the ray passes through the i-th voxel. Otherwise, $d_{ji} = 0$.

By taking the log of both side in Eq. (1) and expanding the log, Eq. (1) is rewritten as

$$\log l'_j = \log l_j + \sum_i d_{ji} \log \alpha_i. \tag{2}$$

By collecting all relationships between the incident ray and attenuated ray, l_j and l'_j using Eq. (2), we obtain the following formulation:

$$L' = DA + L, \tag{3}$$

where

$$L = \begin{bmatrix} \log l_0 \\ \vdots \\ \log l_{N_r-1} \end{bmatrix}, \; L' = \begin{bmatrix} \log l'_0 \\ \vdots \\ \log l'_{N_r-1} \end{bmatrix}, \; A = \begin{bmatrix} \log \alpha_0 \\ \vdots \\ \log \alpha_{N_v-1} \end{bmatrix},$$

$$D = \begin{bmatrix} d_{00} & \cdots & d_{0(N_v-1)} \\ \vdots & \ddots & \vdots \\ d_{(N_r-1)0} & \cdots & d_{(N_r-1)(N_v-1)} \end{bmatrix}.$$

Here, we assume that aperture of the light source and objective lens are enough large to the target cell. On this assumption, an arbitrary pixel $I_\alpha(x, y, s)$ can be similarly expressed by shifting the stage along with (x, y, s) coordinates. Therefore, D and L are regarded as the function of the three parameters x, y, and s. Therefore, by rewriting D as a function of (x, y, s), Eq. (3) is described as

$$L'(x, y, s) = D(x, y, s)A + L. \tag{4}$$

Finally, $I_\alpha(x, y, s)$ is calculated by the total amount of the attenuated rays l'_j:

$$I_\alpha(x, y, s) = \sum_j l'_j(x, y, s). \tag{5}$$

2.2   Estimation of the Voxel Transmittance

Using the model as mentioned in Sect. 2.1, we simulate the observed multi-focus images. When the estimated transmittances of the target voxels are close to the real ones, the intensity value of the simulated multi-focus images $I_\alpha(x, y, s)$ should be the same as the intensity value of the observed images $I(x, y, s)$ by the microscopy. Considering this, the 3D image is reconstructed by minimizing an objective function F:

$$F(\alpha) = E(\alpha) + wTV(\alpha), \tag{6}$$

where $\alpha = (\alpha_0, \alpha_1, \cdots, \alpha_{N_v-1})$ is a vector composed of all the transmittances. The parameter w is a weighted coefficient as a regularization parameter. The gradient descent method is applied to find optimal transmittances which minimize $F(\alpha)$.

The function $E(\alpha)$ in Eq. (6) represents the difference between the intensity value $I(x, y, s)$ in the observed image and $I_\alpha(x, y, s)$ in the simulated image by Eq. (5). The function E is defined as

$$E(\alpha) = \sum_s \sum_x \sum_y (I_\alpha(x, y, s) - I(x, y, s))^2. \tag{7}$$

On the contrary, $TV(\alpha)$ is a regularization function base on a total variation (TV) norm to reconstruct the 3D image smoothly. Practically, the value of $TV(\alpha)$ is calculated by the total transmittance difference between the target voxels and its six neighbor voxels:

$$TV(\alpha) = \sum_{k \in \Phi_i} (\alpha_i - \alpha_k)^2, \tag{8}$$

where Φ_i is the set of the six neighbors of the target i-th voxel.

2.3 Efficient Search of Optimal Transmittances

From Eq. (6), our proposed method finds the optimum transmittances by iteratively updating the transmittances. To find the optimum efficiently and robustly, we introduce the two followings.

2.3.1 Initialization from Input Images

The initial values of the transmittances are important to find the optimum transmittances robustly by the conjugate gradient method. Given a sequence of N_s multi-focus images, we determine the initial transmittances based on the intensity value $I(x, y, s)$ of the original image sequence.

Let us consider that all rays are intersected at the i-th voxel when the intensity $I(x, y, s)$ is calculated. In this case, since all rays pass through the i-th voxel, the transmittance α_i of the i-th voxel strongly influences on the calculation of $I(x, y, s)$ compared with other voxels. Moreover, in our imaging system model, each ray passes through at least N_s voxels. Therefore, the optimal transmittance value of the i-th voxel is approximately regarded as the N_s-th root of $I(x, y, s)$. Considering these, the initial transmittance value $\alpha_i^{(0)}$ of the i-th voxel is calculated by

$$\alpha_i^{(0)} = \sqrt[N_s]{I(x, y, s)}. \tag{9}$$

2.3.2 Coarse-to-Fine Search

From Eqs. (1)–(5), the computational burden in our method depends on the number of rays. When the small number of the rays is used, the estimation of the transmittances can be speeded up. However, the light is discretized roughly by the small number of the rays. Therefore, the use of such rays results in the low accuracy of estimating the transmittances. On the other hand, in the case of using many rays, although the estimation of the transmittances is time-consuming, the reliable transmittances can be obtained.

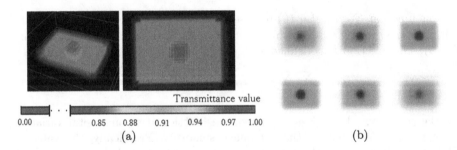

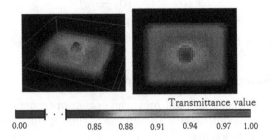

Fig. 2. (a) An artificial 3D cell model; (b) multi-focus images of the cell model (Color figure online).

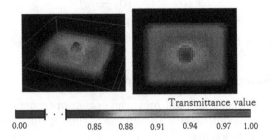

Fig. 3. 3D image of the cell model estimated by our method.

Considering the trade-off between the efficiency and accuracy of estimating the transmittances, we introduce a coarse-to-fine strategy. Firstly, in the coarse step, the transmittances are roughly estimated by using a small number of the rays (in our case, $N_r = 25$). The obtained transmittances in the coarse step are used as the initial values of the transmittances in the following fine step. In the fine step, we find the optimal values of the transmittances by using many rays (in our case, $N_r = 533$).

3   Experimental Results

To evaluate the performance of the proposed method, we made a simulation using synthetic images and experiments using real cell images.

3.1   Simulation Using Synthetic Images

In the simulation, we generate two virtual 3D cell models. Figure 2(a) shows one of them. It consists of a nucleus (red in Fig. 2(a)), a cytoplasm (light blue) and a cell membrane (blue). From real cell images, it is observed that the transmittance values of the nucleus tend to be lower than those of the cytoplasm and the membrane. Based on the observation, the transmittance values of the three components are set to 0.80 (the nucleus), 0.95 (the cytoplasm), and 0.98 (the membrane), respectively.

In addition, Shepp-Logan phantom was used to increase simulation variations. Three types of models were created by randomly changing the position of the ellipse. Figure 4(a) shows one of them.

The imaging system model (Sect. 2.1) is applied to generate the synthetic images of the virtual cells and Shepp-Logan phantom. Here, the number N_r of the rays used in the 3D image reconstruction is set to 533 so that for each voxel shown in Fig. 1, at least one ray passes through the voxel when the maximum blur is occurred in the model. Finally, we obtain 11 multi-focus images with 50×50 [pixel] (Figs. 2(b) and 4(b)).

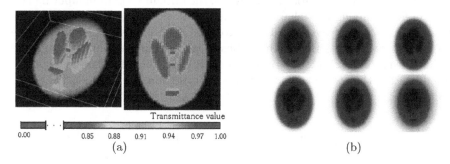

Fig. 4. (a) An artificial 3D Shepp-Logan phantom; (b) multi-focus images of Shepp-Logan phantom.

We verify initialization from input images and coarse-to-fine search (Sect. 2.3.2). In the verification, the 3D images are reconstructed by the proposed methods. The parameter w in Eq. (6) is set to $w = 0.125$. Moreover, the proposed methods are compared by the two methods. First one is the method in which all initial values of the transmittances are set to 0.5. Second one is the method which uses 25 or 533 rays to reconstruct the 3D image.

To measure the accuracy of the reconstructed 3D image, we use the root mean square error (RMSE) between the reconstructed 3D image and their ground truth

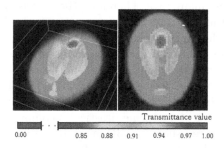

Fig. 5. 3D image of Shepp-Logan phantom estimated by our method.

values. Table 1 shows the average of RMSE and computational time between five 3D models for the each method (Fig. 5).

In the verification about the initialization, from Table 1, the initialization from input images improves the accuracy of reconstructing 3D image compared with the method in which all initial values of transmittances are set to 0.5. If all initial values of transmittances are set to 0.5, the optimal solution could not be obtained at all because of local minimum. Therefore, it is important to set the initial value as close as possible to the optimal solution in our method. Moreover, the computational time for the initialization from input images is shorter than that of the method in which all initial values of transmittances are set to 0.5 using same number of the rays. From these results, the initialization from input images is useful for obtaining the reliable transmittances. In the verification about the coarse-to-fine search, from Table 1, the proposed method using the coarse-to-fine search improves the accuracy of the reconstructing 3D image compared with the methods using only 25 or 533 rays. Moreover, the computational time of the methods using the coarse-to-fine search is shorter than the methods using only 533 rays.

Table 1. Ablation study for initialization and coarse-to-fine methods.

Initial values	N_r	RMSE [$\times 10^{-2}$]	Time [sec]
Initialization from input images	coarse-to-fine (25 to 533)	2.074	575
Initialization from input images	25	2.098	107
Initialization from input images	533	2.087	3,080
Constant value ($\alpha_i^{(0)} = 0.50$)	coarse-to-fine (25 to 533)	37.39	762
Constant value ($\alpha_i^{(0)} = 0.50$)	25	37.86	687
Constant value ($\alpha_i^{(0)} = 0.50$)	533	37.78	19,031

The computational time in the 3D image reconstruction increases according to the number of the used rays in the reconstruction. In the coarse-to-fine search, the first coarse step is to search the optimal transmittances roughly by using a small number of the rays. In the second fine step, we find the optimal values of the transmittances by using many rays. Therefore, the coarse-to-fine search reduces the total number of the used rays in the reconstruction. Moreover, the coarse search enables to find the values of the transmittances closed to the optimal ones while avoiding local minimum. Owing to these, the proposed method using the coarse-to-fine search can find the optimal transmittances efficiently and stably.

Thus, the proposed method using the initialization from input images and the coarse-to-fine search achieves the best accuracy of the 3D images reconstruction while reducing the computational time drastically compared with the methods using only 533 rays. Figure 3 shows the 3D image of the virtual cell estimated by the proposed method using the initialization from input images and the coarse-to-fine search.

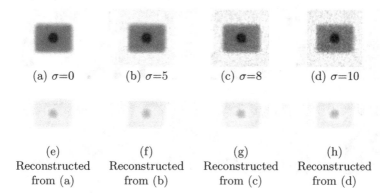

(a) $\sigma=0$ (b) $\sigma=5$ (c) $\sigma=8$ (d) $\sigma=10$

(e)
Reconstructed
from (a)

(f)
Reconstructed
from (b)

(g)
Reconstructed
from (c)

(h)
Reconstructed
from (d)

Fig. 6. Noise analysis for virtual cell model. (a)–(d) are a slice of input image with different noise level. (e)–(h) are the corresponding slice of reconstructed 3D image.

3.1.1 Noise Analysis

We evaluated the reconstruction accuracy under the different noise level in the input images. Practically, zero mean Gaussian noise with standard deviation $\sigma = 5, \sigma = 8$, and $\sigma = 10$ is added the 8bit, 255 levels, of the input images. We reconstruct 3D images from these images by using the initialization from the noisy images and the coarse-to-fine approach (Sect. 2.3.2). Moreover, the parameter w in Eq. (6) is set to $w = 1.5$.

Firstly, Figs. 6 and 7 show input images with Gaussian noise and the estimated 3D images. These images are the 5-th images of the 11 multi-focus images. Figures 6 and 7(a), (e) are original input image and the estimated transmittance image. Similarly, the standard deviation $\sigma = 5$ in (b)(f), $\sigma = 8$ in (c)(g), and $\sigma = 10$ in (d)(h). Moreover, Figs. 8 and 9 show 3D images of a virtual cell and Shepp-Logan phantom. It appears that the noise in the estimated transmittance images is less than the noise in input images due to TV norm.

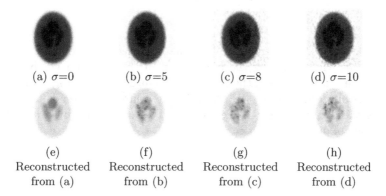

(a) $\sigma=0$ (b) $\sigma=5$ (c) $\sigma=8$ (d) $\sigma=10$

(e)
Reconstructed
from (a)

(f)
Reconstructed
from (b)

(g)
Reconstructed
from (c)

(h)
Reconstructed
from (d)

Fig. 7. Noise analysis for Shepp-Logan phantom. (a)–(d) are a slice of input image with different noise level. (e)–(h) are the corresponding slice of reconstructed 3D image.

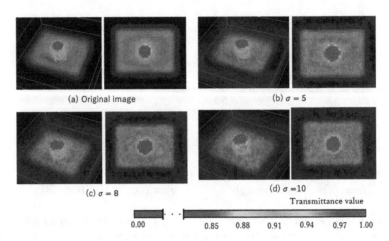

(a) Original image   (b) $\sigma = 5$

(c) $\sigma = 8$ (d) $\sigma = 10$

Transmittance value

0.00   0.85   0.88   0.91   0.94   0.97   1.00

Fig. 8. 3D images of a virtual cell

Secondly, Table 2 shows the average of RMSE and computational time between the five 3D models for the each input image (the original images, and the images with noise ($\sigma = 5, \sigma = 8$, and $\sigma = 10$)). In Table 2, it is quantitatively confirmed that when the noise of the input image increases, the accuracy of reconstructing the 3D image decreases while the calculation time increases.

Table 2. Results of simulation using images with noise.

Standard deviation σ	RMSE [$\times 10^{-2}$]	Time [sec]
Original images	2.745	407
$\sigma = 5$	3.050	735
$\sigma = 8$	3.278	943
$\sigma = 10$	3.403	1147

From the results, it is confirmed that the proposed method can reconstruct the 3D images while reducing the noise effect in the input images by the TV norm. However, in the cases of the images with much noise like Fig. 9(c) and (d), the accuracy of reconstructing 3D image in the contour part tends to be lower. Therefore, the determination of the suitable TV norm according to the image quality is one of our future works.

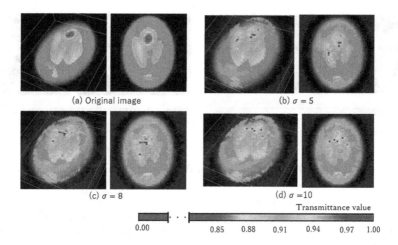

Fig. 9. 3D images of Shepp-Logan Phantom

3.2 Experiment Using Real Cell Images

In the experiment, the proposed method is applied to the multi-focus images of real cell images to reconstruct the 3D image of the real cells. Figure 10(a) and (b) show the multi-focus image sequences of normal and cancer cells. The size and spatial resolution of each cell image is 62×62 [pixel] and 0.92μm$/1$ pixel. To apply the proposed method, the color cell images are converted into the gray scale images.

Figure 11(a) and (b) show the 3D image of the normal and cancer cells reconstructed from Fig. 10, respectively. From the cell images, it is observed that the transmittance in the cell cytoplasm is higher than that of the cell nucleus. The estimated 3D cell image has the same tendency as the real cell images. Since we have no ground-truth of the 3D cell image, from this qualitative evaluation, the proposed method produces the 3D image which capture the characteristic of the cell transmittance.

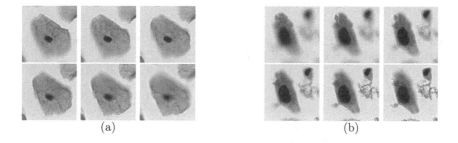

Fig. 10. Multi-focus images of real cells: (a) a normal cell; (b) a cancer cell.

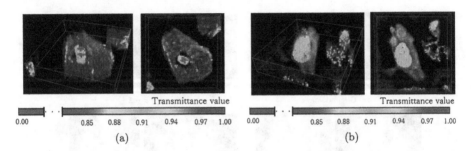

Fig. 11. Reconstructed 3D images of (a) the normal and (b) cancer cells.

It takes about 1,650 [sec] on average to reconstruct 3D image. The average computational time in the experiments is longer than that in the simulation because of the following reason. In the simulation, we assume that the cytoplasm is homogeneous with no other components. In other words, all the voxels in the artificial cell model have almost the same transmittance values. On the contrary, a real cell contain other components such as mitochondria. This means that there are the voxels with various transmittance values in the real cells. Owing to the complex structure of the cell, reconstructing the 3D image of the real cells is time-consuming. One of our future works is to speed up the estimation of the transmittances of real cells with complex structures.

4   Conclusion

We proposed a method for reconstructing the 3D image of a transparent object from multi-focus microscopic images. To achieve this, we model a microscopic imaging system for acquiring the multi-focus microscopic images with different focuses. The optimal values of the transmittances are determined by minimizing the difference between the intensities of the observed image and the simulated image by our model. From the simulation using the virtual cells, it is confirmed that the proposed method can reconstruct the optimal 3D image efficiently and stably. In addition, the 3D image reconstruction from the real cell images is achieved with these proposed methods.

Acknowledgements. This work was supported by JST CREST Grant Number JPMJCR1786 and JSPS KAKENHI Grant number 19H04139, Japan.

References

1. Attota, R.: Through-focus or volumetric type of optical imaging methods: a review. J. Biomed. Opt. **23**, 070901 (2018)
2. S. Nayar., Y. Nakagawa.: Shape from focus. IEEE Transactions on Pattern Analysis and Machine Intelligence, 16(8), 824–831, 1994

3. Pentland, A.P.: A new sense for depth of field. IEEE Trans. Pattern Anal. Mach. Intell. **PAMI-9**(4), 523–531 (1987)
4. Subbarao, M., Gurumoorthy, N.: Depth recovery from blurred edges. In: Proceedings CVPR 1988: Computer Society Conference on Computer Vision and Pattern Recognition, pp. 498–503. IEEE (1988)
5. Zhuo, S., Sim, T.: Defocus map estimation from a single image. Pattern Recogn. **44**(9), 1852–1858 (2011)
6. Brenner, D.J., Hall, E.J.: Computed tomography - an increasing source of radiation exposure. N. Engl. J. Med. **357**(22), 2277–2284 (2007)
7. Figueiras, E., et al.: Optical projection tomography as a tool for 3D imaging of hydrogels. Biomed. Opt. Express **5**(10), 3443–3449 (2014)
8. Tanaka, K., Mukaigawa, Y., Kubo, H., Matsushita, Y., Yagi, Y.: Recovering inner slices of layered translucent objects by multi-frequency illumination. IEEE Trans. Pattern Anal. Mach. Intell. **39**(4), 746–757 (2017)
9. Yoo, S., et al.: 3D image reconstruction from multi-focus microscope: axial super-resolution and multiple-frame processing. In: 2018 IEEE International Conference on Acoustics, Speech and Signal Processing (ICASSP). IEEE (2018)

Block-Wise Authentication and Recovery Scheme for Medical Images Focusing on Content Complexity

Faranak Tohidi[1,2,3], Manoranjan Paul[3(✉)], Mohammad Reza Hooshmandasl[1,2],
Subrata Chakraborty[4,5], and Biswajeet Pradhan[4,5]

[1] The Laboratory of Quantum Information Processing, Yazd University, Yazd, Iran
ftohidi@stu.yazd.ac.ir, hooshmandasl@yazd.ac.ir
[2] Department of Computer Science, Yazd University, Yazd, Iran
[3] School of Computing and Mathematics, Charles Sturt University, Bathurst, Australia
mpaul@csu.edu.au
[4] School of Information, Systems and Modelling, University of Technology Sydney,
Ultimo, Australia
{Subrata.Chakraborty,Biswajeet.Pradhan}@uts.edu.au
[5] Centre for Advanced Modelling and Geospatial Information Systems,
University of Technology Sydney, Ultimo, Australia

Abstract. Digital images are used to transfer most critical data in areas like medical, research, business, military, etc. The images transfer takes place over an unsecured Internet network. Therefore, there is a need for reliable security and protection for these sensitive images. Medical images play an important role in the field of Telemedicine and Tele surgery. Thus, before making any diagnostic decisions and treatments, the authenticity and the integrity of the received medical images need to be verified to avoid misdiagnosis. This paper proposes a block-wise and blind fragile watermarking mechanism for medical image authentication and recovery. By eliminating embedded insignificant data and considering different content complexity for each block during feature extraction and recovery, the capacity of data embedding without loss of quality is increased. This new embedding watermark method can embed a copy of the compressed image inside itself as a watermark to increase the recovered image quality. In our proposed hybrid scheme, the block features are utilized to improve the efficiency of data concealing for authentication and reduce tampering. Therefore, the scheme can achieve better results in terms of the recovered image quality and greater tampering protection, compared with the current schemes.

Keywords: Medical images · Image authentication · Watermarking · Tamper detection · Image recovery · Medical image security

1 Introduction

Today, Patients who live in remote areas are able to be diagnosed by experts with the help of telemedicine. However, this advancement of technology has led to some serious

© Springer Nature Switzerland AG 2020
J. J. Dabrowski et al. (Eds.): PSIVT 2019 Workshops, LNCS 11994, pp. 86–99, 2020.
https://doi.org/10.1007/978-3-030-39770-8_7

security concerns. Medical imagery transmission between experts and patients is an important task in this regard. During the data transfer, this data may be altered by some attacks intentionally or unintentionally. Thus, the authentication and content verification of this kind of important digital data is essential. Furthermore, recent studies show that, due to the rise of software capabilities for editing and modifying digital images, manipulation of radiography data is a serious issue; For example, modified images could be used in illegal claim for medical insurance of a patient or in publishing fraudulent results. The present security frameworks are either using encryption or steganography, or the combination of both to protect against unauthorized access. While these image encryptions are useful for protection against unauthorized access, they are unable to safeguard the authenticity and integrity of the transmitted image when the key is revealed. Furthermore, these methods are not able to reconstruct the original image when it is attacked. It is obvious that integrity and confidentiality are the main issues, because damaging of the medical image during transmission leads to serious problems in medical treatments, like the damage of decisive information, misdiagnosis by physicians and potentially calling into question the reliability of the health care center [1, 2].

Due to the high sensitivity to the modification in some images such as medical imagery, fragile watermarking schemes can be used where authentication is required. Fragile watermarking could be considered as two main groups: pixel-based and block-based schemes. In the pixel-based fragile watermarking approaches, the data pertaining to the watermark is produced utilising the host pixel values. These are then embedded into the host pixels as well. In case of the block-based fragile watermarking approaches, the host image is first segmented into multiple blocks. Each block contains individual data for the watermark, which can be used for authentication through detection and verification of the watermark data. If detection of the watermark data is unsuccessful, it indicates that the image may have been changed. Subsequently the block is then marked as tampered or invalid. From the embedding point of view, watermarking can be categorized into frequency or spatial based. The frequency-based approaches apply various transfer functions such as the *Fast Fourier Transformation* (FFT), *Discrete Cosine Transformation* (DCT), and *Discrete Wavelet Transformation* (DWT) to change pixel values from spatial domain to the coefficients of the frequency domain. Then the watermark data is hidden into those. But the spatial domain uses the pixel values to embed the watermark data directly. Spatial domain usually embed hidden data in the *Least Significant Bits* (LSBs) of pixels' value in order to avoid damaging the image [3–10].

1.1 Related Work

Self-embedding fragile watermarking can be useful in order to identify and then recover after any tampering. In this method the watermark data can be a copy of the compressed image or features of original image itself. The basic features of an image which are chosen as watermark data should include enough information to recover the original image, with higher recovery in the tamper region. A dual watermarking method has been proposed by Lee and Lin to detect tampering within an image and then to recover the original image [5]. In their method tampered area can be recovered by extracting watermarked data from the other intact blocks. This method is appropriate for minor tampering cases only.

Some of watermarking methods suffer from false image production after recovery by using a reference table, because of the block autonomous aspect of image watermarking. Those kinds of watermarking that have not involved any block dependency may be damaged with some special attacks like *Vector Quantization* (VQ) attack [6]. To overcome VQ attack, some block-wise watermarking methods are introduced, such as a fragile watermarking method for verifying and recovering medical images [6]. An image needs to be segmented into same size blocks in order to compute authentication and recovery codes by their method. Singular value decomposition is applied to attain a block authentication code for every 4 × 4 block. The recovery code is the mean value of every 2 × 2 block. Arnold transform is applied to distinguish where these codes should be embedded but embedding both codes in the same block can cause an increase in the rate of false detection. A blind image watermarking method utilising the DWT and the *Singular Value Decomposition* (SVD) has been developed by Thakkar and Srivastava [7]. They used DWT on selecting the region of interest in medical images and produced separate frequency sub-bands for decomposition of these areas. Then the results are combined by the applying SVD on the LL sub-band. Their method is robust and has produced good results in terms of watermarked image quality and in extracting watermarked data successfully, but it is not capable of recovering the medical images when it is altered.

Qin et al. [8] developed a new scheme of compressing the image, named as *Optimal Iterative Block Truncation coding* (OIBTC), which achieved better quality than the traditional *Block Truncation Coding* (BTC). They applied OIBTC to achieve recovery. They have used 4 × 4 block size and 8 × 8 block size. In higher tampering rates, the quality of a recovered image by bigger block size is higher because of more redundancy of the recovery code but in lower tampering rate the block size of 4 × 4 has higher performance, since the recovery code has not been so compressed. In most of the block-wise methods, an image is segmented into the same sized blocks and all blocks are treated equally. It is obvious that the volume of data that can be concealed in a block is limited by the size of the block. A big block size can convey more data, leading to more recovery data. But the ability of detecting and locating of the exact area is less.

Therefore, the size of block can be an important option to have efficient authentication and recovery since there is a trade-off between the size of the block and effective authentication and recovery. In addition, the features of a block can be exploited to enhance the efficiency of data concealing and authentication. It may be better to encode recovery data related to the blocks with small changes and fewer bits. Instead recovery data of the blocks with big changes could be encoded by more bits to boost the quality of the recovered image. This could mean a bigger capacity to hide the recovery data of the smooth blocks is pointless. This capacity can be reserved for hiding the recovery data of more complex blocks. In the proposed method, the complexity of the block has been used to understand the types of the blocks to design different plans of embedding and extracting data to increase the efficiency of authentication and recovery. In the other word, some blocks do not need much capacity for embedding their features, and their dedicated capacities can then be used for other purposes.

2 Proposed Method

The first step for self-embedding watermarking is obtaining the basic features from the image, then embedding this data into the image itself. Thus, an image can be recovered after tampering by extracting and using the watermarked data from intact areas of the image. On one hand, since the data is embedded into the image as watermarked data, the amount of this data should be as minimum as possible so to minimize the decrease in the watermarked image quality. On the contrary, if the amount of data entrenched into the image is larger, the recovered image will be of better quality. Therefore, there is a trade-off between the watermarked and recovered images in terms of their quality. To address this problem and have high quality for both the watermarked and the recovered images, the following steps should be considered: firstly, the selected data as watermarked data should be as efficient as possible, so that watermarked data is able to recover the tampered image with higher quality. Secondly, watermarked data should be as compressed as possible so that embedding them as watermark data into the image decreases the original image quality as little as possible.

To achieve this aim, a new hybrid method for compressing and obtaining the efficient features of an image will be introduced. This method discovers and pinpoints modifications in an image and recovers the altered areas. The information hidden in the image or the watermark data are divided into authentication code and recovery code, leading to greater accuracy. The authentication code is used to identify and trace the regions of tampered areas, and the recovery code can be used in case of tampering to recover the original image. In some cases, not only some areas of the image are destroyed but also their recovery codes may have been lost as well as a result of tampering. Therefore, these regions cannot be salvaged, and the quality of the recovered image will decrease. For this reason, as well as obtaining a better quality of a recovered image, two different copies of a compressed image will be embedded into the original image as the watermark data.

Three kinds of the watermark data should be provided for every block of size 8 × 8. The first kind of watermark data is named as the authentication code (16 bits) which can be used to identify the tampered blocks, the second and third kinds of watermark data are recovery codes, which are applied for recovery of the damaged content of the tampered image. The authentication code is entrenched inside the block itself and the recovery codes are entrenched into the mapped block of the image in order to have block dependency and being able to deal with the VQ attack. Due to the fact that replacing only two LSBs of pixels in image may not decrease the quality of the image noticeably, these two LSBs in all blocks are reserved for embedding data. Recovery codes can be achieved with the help of OIBTC and average pixels values of the block.

The Block Truncation Coding (BTC) is an effective image compressing algorithm. In this algorithm an original image with size n × n should be divided into m × m non-overlapping blocks. The average value (μ) and the standard deviation (σ) will be calculated for every block using (1, 2):

$$\mu = \frac{1}{m} \sum_{i=1}^{m} x_i \tag{1}$$

$$\sigma = \sqrt{\frac{1}{m} \sum_{i=1}^{m} (xi - \mu)^2} \tag{2}$$

All pixels in the block are categorized into two sets, in a way that when the intensity of a pixel is more than the mean value of the block, it is considered as the first set. Otherwise, it belongs to the other set. There is a bit map for every block as well. The corresponding bit for the pixels of the first set are zeros and for the second set pixels are ones. Any block in the image can be compressed by following above steps. Then an image block will be decompressed by substituting the ones with high reconstruction level (M_1) and the zeros by low reconstruction level (M_0) using the following Eqs. (3, 4) [11–16].

$$M_0 = \mu - \sigma \sqrt{\frac{m^+}{m^-}} \tag{3}$$

$$M_1 = \mu + \sigma \sqrt{\frac{m^-}{m^+}} \tag{4}$$

Where $m+$ is the number of pixels for which their values are greater than μ and $m-$ is the number of pixels that are less than. To improve the visual quality of BTC-decompressed image, [8] has proposed a new OIBTC algorithm for compressing an image. In OIBTC new low and high reconstruction levels have been introduced as M_l and M_h, which can be calculated by minimizing the distortion for each block through following steps:

1. Every block is arranged in ascending order of its pixels' values, i.e.,

$$S = \{p_1, p_2, \ldots, p_m\}$$

    In which p_i are the pixels in the block and $p_1 < p_2 < \ldots < p_m$
2. Each block should be divided into two segments, and for each segment the mean value should be calculated as

$$S_l^k = \{p_1, p_2, \ldots, p_k\}, S_h^k = \{p_{k+1}, p_{k+2}, \ldots, p_m\}$$

    In which S_l^k and S_h^k are these two segments.
3. In each block, the mean values of the two above sets $\left(M_l^k \text{ and } M_h^k\right)$ are considered as low and high reconstruction levels and the distortion should be computed for the block by (5):

$$d^k = d_l^k + d_h^k = \sum_{i=1}^{k} (p_i - M_l^k)^2 + \sum_{i=k+1}^{i=m} (p_i - M_h^k)^2 \tag{5}$$

    The distortion for the whole block is d^k while d_l^k and d_h^k are distortion for each segment and p_i are the real amount of pixels in the block.
4. Steps 2 and 3 should be repeated to obtain minimum distortion. Where the distortion is minimum, M_l^k and M_h^k can be used as the low and high reconstruction levels (M_l and M_h) of the block.

After generating the recovery codes (it will be introduced in Sect. 2.1 and 2.2), these codes should be embedded in other blocks. Arnold transformation can be applied as a mapping function to find the suitable block for embedding the recovery codes. Using this function helps with distributing the recovery data into different blocks. A digital image is partitioned into blocks and each block has the address of (x, y). Arnold transform maps one block to another block using (6).

$$\begin{bmatrix} x^{'} \\ y^{'} \end{bmatrix} = \begin{bmatrix} 1 & K_1 \\ K_2 & K_1 K_2 + 1 \end{bmatrix} \begin{bmatrix} x \\ y \end{bmatrix} mod N \qquad (6)$$

Where "N" is the number of all blocks in the image. K_1 and K_2 are used as keys. The embedding locations of two recovery codes of each block are different and are calculated by two keys.

2.1 Producing Authentication and Recovery Data

The first and the second LSBs of all pixels should be replaced with zero during the process of authentication code calculation, since LSBs will be substituted with water-marked data and must not be assessed. The authentication code for each block is 16 bits and can be generated through a Hash function. All 64 pixels which are inside the 8×8 block and the ordering numbers of them should be included in the hash function. The authentication code is then included in the block itself.

To obtain the recovery code, a distortion criteria D has been used to select which option of compression is more suitable for each block (unlike as presented in [8]). Each block has been treated differently regarding its complexity in our work. Some blocks do not need as much capacity to embed their features. These blocks are considered as smooth blocks. But some other blocks need more capacity to embed their features as they are more complex or textured. Since every smooth block can be recovered by less information, their dedicated locations can be reserved for embedding another copy related to the other blocks. For every 8×8 block these following four compression methods are available to choose in order (methods are arranged in order of descending compression rates):

1. An average pixels values of the 8×8 block
2. Four average pixels values related to four 4×4 blocks inside the 8×8 block
3. An 8×8 OIBTC compression
4. Four 4×4 OIBTC compression related to four 4×4 blocks inside the 8×8 block

In order to efficiently exploit the available capacity and to embed more data, as well as having a high-quality watermarked image, a threshold for distortion should be set. Each block should have its own limitation to extract its basic features depending on its content complexity. Hence any of the four compression methods above whose distortion is less than the distortion threshold level and having greater compression rate, should be applied for selecting the first recovery data. Thus, the option that presents the highest compression rate is the priority if its calculated distortion is less than the threshold. These kinds of blocks are very smooth and the first copy in this case is just the mean value of the 8×8 block. Otherwise, the distortion should be calculated for the second option in a way that the block should be divided into four 4×4 blocks. The average mean value for each 4×4 block and their distortion should be calculated and if their total distortion is not less than threshold as well, the next option is our next priority using a similar procedure. The last priority is four 4 × 4 OIBTC which may be selected when the block is quite complex.

The value of threshold can be selected according to the complexity of the image and predicted tampering rate. If the threshold is selected at a lower level the distortion for the first copy will be low. Consequently the quality of the recovered block by the first copy will be high. But it should be considered that in the higher tampering rate because of high probability of losing the first copy, we have to use the backup recovery data therefore reasonable quality for the second copy is also important. Hence enough room should be created for better backup recovery as well. In this work, in order to find the suitable threshold, a copy of the compressed image by 8 × 8 OIBTC should be calculated then average value of distortion for all 8 × 8 blocks in the image can be set as a threshold. Two bits are also allocated as indicators to demonstrate which compression method has been used. The distortion is calculated by (7) for each 8 × 8 block.

$$D = \sum_{i=1}^{i=8} \sum_{j=1}^{j=8} (p_{i,j} - c_{i,j})^2 \tag{7}$$

Where D denotes the distortion for each 8 × 8 block, $p_{i,j}$, and $c_{i,j}$ are the original pixel value and the value of pixel after compression.

2.2 Reducing the Number of Bits for Embedding

Reducing the number of bits which are needed to embed as watermark data is possible by exploiting the differences between nearby values. Since any of M_l and M_h (low and high reconstruction levels in OIBTC compression) can be displayed by 6 bits separately and both belong to the same image block, 10 bits should be sufficient for both. Here 6 bits are required for the mean values of M_l and M_h and 4 bits for the absolute difference between their mean values and any value of M_l or M_h. Instead of real values of M_l and M_h the mean value and the absolute difference value can be embedded. Then in the receiver side, the real values for M_l and M_h can be calculated conveniently by subtracting and adding the difference value with the mean value separately. Hence, it is not required to embed all 12 bits for every block and more capacity will be remaining to embed more useful data (unlike [8]).

2.3 Watermark Embedding Process

Every 8 × 8 block has 64 pixels which watermarked data is embedded in 2 LSBs of these pixels. The 16 bits of the LSBs are earmarked for authentication purposes. Two bits of the LSBs are dedicated for distinguishing which compression method has been done. The rest of the LSBs (which are 110 bits) are reserved for recovery purposes including the first and backup recovery codes. After embedding the first copy with the help of reduced bit numbers, and considering texture of every block, there are still spaces for embedding the other copy for each block. It should be mentioned that, the type of the other copy is dependent on the first copy and how much capacity is still available for embedding more data. The total capacity in each block for embedding data is restricted to 128 bits to be able to have high quality watermarked image. The vacant capacity to embed the second copy can be calculated by considering the occupied capacity that has been used by the first copy. In this way one of the embedded copies will have better quality and the other one is more compressed in every block. Thus to efficiently use the remaining capacity of the block, there are four options as follows:

- First copy is 8 × 8 OIBTC compression, second copy should be four average pixels value of four 4 × 4 blocks.
- First copy is four 4 × 4 OIBTC compression, second copy should be an average pixels value of 8 × 8 block.
- First copy is an average pixels value of 8 × 8 block, second copy should be four 4 × 4 OIBTC compression.
- First copy is four average pixels value of four 4 × 4 blocks, second copy should be 8 × 8 OIBTC compression.

2.4   Detecting and Localizing Tampered Area

For detection of tampering and trace the location of tampered area, the image is divided into 8 × 8 blocks and the 2 LSBs of all pixels are replaced with zeros. For each of the blocks the information associated with the current block should be supplied into the hash function. Clearly all the 64 pixels which are inside the 8 × 8 block and the ordering numbers of them should be included in the hash function. The obtained authentication code from each block is compared with the amount of Hash function related to that block to recognize if the block is tampered. If this information is not identical it shows that the block has been tampered with. Since hash function is sensitive to even a one bit change of input, any modification will be detected for every block. If tampering is detected, extraction of the recovery code from destination blocks is required.

2.5   Recovery of Tampered Image

If a block is detected as tampered by comparing its authentication code with the content, it can be recovered by extracting the recovery information from the intact areas of the image. Recovery data include first and backup recovery data. As the probability of losing first recovery data related to a tampered block, there is a second opportunity to recover the tampered block with the assistance of the backup recovery data. In case of tampering, the addresses of destinations for the first recovery data and the backup recovery data can be calculated by the reverse of Arnold transformation with previous keys. Then the other authentication checks should be done to ensure that the blocks that contained the first and backup data are still intact. If both are intact in regard to the indicator bits, the copy which is more detailed will be chosen for obtaining better results. Otherwise any of the copies which is available and intact can be used. If both copies had been tampered with, the recovery of the block is done with the help of mean values of their obtainable undamaged neighbouring blocks. Through the above steps and decompression of the relevant tampered blocks pixels could be recovered. Then by combining the intact blocks and the recovered blocks the recovered image can be reconstructed.

3 Experimental Results

Performance evaluation of our proposed scheme has been conducted on the watermarked image quality and recovered image quality. The experiment has been conducted on some standard 512×512 images when tampering rates (t) were below 50% and the results are shown in Table 1. The watermarked image quality is more than 43 dB for all images. The quality of recovered images has been compared with the watermarked image quality with two standard quality measurements (The Structural SIMilarity (SSIM) and Peak Signal-to-Noise Ratio (PSNR)). Figures 1 2, 3 and 4 show the results of encoding. In these figures, three encoded images are presented to demonstrate that in the proposed hybrid method some useless data has been eliminated during preparation of data for the first copy in order to make room for embedding one more but different copy as backup recovery data. As it can clearly be seen in the figures, more textured blocks have more data to embed, but the dedicated capacity for a smooth block has been used by embedding one more complete backup copy related to another block. Smooth blocks in hybrid method encoded figures are shown white.

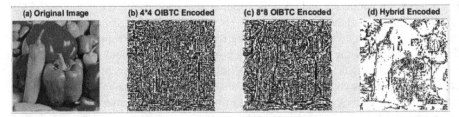

Fig. 1. (a) Pepper image, (b) OIBTC (4×4) encoded, (c) OIBTC (8×8) encoded, (d) Proposed Hybrid Scheme encoded for the first copy

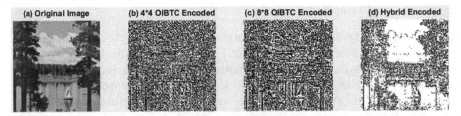

Fig. 2. (a) Lake Image, (b) OIBTC (4×4) encoded, (c) OIBTC (8×8) encoded, (d) Proposed Hybrid Scheme encoded for the first copy

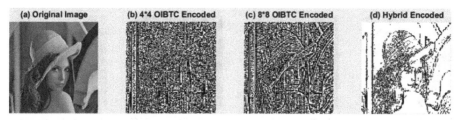

Fig. 3. (a) Lena image, (b) OIBTC (4 × 4) encoded, (c) OIBTC (8 × 8) encoded, (d) Proposed Hybrid Scheme encoded for the first copy

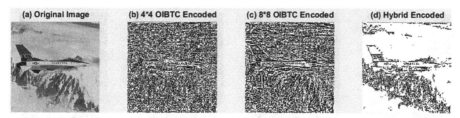

Fig. 4. (a) Plane image, (b) OIBTC (4 × 4) encoded, (c) OIBTC (8 × 8) encoded, (d) Proposed Hybrid Scheme encoded for the first copy

Figures 5 and 6 show the results of tampering detection, localization and recovery by the proposed hybrid method. The 512×512 standard medical images are included in our figure results also since the proposed method can work on medical images as well. Figure 7 shows the results of watermarking on the original medical image and the results of recovery after tampering using the proposed method.

Fig. 5. (a) Original image (b) Tampered image (tampering rate $= 19\%$), (c) Detected tampering (d) Recovered image

In the proposed hybrid method, two different copies of each block are available as the watermark data. While in 8×8 OIBTC method, according the amount of capacity of 2 LSBs and redundancy of data, at most one half of the blocks can have a second opportunity of another copy. In 4×4 OIBTC method, there is no second chance of having another copy. For this reason the method presented here could be more suitable for higher tampering rates since the probability of losing the first copy is higher. Furthermore, it can be more suitable for less textured images as presented in Table 1. Images which are more textured, e.g. Barbara and Mandril, the quality of recovered image is lower especially

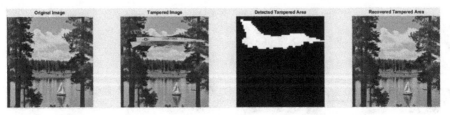

Fig. 6. (a) Original image (b) Tampered image (tampering rate = 25%), (c) Detected tampering (d) Recovered image

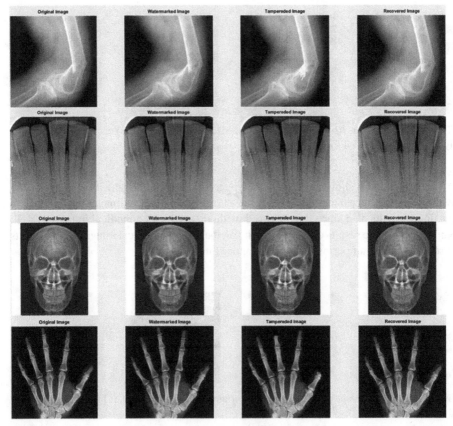

Fig. 7. (a) Original image (b) Watermarked image (c) Tampered image (d) Recovered image

when tampering rate is low compared with using just OIBTC. It is demonstrated that for most images with different tampering rates the proposed hybrid method has better performance.

Table 1. Comparison the results of Proposed Hybrid Scheme with 4 × 4 OIBTC [8] and 8 × 8 OIBTC [8] in terms of SSIM and PSNR for different standard images when tampering rates are different (the minimum values are shown for all SSIMs and PSNRs)

Standard images	8 × 8 OIBTC [8]		4 × 4 OIBTC [8]		Proposed Hybrid Scheme		(t) Tampering rate %
	SSIM	PSNR (dB)	SSIM	PSNR (dB)	SSIM	PSNR (dB)	
Lena	0.9036	30.16	–	–	**0.9162**	**31.84**	45 < t < 50
Lena	0.9534	33.92	0.9580	35.08	**0.9581**	**35.69**	25 < t < 30
Lena	0.9812	39.26	0.9855	41.66	**0.9839**	**42.02**	10 < t < 12
Barbara	0.8645	25.08	–	–	**0.8935**	**26.19**	45 < t < 50
Barbara	0.9384	28.98	**0.9425**	**29.14**	0.9422	29.02	25 < t < 30
Barbara	0.9721	32.99	**0.9766**	**33.43**	0.9701	32.24	10 < t < 12
Mandril	0.8474	26.66	–	–	**0.8550**	**27.01**	45 < t < 50
Mandril	0.9058	27.78	0.9232	28.68	**0.9288**	**28.92**	25 < t < 30
Mandril	0.9469	30.03	**0.9527**	**31.28**	0.9501	30.89	10 < t < 12
Woman-Darkhair	0.9383	35.29	–	–	**0.9521**	**38.13**	45 < t < 50
Woman-Darkhair	0.9673	38.29	**0.9766**	41.41	0.9759	**41.52**	25 < t < 30
Woman-Darkhair	0.9784	38.45	0.9816	38.14	**0.9842**	**40.15**	10 < t < 12
Woman-Blonde	0.8799	29.10	–	–	**0.8950**	**30.01**	45 < t < 50
Woman-Blonde	0.9405	33.73	0.9389	33.85	**0.9482**	**35.01**	25 < t < 30
Woman-Blonde	0.9651	35.09	0.9682	36.22	**0.9716**	**36.97**	10 < t < 12
Living room	0.8574	27.43	–	–	**0.8855**	**28.94**	45 < t < 50
Living room	0.9287	32.28	0.9296	32.36	**0.9416**	**33.54**	25 < t < 30
Living room	0.9687	37.22	0.9716	38.49	**0.9752**	**38.86**	10 < t < 12
Pepper	0.8883	28.53	–	–	**0.9098**	**30.43**	45 < t < 50
Pepper	0.9407	31.77	0.9539	33.04	**0.9543**	**33.94**	25 < t < 30
Pepper	0.9715	34.71	0.9789	36.21	**0.9800**	**37.65**	10 < t < 12
Lake	0.9475	30.80	–	–	**0.9622**	**32.65**	45 < t < 50
Lake	0.9737	33.98	0.9758	34.44	**0.9800**	**35.89**	25 < t < 30
Lake	0.9870	37.97	0.9895	38.99	**0.9912**	**40.42**	10 < t < 12
JetPlane	0.9582	31.45	–	–	**0.9658**	**32.62**	45 < t < 50
JetPlane	0.9878	42.47	0.9904	45.77	**0.9918**	**46.31**	25 < t < 30
JetPlane	0.9915	45.69	0.9938	47.27	**0.9940**	**48.27**	10 < t < 12
CameraMan	0.9610	30.43	–	–	**0.9691**	**32.15**	45 < t < 50
CameraMan	0.9760	32.06	**0.9816**	33.45	0.9812	**34.82**	25 < t < 30
CameraMan	0.9825	38.23	0.9930	43.81	**0.9932**	**43.89**	10 < t < 12
House	0.9507	31.87	–	–	**0.9785**	**36.84**	45 < t < 50
House	0.9769	34.64	0.9591	35.18	**0.9934**	**41.49**	25 < t < 30
House	0.9889	42.59	0.9901	45.61	**0.9972**	**47.76**	10 < t < 12

4 Conclusion

In this work, an image security scheme which can be applicable for sensitive medical images has been developed. This method not only provides excellent authentication detection, but also is able to recover the original image well, when it is necessary. To achieve this aim, an image is divided into set of pixel blocks, then watermarked data including authentication code and recovery codes is computed for each block. Authentication code for each block is 16 bits and is produced by a Hash function and should be hidden into the block itself. In order to authenticate an image, authentication code can be extracted and compared with the result of the hash function on the contents of the block. The OIBTC compression and the mean value are exploited for each block to generate recovery information. Another recovery code is available since there is a probability of losing one of the recovery codes as a result of tampering. Recovery codes are scrambled inside the image blocks to have better reconstruction of the image in case of tampering. The proposed method can embed two compressed copies of the image inside the image itself with high quality by applying two new ways; extracting different features depending on the types of blocks then reducing the number of needed bits for embedding as well. Experimental results demonstrate conclusively that this scheme can achieve superior performance for tampering detection, localization and recovery, especially when tampering rate is high. The proposed hybrid method uses block size of 8×8 for authentication code and block size of 4×4 or 8×8 for recovery code depending on the texture of the block. Although our proposed method showed good performance in recovery of image after high level of tampering, the accuracy of tamper localization could be improved further by considering adaptive block size for authentication code as well.

References

1. Singh, J., Patel, A.K.: An effective telemedicine security using wavelet based watermarking. In: IEEE International Conference on Computational Intelligence and Computing Research (ICCIC), pp. 1–6 (2016)
2. Rocek, A., Slavicek, K., Dostal, O., Javorník, M.: A new approach to fully-reversible watermarking in medical imaging with breakthrough visibility. Biomed. Sig. Process. Control **29**, 44–52 (2016)
3. Qin, C., Ji, P., Zhang, X., Dong, J., Wang, J.: Fragile image watermarking with pixel-wise recovery based on overlapping embedding strategy. Sig. Process. **138**, 280–293 (2017)
4. Dhole, V.S., Patil, N.N.: Self-embedding fragile watermarking for imagetampering detection and image recovery using self recovery blocks. In: IEEE International Conference on Computing Communication Control and Automation, (ICCUBEA) (2015)
5. Lee, T.Y., Lin, S.D.: Dual watermark for image tamper detection and recovery. Pattern Recognit. **41**(11), 3497–3506 (2008)
6. Shehab, A., et al.: Secure and robust fragile watermarking scheme for medical images. IEEE Access **6**, 10269–10278 (2018)
7. Thakkar, F.N., Kumar Srivastava, V.: A blind medical image watermarking: DWT-SVD based robust and secure approach for telemedicine applications. Multimedia Tools Appl. **76**(3), 3669–3697 (2017)

8. Qin, C., Ji, P., Chang, C.-C., Dong, J., Sun, X.: Non-uniform watermark sharing based on optimal iterative BTC for image tampering recovery. IEEE Multimedia **25**, 36–48 (2018)
9. Sing, D., Sing, S.K.: Effective self-embedding watermarking scheme for image tampered detection and localization with recovery capability. J. Vis. Commun. Image Represent. **38**, 775–789 (2016)
10. Joshi, A.M., Darji, A., Mishra, V.: Design and implementation of real-time image watermarking. In: IEEE International Conference on Signal Processing, Communications and Computing (ICSPCC), pp. 1–5 (2011)
11. Sun, W., Lu, Z.M., Wen, Y.C., Yu, F.X., Shen, R.J.: High performance reversible data hiding for block truncation coding compressed images. Sig. Image Video Process. **7**(2), 297–306 (2013)
12. Mohammad, N., Sun, X., Yang, H.: An adaptive visible watermarking algorithm for BTC compressed images. Inf. Technol. J. **13**(3), 536–541 (2014)
13. Mohammad, N., Sun, X., Yang, H.: An excellent image data hiding algorithm based on BTC. Inf. Technol. J. **10**(7), 1415–1420 (2011)
14. Tohidi, F., Abdul Manaf, A.B., Zamani, M., Jamshidi, H.: Improving the capacity of watermarking techniques by using block truncation coding. JDCTA **7**(14), 33 (2013)
15. Ji, P., Qin, C., Tang, Z.: Fragile watermarking with self-recovery capability via absolute moment block truncation coding. In: Sun, X., Liu, A., Chao, H.-C., Bertino, E. (eds.) ICCCS 2016. LNCS, vol. 10039, pp. 104–113. Springer, Cham (2016). https://doi.org/10.1007/978-3-319-48671-0_10
16. Chang, C.C., Chen, T.S., Wang, Y.K., Liu, Y.: A reversible data hiding scheme based on absolute moment block truncation coding compression using exclusive OR operator. Multimedia Tools Appl. **77**(7), 9039–9053 (2018)

GAN-Based Method for Synthesizing Multi-focus Cell Images

Ken'ich Morooka[1]([✉]), Xueru Zhang[1], Shoko Miyauchi[1], Ryo Kurazume[1],
and Eiji Ohno[2]

[1] Graduate School of Information Science and Electrical Engineering,
Kyushu University, Fukuoka 819-0395, Japan
`morooka@ait.kyushu-u.ac.jp`
[2] Faculty of Health Sciences, Kyoto Tachibana University, Kyoto 607-8175, Japan

Abstract. This paper presents a method for synthesizing multi-focus cell images by using generative adversarial networks (GANs). The proposed method, called multi-focus image GAN (MI-GAN), consists of two generators. A base image generator synthesizes a 2D base cell image from random noise. Using the generated base image, a multi-focus cell image generator produces 11 realistic multi-focus images of the cell while considering the relationships between the images acquired at successive focus points. From experimental results, MI-GAN achieves the good performance to generate realistic multi-focus cell images.

Keywords: Multi-focus pathological images · GAN · Image synthesis

1 Introduction

Cervical cancer screening is useful for early detection of cancers with less invasive natures. In the screening, cytotechnologists observe a tissue sample taken out from human body, and find pre-cancerous and cancer cells from the sample. Generally, one sample includes tens of thousands of cells. Among them, the number of cancer cells is much smaller than that of normal cells. Moreover, in the case of cervical cancer screening in Japan, only 120 of every 10,000 people may carry cancer cells, and 7 of them will be diagnosed as suffering from cancer. Owing to these, the detection of cancer cells is a hard and time-consuming task.

Recently, instead of the sample, whole slide images (WSIs) have become a common method for not only cancer screening but also another clinical applications [1]. WSIs are high resolution digital images with gigapixels acquired by scanning the enter sample and varying focus points. The use of WSIs enables to computerize the cancer screening. By applying image processing techniques, WSI has the potential to improve the accuracy and efficiency of the cancer screening including web-based remote diagnosis.

Supported by JST CREST Grant Number JPMJCR1786 and JSPS KAKENHI Grant Number JP19H04139, Japan.

J. J. Dabrowski et al. (Eds.): PSIVT 2019 Workshops, LNCS 11994, pp. 100–107, 2020.
https://doi.org/10.1007/978-3-030-39770-8_8

Now, we have been developing an automatic system of cervical cancer screening using WSI. The construction of the system needs many WSIs including cancer and normal cells. However, as stated above, cancer cell images are difficult to collect compared with the case of normal cells. Therefore, there is a serious problem of the imbalance between normal and cancer cell images. The data imbalance makes it difficult to construct the system with acceptable accuracy.

Here, generative adversarial networks (GANs) [2] have achieved great success at generating realistic images. Recent researches [3–7] have developed GAN-based methods for pathological images. Hou et al. [3] applied GAN to synthesize image patches to generate large-scale histopathological images by integrating the patches. Hu et al. [4] proposed a GAN-based unsupervised learning of the visual attributions of cells. Another GAN application to pathological images is a stain normalization of the images. One challenge of using pathological images is their color or stain variations. To overcome the problem, GAN-based stain normalization methods [5–7] have been developed to transfer the stain style of a microscopic image into another one.

Most of GAN-based methods have focused on single-focus images including natural and pathological images. On the contrary, considering the WSI generation, WSI is also regarded as a sequence of multi-focus cytopathological images acquired at different focus. However, there are few GAN-based methods whose targets are the multi-focus images.

When the multi-focus images is regarded as an image sequence, the generation of multi-focus images is related to realistic video generation [8–10]. Generally, the aim of the video generation is to capture the changes of the appearance and motion of a target. On the contrary, in our case, GAN needs to learn the appearance changes of cells by varying a focus setting. This difference makes it difficult to apply previous GANs for video generation to the synthesis of multi-focus images.

In this paper, we propose a new GAN-based method, called multi-focus image GAN (MI-GAN), for synthesizing multi-focus cell images to construct virtual WSIs. MI-GAN is composed of two phases. The first phase is to from random noise, produce a base cell image which is in focus in the multi-focus images. In the second phase, MI-GAN produces realistic multi-focus images of the cell considering the relationships between the images acquired at successive focus points.

2 Method

Figure 1 shows the architecture of our proposed MI-GAN system which generates a sequence of 11 multi-focus images of a cell. The size of each generated image is 64×64[pixel]. Here, we denote $I_{-5}, \ldots, I_{+5}$ as the 11 images. Especially, I_0 is a base cell image which is in focus in the multi-focus images.

The MI-GAN consists of two generators. A base image generator G_1 synthesizes a 2D base cell image I_0 from random noise. Using the generated base image I_0, a multi-focus cell image generator G_2 produces 11 realistic multi-focus images of the cell. The two generators are trained independently. In the following, we explain the architectures and training of the two generators.

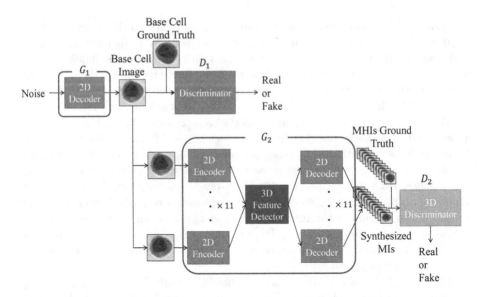

Fig. 1. Architecture of MI-GAN.

2.1 Base Image Generator

As shown in Fig. 2, the framework of constructing the base image generator is based on DCGAN [11]. Given a 100 dimensional random noise Z, the base image generator outputs the base image with size 64×64 [pixel]. In the base image generator, there are four up-sampling convolution layers. Batch normalization and Rectified Liner Unit (ReLU) activation are applied after each convolution layer. Moreover, the kernel size of the convolution layer is 6×6 while both the stride and padding sizes are 2. The discriminator is a feed-forward network with six convolution layers. The kernel size of the convolution layer is 5×5.

In the training of the base image generator, we use the loss function used in WGAN-GP [12] to stably synthesize images with acceptable quality. In the WGAN-GP, the loss function $\mathcal{L}_G^{(1)}$ of the generator G_1 is defined by

$$\mathcal{L}_G^{(1)} = -\mathbb{E}_{I \sim P_g}[D_1(I)]. \tag{1}$$

On the contrary, the loss function $\mathcal{L}_D^{(1)}$ of the discriminator D_1 is formulated as

$$\mathcal{L}_D^{(1)} = \mathbb{E}_{I \sim P_g}[D_1(I)] - \mathbb{E}_{I^* \sim P_r}[D_1(I^*)] + \lambda_1 \mathbb{E}_{\hat{I} \sim p_{\hat{I}}}[(\|\nabla_{\hat{I}} D_1(\hat{I})\|_2 - 1)^2] \tag{2}$$

where I^* and I are the real and synthesized base images of cells. The value of λ_1 in our method is set to 10. In Eq. (2), $\hat{I}$ is calculated by

$$\hat{I} = \epsilon_1 I^* + (1 - \epsilon_1)I \tag{3}$$

where ϵ_1 is a random number follow $U \sim [0, 1]$.

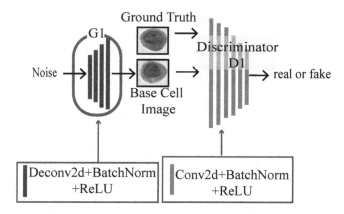

Fig. 2. Architecture of base image generation network.

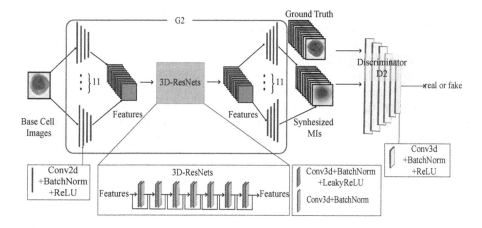

Fig. 3. Architecture of multi-focus cell image generation network.

2.2 Multi-focus Cell Image Generator

Unlike general generators using random noise as the input data, the multi-focus cell image generator G_2 produces 10 multi-focus cell images from the base image. Here, cycleGAN [13] converts a given real image into another type image. Inspired by cycleGAN, as shown in Fig. 3, the multi-focus cell image generator is composed of three parts: an 2D encoder, a 3D feature map generation, and a 2D decoder.

The encoder part includes 11 networks, each of which uses the base image I_0 as the input image to output a candidate sample of the cell image acquired at the corresponding focus point. The input matrix of the feature map generation part is obtained by concatenating 11 candidate samples extracted from the 11 networks of the encoder part. The size of the input matrix is $11 \times 3 \times 4 \times 4$.

3D ResNet with seven layers is employed to transform the input matrix into a 3D feature map of a sequence of multi-focus images while considering the relationships between the images acquired at successive focus points. In the decoder part, the feature matrix is divided into 11 2D feature maps with size of $3 \times 4 \times 4$. Each 2D feature map is inputted to the corresponding 2D-decoder part to synthesize the multi-focus cell image.

In the encoder part, there are four 2D down-sampling convolution layers. On the contrary, the decoder part has four 2D up-sampling convolution layers. In both the encoder and decoder parts, batch normalization and Rectified Liner Unit (ReLU) activation are applied after each convolution layer. Moreover, the kernel size of the 2D convolution layer is 6×6 while both the stride and padding sizes are 2.

The feature map generation part is constructed by 3D ResNet with seven layers. Each layer consists of two 3D convolution sub-layers. In the first sub-layers, we apply batch normalization and LeakyReLU to the sub-layer while batch normalization is applied to the second sub-layer. In both the sub-layer, the kernel size of the convolution layer is 3×3. Moreover, to keep the output size of 3D ResNets unchanged, we use padding of $1 \times 1 \times 1$ at each convolution.

The discriminator D_2 is a feed-forward network with six 3D down-sampling convolution layers. Batch normalization and ReLU activation are applied after each convolution layer. The kernel size of the convolution layer is 5×5 while both the stride and padding sizes are 2.

Similar with the training of the base image generator, the multi-focus cell image generator is trained by the 3D version of the WGAN-GP loss function. Practically, the loss function $\mathcal{L}_G^{(2)}$ of the multi-focus cell image generator G_2 is described by

$$\mathcal{L}_G^{(2)} = -\mathbb{E}_{V \sim P_g}[D_2(V)]. \tag{4}$$

On the contrary, the loss function $\mathcal{L}_D^{(2)}$ of the discriminator D_2 is defined as

$$\mathcal{L}_D^{(2)} = \mathbb{E}_{V \sim P_g}[D_2(V)] - \mathbb{E}_{V^* \sim P_r}[D_2(V^*)] + \lambda_2 \mathbb{E}_{\hat{V} \sim p_{\hat{V}}}[(\|\nabla_{\hat{V}} D_2(\hat{V})\|_2 - 1)^2] \tag{5}$$

where V^* and V are the sequences of real and synthesized multi-focus images of cells. The value of λ_2 in our method is set to 10. In Eq. (5), $\hat{V}$ is calculated by

$$\hat{V} = \epsilon_2 V^* + (1 - \epsilon_2)V \tag{6}$$

where ϵ_2 is a random number follow $U \sim [0, 1]$.

3   Experimental Results

To verify the applicability of the proposed method, we made experiments of synthesizing multi-focus images of cells. In our experiments, a digital slide scanner (Hamamatsu Photonics: Nanozoomer-XR) is used to acquire WSI of a sample including many cells. WSI consists of 11 multi-focus images of the sample at different focus. Each WSI has $75,000 \times 75,000$ [pixel] while the spatial resolution

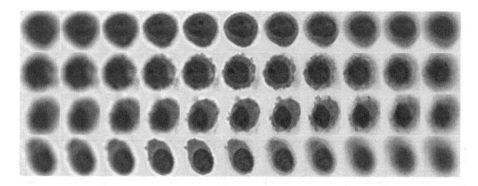

Fig. 4. Examples of real multi-focus images of SiHa cells.

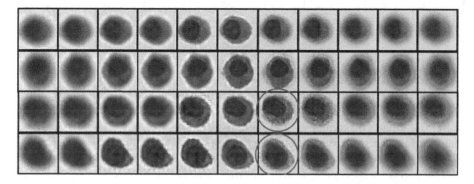

Fig. 5. Synthesized multi-focus SiHa images by MI-GAN1.

of each image in WSI is 0.23 [μm/pixel]. The multi-focus images of a target cell are extracted automatically from the WSI. The size of each cell image is 64×64 [pixel]. The proposed method is implemented on a commercial desktop computer (Quadro GP100 16 GB and Pytorch framework).

Firstly, we constructed MI-GAN, called MI-GAN1, for generating multi-focus images of SiHa cell which is one of human cervical cancer cell lines. Figure 4 shows the examples of the real multi-focus images of SiHa cell. the MI-GAN1 construction uses 1,100 images of SiHa cells. In addition, to prevent the proposed system overfitting, we perform data augmentation as follows: 90, 180, and 270 [deg] rotation of the original data, and a mirror flip of the up-down and left-right directions. Finally, MI-GAN1 is constructed by using 6,600 SiHa images.

The proposed method synthesized the sequences of multi-focus SiHa images as shown in Fig. 5. From these figures, the proposed method can generate realistic multi-focus SiHa images compared with real SiHa cell images in Fig. 4. Moreover, the quality of the synthesized cell images is evaluated by some experienced cytotechnologists. We got the comment of the experienced cytotechnologists that the synthesized cell images are very similar with real cell images.

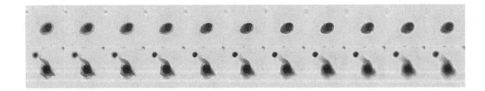

Fig. 6. Examples of real multi-focus images of cancer cells.

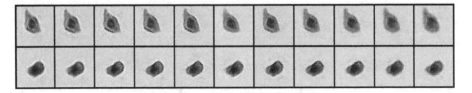

Fig. 7. Synthesized multi-focus images of cancer cells by MI-GAN2.

However, MI-GAN1 generates some multi-focus images with low quality. The red circles in Fig. 5 illustrate the example of the low quality cell images obtained by MI-GAN1. The figures include some noises in the smooth region of cell cytoplasm and unnatural change of the cell nuclear shape between successive images. The solutions for this problem include the improvement of the network architecture and the definition of the loss function.

The second experiment is to construct another MI-GAN, called the MI-GAN2, for generating multi-focus images of real cancer cells (Fig. 6). The number of real cancer cell images is 541 and about half of SiHa cell images used in the MI-GAN1 construction. Therefore, a transfer learning is applied to construct MI-GAN2. Practically, the trained MI-GAN1 using SiHa cell images is used as the initial architecture of MI-GAN2. Moreover, the data augmentation is applied to increase the number of the cancer cell images. Using the cancer cell images, MI-GAN2 is trained to synthesize multi-focus images of cancer cells.

The generated multi-focus images of cancer cells is illustrated in Fig. 7. As with the generation of SiHa cell image, the proposed method reconstructs multi-focus images of cancer cells with acceptable quality compared with real cancer cell images. From the results, the pretrained GAN by using one type of cells is useful to construct GAN for producing another type of cells.

4   Conclusion

We propose a GAN-based method, MI-GAN, for synthesizing multi-focus images of cells. The synthesis process using MI-GAN is composed of two phases. In the first phase, from random noise, the proposed method, MI-GAN produces a base cell image which is in focus in the multi-focus images. In the second phase, the MI-GAN produces realistic multi-focus images of the cell considering the relationships between the images acquired at successive focus points. From the experimental results, MI-GAN achieves the good performance to generate realistic multi-focus cell images. One of our future works is to establish metrics for evaluating the generated multi-focus cell images such as the visual tuning test [14].

References

1. Farahani, N., Parwani, A.V., Pantanowitz, L.: Whole slide imaging in pathology: advantages, limitations, and emerging perspectives. Pathol. Lab. Med. Int. **7**, 23–33 (2015)
2. Goodfellow, I.J., et al.: Generative adversarial networks. In: Advances in Neural Information Processing Systems, vol. 3, pp. 2672–2680 (2014)
3. Hou, L., et al.: Unsupervised histopathology image synthesis. arXiv preprint arXiv:1712.05021 (2017)
4. Hu, B., et al.: Unsupervised learning for cell-level visual representation with generative adversarial networks. IEEE J. Biomed. Health inform. **23**, 1316–1328 (2019)
5. Cho, H., et al.: Neural stain-style transfer learning using gan for histopathological images. arXiv preprint arXiv:1710.08543 (2017)
6. Shaban, M.T., et al.: Staingan: stain style transfer for digital histological images. arXiv preprint arXiv:1804.01601 (2018)
7. Zanjani, F.G., et al.: Histopathology stain-color normalization using deep generative models (2018)
8. Nam, S., Ma, C., Chai, M., Brendel, W., Xu, N., Joo Kim, S.: End-to-end time-lapse video synthesis from a single outdoor image. In: CVPR 2019, pp. 1409–1418 (2019)
9. Xiong, W., Luo, W., Ma, L., Liu, W., Luo, J.: Learning to generate time-lapse videos using multi-stage dynamic generative adversarial networks. In: CVPR 2019, pp. 2364–2373 (2018)
10. Ying, G., Zou, Y., Wan, L., Hu, Y., Feng, J.: Better guider predicts future better: difference guided generative adversarial networks. In: Jawahar, C.V., Li, H., Mori, G., Schindler, K. (eds.) ACCV 2018. LNCS, vol. 11366, pp. 277–292. Springer, Cham (2019). https://doi.org/10.1007/978-3-030-20876-9_18
11. Radford, A., et al.: Unsupervised representation learning with deep convolutional generative adversarial networks. In: International Conference on Learning Representations (ICLR) (2016)
12. Gulrajani, I., et al.: Improved training of Wasserstein GANs. In: Advances in Neural Information Processing Systems (2017)
13. Zhu, J.Y., Park, T., Isola, P., Efros, A.A.: Unpaired image-to-image translation using cycle-consistent adversarial networks. In: IEEE International Conference on Computer Vision (ICCV), pp. 2242–2251 (2017)
14. Salimans, T., Goodfellow, I., Zaremba, W., Cheung, V., Radford, A., Chen, X.: Improved techniques for training GANs. In: Proceedings of Advances in Neural Information Processing Systems (NIPS), pp. 2234–2242 (2016)

International Workshop on Deep Learning for Video and Image Analysis

Improving Image-Based Localization with Deep Learning: The Impact of the Loss Function

Isaac Ronald Ward$^{(\boxtimes)}$, M. A. Asim K. Jalwana, and Mohammed Bennamoun

University of Western Australia, Perth, Australia
isaac.ward@uwa.edu.au

Abstract. This work investigates the impact of the loss function on the performance of Neural Networks, in the context of a monocular, RGB-only, image localization task. A common technique used when regressing a camera's pose from an image is to formulate the loss as a linear combination of positional and rotational mean squared error (using tuned hyperparameters as coefficients). In this work we observe that changes to rotation and position mutually affect the captured image, and in order to improve performance, a pose regression network's loss function should include a term which combines the error of both of these coupled quantities. Based on task specific observations and experimental tuning, we present said loss term, and create a new model by appending this loss term to the loss function of the pre-existing pose regression network 'PoseNet'. We achieve improvements in the localization accuracy of the network for indoor scenes; with reductions of up to 26.7% and 24.0% in the median positional and rotational error respectively, when compared to the default PoseNet.

1 Introduction

In Convolutional Neural Networks (CNNs) and other Neural Network (NN) based architectures, a 'loss' function is provided which quantifies the error between the ground truth and the NN's prediction. This scalar quantity is used during the backpropagation process, essentially 'informing' the NN on how to adjust its trainable parameters. Naturally, the design of this loss function greatly affects the training process, yet simple metrics such as mean squared error (MSE) are often used in place of more intuitive, task specific loss functions. In this work, we explore the design and subsequent impact of a NN's loss function in the context of a monocular, RGB-only, image localization task.

The problem of image localization—that is; extracting the position and rotation (herein referred to collectively as the 'pose') of a camera, directly from an image—has been approached using a variety of traditional and deep learning based techniques in the recent years (Fig. 1).

The problem remains exceedingly relevant as it lies at the heart of numerous technologies in Computer Vision (CV) and robotics, e.g.geo-tagging, augmented reality and robotic navigation.

© Springer Nature Switzerland AG 2020
J. J. Dabrowski et al. (Eds.): PSIVT 2019 Workshops, LNCS 11994, pp. 111–124, 2020.
https://doi.org/10.1007/978-3-030-39770-8_9

Fig. 1. A sample of the predicted pose positions (purple) generated for the ground truth poses (orange) in the *7Scenes Heads* scene using our proposed model. The scene's origin (white) and SfM reconstruction is rendered for reference. Image best viewed in color. The *Heads* scene has been rendered in blue to contrast with the plotted data points. (Color figure online)

More colloquially, the problem can be understood as trying to find out where you are, and where you are looking, by considering only the information present in an RGB image.

CNN based approaches to image localization—such as PoseNet [4]—have found success in the recent years due to the availability of large datasets and powerful training hardware, but the performance gap between these systems and the more accurate SIFT feature-based pipelines remains large. For example, the SIFT-based Active Search algorithm [12] remains as a reminder that significant improvements need to be made before CNN techniques can be considered competitive when localizing images.

However, CNN-based approaches do possess number of characteristics which qualify them to handle this task well. Namely, CNNs are robust to changes in illumination and occlusion [9], they can operate in close to real time [7] (∼30 frames per second) and can be trained from labelled data (which can easily be gathered via Structure from Motion (SfM) for any arbitrary scene [13,14]). CNN based systems also tend to excel in textureless environments where SIFT based methods would typically fail [1]. They are also proven to operate well using purely RGB image data—making them an ideal solution for localizing small, cheap, robotic devices such as drones and unmanned ground vehicles. The major concern of this work is to extend existing pipelines whilst ensuring that the benefits provided by CNNs are *preserved*.

A key observation when considering existing CNN approaches is how position and rotation are treated separately in the loss function. It can be observed that altering a camera's position *or* rotation both affect the image produced, and hence the error in the regressed position and the regressed rotation cannot be decoupled—each mutually affects the other. In order to optimize a CNN for regressing a camera's pose accurately, a loss term should be used which combines both distinct quantities in an intuitive fashion.

This publication thus offers the following key contributions:

1. The formulation of a loss term which considers the error in both the regressed position *and* rotation (Sect. 3).
2. Comparison of a CNN trained with and without this loss term on common RGB image localization datasets (Sect. 5).
3. An indoor image localization dataset (the *Gemini* dataset) with over 3000 pose-labelled images per-scene (Sect. 4.1).

2   Related Work

This work builds chiefly on the PoseNet architecture (a camera pose regression network [4]). PoseNet was one of the first CNNs to regress the 6 degrees of freedom in a camera's pose. The network is pretrained on object detection datasets in order to maximize the quality of feature extraction, which occurs in the first stage of the network. It only requires a single RGB image as input, unlike other networks [11,17], and operates in real time.

Notably, PoseNet is able to localize traditionally difficult-to-localize images, specifically those with large textureless areas (where SIFT-based methods fail). PoseNet's end-to-end nature and relatively simple 'one-step' training process makes it perfect for the purpose of modification, and in the case of this work, this comes in the form of changing its loss function.

PoseNet has had its loss function augmented in prior works. In [3] it was demonstrated that changing a pose regression network's loss function is sufficient enough to cause an improvement in performance. The network was similarly 'upgraded' in [18] using LSTMs to correlate features at the CNN's output. Additional improvements to the network were completed in [2], where a Bayesian CNN implementation was used to estimate re-localization accuracy.

More complex CNN approaches do exist [8–10]. For example, the pipeline outlined in [5] uses a CNN to regress the relative poses between a set of images which are *similar* to a query image. These relative pose estimates are coalesced in a fusion algorithm which produces an estimate for the camera pose of the query image.

Depth data has also been incorporated into the inputs of pose regression networks (to improve performance by leveraging multi-modal input information). These RGB-D input pipelines are commonplace in the image localization literature [1], and typically boast higher localization accuracy at the cost of requiring additional sensors, data and computation.

A variety of non-CNN solutions exist, with one of the more notable solutions being the Active Search algorithm [12], which uses SIFT features to inform a matching process. SIFT descriptors are calculated over the query image and are directly compared to a known 3D model's SIFT features. SIFT and other non-CNN learned descriptors have been used to achieve high localization accuracy, but these descriptors tend to be susceptible to changes in the environment, and they often necessitate systems with large amounts of memory and computational power (comparatively to CNNs) [4].

The primary focus of this work is quantifying the impact of the loss function when training a pose regression CNN. Hence, we do not draw direct comparisons between the proposed model and significantly different pipelines—such as SIFT-based feature matching algorithms or PoseNet variations with highly modified architectures. Moreover, for the purpose of maximizing the number of available benchmark datasets, we consider pose regressors which handle *purely* RGB query images. In this way, this work deals specifically with CNN solutions to the *monocular*, RGB-only image localization task.

3   Formulating the Proposed Loss Term

When trying to accurately regress one's pose based on visual data alone, the error in the two terms which define pose—position and rotation—obviously needs to be minimized. If these error terms were entirely minimized, the camera would be in the correct location and would be 'looking' in the correct direction.

Formally, pose regression networks—such as the default PoseNet—are trained to regress an estimate $\hat{\vec{p}}$ for a camera's true pose $\vec{p}$. They do this by calculating the loss after every training iteration, which is formulated as the MSE between the predicted position $\hat{\vec{x}}$ and the true position $\vec{x}$, plus the MSE between the predicted rotation $\hat{\vec{q}}$ and the true rotation $\vec{q}$. Note that rotations are encoded as quaternions, since the space of rotations is continuous, and results can be easily normalized to the unit sphere in order to ensure valid rotations. Hyperparameters α and β control the balance between positional and rotational error, as illustrated in Eq. (1). In practice, RGB-only pose regression networks reach a maximum localization accuracy when minimizing these error terms independently.

$$\mathcal{L}_{default} = \alpha \cdot \|\hat{\vec{x}} - \vec{x}\| + \beta \cdot \|\hat{\vec{q}} - \vec{q}\| \tag{1}$$

Rather than considering position and rotation as two separate quantities, we consider them together as a line in 3D space: the line travels in a direction defined by the rotation, and must travel through the position vector defined by the position $\vec{x}$. We then introduce a 'line-of-sight' term which constrains our predictions to lie on this line. The line-of-sight term considers the cosine similarity between the direction of the pose $\vec{p}$ and the direction of the difference vector $\vec{d} = \vec{x} - \hat{\vec{x}}$, as per Eq. (2) and Fig. 2. This term is only zero when the predicted position lies on the line defined by the ground truth pose, hence constraining the pose regression objective further. In the context of image localization, this ensures that the predicted poses lie on the line-of-sight defined in the ground truth image.

$$1 - \cos\theta = 1 - \frac{\vec{p} \cdot \vec{d}}{\|\vec{p}\| \cdot \|\vec{d}\|} \tag{2}$$

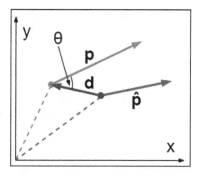

Fig. 2. The important quantities required in the calculation of the proposed loss term in 2D. This process naturally extends to 3D. The Euclidean dot product formula is used to calculate a value for θ.

We modify the default loss function presented in Eq. (1) by adding a weighted contribution of the line-of-sight loss term, producing the proposed loss function in Eq. (3). In practice, the value of γ is chosen to roughly reflect the scale of the scene being considered, and is found via a hyperparameter grid search. Note that the line-of-sight term can contribute to the loss through multiplication, higher order terms, etc. but it was determined that weighted addition produced the best performing networks.

$$\mathcal{L}_{proposed} = L_{default} + \gamma \cdot (1 - \cos\theta) \qquad (3)$$

In short, the final loss function used to train the proposed model (Eq. (3)) is the result of an exploration in the space of possible loss terms, and the term's design was informed by task specific observations and experimentation.

4   Experiments

Our experiments are naturally centred around testing the performance of the proposed model (defined in Sect. 3). This performance is defined with respect to the following criteria:

- **Accuracy**: the system should be able to regress a camera's pose with a level of positional and rotational accuracy that is competitive with similar classes of algorithms. Accuracy is reported using per-scene and average median positional and rotational error (See Sect. 5.1).
- **Robustness**: the system should be robust to perceptual aliasing, motion blur and other challenges posed by the considered datasets (See Sect. 5.2 and Fig. 8).
- **Time performance**: evaluation should occur in real-time (~30 frames per second), such that the system is suitable in hardware limited real-time applications, or on platforms with RGB-only image sensors, e.g. on mobile phones (See Sect. 5.3).

We compare our proposed model against the default PoseNet and other PoseNet variants.

4.1 Datasets

The following datasets are used to benchmark model performance. Each scene's recommended train and test split is used throughout the following experiments (Figs. 3, 4, 5 and 6).

Chess   Fire   Heads   Office   Pumpkin   Red Kitchen   Stairs

Fig. 3. Sample images from each of the 7 scenes in the *7Scenes* dataset.

Great Court   Kings College   Old Hospital   Shop Facade   St Mary's   Street
                                                                 Church

Fig. 4. Sample images from each of the 6 scenes in the *Cambridge Landmarks* dataset.

Office   Meeting   Kitchen   Conference   Coffee Room

Fig. 5. Sample images from each of the 5 scenes in the *University* dataset.

Fig. 6. Sample images from the 2 scenes in the *Gemini* dataset.

7Scenes [15]. 7 indoor locations in a domestic office context. The dataset features large training and testing sets (in the thousands). The camera paths move continuously while gathering images in distinct sequences. Images include motion blur, featureless spaces and specular reflections (see Fig. 8), making this a challenging dataset, and one that has been used prolifically in the image localization literature. The ground truths poses are gathered with KinectFusion, and the RGB-D frames each have resolutions of 640 × 480 px.

Cambridge Landmarks [2,4]. 6 outdoor locations in and around Cambridge, The United Kingdom. The larger spatial extent and restricted dataset size make this a challenging dataset to learn to regress pose from—methods akin to the one presented in this work typically only deliver positional accuracy in the scale of metres. However, the dataset does provide a common point of comparison, and also includes large expanses of texture-less surfaces. Ground truth poses are generated by a SfM process, so some comparison can be drawn between this dataset and the one created in this work.

University [5]. 5 indoor scenes in a university context. Ground truth poses are gathered using odometry estimates and "manually generated location constraints in a pose-graph optimization framework" [5]. The dataset, similarly to *7Scenes*, includes challenging frames with high degrees of perceptual aliasing, where multiple frames (with different poses) give rise to similar images [20]. Although the scenes are registered to a common coordinate system in the *University* dataset and thus a network *could* be trained on the full dataset, the models created in this work are trained and tested *scene-wise* for the purpose of consistency.

Gemini[1]. 2 indoor scenes in a university lab context. This dataset was created for the purpose of studying the effect of texture and colour on pose regression networks: both scenes survey the same environment, with one scene including decor (posters, screen-savers, paintings etc.) and the other deliberately *not* including visually rich, textured, and colorful decor. As such the two scenes are labelled *Decor* and *Plain*. A photogrammetry pipeline (COLMAP [14]) was used to generate the ground truth poses. Images were captured in 15 separate video sequences using a FujiFilm X-T20 with a 23 mm prime autofocus lens (in order to ensure a fixed calibration matrix between sequences). Visualizations of the *with decor* scene are provided in Fig. 7.

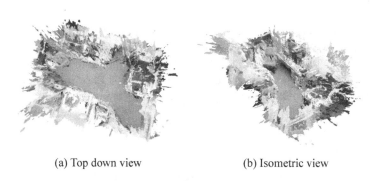

(a) Top down view   (b) Isometric view

Fig. 7. (a) – (b) Varying views of the *Gemini* dataset.

---

[1] This dataset has been made available at https://github.com/anon-datasets/gemini.

4.2 Architecture and Training

As stated, we primarily experiment with the PoseNet architecture (using TensorFlow). For the purpose of brevity we redirect the reader to the original publication [4], as here we only describe crucial elements of the network's design and operation.

The PoseNet architecture is in itself based on the GoogLeNet architecture [16], a 22 layer deep network which performs classification and detection. PoseNet extracts GoogLeNet's early feature extracting layers, and replaces the final three softmax classifiers with affine regressors. The network is pretrained using large classification datasets such as *Places* [21].

Strictly, the default loss function used is not exactly as defined in Eq. (1). Instead, PoseNet uses the predictions from all three affine regressors (hence there are three predictions for each quantity). We label the ith affine regressor's hyperparameters and predictions using a subscript i, as per Eq. (4). All three affine regressors' predictions are used in the loss function, but each have different hyperparameter weightings: $\alpha_1 = \alpha_2 = 0.3$, $\alpha_3 = 1$, $\beta_1 = \beta_2 = 150$ and $\beta_3 = 500$.

$$\mathcal{L}_{default} = \alpha_i \cdot \|\hat{\vec{x}}_i - \vec{x}\| + \beta_i \cdot \|\hat{\vec{q}}_i - \vec{q}\| \tag{4}$$

In order to demonstrate the consistency and generalization of the proposed network, we train against all scenes in all datasets using the same experimental setup. For each scene we train PoseNet using the default loss (Eq. (4)) and the proposed loss (Eq. (3)) *with* the contribution from all three affine regressors. Each model is trained per-scene over 300,000 iterations with a batch size of 75 on a Tesla K40c, which takes ~10 h to complete.

5 Results

We compare our proposed model to PoseNet and one of its variants—Bayesian PoseNet [18]—in Table 1. This is to show the proposed model's performance when compared to other variants of PoseNet with modified loss functions. We then provide results specifically comparing the default PoseNet to our proposed model in Table 2. A discussion of our system's performance regarding the criteria outlined in Sect. 4 follows.

5.1 Accuracy

It is observed that the proposed model outperforms the default version of PoseNet in approximately half the *7Scenes* scenes—particularly the *Stairs* scene. In the *Stairs* scene, repetitious structures, e.g.staircases, make localization harder, yet the proposed model is robust to such challenges. The network is outperformed in others scenes; namely outdoor datasets with large spatial extents, but in general, performance is improved for the indoor datasets *7Scenes*, *University* and *Gemini*.

Table 1. The results of various pose regression networks for various image localization datasets. Median positional and rotational error is reported in the form: **metres, degrees**. The lowest errors are emboldened. Note that our proposed model is competitive in *indoor* datasets with respect to median positional error.

Scene	Bayesian PoseNet [2]	Default PoseNet [4]	Proposed model
Chess	0.37, 7.24	0.32, 8.12	**0.31, 7.04**
Fire	**0.43**, 13.7	0.47, 14.4	0.49, **13.3**
Heads	0.31, **12.0**	0.29, **12.0**	**0.24**, 15.7
Office	0.48, 8.04	0.48, **7.68**	**0.40**, 10.0
Pumpkin	0.61, **7.07**	**0.47**, 8.42	0.49, 9.50
Red Kit.	0.58, **7.54**	0.58, 11.3	**0.53**, 7.98
Stairs	**0.48, 13.1**	0.56, 15.4	**0.48**, 14.7
Average	0.47, **9.81**	0.45, 11.0	**0.42**, 11.2
Street	–	3.67, 6.50	–
King's Col.	**1.74**, 4.06	1.92, 5.40	2.28, **4.05**
Old Hosp.	2.57, **5.14**	**2.31**, 5.38	3.90, 8.75
Shop Fac.	**1.25, 7.54**	1.46, 8.08	2.48, 10.2
St Mary's	**2.11**, 8.38	2.65, 8.48	3.02, **7.79**
Average^a	**1.92, 6.28**	2.09, 6.84	2.92, 7.70

^{a} Average calculated using only the scenes: *King's College, Old Hospital, Shop Facade & St Mary's Church* as full dataset performance is not available for all pipelines.

Table 2. A study on the direct effects of using our proposed loss function, instead of the default loss function when training PoseNet. Median positional and rotational error is reported in the form: **metres, degrees**. The lowest errors of each group are emboldened. Note that our contribution majorly outperforms the default PoseNet in both median positional and median rotational error throughout the *University* dataset and the *Gemini* dataset. In the *Gemini* dataset, decreases of 26.7% and 24.0% in the median positional and rotational error are observed in the *Decor* scene, and an overall increase in accuracy demonstrates the proposed model's robustness to textureless indoor environments (when compared to the default PoseNet).

Scene	Default PoseNet [4]	Proposed model
Office (University)	1.05, 16.2	**0.91, 11.0**
Meeting	1.78, 10.1	**1.30, 9.58**
Kitchen	**1.19, 12.5**	1.25, 15.5
Conference	2.88, 13.3	**2.83**, 15.8
Coffee Room	1.41, 14.9	**1.21, 13.3**
Average	1.66, 13.4	**1.50, 13.0**
Plain	1.27, **7.87**	**1.14**, 7.90
Decor	0.15, 1.17	**0.11, 0.89**
Average	0.71, 4.52	**0.63, 4.40**

A set of cumulative histograms for six of the evaluated scenes are provided in Table 3, where we compare the distribution of the positional errors and rotational errors. Median values (provided in Tables 1 and 2) are plotted for reference.

The proposed model's errors are strictly less than the default PoseNet's throughout the majority of the *Chess* and *Coffee Room* distributions. However, the default PoseNet outperforms our proposed model with respect to rotational accuracy in the 10°–30° range in the *Coffee Room* scene.

Note the lesser performance observed from the proposed model on the *King's College* scene; where the positional errors distributions for the two networks are nearly aligned. Moreover, the default PoseNet more accurately regresses rotation in this outdoor scene. See Sects. 5.2 and 6 for further discussion.

5.2   Robustness

The robustness of our system to challenging test frames—that is, images with motion blur, repeated structures or demonstrating perceptual aliasing [6]—can be determined via the cumulative histograms in Table 3. For the purpose of visualization, some difficult testing images from the *7Scenes* dataset are displayed in Fig. 8.

The hardest frames in the test set by definition produce the greatest errors. Consider the positional error for the *Meeting* scene: our proposed model reaches a value of 1.0 on the y-axis before the default PoseNet does, meaning that the *hardest* frames in the test set have their position regressed more accurately. This analysis extends to each of the cumulative histograms in Table 3, thus confirming our proposed loss function's robustness to difficult test scenarios, as the frames of greatest error consistently have less than or comparable errors when compared to the default PoseNet.

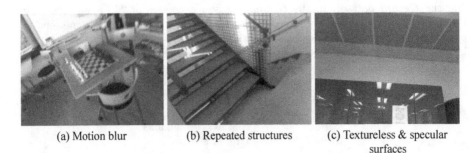

(a) Motion blur   (b) Repeated structures   (c) Textureless & specular
                                                          surfaces

Fig. 8. (a) – (c) Images from the *7Scenes* dataset where accurately regressing pose is challenging.

Moreover, the proposed model significantly exceeds the default PoseNet's performance throughout the *Gemini* dataset. The performance gap in the *Plain* scene proves that our model is more robust to textureless spaces than the default PoseNet.

Table 3. Cumulative histograms of positional and rotational errors, with median values plotted as a dotted line. Note that the proposed model's positional error distribution is strictly less than (shifted to the left of) the default PoseNet's positional error distribution for the indoor scenes (except *Conference*, where performance is comparable). Additionally, the maximum error of the proposed model is lower in the scenes *Meeting*, *Coffee Room* and *Kitchen*, meaning that our implementation is robust to some of the most difficult frames offered by the *University* dataset. Images best viewed in colour.

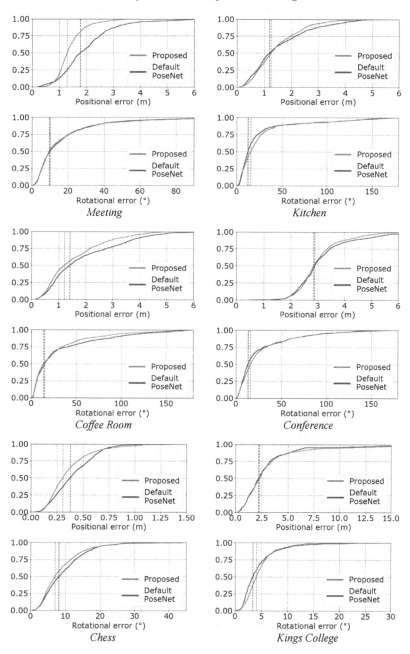

5.3   Efficiency

Training Time. The duration of the training stage compared between our implementation and default PoseNet is by design, very similar, and highly competitive when compared to the other systems analyzed in Table 1. This is due to the relatively inexpensive computing cost of introducing a simple line-of-sight loss term into the network's overall loss function. The average training time for default PoseNet and for our augmented PoseNet over the University dataset is 10 : 21 : 31 and 10 : 23 : 33 respectively (HH:MM:SS), where both tests are ran on the same hardware.

Testing Time. The network operation during the test time is naturally not affected by the loss function augmentation. The time performance when testing is similar to that of the default PoseNet and in general is competitive amongst camera localization pipelines (especially feature based matching techniques). We observe a total elapsed time of 16.04 s when evaluating the entire *Coffee Room* scene testing set, whereas it takes 16.03 s using the default PoseNet. In other words, both systems take ∼16.8 ms to complete a single inference on our hardware.

Memory Cost. Memory cost in general for CNNs is low—only the weights for the trained layers and the input image need to be loaded into memory. When compared to feature matching techniques, which need to store feature vectors for all instances in the test set, or SIFT-based matching methods with large memory and computational overheads, CNN approaches are in general quite desirable—especially in resource constrained environments. Both the proposed model and the default PoseNet take 8015MiB and 10947MiB to train and test respectively (as reported by *nvidia-smi*). For interest, the network weights for the proposed model's TensorFlow implementation total only 200 MB.

6   Discussion and Future Work

Experimental results confirm that the proposed loss term has a positive impact on robustness and accuracy, whilst maintaining speed, memory usage, and robustness (to textureless spaces and so forth).

The network *is* outperformed by the SIFT-based image localization algorithm 'Active Search' [12], indicating that there is still some work required until the gap between SIFT-based algorithms and CNNs is closed (in the context of RGB-only image localization). However, SIFT localization operates on a much longer timescale, and can be highly computationally expensive depending on the dataset and pipeline being used [19].

Ultimately, the loss function described in this work illustrates that intuitive loss terms, designed with respect to a specific task (in this case image localization) can positively impact the performance of deep networks.

Possible avenues for future work include extending this loss function design methodology to other CV tasks, in order to achieve higher performance, or to consider RGB-D pipelines. An investigation on the effect that such loss terms have on the convergence rate, and upper performance limit of NNs could also be explored.

7   Conclusion

In summary, the effect of adding a line-of-sight loss term to an existing pose regression network is investigated. The performance of the proposed model is compared to other similar models across common image localization benchmarks and the newly introduced *Gemini* dataset. Improvements to performance in the image localization task are observed, without any drastic increase in evaluation speed or training time. Particularly, the median positional accuracy is—on average—increased for indoor datasets when compared to a version of the model without the suggested loss term.

This work suggests that means squared error between the ground truth and the regressed predictions—although often used as a measure of loss for many Neural Networks—can be improved upon. Specifically, loss functions designed with the network's task in mind may yield better performing models. For pose regression networks, the distinct and coupled nature of positional and rotational quantities needs to be considered when designing a network's loss function.

References

1. Brachmann, E., Rother, C.: Learning less is more - 6D camera localization via 3D surface regression. In: Conference on Computer Vision and Pattern Recognition (CVPR) abs/1711.10228 (2017). http://arxiv.org/abs/1711.10228
2. Kendall, A., Cipolla, R.: Modelling uncertainty in deep learning for camera relocalization. In: International Conference on Robotics and Automation (ICRA) abs/1509.05909 (2015). http://arxiv.org/abs/1509.05909
3. Kendall, A., Cipolla, R.: Geometric loss functions for camera pose regression with deep learning. In: Conference on Computer Vision and Pattern Recognition (CVPR), April 2017. http://arxiv.org/abs/1704.00390
4. Kendall, A., Grimes, M., Cipolla, R.: PoseNet: a convolutional network for real-time 6-DOF camera relocalization. In: International Conference on Computer Vision (ICCV), May 2015. http://arxiv.org/abs/1505.07427
5. Laskar, Z., Melekhov, I., Kalia, S., Kannala, J.: Camera relocalization by computing pairwise relative poses using convolutional neural network. In: International Conference on Computer Vision (ICCV) (2017)
6. Li, X., Ylioinas, J., Kannala, J.: Full-frame scene coordinate regression for image-based localization. Robot.: Sci. Syst. (2018). http://arxiv.org/abs/1802.03237
7. Massiceti, D., Krull, A., Brachmann, E., Rother, C., Torr, P.H.S.: Random forests versus neural networks - what's best for camera relocalization? In: International Conference on Robotics and Automation (ICRA) abs/1609.05797 (2016). http://arxiv.org/abs/1609.05797
8. Melekhov, I., Kannala, J., Rahtu, E.: Relative camera pose estimation using convolutional neural networks. In: Advanced Concepts for Intelligent Vision Systems (ACIVS) abs/1702.01381 (2017). http://arxiv.org/abs/1702.01381

9. Melekhov, I., Ylioinas, J., Kannala, J., Rahtu, E.: Image-based localization using hourglass networks. In: International Conference on Computer Vision Workshops (ICCVW) abs/1703.07971 (2017). http://arxiv.org/abs/1703.07971
10. Purkait, P., Zhao, C., Zach, C.: SPP-Net: deep absolute pose regression with synthetic views. In: British Machine Vision Conference (BMVC) abs/1712.03452 (2017). http://arxiv.org/abs/1712.03452
11. Radwan, N., Valada, A., Burgard, W.: VLocNet++: deep multitask learning for semantic visual localization and odometry. Robot. Autom. Lett. (RAL) **3** (2018). http://arxiv.org/abs/1804.08366
12. Sattler, T., Leibe, B., Kobbelt, L.: Efficient and effective prioritized matching for large-scale image-based localization. Trans. Pattern Anal. Mach. Intell. (PAMI) **39**(09), 1744–1756 (2017). https://doi.org/10.1109/TPAMI.2016.2611662
13. Schönberger, J.L., Zheng, E., Frahm, J.-M., Pollefeys, M.: Pixelwise view selection for unstructured multi-view stereo. In: Leibe, B., Matas, J., Sebe, N., Welling, M. (eds.) ECCV 2016. LNCS, vol. 9907, pp. 501–518. Springer, Cham (2016). https://doi.org/10.1007/978-3-319-46487-9_31
14. Schönberger, J.L., Frahm, J.: Structure-from-motion revisited. In: Conference on Computer Vision and Pattern Recognition (CVPR), pp. 4104–4113, June 2016. https://doi.org/10.1109/CVPR.2016.445
15. Shotton, J., Glocker, B., Zach, C., Izadi, S., Criminisi, A., Fitzgibbon, A.: Scene coordinate regression forests for camera relocalization in RGB-D images. In: Conference on Computer Vision and Pattern Recognition (CVPR), pp. 2930–2937 (2013). https://doi.org/10.1109/CVPR.2013.377
16. Szegedy, C., et al.: Going deeper with convolutions. In: Conference on Computer Vision and Pattern Recognition (CVPR) abs/1409.4842 (2014). http://arxiv.org/abs/1409.4842
17. Valada, A., Radwan, N., Burgard, W.: Deep auxiliary learning for visual localization and odometry. In: International Conference on Robotics and Automation (ICRA) abs/1803.03642 (2018). http://arxiv.org/abs/1803.03642
18. Walch, F., Hazirbas, C., Leal-Taixé, L., Sattler, T., Hilsenbeck, S., Cremers, D.: Image-based localization using LSTMs for structured feature correlation. In: International Conference on Computer Vision (ICCV), November 2016. http://arxiv.org/abs/1611.07890
19. Wu, C.: Towards linear-time incremental structure from motion. In: International Conference on 3D Vision (3DV), pp. 127–134, June 2013. https://doi.org/10.1109/3DV.2013.25
20. Zaval, L., Gureckis, T.M.: The impact of perceptual aliasing on exploration and learning in a dynamic decision making task. In: Proceedings of the Annual Meeting of the Cognitive Science Society (2010)
21. Zhou, B., Lapedriza, A., Xiao, J., Torralba, A., Oliva, A.: Learning deep features for scene recognition using places database. In: Ghahramani, Z., Welling, M., Cortes, C., Lawrence, N.D., Weinberger, K.Q. (eds.) Advances in Neural Information Processing Systems 27, pp. 487–495. Curran Associates, Inc. (2014)

Face-Based Age and Gender Classification Using Deep Learning Model

Olatunbosun Agbo-Ajala and Serestina Viriri[✉]

School of Mathematics, Statistics and Computer Science,
University of KwaZulu-Natal, Westville, Durban 4000, South Africa
ajalabosun@gmail.com, viriris@ukzn.ac.za

Abstract. Age and gender classification of human's face is an important research focus, having many application areas. Recently, Convolutional Neural Networks (CNNs) model has proven to be the most suitable method for the classification task, especially of unconstrained real-world faces. This could be as a result of its expertise in feature extraction and classification of face images. Availability of both high-end computers and large training data also contributed to its usage. In this paper, we, therefore, propose a novel CNN-based model to extract discriminative features from unconstrained real-life face images and classify those images into age and gender. We approach the large variations attributed to those unconstrained real-life faces with a robust image preprocessing algorithm and a pretraining on a large IMDb-WIKI dataset containing noisy and unfiltered age and genders labels. We also adopted a dropout and data augmentation regularization method to overcome the risk of overfitting and allow our model generalize on the test images. We show that well-designed network architecture and properly tuned training hyperparameters, give better results. The experimental results on OIU-Adience dataset confirm that our model outperforms other studies on the same dataset, showing significant performance in terms of classification accuracy. The proposed method achieves classification accuracy values of 84.8% on age group and classification accuracy of 89.7% on gender.

Keywords: Adience dataset · Age classification · Convolutional neural network · Unconstrained images

1 Introduction

Facial recognition is an interesting [9], and prevalent problem recently [18] because of its many popular real-world application areas, ranging from entertainment [31], security control [1], cosmetology [15], to biometrics [6,14]. Age and gender classification of faces, in particular, has rapidly gained more popularity among others [12]; it plays a very significant role in our social lives in which we rely on the two attributes of the face for our daily interactions [20].

J. J. Dabrowski et al. (Eds.): PSIVT 2019 Workshops, LNCS 11994, pp. 125–137, 2020.
https://doi.org/10.1007/978-3-030-39770-8_10

Age and gender classification tasks have been approached with some many methods, many of which are incapable of solving the two problems accurately. Most of the popular approaches have been handcrafted which manually engineer features from the face, and focuses on extracting handcrafted features to explore the discriminative information needed for the estimation task [16,19,25,30]. Different machine learning methods studied by many researchers for age and gender classification were only efficient on face images captured under controlled conditions; few of those methods are designed to handle the many challenges of unconstrained real-life imaging conditions achieving unsatisfactory results [4,7].

Recently, Convolution Neural Networks (CNNs) has proven to be the most suitable method for facial recognition, especially in age and gender classification. It can classify the age and gender of face images relying on its good feature extraction technique [2,5,11,21,26,29]. Availability of both large data for training and high-end computer machines, also help in the adoption of the deep CNN methods for the classification task. This consequently shows its relevance to classify unconstrained real-world age and gender tasks automatically achieving significant performance over existing methods [17,24,27,32]. We, therefore, present a CNN-based model (in Fig. 1) for age group and gender classification of unfiltered real-life face images of individuals. Our main contributions are as follows:

1. We propose a new CNN model to process age and gender classification of unconstrained real-life faces where we categorize the facial analysis task as a classification problem, that considers each age and gender as a class label.
2. We design a robust face detection and alignment algorithms that localize face in the image, detect facial landmarks of unconstrained faces in real-time and transform the image into an output coordinate space.
3. We also pre-train our model on a very large facial aging dataset containing unconstrained age and gender labels, to learn the bias and particularities of the dataset and also to avoid overfitting.
4. Finally, we employ two popular datasets benchmark for training and validation. The experimental results when evaluated on OIU-Adience benchmark dataset for age and gender classification, show that our novel CNN model achieves better performance compared with state-of-the-art on the same dataset and hence can satisfy the requirements of many real-world applications.

The remainder of this paper is arranged as follows: Sect. 2 briefly studies the related works in age and gender classification, Sect. 3 describes our proposed approach, Sect. 4 presents the experiments and the experimental analysis on OIU-Adience dataset of unconstrained faces with age and gender labels and then discusses the achieved results while conclusion and future works are drawn in Sect. 5.

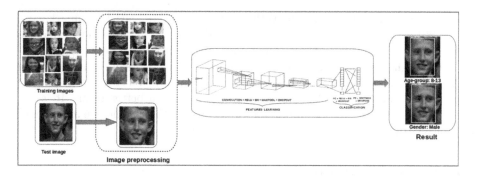

Fig. 1. The pipeline of our proposed model

2   Related Works

In the past years, several methods have been proposed to solve the age and gender classification problem. Some of those methods focus more on constrained images while only a few studies age and gender classification of unconstrained real-world faces. Recently, CNN has received increasing attention in the computer vision community especially for classifying age and gender of face images from uncontrolled imaging environment [11]. To mention a few, Eidinger *et al.* [12] studied age and gender classification of face images acquired in challenging in-the-wild scenarios. Firstly, they collected face images of people labeled for age and gender from online image repositories. They also proposed a dropout-SVM approach for the estimation task with a robust face alignment technique to prepare the in-the-wild images for better result. Their approach achieved a better result when compared to the state-of-the-art. Levi and Hassner [20] also investigated a five-layer CNN method to classify the age and gender of the person using the faces collected from unconstrained settings. The model is trained and evaluated on Adience benchmark for age and gender estimation where the results reflect a remarkable baseline for CNN-based models and can improve with better system design. Subhani and Anto in [29] proposed a five-layer CNN based architecture for age and gender classifications on Adience benchmark images using direct Convolutional Neural System engineering. The model achieved a better result than the current state-of-the-art methods when evaluated on Adience dataset. Zhang *et al.* [32] developed a novel CNN-based model for age group and gender classifications of the in-the-wild images, named "Residual Networks of Residual Networks (RoR)". RoR model was initially pretrained on ImageNet dataset, then finetuned on IMDB-WIKI dataset to learn the peculiarity of each dataset before finally finetuning on Adience benchmark dataset. The experimental results achieved new state-of-the-art results on Adience dataset. In 2018, Duan *et al.* [10] proposed a hybrid novel age estimation model named CNN2ELM, to predict the age and gender of face images. CNN2ELM includes three convolutional neural networks (CNN) models and two extreme learning machine (ELM) structures. The models are pretrained on the ImageNet dataset before finetuning on the IMDB-WIKI, MORPH-II, Adience benchmark, and LAP-2016 datasets. The three CNNs are used for features extraction while the two ELM structures classify the age group and gender.

Although most of the methods discussed above made lots of improvement on age and gender classification, where some are aimed at unconstrained imaging conditions, our novel CNN structure can still achieve a better result. It is not only suitable on constrained images but also able to classify the age and gender of unconstrained real-life facial images.

3   Proposed Approach

The approach for the age group and gender classification of unconstrained real-life face images as presented in Fig. 1, consists of the following main components:

3.1   Face Detection

The image preprocessing stage starts with face detection to detect an input image by localizing face in the image before detecting the key facial structures on the face object of interest. To accomplish this task, we employ a dlib library that uses "pre-trained HOG + Linear SVM". The detector, an improvement of [8] and [23], is an effective and reliable model to localize the face in the image; it can locate the bounding box (x, y)-coordinates of a face in an image.

3.2   Landmark Detection and Face Alignment

Given the face region from face detection phase, we can then apply a face landmark method to detect the key facial structures on the face area of interest including the mouth, right eyebrow, left eyebrow, right eye, left eye, nose, and jaw. The designed landmark detector algorithm detects facial landmarks of unconstrained faces in real-time.

Also, before we pass our face images through our CNN model for training and evaluation, there is a need to normalize and align the face images to obtain better accuracy. The goal of this is to warp and transform the images into an output coordinate space. Having achieved the (x, y)-coordinates of the eyes through landmark detection, we then compute the angle between them and generate their midpoint. An affine transformation is then applied to warp the images into a new output coordinate space for centered images, an equally scaled, and well-rotated eyes lying along a horizontal line.

3.3   Architecture of Our CNN Model

In this section, we describe the design of our novel CNN structure in Fig. 2. Our network architecture includes two stages: feature extraction and classification. The feature extraction stage contains the convolutional layer, activation layer (rectified linear unit (ReLU)), batch normalization (instead of the deprecated

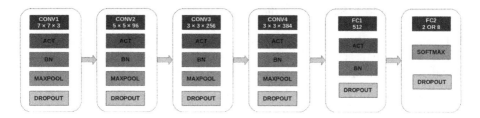

Fig. 2. The pipeline of our proposed model

Local Response Normalization), max-pooling layer, and a dropout. The feature extraction stage has four convolutional layers with their corresponding parameters, including the number of each filter, the kernel size of each filter, the stride, etc. The first convolutional layer consists of 96, 7 × 7 kernels and a stride of 4 × 4. The second, third and fourth series of convolutional layers applied the same structure as the first but with different filter and filter size. Second convolutional layer consist of 256, 5 × 5 filters, third is near identical to the second convolutional layers but with an increase in the number of filters to 384 and a reduction of the filter size to 3 × 3. The last and fourth convolutional layer set has a filter of 256 and a filter size of 3 × 3. All the convolutional layers have a fixed dropout of 25% to improve generalization and reduce overfitting.

The classification stage contains two fully-connected layers that classify the age group and gender tasks. The first fully-connected layers contain 512 neurons, followed by a ReLU, batch normalization and a dropout layer at a dropout ratio of 50%. The last fully-connected layer output 512 features which are densely mapped to 8 or 2 neurons for classification tasks. A softmax with cross-entropy loss function is adopted to obtain a probability for each class.

Cross-Entropy: Cross-entropy loss measures the performance of a classification model and generates an output that is between 0 and 1. Cross-entropy loss decreases as the predicted probability converges to the correct label; the lower the cross-entropy result, the better the classification model to generalize.

In binary classification, with the number of classes N equals 2, it is therefore defined as:

$$- (z \log(p) + (1 - z) \log(1 - p)) \tag{1}$$

but for multi-class classification with N > 2, we calculate a separate loss for each label of observation and then sum the outcome (see Eq. 2).

$$- \sum_{c=1}^{N} z_{o,c} \log(p_{o,c}) \tag{2}$$

where N is the number of classes, z is the binary indicator (0 or 1) if class label c is the actual classification for observation o, log is the natural log, and p is the predicted probability observation o of class label c.

Table 1. Summary of the popular Facial Aging Databases

Database	Database size	#Subjects	Age range	Age type	Year	In-the-wild?
OIU-Adience [12]	26,580	2,284	0–60+	Age group	2014	Yes
IMDb-WIKI [32]	523,051	20,284	0–100	Real	2016	Yes

3.4 System Training

In this section, we present the training details of the two classifiers for age group and gender on Adience dataset that correctly predict the age group and the gender of unconstrained face images. The age classifier will be responsible for predicting the age of eight different classes while gender classifier will classify gender into two classes. We initially pre-train the two CNN based classifiers on a very large IMDb-WIKI benchmark dataset containing unconstrained real-life faces with age and gender label. This is important so that the two classifiers will learn the bias from large image samples to generalize on the test image samples and also reduce the risk of overfitting. For IMDb-WIKI dataset, we split into two: 90% for training, and 10% for validation while 70% of OIU-Adience images is used for training and the remaining 30% is equally split, 15% for validation and 15% for testing. The images in the datasets were originally rescaled to 256×256 pixel, then cropped to 224×224 pixel before being passed into the network. We also train the network using a batch size of 64. The optimization of the proposed model for the classifiers is carried out by using a stochastic gradient descent method with mini-batches of size 256 and a momentum value of 0.9 with a weight decay of 0.0005. The training starts with an initial learning rate of 0.0001 then decrease by a factor of 10 whenever there is no improvement in the accuracy result. The training on the classifiers is terminated when the network begins to overfit on the validation set. To further improve our model performance, we employ data augmentation on both the training and testing images and also utilize dropout regularization methods. We calculate SGD as defined in Eq. 3:

$$\beta = \beta - \eta \cdot \nabla_\beta J(\beta; x^{(i)}; y^{(i)}) \tag{3}$$

where η is defined as the learning rate, $\nabla_\beta J$, the gradient of the loss term with respect to the weight vector β.

4 Experiments

In this section, we describe the specifications of the employed OIU-Adience and IMDb-WIKI benchmark databases, and experimental analysis of our model on OIU-Adience benchmark with age and gender labels.

4.1 Description of the Dataset

We employ two standard facial aging datasets to train and validate our approach. We initially train our model on IMDb-WIKI database [32] and then finetune it on the original OIU-Adience benchmark [12] of unconstrained facial images.

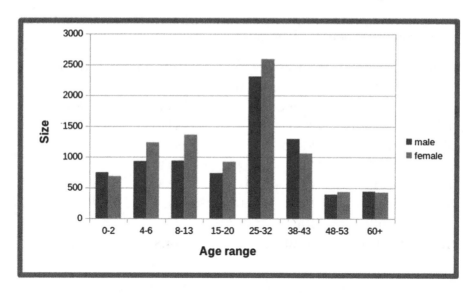

Fig. 3. Age group and gender distribution of face images in OIU-Adience dataset.

OIU-Adience dataset [12] consists of about 26,000 face images from ideal real-life and unconstrained environments. Hence, It reflects all the features that are expected of an image collected from challenging uncontrolled scenarios with a high degree of variations in noise, pose, appearance among others. It has eight different age categories (0–2, 4–6, 8–13, 15–20, 25–32, 38–43, 48–53, 60+) and two gender labels.

IMDb-WIKI database [32] is the largest publicly available dataset for age estimation of people in the wild, containing more than half a million images with accurate age labels between 0 and 100 years. For the IMDb-WIKI dataset, the images were crawled from IMDb and Wikipedia; IMDb contains 460,723 images of 20,284 celebrities and Wikipedia with 62,328 images. The images of IMDb-WIKI dataset are obtained directly from the website, as such the dataset contains many low-quality images, such as "human comic" images, sketch images, severe facial mask, full body images, multi-person images, blank images, and so on.. The specification of the datasets is highlighted in Table 1 while the detailed distribution of OIU-Adience images for the age and gender categories, is presented in Fig. 3.

4.2 Experimental Results and Discussion

A novel CNN model which classify unconstrained face images to age group and gender has been proposed. Different empirical experiments have been carried out to evaluate the performance of the proposed approach for classifying a person to the correct age group and gender on Adience dataset. The performance of the two classifiers is measured by two standard metrics common in the literature: confusion matrix and accuracy.

Table 2. Results in literature for Age group and Gender classification on OIU-Adience benchmark using classification accuracy.

Reference	Year	Approach	Age group (%)	Gender (%)
[12]	2014	Dropout SVM + LBP	45.1	–
[20]	2015	3C2FC	50.7	86.8
[13]	2016	3C3FC	54.5	80.8
[3]	2017	FFNN	58.5	–
[24]	2017	VGG	59.9	–
[11]	2018	CNN + ELM	52.3	88.2
[21]	2018	CNN + focal Loss	54.0	–
[10]	2018	RAGN	66.5	–
Proposed	**2019**	**4C2FC**	**84.8**	**89.7**

Confusion Matrix [22]. This evaluates the performance of multi-class age group and binary gender classification model on sets of test images. The metric summarizes the performance of the classification algorithm in a table with four different combinations of predicted and actual classes. We therefore presents a confusion matrix to the eight classes (0–2, 4–6, 8–13, 15–20, 25–32, 38–43, 48–53, 60+) age grouping results and for binary class gender classification results. The metric generates the results of our proposed method on OIU-Adience dataset for age group and gender classification.

Accuracy [28]. This calculates the closeness of the measured (predicted) value to the standard or known (ground truth) value. It is calculated as the percentage of face images that were classified into correct age-groups (or gender). It measures the proportion of true results (both true positives and true negatives) among the total number of face image samples tested (see Eq. 4).

$$\text{Accuracy} = \frac{TP + TN}{TP + TN + FP + FN} \tag{4}$$

where TP is the number of true positive value, TN is the number of true negative value, FP is the number of false positive value, and FN is the number of false negative value.

It is important to comment that the variation in the classification result for age and gender as presented in Fig. 5(a) and (b) respectively, is attributed to the different number of samples for age and gender annotations which are not evenly distributed, and also the peculiarity of each class.

From the confusion matrix table in Fig. 5(a), it is noticed that the 8–13 and 0–2 age group labels are estimated with the highest accuracy compared to the other age groups. In the case of the 0–2 age group, this could be attributed to the fact that face images of infants contain distinctive features that enable the classifier to distinguish this age group easily. For 8–13 group, that might be as a result of its size and distinctive features in those image category. 48–53 age group label was recorded with the lowest accuracy, the result might be as a result of its small size. The confusion matrix of the gender classification is presented Fig. 5(b). From this figure, we see that our approach recognizes males easily compared to females, achieving better accuracy.

In addition to applying a confusion matrix metric, we also evaluate the accuracy of the best configuration of our method in terms of classification accuracy, on OIU-Adience benchmark dataset, and compare our results with the state of the art methods. Table 2 compares the accuracy of the best configuration of our method with that of state-of-the-art techniques for the OIU-Adience dataset. For the Age group Classification, our model achieves a classification accuracy of 84.8%, and this improves over best-reported state of the art result for accuracy in Duan *et al.* [10] by 18.3%. We also evaluate our method for classifying a person to the correct gender on the same OIU-Adience dataset where we train the model for classification of two gender classes, and report the result on classification accuracy with pre-training on the IMDb-WIKI dataset, and finetuning on the original dataset. As presented in Fig. 4(b), we achieve an accuracy of 89.7% compared to the previous state-of-the-art of 88.2% reported in Duan *et al.* [11]. Our approach, therefore, achieves the best results not only on the age group estimation but also on gender classification; it outperforms the current state-of-the-art methods. The graphs in Fig. 4(a) and (b) present the results of the two classifications on the OIU-Adience dataset.

As presented in Figs. 6, 7 and 8, it is recorded that our model can correctly predict the age group and gender of faces. However, there are few cases where face images were incorrectly classified, this is could be as a result of different degree of variability attributed to unconstrained images including low resolution, non-frontal, lighting conditions, and heavy makeup (see Fig. 9).

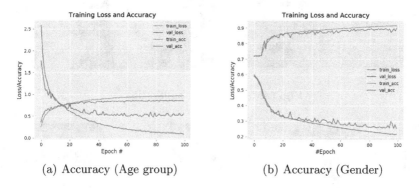

(a) Accuracy (Age group)   (b) Accuracy (Gender)

Fig. 4. Graphs of accuracy results for age group and gender classification.

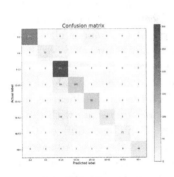
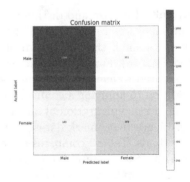

(a) Confusion matrix (Age group)   (b) Confusion matrix (Gender)

Fig. 5. Graphs of confusion matrix results for age group and gender classification.

Fig. 6. Age group classification

Fig. 7. Male: gender classification

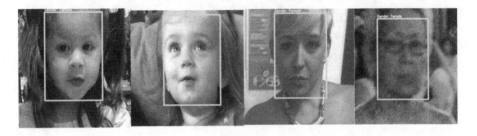

Fig. 8. Female: gender classification

Fig. 9. Faces with misclassification

5   Conclusions and Future Work

The proposed CNN-based classification model is designed for the age group and gender classification of unconstrained real-life faces. The novel approach relied on the features extraction ability and classification proficient of the CNN architecture. The satisfactory performance of the classification model is attributed mainly to our new CNN architecture, that was initially pre-trained on very large IMDb-WIKI dataset before being fine-tuned on the original dataset. Robust face detection and good alignment technique also contributed greatly to the classification accuracy of the approach. An extensive evaluation of the newly-designed model on OIU-Adience benchmark for age and gender classification, confirms the applicability of our method on unconstrained real-world face images. Exact age and gender classification of human's face will be an interesting research field to study in the future.

References

1. Abbas, A.R., Kareem, A.R.: Intelligent age estimation from facial images using machine learning techniques. Iraqi J. Sci. **59**(2A), 724–732 (2018). https://doi.org/10.24996/ijs.2018.59.2a.10, http://scbaghdad.edu.iq/eijs/index.php/eijs/article/view/247/116
2. Agbo-Ajala, O., Viriri, S.: Age estimation of real-time faces using convolutional neural network. In: Nguyen, N.T., Chbeir, R., Exposito, E., Aniorté, P., Trawiński, B. (eds.) ICCCI 2019. LNCS (LNAI), vol. 11683, pp. 316–327. Springer, Cham (2019). https://doi.org/10.1007/978-3-030-28377-3_26
3. Anand, A., Labati, R.D., Genovese, A., Munoz, E., Piuri, V., Scotti, F.: Age estimation based on face images and pre-trained convolutional neural networks. In: Proceedings of 2017 IEEE Symposium Series on Computational Intelligence, SSCI 2017, pp. 1–7 (2017). https://doi.org/10.1109/SSCI.2017.8285381, http://ieeexplore.ieee.org/document/8285381/
4. Angulu, R., Tapamo, J.R., Adewumi, A.O.: Human age estimation using Multi-Frequency Biologically Inspired Features (MF-BIF). In: 2017 IEEE AFRICON: Science, Technology and Innovation for Africa, AFRICON 2017, pp. 26–31, no. September (2017). https://doi.org/10.1109/AFRCON.2017.8095450
5. Antipov, G., Baccouche, M., Berrani, S.A., Dugelay, J.L.: Effective training of convolutional neural networks for face-based gender and age prediction. Pattern Recogn. **72**, 15–26 (2017). https://doi.org/10.1016/j.patcog.2017.06.031
6. Bouchrika, I., Harrati, N., Ladjailia, A., Khedairia, S.: Age estimation from facial images based on hierarchical feature selection. In: 16th International Conference on

Sciences and Techniques of Automatic Control and Computer Engineering, STA 2015 (STA 2015), pp. 393–397 (2016). https://doi.org/10.1109/STA.2015.7505156

7. Choi, S.E., Lee, Y.J., Lee, S.J., Park, K.R., Kim, J.: Age estimation using a hierarchical classifier based on global and local facial features. Pattern Recogn. 44(6), 1262–1281 (2011). https://doi.org/10.1016/j.patcog.2010.12.005. https://www.sciencedirect.com/science/article/abs/pii/S0031320310005704?via%3Dihub

8. Dalal, N., Triggs, B.: Histograms of oriented gradients for human detection. In: Proceedings of 2005 IEEE Computer Society Conference on Computer Vision and Pattern Recognition, CVPR 2005 I(8), pp. 886–893 (2005). https://doi.org/10.1109/CVPR.2005.177

9. Drobnyh, K.A., Polovinkin, A.N.: Using supervised deep learning for human age estimation problem. ISPRS - Int. Arch. Photogramm. Remote Sens. Spat. Inf. Sci. XLII–2/W4(May), 97–100 (2017). https://doi.org/10.5194/isprs-archives-XLII-2-W4-97-2017. https://www.int-arch-photogramm-remote-sens-spatial-inf-sci.net/XLII-2-W4/97/2017/

10. Duan, M., Li, K., Li, K.: An ensemble CNN2ELM for age estimation. IEEE Trans. Inf. Forensics Secur. 13(3), 758–772 (2018). https://doi.org/10.1109/TIFS.2017.2766583

11. Duan, M., Li, K., Yang, C., Li, K.: A hybrid deep learning CNN-ELM for age and gender classification. Neurocomputing 275, 448–461 (2018). https://doi.org/10.1016/j.neucom.2017.08.062

12. Eidinger, E., Enbar, R., Hassner, T.: Age and gender estimation of unfiltered faces. IEEE Trans. Inf. Forensics Secur. 9(12), 2170–2179 (2014). https://doi.org/10.1109/TIFS.2014.2359646. http://www.adience.com

13. Ekmekji, A.: Convolutional Neural Networks for Age and Gender Classification. Stanford University (2016). https://doi.org/10.1016/S0378-7753(96)02544-X

14. Escalera, S., et al.: ChaLearn looking at people 2015 new competitions: age estimation and cultural event recognition. In: Proceedings of the International Joint Conference on Neural Networks, September 2015 (2015). https://doi.org/10.1109/IJCNN.2015.7280614

15. Fu, Y., Guo, G., Huang, T.S.: Age synthesis and estimation via faces: a survey. IEEE Trans. Pattern Anal. Mach. Intell. 32(11), 1955–1976 (2010). https://doi.org/10.1109/TPAMI.2010.36

16. Guo, G., Fu, Y., Dyer, C.R., Huang, T.S.: Image-based human age estimation by manifold learning and locally adjusted robust regression. IEEE Trans. Image Process. 17(7), 1178–1188 (2008). https://doi.org/10.1109/TIP.2008.924280

17. Huang, J., Li, B., Zhu, J., Chen, J.: Age classification with deep learning face representation. Multimedia Tools Appl. 76(19), 20231–20247 (2017). https://doi.org/10.1007/s11042-017-4646-5

18. Huerta, I., Fernández, C., Segura, C., Hernando, J., Prati, A.: A deep analysis on age estimation. Pattern Recogn. Lett. 68, 239–249 (2015). https://doi.org/10.1016/j.patrec.2015.06.006

19. Kannan, E., Nair, R.R., Visu, P., Koteeswaran, S.: Human age manifold learning scheme and curve fitting for aging features. Int. J. 1, 490–494 (2011)

20. Levi, G., Hassncer, T.: Age and gender classification using convolutional neural networks. In: IEEE Computer Society Conference on Computer Vision and Pattern Recognition Workshops, October 2015, pp. 34–42 (2015). https://doi.org/10.1109/CVPRW.2015.7301352, http://ieeexplore.ieee.org/document/7301352/

21. Liu, W., Chen, L., Chen, Y.: Age classification using convolutional neural networks with the multi-class focal loss. IOP Conf. Ser.: Mater. Sci. Eng. 428(1) (2018). https://doi.org/10.1088/1757-899X/428/1/012043

22. Malli, R.C., Aygun, M., Ekenel, H.K.: Apparent age estimation using ensemble of deep learning models. In: IEEE Computer Society Conference on Computer Vision and Pattern Recognition Workshops, pp. 714–721 (2016). https://doi.org/10.1109/CVPRW.2016.94, http://arxiv.org/abs/1606.02909
23. Felzenszwalb, P.F., Girshick, R.B., McAllester, D., Ramanan, D.: Object detection with discriminatively trained part-based models. Computer **47**(2), 6–7 (2008). https://doi.org/10.1109/MC.2014.42
24. Qawaqneh, Z., Mallouh, A.A., Barkana, B.D.: Deep convolutional neural network for age estimation based on VGG-face model. arXiv, September 2017. http://arxiv.org/abs/1709.01664
25. Ramanathan, N., Chellappa, R.: Modeling age progression in young faces. In: Proceedings of the IEEE Computer Society Conference on Computer Vision and Pattern Recognition, vol. 1, pp. 387–394 (2006). https://doi.org/10.1109/CVPR.2006.187
26. Ranjan, R., Sankaranarayanan, S., Castillo, C.D., Chellappa, R.: An all-in-one convolutional neural network for face analysis. In: Proceedings of 12th IEEE International Conference on Automatic Face and Gesture Recognition, FG 2017–1st International Workshop on Adaptive Shot Learning for Gesture Understanding and Production, ASL4GUP 2017, Biometrics in the Wild, Bwild 2017, Heteroge, pp. 17–24 (2017). https://doi.org/10.1109/FG.2017.137
27. Ranjan, R., et al.: Unconstrained age estimation with deep convolutional neural networks. In: Proceedings of the IEEE International Conference on Computer Vision, pp. 351–359 (2015). https://doi.org/10.1109/ICCVW.2015.54, http://ieeexplore.ieee.org/document/7406403/
28. Selim, M., Raheja, S., Stricker, D.: Real-time human age estimation based on facial images using uniform local binary patterns. In: Visigrapp, pp. 408–415 (2015). https://doi.org/10.5220/0005311604080415
29. Shaik, S., Micheal, A.A.: Automatic age and gender recognition in human face image dataset using convolutional neural network system. Int. J. Adv. Res. Comput. Sci. Manag. Stud. **4**(2), 14–23 (2016)
30. Srivastava, A., Tiwari, R.G.: Human age estimation techniques using facial features. Imp. J. Interdisc. Res. **2**(9), 823–827 (2016)
31. Vairavan, T., Vani, K.: An efficient age estimation system with facial makeover images based on key points selection. Int. Arab J. Inf. Technol. **14**(1), 8–18 (2017)
32. Zhang, K., et al.: Age group and gender estimation in the wild with deep RoR architecture. IEEE Access **5**(X), 22492–22503 (2017). https://doi.org/10.1109/ACCESS.2017.2761849

SO-Net: Joint Semantic Segmentation and Obstacle Detection Using Deep Fusion of Monocular Camera and Radar

V. John[1(✉)], M. K. Nithilan[1], S. Mita[1], H. Tehrani[1,2], R. S. Sudheesh[2], and P. P. Lalu[2]

[1] Research Center for Smart Vehicles, Toyota Technological Institute, Nagoya, Japan
{vijayjohn,mknithilan,smita}@toyota-ti.ac.jp
[2] Nodal Center for Robotics and Artificial Intelligence,
Government Engineering College, Thrissur, India
{rssudheesh,lalupp}@gectcr.ac.in

Abstract. Vision-based semantic segmentation and obstacle detection are important perception tasks for autonomous driving. Vision-based semantic segmentation and obstacle detection are performed using separate frameworks resulting in increased computational complexity. Vision-based perception using deep learning reports state-of-the-art accuracy, but the performance is susceptible to variations in the environment. In this paper, we propose a radar and vision-based deep learning perception framework termed as the SO-Net to address the limitations of vision-based perception. The SO-Net also integrates the semantic segmentation and object detection within a single framework. The proposed SO-Net contains two input branches and two output branches. The SO-Net input branches correspond to vision and radar feature extraction branches. The output branches correspond to object detection and semantic segmentation branches. The performance of the proposed framework is validated on the Nuscenes public dataset. The results show that the SO-Net improves the accuracy of the vision-only-based perception tasks. The SO-Net also reports reduced computational complexity compared to separate semantic segmentation and object detection frameworks.

Keywords: Joint learning · Sensor fusion · Radar · Monocular camera

1 Introduction

Vehicle detection and free space semantic segmentation are important perception tasks that has been researched extensively [8,9]. Generally these tasks are independently explored and modeled using the monocular camera. By independently modeling these tasks, the resulting computational complexity is high. Additionally, the camera-based perception frameworks are affected by challenging environmental conditions.

In this paper, we propose to address both these issues using the SO-Net. Firstly, we address the environmental challenges by performing a deep fusion

© Springer Nature Switzerland AG 2020
J. J. Dabrowski et al. (Eds.): PSIVT 2019 Workshops, LNCS 11994, pp. 138–148, 2020.
https://doi.org/10.1007/978-3-030-39770-8_11

of radar and vision features. Secondly, for the high computational complexity, we formulate a joint multi-task deep learning framework which simultaneously performs semantic segmentation and object detection.

The main motivation for formulating a joint multi-task deep learning framework is to reduce the computational complexity, while achieving real-time performance. We propose to achieve computationally complexity by sharing the features extracted by deep learning layers for multiple tasks.

In sensor fusion methodologies, sensors with complementary features are fused together to enhance robustness. In case of radar and vision sensors, the features are complementary. The vision features are descriptive and provide delineation of objects, but are noisy in adverse conditions. Radar features are not affected by adverse conditions caused by illumination variation, rain, snow and fog [11,12], but are sparse and do not provide delineation of objects. By fusing the radar and vision sensors, we can improve the robustness of perception. Examples of radar features in challenging scenes are shown in Fig. 1.

In this research, we propose the SO-Net, which is an extension of RV-Net [18]. The SO-Net is a perception network containing two feature extraction branches and two output branches. The two feature extraction branches contain separate branches for the camera-based images and the radar-based features. The output branches correspond to vehicle detection and free space semantic segmentation branches.

The main contribution of the paper is as follows:

- A novel deep learning-based joint multi-task framework termed as the SO-Net using radar and vision.

The SO-Net is validated using the Nuscenes public dataset [2]. The experimental results show that the proposed framework effectively fuses the camera and radar features, while reporting reduced computational complexity for vehicle detection and free space semantic segmentation.

The remainder of the paper is structured as follows. The literature is reviewed in Sect. 2 and the SO-Net is presented in Sect. 3. The experimental results are presented in Sect. 4. Finally, the paper is concluded in Sect. 5.

Fig. 1. An illustration of the radar features overlaid on the camera images in the Nuscenes dataset.

2   Literature Review

To our understanding, no one has explored the possibility to use radar and camera pipeline for multi-task learning. Multi-task learning is the joint learning of multiple perception tasks. The main advantage of joint learning is the reduction of computational complexity. Recently, multi-task learning has received much attention [6,13].

We perform radar-vision fusion within a multitask framework. Generally, radar-vision fusion for perception is performed as early-stage fusion [1,4,17], late-stage fusion methods [7,19,20] and feature-level fusion [3,18]. In early-stage fusion, the radar features identify candidate regions for vision-based perception tasks [1,5,10,14,17]. In late stage fusion, independent vision and radar pipelines are utilized for the perception tasks. The results obtained by the independent pipelines are fused in the final step [7,20].

Compared to the above two methods of fusion, the feature-level fusion is more suited for deep learning-based multi-task learning [3]. In feature-level fusion a single pipeline is adopted for perception. Recently, John et al. [18] proposed the RVNet to fuse radar and vision fusion for obstacle detection using feature level vision. The authors show that the feature-level fusion framework reports state-of-the-art performance with real-time computational complexity.

In this paper, we extend the RVNet to a multi-task learning framework, where the radar and vision features extracted in the input branches are shared in the output branches. By sharing the features, the proposed SO-Net performs free space segmentation and vehicle detection while reducing the computational complexity.

3   Algorithm

The SO-Net is a deep learning framework which performs sensor fusion of camera and radar features for semantic segmentation and vehicle detection. The SO-Net architecture, based on the RVNet, contains two input branches for feature extraction and output branches for vehicle detection and semantic segmentation.

The semantic segmentation framework can be utilized to detect the vehicles instead of the separate vehicle detection output branch. However, the semantic segmentation framework does not provide the instances of vehicles for tracking. The instances of vehicles are provided by the instance segmentation framework. However, the instance segmentation framework utilizes a bounding box-based obstacle detector in its initial step [16]. Thus in our work, we propose to utilize an obstacle detection branch and semantic segmentation branch. An overview of SO-Net modules are shown in Fig. 2.

3.1   SO-Net Architecture

Feature Extraction Branches. The SO-Net has two input feature extraction branches which extract the features from the front camera image I and the

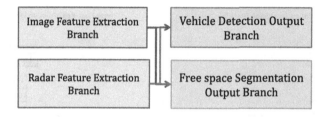

Fig. 2. An overview of the input and output branches of the SO-Net. The input feature maps are shared across the two output branches.

"sparse radar image" S. The "sparse radar image" is a 3-channel image of size (224×224), where each non-zero pixel in the S contains the depth, lateral velocity and longitudinal velocity radar features. The velocity features are compensated by the ego-motion of the vehicle. The two feature extraction branches extract image-specific and radar-specific features, respectively. Each randomly initialised input branch contains multiple encoding convolutional layers and pooling layers. These specific features maps are shared with the two output branches. The detailed architecture of the feature extraction branches are given in Fig. 3.

Vehicle Detection Output Branch. The radar and image feature maps are fused in the vehicle detection output branch. The vehicle detection branch is based on the tiny Yolo3 network. The fusion of the radar and image feature maps in the output branches are performed by concatenation, 1×1 2D convolution and up-sampling. The vehicle detection output branch detects vehicles in two sub-branches. In the first sub-branch, small and medium vehicles are detected. In the second sub-branch, big vehicles are detected. For both the sub-branches, the YOLOv3 loss function [15] is used within the binary classification framework.

Free Space Semantic Segmentation Output Branch. The second output branch performs semantic segmentation for estimating the free space for the vehicle. The free space represents the drivable area on the road surface. In this work, we define everything other than the free space as the background.

For the semantic segmentation framework, an encoder-decoder architecture is utilized. The radar and vision features obtained in the encoding layers are shared and fused in the output branch using the skip connections. In the skip connections, the vision and radar features at the different encoding levels are transferred individually to the corresponding semantic segmentation output branch. The feature maps are effectively fused using concatenation layer. Details of the encoder-decoder architecture are found in Fig. 3. We use a sigmoid activation function at the output layer for the binary semantic segmentation.

Training. The SO-Net is trained with the image, radar points and ground truth annotations from the Nuscenes dataset. For the semantic segmentation,

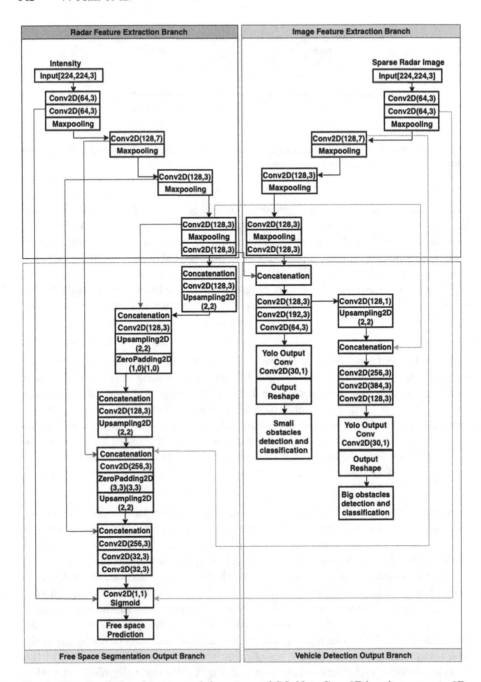

Fig. 3. The detailed architecture of the proposed SO-Net. Conv2D(m,n) represents 2D convolution with m filters with size $n \times n$ and stride 1. Maxpooling 2D is performed with size (2,2). The zero-padding 2D pads as following (top, bottom), (left, right). The Yolo output conv (Conv2D(30,1)) and the output reshape are based on the YOLOv3 framework.

we manually annotate the free space for the images in the Nuscenes dataset as the dataset doesn't contain semantic information. The SO-Net is trained with an Adam optimizer with learning rate of 0.001.

3.2 SO-Net Variants

We propose different variations of the proposed SO-Net to understand how each input branch contributes to the learning.

Fusion for Vehicle Detection. The camera and radar features are utilized for the vehicle detection task alone, instead of the joint multi-task learning (Fig. 4(a)). The architecture is similar to the SO-Net in Fig. 3, with the omission of the segmentation branch.

Fusion for Semantic Segmentation. The camera and radar features are utilized for the semantic segmentation task alone, instead of the joint multi-task learning (Fig. 4(b)). The architecture is similar to the SO-Net in Fig. 3, with the omission of the vehicle detection branch.

Camera-Only for Vehicle Detection. The camera features "alone" are utilized for the vehicle detection task, instead of the sensor fusion for the joint multi-task learning (Fig. 4(c)). The architecture is similar to the SO-Net in Fig. 3, with the omission of the radar-input branch and segmentation branch.

Camera-Only for Semantic Segmentation. The camera features "alone" are utilized for the semantic segmentation task, instead of the sensor fusion for the joint multi-task learning (Fig. 4(d)). The architecture is similar to the SO-Net in Fig. 3, with the omission of the radar-input branch and vehicle detection branch.

4 Experimental Section

Dataset: The different algorithms are validated on the Nuscenes dataset with 308 training and 114 testing samples. The training data contain scenes from rainy weather and night-time. Example scenes from the dataset are shown in Fig. 1.

Algorithm Parameters: The proposed algorithm and its variants were trained with batch size 8 and epochs 20 using the early stopping strategy. The algorithms were implemented on Nvidia Geforce 1080 Ubuntu 18.04 machine using TensorFlow 2.0. The performance of the networks are reported using accuracy and computational time.

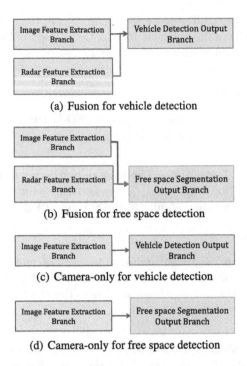

(a) Fusion for vehicle detection

(b) Fusion for free space detection

(c) Camera-only for vehicle detection

(d) Camera-only for free space detection

Fig. 4. SO-Net variants.

Table 1. Comparative Analysis of the SO-Net and vehicle detection variants. Note that the proposed network reports computational time for the joint tasks, while the variants report the time for the individual tasks. The total time for joint tasks are given in the total time.

Algo.	Detection accuracy	Computational time (ms)
SO-Net (proposed)	42.34	25
Fusion vehicle detection	**46.35**	15
Camera-alone vehicle detection	35.21	7

Table 2. Comparative Analysis of the SO-Net and semantic segmentation variants. Note that the proposed network reports computational time for the joint tasks, while the variants report the time for the individual tasks.

Algo.	Semantic segmentation accuracy	Computational time (ms)
SO-Net (proposed)	**99.1**	25
Fusion semantic seg	98.6	20
Camera-alone semantic seg	98.5	15

Fig. 5. Results for the SO-Net and fusion network variants. Yellow rectangle denotes the detected vehicles, while the green oval denotes the missed vehicles. (Color figure online)

Error Measures: The performance of the vehicle detection for the networks are reported using the Average Precision (AP) with IOU (intersection over threshold) of 0.5. In case of the semantic segmentation, we report the per-pixel classification accuracy for free space segmentation.

Results. The performance of the different algorithms tabulated in Tables 1 and 2 show that the segmentation accuracy of the proposed SO-Net and vehicle detection accuracy of the fused vehicle detection framework are better than the variants. The computational time of all the algorithms are real-time in the order of 10–25 ms.

Discussion. The results tabulated in Tables 1 and 2 show that performance of the SO-Net is similar to the fusion network variants, with marginally inferior vehicle detection accuracy and superior semantic segmentation accuracy. However, the SO-Net reports improved computational complexity. The two fusion network variants, fusion with vehicle detection and fusion with semantic segmentation, report a combined computational time of (vehicle det-15 + semantic seg-20) 35 ms per frame. The proposed SO-Net reports a reduced computational time of 25 ms with similar performance as shown in Table 3 (Fig. 5).

Fig. 6. Results for the SO-Net and camera-only network variants. Yellow rectangle denotes the detected vehicles, while the green oval denotes the missed vehicles. (Color figure online)

In the case of comparison with the camera-only network variants, the SO-Net reports better accuracy for both vehicle detection and semantic segmentation tasks, with similar computational complexity. The two camera-only network variants report a combined computational time of (vehicle det-7 + semantic seg-15) 22 ms per frame, which is similar to the SO-Net as shown in Table 3.

Table 3. Computational time of the SO-Net and its variants.

Alg.	Computational time (ms)
SO-Net (proposed)	25
Fusion semantic seg + Fusion vehicle det	$20 + 15 = 35$
Camera-alone semantic seg + Camera-alone vehicle det	$15 + 7 = 22$

The observed results show the effectiveness of sensor fusion for vehicle detection and semantic segmentation. The SO-Net and fusion network variants both report better accuracy than the camera-only network variants. In case of the computational complexity, we see that the multi-task learning based SO-net reports reduced the computational complexity compared to the individual fusion networks (Fig. 6).

5 Conclusion

A deep sensor fusion and joint learning framework termed as the SO-Net is proposed for the sensor fusion of camera-radar. The SO-Net is a multi-task learning framework, where the vehicle detection and free space segmentation is performed using a single network. The SO-Net contains two independent feature extraction branches, which extract radar and camera specific features. The multi-task learning is performed using two output branches. The proposed network is validated on the Nuscenes dataset and perform comparative analysis with variants. The results show that sensor fusion improves the vehicle detection and semantic segmentation accuracy, while reporting reduced computational time. In our future work, we will consider the fusion of additional sensors.

References

1. Bombini, L., Cerri, P., Medici, P., Aless, G.: Radar-vision fusion for vehicle detection. In: International Workshop on Intelligent Transportation, pp. 65–70 (2006)
2. Caesar, H., et al.: nuScenes: a multimodal dataset for autonomous driving. CoRR abs/1903.11027 (2019)
3. Chadwick, S., Maddern, W., Newman, P.: Distant vehicle detection using radar and vision. CoRR abs/1901.10951 (2019)
4. Fang, Y., Masaki, I., Horn, B.: Depth-based target segmentation for intelligent vehicles: fusion of radar and binocular stereo. IEEE Trans. Intell. Transp. Syst. **3**(3), 196–202 (2002)
5. Gaisser, F., Jonker, P.P.: Road user detection with convolutional neural networks: an application to the autonomous shuttle WEpod. In: International Conference on Machine Vision Applications (MVA), pp. 101–104 (2017)
6. Sistu, G., Leang, I., Yogamani, S.: Real-time joint object detection and semantic segmentation network for automated driving (2018)
7. Garcia, F., Cerri, P., Broggi, A., de la Escalera, A., Armingol, J.M.: Data fusion for overtaking vehicle detection based on radar and optical flow. In: 2012 IEEE Intelligent Vehicles Symposium, pp. 494–499 (2012)
8. Jazayeri, A., Cai, H., Zheng, J.Y., Tuceryan, M.: Vehicle detection and tracking in car video based on motion model. IEEE Trans. Intell. Transp. Syst. **12**(2), 583–595 (2011)
9. John, V., Karunakaran, N.M., Guo, C., Kidono, K., Mita, S.: Free space, visible and missing lane marker estimation using the PsiNet and extra trees regression. In: 24th International Conference on Pattern Recognition, pp. 189–194 (2018)
10. Kato, T., Ninomiya, Y., Masaki, I.: An obstacle detection method by fusion of radar and motion stereo. IEEE Trans. Intell. Transp. Syst. **3**(3), 182–188 (2002)
11. Macaveiu, A., Campeanu, A., Nafornita, I.: Kalman-based tracker for multiple radar targets. In: 2014 10th International Conference on Communications (COMM), pp. 1–4 (2014)

12. Manjunath, A., Liu, Y., Henriques, B., Engstle, A.: Radar based object detection and tracking for autonomous driving. In: 2018 IEEE MTT-S International Conference on Microwaves for Intelligent Mobility (ICMIM), pp. 1–4 (2018)
13. Teichmann, M., Weber, M., Zoellner, M., Cipolla, R., Urtasun, R.: MultiNet: real-time joint semantic reasoning for autonomous driving (2018)
14. Milch, S., Behrens, M.: Pedestrian detection with radar and computer vision (2001)
15. Redmon, J., Farhadi, A.: YOLOv3: an incremental improvement (2018). http://arxiv.org/abs/1804.02767
16. Shao, L., Tian, Y., Bohg, J.: ClusterNet: instance segmentation in RGB-D images. arXiv (2018). https://arxiv.org/abs/1807.08894
17. Sugimoto, S., Tateda, H., Takahashi, H., Okutomi, M.: Obstacle detection using millimeter-wave radar and its visualization on image sequence. In: 2004 Proceedings of the 17th International Conference on Pattern Recognition. ICPR 2004, vol. 3, pp. 342–345 (2004)
18. John, V., Mita, S.: RVNet: deep sensor fusion of monocular camera and radar for image-based obstacle detection in challenging environments. In: Lee, C., Su, Z., Sugimoto, A. (eds.) PSIVT 2019. LNCS, vol. 11854, pp. 351–364. Springer, Cham (2019). https://doi.org/10.1007/978-3-030-34879-3_27
19. Wang, X., Xu, L., Sun, H., Xin, J., Zheng, N.: On-road vehicle detection and tracking using MMW radar and monovision fusion. IEEE Trans. Intell. Transp. Syst. **17**(7), 2075–2084 (2016)
20. Zhong, Z., Liu, S., Mathew, M., Dubey, A.: Camera radar fusion for increased reliability in ADAS applications. Electron. Imaging Auton. Veh. Mach. **1**(4), 258–258 (2018)

Deep Forest Approach for Facial Expression Recognition

Olufisayo Ekundayo and Serestina Viriri[✉]

School of Mathematics, Statistics and Computer Science,
University of KwaZulu-Natal, Durban 4000, South Africa
sunfis1979@gmail.com, viriris@ukzn.ac.za

Abstract. Facial Expression Recognition is a prospective area in Computer Vision (CV) and Human-Computer Interaction (HCI), with vast areas of application. The major concept in facial expression recognition is the categorization of facial expression images into six basic emotion states, and this is accompanied with many challenges. Several methods have been explored in search of an optimal solution, in the development of a facial expression recognition system. Presently, Deep Neural Network is the state-of-the-art method in the field with promising results, but it is incapacitated with the volume of data available for Facial Expression Recognition task. Therefore, there is a need for a method with Deep Learning feature and the dynamic ability for both large and small volume of data available in the field. This work is proposing a Deep Forest tree method that implements layer by layer feature of Deep Learning and minimizes overfitting regardless of data size. The experiments conducted on both Cohn Kanade (CK+) and Binghamton University 3D Facial Expression (BU-3DFE) datasets, prove that Deep Forest provides promising results with an impressive reduction in computational time.

Keywords: Facial Expression Recognition · Deep Neural Network · Deep Forest

1 Introduction

Deep forest learning is a recent method initiated by [14, 21] with the motive of approaching classification and regression problems by making a conventional classifier (shallow learners) like the random forest (decision tree) to learn deep. The prevalence of Deep Neural Network (DNN) in Machine Learning (ML) and Artificial Intelligence (AI) can never be overemphasised. Deep learning is said to be as old as Artificial Neural Network (ANN) but went into hibernation due to its computational complexity and the demand for the large volume of data [5]. In the recent years, the availability of sophisticated computational resources and invention of the internet that give room for the collection of large datasets play a remarkable role in bringing deep learning back into the forefront of machine learning models. Deep learning has proven its worth in several areas of classification and regression computation with an efficient and optimal solution.

© Springer Nature Switzerland AG 2020
J. J. Dabrowski et al. (Eds.): PSIVT 2019 Workshops, LNCS 11994, pp. 149–161, 2020.
https://doi.org/10.1007/978-3-030-39770-8_12

Beyond reasonable doubt, deep learning outperformed the conventional classifiers in most machine learning tasks like; image processing, computer vision, pattern matching, biometrics, bioinformatics, speech processing and recognition, etc. Nevertheless, despite the computational prowess of Deep learning, its quest for large datasets and computational resources consumption is still a challenge. Therefore, there is a need to explore other machine learning models and see the opportunities to enhance their capability for better efficiency and accuracy.

Deep forest is still very new in machine learning and this implies that its application is yet to be explored. Both Forward Thinking Random Forest and gcForest are the popularly available deep forest models. And the reports of the models give the similar performance even if not more, as DNN in their experiments on MNIST dataset, with additional advantages of low computational time, limited hyper-parameter tuning and dynamic adaptation to the quantity of available dataset. Our task in this paper is to develop a deep learning model from the ensemble of forest trees for the classification of facial expression into six basic emotions, while depending on the forest tree inherent affinity for multiclass problems. Facial expression recognition is a multi-class problem and its goal is to detect human affective state from the deformation experience in the face due to facial muscles response to emotion states. To the best of our knowledge, this work is the first of its kind that engages a layer by layer enssemble of forest tree approach to the task of facial expression classification.

In this paper; Sect. 2 contains the details description of the related works, it captures the performances and the limitations of some of the classification models on facial expression recognition data. Section 3 contains a brief introduction to random forest and the description of the proposed deep forest framework for facial expression recognition. In Sect. 4 we discuss the databases for the experiments while Sect. 5 contains details of the experiment performed and the result analysis. Section 6 is the conclusion of the work.

2   Related Works

The complexity of facial expression and the subtle variations in its transition give rise to several challenges experienced in the field. One of the major challenges of facial expression is its classification into the six category of classes proposed by [9]. Many classifiers and regression algorithms have been proposed severally to address the challenge, the methods include Support Vector Machine (SVM) [15], Boosting Algorithm (AdaBoost) [7], Convolution Neural Network (CNN) [2] Decision Tree [18], Random Forest [4], Artificial Neural Network (ANN) [19], to mention a few. The listed classifiers have reportedly produced various promising results depending on the approach.

The impressive performance of Decision tree towards classification problems makes its evident application in several machine learning fields. [18] used decision tree to classify feature extracted from a distance based feature extraction method. Although there are not many works in facial expression recognition with decision tree method because of overfitting challenge in its performance with high dimensional data [16], the available ones are either presented its boosting (AdaBoost) or an ensemble (forest tree) version. Decision tree has been graciously enhanced by the introduction of Forest tree [3]. A random forest tree is an ensemble of learner algorithms in which individual learner is considered to be a weak learner. Decision tree algorithm has been widely explored as a weak learner for random forest tree, and this is likely the reason for describing a random forest as the ensemble of decision trees. [6] in their work extends the capability of random forest tree to a spatiotemporal environment, where subtle facial expression dynamics is more pronounced. The model conditioned random forest pair-wisely on the expression label of two successive frames whereby the transitional variation of the present expression in the sequence is minimized by the condition on the most recent previous frame. [12] hybridized deep learning and decision tree, and the hybridization was based on the representation learning of deep learning feature and the divide and conquer techniques of decision tree properties. A differentiable backpropagation was employed to enhance the decision tree to achieve an end to end learning, and also preserving representation learning at the lower layers of the network. So that the representation learning would minimize any likely uncertainty that could emerge from split nodes and thus minimized the loss function. The concept of Deep Forest is beyond the integration of decision tree into Deep Neural Network as proposed in [12]. [14,21] thoroughly highlighted; computation complexity cost as a result of using backpropagation for the multilayers training of nonlinear activation function, massive consumption of memory during the training of complex DNN models, overfitting and non-generalization to small volume of data and complexity in hyperparameter tuning; as the challenges encountered while implementing Deep Neural Network. Therefore, there is a need for a deep learning model type that would minimize the challenges in the existing deep learning models. [14] proposed a deep learning model (Forward Thinking Deep Random Forest) different from ANN, in which the neurons were replaced by a shallow classifier. The network of the proposed model was formed by layers of Random Forest, and decision tree which is the building blocks of forest tree was used in place of neurons. The model was made to train layer by layer as opposed to the once-off training complexity and rigidity experienced in DNN. Likewise, the evolving Deep Forest learning (gcForest) proposed by [21] ensures diversity in its architecture, where the architecture consists of layers with different random forests. Both models successfully implement deep learning from Random Forest without backpropagation. Although the mode of achieving this slightly differs, while gcForest ensures connection to the subsequent layer using the output of the random forest of the preceding layer, the connection to the subsequent layer in FTDRF is the output of the decision tree in the random forest of the preceding layer. As earlier stated, it was reported that both models outperform DNN on the performance evaluation experiment on MNIST datasets.

3 Deep Forest Learning

Before providing the details of Deep Forest learning operations, it suffices to discuss the basic concept of Random Forest tree.

3.1 Random Forest

Random Forest tree was introduced by Breiman [3], before the advent of Breiman's work, tree learning algorithm (decision tree) had been in existence, the algorithm was effective and efficient. Its implementation could either be shallow or a full grown tree (deep tree). Shallow tree learning model has a great affinity for overfitting resulting from the model high bias and low variance features, which is often addressed by boosting (AdaBoost) algorithm. Breiman established the ensemble idea on the early works of [1, 8, 20] and proposed a random forest algorithm which is efficient for both regression and classification tasks. Breiman implements both bootstrapping and bagging techniques by randomly creates several bootstrap samples from a raw data distribution so that each new sample will act as another independent dataset drawn from the true distribution. And after fit, a weak learner (decision tree) to each of the samples created. Lastly, computes the average of the aggregate output. The operation that would be performed on the aggregate of the output of the weak classifiers is determined by the task (classification or regression). In case of a regression problem, the aggregate is the average of all the learners' output and if classification the class with the highest volt is favoured. Random forest is known for its fast and easy implementation, scalable with the volume of information and at the same time maintain sufficient statistical efficiency. It could be adopted for several prediction problems with few parameter tuning, and retaining its accuracy irrespectives of data size.

3.2 Proposed Facial Expression Deep Forest Famework

Deep forest learning architecture as presented in Fig. 1 is a layer by layer architecture in which each layer comprises of many forests, a layer links with its successive layer by passing the output of the forest tree as input to the next layer in the architecture. This work enhance the deep forest model proposed by [21] by introduction of trees with different features at strategic positions for better performance. The model consists of two phases; the feature learning phase and the deep forest learning phase. The feature learning phase is integrated for the purpose of feature extraction similar to convolution operation in DNN. It uses windows of different sizes to scan the raw images (face expression images), in a process of obtaining a class representative vector. The class vector is a N-dimensional feature vector extracted from a member of a class and then use for the training of the Deep Forest.

The second phase is the main deep forest structure; a cascade structure in the form of a progressive nested structure of different forest trees. The model implements four different forest trees classifiers (two Random Forest, ExtraTree and Logistic Regression classifiers), and each of the forest trees contains 500 trees. The difference between the forest trees is in their mode of selecting the representing feature for a split at every node of the tree.

The learning principle of the deep forest is the layer to layer connectivity, that is, a layer communicates with its immediate predecessor layer by taking as input, the forest tree output o f the preceding layer. The efficiency of the cascade structure lies in its ability to concatenate the original input with the features inherited at each layer. The motive is to update each layer with the original pattern and also to make the layer achieves reliable predictions. The concatenation of the original input layer thus enhances the generalization of the structure. Each layer is an ensemble of forests, the connection from one layer to another layer is done through the output of the forests. Forest processes start with bagging (bootstrap Aggregation). If there is N data sample, then some numbers n subsets of R randomly chosen samples with replacement is created such that each subset is used to train a tree, and the aggregate forest contains n trees. The tree growth for each of the forests starts from the root with the whole dataset, then each node containing an associate sample is split into two with reference to the randomly selected feature from the Forest. The two subsets are then distributed on the two children nodes, and the splitting continues until there is a pure sample of a class at the leaf node of the tree or the predefined condition is satisfied.

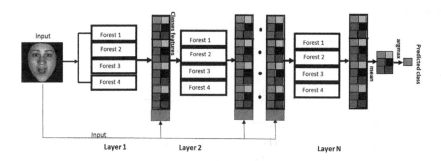

Fig. 1. Deep forest architecture

For each instance of a class, class distribution estimation is computed, and then averaging across all trees for each forest. This becomes the class vector to be concatenated with the original feature vector and send to the cascade next layer as input. Which implies each class will have one class vector, the number of augmented features extracted depends on the number of class multiply by the number of trees in the deep forest model. In order to control overfitting, K-fold is used to generate the class vector for each forest. At every layer expansion, cascade performance evaluation is estimated. At a point in the training where there is no significant improvement in the performance, the training is halt. This account for the control that Deep Forest has over its architecture.

3.3 Mathematical Illustration of the Framework

Data description Let $\chi = R^m$ represent the input space, and let $Y = y_1, \ldots\ldots y_c$ be the output space. Then every sample $x_i \in \chi$ has corresponding $y_i \in Y$ the training sample Δ_m is:

$$\Delta_m = (x_1, y_1), \ldots\ldots\ldots, (x_m, y_m)$$

At each layer there are forests and each forest contains learning algorithms that could be regarded as functions which give the image of the input data as the output of the forest. Then each forest in the first layer, L_1 contains set of learning function say α^{l1} with general behaviour: $\alpha^{l1} : \chi_i \to \chi_i^{l1}$ where χ_i is the input data into the layer1 and χ_i^{l1} is the image of χ_i then all functions in layer1 are represented as:

$$\alpha^{l1} = \alpha_1^{l1}, \ldots\ldots\ldots, \alpha_n^{l1}$$
$$\chi_i^{l1} = \alpha_1^{l1}(\chi_i), \ldots\ldots\ldots \alpha_n^{l1}(\chi_i)$$

this implies that a new data is gotten at layer 1, which means:

$$\Delta_m = \Delta_m^{l1} = (\chi_1^{l1}, y_1), \ldots\ldots, (\chi_m^{l1}, y_m)$$

The process continues as long as there is a significant performance in the model at every successive layer. At every layer k in the model where tree is appreciable improve in the performance of the model, it suffices to recall that the input to layer k is $\chi_i^{(k-1)}$

$$\chi_i^{lk} = \chi_1^{lk} \times \chi_2^{lk} \times \ldots\ldots\ldots \times \chi_n^{lk}$$
$$\chi_i^{lk} = \alpha_1^{lk}(\chi_i), \ldots\ldots\ldots, \alpha_n^{lk}(\chi_i)$$

the output of layer k is:

$$\Delta_m^{lk} = (\chi_1^{lk}, y_1), \ldots\ldots\ldots (\chi_m^{lk}, y_m)$$

the layer stop growing at layer n where there is no significant increase in performance of the model. At layer n there is an assurance of having $\chi_i^{l(n-1)}$ converging closely to y_i. Note that, the output of each layer is the average of the probability distribution for instances in the leaf node of the trees for each forest. Let $P = p_1, \ldots\ldots\ldots, p_t$ be the class vector probability of each node of the tree. For each sample of input $\chi_i^{l(n-1)}$ the probability vector of the leaf node is given as:

$$P_i^{ln}(\chi_i^{l(n-1)}) = (P_1^{ln}(\chi_i^{l(n-1)}), \ldots\ldots\ldots, P_t^{ln}(\chi_i^{l(n-1)}))$$

then the output of Forest β in a layer l^n is the average of the probability vectors of all trees in the forest; as given in (1):

$$\beta_j = \frac{1}{J} \sum_{j=1}^{J} P_j(\chi_t) \tag{1}$$

where J is the number of trees in a Forest and T is the number of class vector estimation at the leaf node.

4   Database

In this section we briefly introduce the two databases (BU-3DFE and CK+) that we are proposing for the experiment here. Figures 2 and 3 are the respective samples of the expression images in BU-3DFE and CK+.

Fig. 2. Selected expression images samples from BU-3DFE datasets. The arrangement from left: Angry, Disgust, Fear, Happy, Sad and Surprise

4.1   Binghamton University 3D Facial Expression (BU-3DFE)

This database was introduced at Binghamton University by [17], it contains 100 subjects with 2500 facial expression models. 56 of the subjects were female and 44 were male, the age group ranges from 18 years to 70 years old, with a variety of ethnic/racial ancestries, including White, Black, East-Asian, Middle-east Asian, Indian, and Hispanic Latino. 3D face scanner was used to capture seven expressions from each subject, in the process, four intensity levels were captured alongside for each of the 6 basic prototypical expressions. Associated with each expression shape model, is a corresponding facial texture image captured at two views (about +45° and −45°). As a result, the database consists of 2,500 two view's texture images and 2,500 geometric shape models.

Fig. 3. Selected expression images for each of the emotion states from CK+ datasets. The arrangement from left: Angry, Disgust, Fear, Happy, Sad and Surprise

4.2   Cohn Kanade and Cohn Kanade Extension (CK and CK+) Database

[11] released a facial expression database in 2000, the database contains 97 subjects between the ages of 18 and 30; 65 were female and the remaining 35 were male. The subjects were chosen from multicultural people and races. There were 486 sequences collected from the subjects and each sequence started from neutral expression and ended at the peak of the expression. The peak of the expressions was fully FACS coded and emotion labeled, but the label was not validated. [13] itemized three challenges with CK databases challenges; invalidation of emotion labels because it did not depict what was actually performed. Unavailable common performance metrics for algorithm performance evaluation, as a result of no standard protocol for a common database. [13], having identified the challenges with CK database proposed its extension termed extended Cohn Kanade (CK+) database. In CK+ the number of subjects was increased by 27 and the number of sequence by 22, there were slight changes in the metadata also, age group of the subject ranged between 18 and 50, male was 31, and female was 69. The emotion labels were revised and validated using FACS investigator guide as a reference and confirmed by appropriate expert researchers. Leave-one-out subject cross-validation and area underneath the Receiver Operator Characteristics curve were proposed as metrics for Algorithm performance evaluation.

5   Experiment

The experiment was conducted on two datasets; the Cohn Kanade extension (CK+) and the Binghamton University 3D Facial Expression (BU-3DFE) datasets. We used only the peak images for the six basic emotion states (Anger, Disgust, Fear, Happy, Sad, Surprise) of 2D images from each of the data sets, and the total number of expression images used from BU-3DFE is 600 (100 images per emotion, 54 female and 46 male). In CK+ dataset; the total number of images extracted was 309 but the number of images per emotion varied (AN = 45, DI = 59, FE = 25, HA = 69, SA = 28, SU = 83). We split each of the extracted data into two; the training set (80%) and the validation set (20%). The training set was used to train the forest and the validation set was used for the performance evaluation. The model depth (the number of layers) is automatically determined, each layer consists of three different pairs of forests, and each forest contains 500 trees.

Before feeding the images as input for processing data processing techniques such as face detection, face alignment and histogram equalization were applied on the data so as to minimise data redundancy and intensity variation that may possibly challenge the performance of the system. As earlier stated we split the input into the training data and the validation data. Growing the forests with the training data set, we used 5-fold cross-validation to minimized chances of overfitting.

We tested the trained model on the validation set and passed each instance of the validation as representative feature to the cascade forest classification process. The output of the cascade forest returned probability predictions from each forest in the last layer of the cascade. As a result, the mean of the predictions was computed, and finally, the class with maximum value is the outcome of the prediction. For performance evaluation we use accuracy as our metrics and also employ confusion matrix for proper analysis of the result.

Furthermore, we conducted an investigation on the effect of number of classifiers on the behaviour of Deep Forest model. Initially, on both datasets (CK+ and BU-3DFE) we used 4 forest classifiers, and obtained average accuracy of 93.22% with only 5 layers added and 7 estimators in each layer for CK+ dataset. When each of the classifiers was doubled, the accuracy remained but ten layers were added with 7 estimators in each layer. This is different in the case of BU-3DFE dataset, the initial 4 classifiers gave accuracy of 57.98% and added 8 layers with 8 estimators in each layer. When each of the classifiers was doubled, the accuracy increased by almost 10% and added 10 layers with 8 estimators in each layer. Summary of the investigation is provided in Table 1.

Table 1. Summary of the investigation conducted on the Deep Forest model with increase in number of classifiers

Database	Classifiers	Layers	Estimators	Accuracy
CK+	4	5	7	93.22%
CK+	8	10	7	93.22%
BU-3DFE	4	8	8	57.98%
BU-3DFE	8	10	8	65.53%

Table 2. The result comparison of FERAtt (Facial Expression Recognition with Attention Net) with Deep Forest learning

Author	Database	Method	Accuracy
Fernandez et al. [10]	BU-3DFE	FERAtt	75.22%
Our	BU-3DFE	Deep Forest	65.53%
Fernandez et al. [10]	CK+	FERAtt	86.67%
Our	CK+	Deep Forest	93.22%

5.1 Result

Figures 4 and 6 are the confusion matrices of the model probabilistic predictions accuracy on the BU-3DFE and CK+ respectively. Also, Figs. 5 and 7 are the graph of average recognition rate on the test data of BU-3DFE and CK+.

Confusion matrix

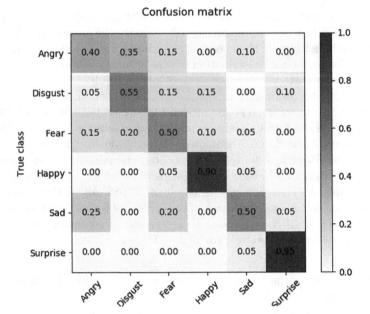

Fig. 4. Confusion matrix of Deep Forest predictions on BU-3DFE dataset

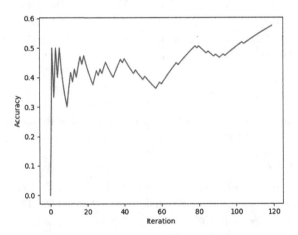

Fig. 5. The graph of the recognition rate against number of predictions of BU-3DFE test data

In Fig. 4, the prediction of the model is most for the surprise at 95%. Followed by happy at 90% then disgust at 55%, both sad and fear have 50% prediction accuracy and angry has the least prediction at 40%. Figure 6 shows that the model gives 100% prediction for Angry, disgust, Fear and happy instances, 94% for surprise and 40% for sad.

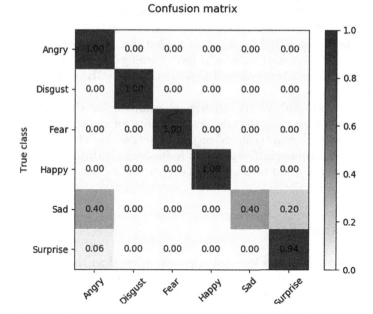

Fig. 6. Confusion matrix of Deep Forest predictions on CK+ dataset

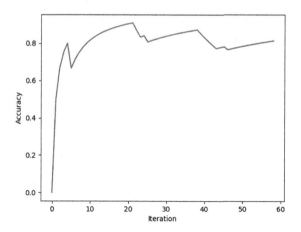

Fig. 7. The graph of the recognition rate against number of predictions of CK+ test data

We justify the performance of Deep forest on Facial expression classification by comparing its performance with the state of the art DNN method (FERAtt) [10]. Table 2, presents both our result and FERAtt result and clearly Deep forest gives better accuracy (93.22%) than the accuracy achieved in FERAtt (86.67%) on CK+ dataset. while accuracy gotten with FERAatt (75.22%) on BU3DFE dataset is more than Deep Forest (65.53%). But it should be noted that FERAtt could not use a small dataset, because the authors reported that the data were augmented and also combined with Coco data. Also FERAtt demands for high computing device like GPU for its appreciable time of computation, unlike the Deep Forest that performed its layer by layer learning on the available computing device (intel(R)Core(TM)i7-4770sCPU @3.10 GHz 3.10 GHz and RAM: 8 GB) at an appreciable time.

Obviously, the result of the experiment compliments the claim of [21]. It shows that Deep Forest has the inherent capability for small datasets. The average prediction accuracy of the model on CK+ (309 data) is 93.22% and BU-3DFE (600) is 65.53%. Although, Deep Forest is challenge with the issue of memory consumption, yet it could be a an alternative to DNN if its features are greatly explored.

6   Conclusion

We have presented a Deep learning approach other than the popularly known DNN for Facial Expression Recognition. And our work proved that Deep forest could preform very well even in a wild environment and with a sparsely distributed and unbalanced dataset. Also the outcome of the further investigation conducted in the experiment, is the evidence of dynamic control behaviour of deep forest over its model. The result of this work is an incite for exploring possibilities of enhancing Deep Forest model, which is the focus of the future work.

References

1. Amit, Y., Geman, D.: Shape quantization and recognition with randomized trees. Neural Comput. **9**(7), 1545–1588 (1997). https://doi.org/10.1162/neco.1997.9.7. 1545
2. Anggraeni, D., Wulandari, A., Barasaruddin, T., Yanti, D.: Enhancing CNN with preprocessing stage in automatic emotion enhancing CNN with preprocessing stage in automatic emotion recognition recognition. Procedia Comput. Sci. **116**, 523–529 (2017). https://doi.org/10.1016/j.procs.2017.10.038
3. Breiman, L.: Random forests. Mach. Learn. **45**(5), 1–33 (2001). https://doi.org/10.1023/A:1010933404324
4. Chen, J., Zhang, M., Xue, X., Xu, R., Zhang, K.: An action unit based hierarchical random forest model to facial expression recognition. In: International Conference on Pattern Recognition Application and Methods, ICPRAM, pp. 753–760 (2017). https://doi.org/10.5220/0006274707530760
5. Chollet, F.: Deep Learning with Python. Manning Publications Co., Shelter Island (2018)
6. Dapogny, A., Bailly, K., Dubuisson, S.: Pairwise conditional random forests for facial expression recognition. In: Proceedings of the IEEE International Conference on Computer Vision, vol. 2015 Inter, pp. 3783–3791 (2015). https://doi.org/10.1109/ICCV.2015.431

7. Deng, H., Zhu, J., Lyu, M.R., King, I.: Two-stage multi-class AdaBoost for facial expression recognition. In: IEEE International Conference on Neural Networks - Conference Proceedings, no. 1, pp. 3005–3010 (2007). https://doi.org/10.1109/ IJCNN.2007.4371439

8. Dietterich, T.G.: Ensemble methods in machine learning. In: Kittler, J., Roli, F. (eds.) MCS 2000. LNCS, vol. 1857, pp. 1–15. Springer, Heidelberg (2000). https:// doi.org/10.1007/3-540-45014-9_1

9. Ekman, P.: An argument for basic emotions. Cogn. Emot. **6**, 169 (1992). https:// doi.org/10.1080/02699939208411068.   http://www.tandfonline.com/loi/pcem20, http://dx.doi.org/10.1080/02699939208411068

10. Fernandez, P.D.M., Peña, F.A.G., Ren, T.I., Cunha, A.: FERAtt: facial expression recognition with attention net. In: IEEE Xplore (2019). http://arxiv.org/abs/1902. 03284

11. Kanade, T., Cohn, J.F., Tian, Y.: Comprehensive database for facial expression analysis the robotics institute. In: Proceedings of the 4th IEEE International Conference on Automatic Face and Gesture Recognition, pp. 46–53 (2000). https:// doi.org/10.1109/AFGR.2000.840611

12. Kontschieder, P., Fiterau, M., Criminisi, A., Bul, S.R., Kessler, F.B.: Deep neural decision forests. In: International Joint Conference on Artificial Intelligence, pp. 4190–4194 (2016)

13. Lucey, P., Cohn, J.F., Kanade, T., Saragih, J., Ambadar, Z., Matthews, I.: The extended Cohn-Kanade dataset (CK+): a complete dataset for action unit and emotion-specified expression. In: 2010 IEEE Computer Society Conference on Computer Vision and Pattern Recognition - Workshops, CVPRW 2010, pp. 94–101, July 2010. https://doi.org/10.1109/CVPRW.2010.5543262

14. Miller, K., Hettinger, C., Humpherys, J., Jarvis, T., Kartchner, D.: Forward thinking : building deep random forests. In: 31st Conference on Neural Information Processing Systems (NIPS 2017), pp. 1–8. NIPS (2017)

15. Vasanth, P.C., Nataraj, K.R.: Facial expression recognition using SVM classifier. Indones. J. Electr. Eng. Inf. (IJEEI) **3**(1), 16–20 (2015). https://doi.org/10.11591/ ijeei.v3i1.126

16. Rokach, L., Maimon, O.: Classification trees. In: Maimon, O., Rokach, L. (eds.) Data Mining and Knowledge Discovery Handbook, pp. 149–174. Springer, Boston (2009). https://doi.org/10.1007/978-0-387-09823-4_9. Chap. 9

17. Rosato, M.J.: A 3D facial expression database for facial behavior research a 3D facial expression database for facial behavior research. In: International Conference on Automatic Face and Gesture Recognition (FGR 2006), pp. 211–216, May 2006 (2016). https://doi.org/10.1109/FGR.2006.6

18. Salmam, F.Z., Madani, A., Kissi, M.: Facial expression recognition using decision trees. In: Proceedings - Computer Graphics, Imaging and Visualization: New Techniques and Trends, CGiV 2016, pp. 125–130. IEEE (2016). https://doi.org/ 10.1109/CGiV.2016.33

19. Su, M.C., Hsieh, Y., Huang, D.Y.: A simple approach to facial expression recognition. In: International Conference on Computer Engineering and Applications, pp. 458–461, January 2007 (2014)

20. Ho, T.K.: The random subspace method for constructing decision forests. IEEE Trans. Pattern Anal. Mach. Intell. **20**(8), 832–844 (1998)

21. Zhou, Z.H., Feng, J.: Deep forest : towards an alternative to deep neural networks. In: International Joint Conference on Artificial Intelligence (IJCAI-17), pp. 3553– 3559 (2017)

Weed Density Estimation Using Semantic Segmentation

Muhammad Hamza Asad and Abdul Bais[✉]

Electronic Systems Engineering, Faculty of Engineering and Applied Science,
University of Regina, Regina, SK, Canada
{maq541,abdul.bais}@uregina.ca

Abstract. Use of herbicides is rising globally to enhance crop yield and meet the ever increasing food demand. It adversely impacts environment and biosphere. To rationalize its use, variable rate herbicide based on weed densities mapping is a promising technique. Estimation of weed densities depends upon precise detection and mapping of weeds in the field. Recently, semantic segmentation is studied in precision agriculture due to its power to detect and segment objects in images. However, due to extremely difficult and time consuming job of labelling the pixels in agriculture images, its application is limited. To accelerate labelling process for semantic segmentation, a two step manual labelling procedure is proposed in this paper. The proposed method is tested on oat field imagery. It has shown improved intersection over union values as semantic models are trained on a comparatively bigger labelled real dataset. The method demonstrates intersection over union value of 81.28% for weeds and mean intersection over union value of 90.445%.

Keywords: Weed density · Semantic segmentation · Variable rate

1 Introduction

Approximately one third of all pest related agriculture production losses are attributed to weeds [1]. Weeds reduce crop yield by sharing nutrients, moisture and sunlight with host plants in an adaptive and competitive process [2]. Herbicide application is a common agriculture practice in mitigating the impact of weeds on crop yield. In USA, it constitutes two third of all chemical application to agricultural fields [3]. Increasing trend of chemical application have raised environmental, biological and sustainability concerns. Recent studies have shown their detrimental effects on human health [4]. To reduce harmful effects of chemicals while ensuring profitability of farmers, precision agriculture proposes site specific variable rate application of herbicides which requires accurate mapping

This work is supported by Mitacs Accelerate grant entitled "Weed Classification and Density Estimation for Variable Rate Herbicide Prescription". We would like to thank CropPro Consulting (https://www.croppro.ca), our industry partner, for their financial and in kind support.

J. J. Dabrowski et al. (Eds.): PSIVT 2019 Workshops, LNCS 11994, pp. 162–171, 2020.
https://doi.org/10.1007/978-3-030-39770-8_13

of weed densities [5,6]. Weed mapping on a large scale is a challenging task due to spectral similarity of weeds and host plants.

Weed mapping techniques can be classified into two broad categories: interline and intraline. The former assumes that host plants are planted in rows and everything outside of plant rows is weed [7]. This technique has inherit flaw of misclassifying intra row weeds as host plants and inter-row host plants as weeds. Intra-line approaches attempt to address these flaws by extracting shape features of plants and classifying them into host plant and weeds. With the advent of deep learning techniques, image classification tasks have become easier due to automated feature extraction. In precision agriculture, different deep learning based classification techniques are being employed. Semantic segmentation is a promising pixel level classification technique for weed density mapping. The bottleneck for this technique is labelling of data at pixel level which is time consuming. Recent works have concentrated on synthetic data for training semantic segmentation models and then employing them for real data. Training models on synthetic data do not generalize well on real datasets.

In this paper, semantic segmentation technique is used on the images acquired from oat fields in Saskatchewan for weed density estimation. The paper makes following contributions:

1. It proposes a two step manual labelling procedure for pixels in agriculture images.
2. Semantic segmentation is employed on a real oat field imagery for both training and testing.

The proposed methodology has shown Intersection Over Union (IOU) value of 81.28% for weeds and Mean Intersection Over Union (MIOU) value of 90.445%. Remainder of the paper is organized as follows: Sect. 2 surveys related works, Sect. 3 explains methodology, Sect. 4 discusses results and Sect. 5 concludes the paper.

2   Related Work

Distribution of weeds is not uniform in field. Its patchiness character prompts site specific weed management. Garibay et al. study site specific weed control by thresholding weed density for herbicide spray [8]. Site specific weed control is not readily adopted by farmers due to accuracy concerns, unavailability of robust weed recognition system and limitation of spraying machinery [9]. Castaldi et al. use Unmanned Aerial Vehicle (UAV) imagery to explore the economic potential of patch spraying and its effects on crop yield [10]. Korres et al. study relationship of soil properties and weed types with focus on weeds along highways [11]. Metcalfe et al. demonstrate correlation between weed and soil properties and make prediction of weed patches in wheat field with the objective to make cite specific weed control more effective [12].

Apart from weed patch prediction based on soil properties, weed detection using computer vision techniques is also widely studied. Traditionally, weed detection involves following four steps [13]:

1. RGB or multispectral image acquisition through UAV or ground moving equipment.
2. Background and foreground (vegetation) segmentation.
3. Feature extraction from images like shape and colours.
4. Classification of images based on extracted features.

Saari et al. study UAV and ground equipment mounted sensors for higher resolution imagery [14]. For background segmentation, numerous techniques like Otsu-Adaptive Thresholding, clustering algorithms and principle component analysis are employed to separate vegetation from soil [5,15,16]. These colour based segmentation techniques do not perform well under varying sunlight, weather conditions and shadows. Feature extraction and classification techniques can be further categorized in two main classes, interline approach and intraline approaches. Bah et al. implement interline approach using normalized Hough transform to detect crop rows [17]. This approach has disadvantage of misclassifying interline crop plants as weed and intraline weeds as host plants. Contrary to this, intraline approach assumes that weeds can be both interline and intraline [18]. For the purpose, extra features like texture and shape are extracted from weed and host plants to classify images [19]. Lastly, different machine learning techniques like support vector machines and artificial neural network are used to classify based on extracted features [20].

Deep learning has emerged as a powerful machine learning tool in the field of computer vision because of its ability to extract features automatically [21]. Dyrmann et al. detect the location of monocot and dicot weeds in cereal field images using Convolutional Neural Networks (CNN) [22]. Yu et al. apply object detection techniques like VGGNet, GoogLeNet and DetectNet for detecting weeds in turf-grass [23]. Semantic segmentation techniques are also being implemented. Bottleneck in semantic segmentation is pixel wise labelling of images. Dyrmann et al. overcome this problem by synthesizing training images and labels. Weeds and host plants are placed in randomly overlapping and nonoverlapping configurations [24]. Potena et al. use a small representative dataset to label large dataset for semantic segmentation [25]. To compensate the unavailability of large labelled data for semantic segmentation, Milioto et al. input vegetation indexes as additional variables to segmentation model [26]. These studies lack fully labelled real images at pixel level for semantic segmentation which is the focus of this work.

3   Methodology

The objective of the study is to estimate weed density for crops grown in Canadian Prairies. The weed density mapping will be used for variable rate herbicide application. Approach adopted in this paper can be summarized in three steps. First step is acquisition of images and second is labelling the pixels in a two step procedure. Third step is to train semantic segmentation model for automating weed mapping and weed density calculation. Following sub sections give details about these steps.

3.1   Two Step Manual Labelling

For deep learning applications in precision agriculture, large number of labelled agriculture images are not available [27]. Semantic segmentation requires images to be labelled at pixel level which is time consuming. In this study, focus is on developing an efficient and effective way of labelling RGB images. A two step manual labelling procedure is proposed as follows.

Background Removal Using Maximum Likelihood Segmentation. In first step, images are preprocessed by segmenting background and foreground using Maximum Likelihood Segmentation (MLS) [28]. Background removal is performed for two reasons, first is to label background pixels and second reason is to facilitate manual labelling of weeds as with background there are chances that some weed plants are missed in a highly varied background from being labelled. ARCGIS is used as a tool for this purpose. Unlike rule based scheme applied to all images, in our procedure we are making batch of similar images and then training MLS on each batch separately for background removal. MLS is applied in batches because RGB images vary in leave colours, light conditions, soil colour, moisture content of soil, mix of dead plants and some of images contain shadow of the sensing equipment. Figure 1 shows the instances of variations in the images.

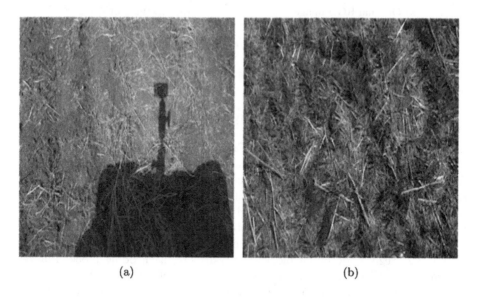

(a)   (b)

Fig. 1. Examples of images with shadows, varying sunlight and colours

Manual Labelling. In second step, minority class pixels are manually labelled using Labelme software package [29]. Instead of labelling both crop and weeds, only weeds are labelled assuming it to be a minority class in images. The crop pixels are zeroed out like background pixels in first step. Minority class labelling dramatically reduces time for manual labelling of pixels. Figure 2 is an example of manually labelled image.

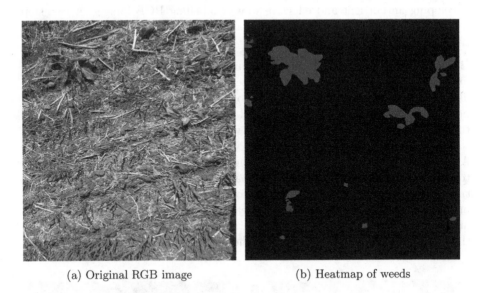

(a) Original RGB image   (b) Heatmap of weeds

Fig. 2. Manual labelling of minority class pixels

3.2 Semantic Segmentation

Semantic segmentation has seen great progress in recent years thanks to advent of deep learning techniques. Deep learning based semantic segmentation consists of encoding and decoding blocks. Encoding block downsamples the image and extracts features out of it and decoder block up samples to target mask size. The network architecture of encoder and decoder blocks is determined by meta-architecture scheme like UNET [30] and SegNet [31]. The paper makes comparison of UNET and SegNet on given dataset. In UNET, whole feature map is transferred from encoder block to decoder block while in SegNet only pooling indexes are transferred from encoder block to decoder block. In both UNET and SegNet, decoding blocks are transpose of encoding block. Phased upsampling in UNET and SegNet improve accuracy of network [32].

After semantic segmentation is performed on images, weed densities are estimated by following equation:

$$Weed\ density\ (w_d) = \frac{Weed\ pixels\ in\ a\ image}{Total\ pixels} \tag{1}$$

Crop pixels are not separately classified because the objective of the study is to estimate weed density (w_d) for variable rate herbicide application. However, crop density (c_d) can be estimated by subtracting weed density from background segmented vegetation density (v_d) given by following equation:

$$c_d = v_d - w_d \tag{2}$$

where v_d is the vegetation density and c_d is the crop density in the image.

4 Results Discussion

The study is conducted in collaboration with CropPro consulting, Canada. RGB images are collected from three oat fields at early growth stage using quad mounted Sony DSC-RX100M2 camera. A total of 2109 images are collected in a grid pattern of 60 ft by 80 ft. The dataset is augmented to 4702 images using different combinations of flipping, rotation, shearing, scaling, noise addition, colour variations and blurry effects. The original images are divided into four tiles of 800×544 to deal with memory constraints as downsampling would remove details from the images.

For semantic segmentation UNET and SegNet are used with VGG16 and ResNet-50 as base models. To evaluate and fine tune models, dataset is divided into train, validation and test dataset with split ratio of 70%, 15% and 15% respectively. Thereafter it is augmented to avoid overfitting and better generalization. The trained models are evaluated on accuracy, precision, recall, F1, IOU, MIOU and Frequency Weighted Intersection Over Union (FWIOU). F1 score, IOU, MIOU and FWIOU are given by following equations:

$$F1 = \frac{2 \cdot precision \cdot recall}{precision + recall} \tag{3}$$

$$IOU = \frac{Area\ of\ overlap}{Area\ of\ union} \tag{4}$$

$$MIOU = \frac{IOU_i + IOU_j}{k} \tag{5}$$

$$FWIOU = w_i \times IOU_i + w_j \times IOU_j \tag{6}$$

where w_i and w_j are the weights of each class and k is number of pixel classes.

Table 1 summarizes the metrics for evaluation on test dataset. For comparison purpose, accuracy for majority class classifier is calculated to be 98.27%. Accuracy of the UNET model exceeds this by 1.30% while that of SegNet model exceeds majority class classifier (MCC) by 1.37%. SegNet performance is comparatively better than UNET. IOU for weed class is 81.28% for SegNet model. MIOU and FWIOU values for SegNet model are 90.445% and 99.29%.

Table 1. Evaluation metrics

Metric	UNET with VGG16	SegNet with ResNet-50
MCC accuracy	98.27%	98.27%
Accuracy	99.55%	99.62%
Precision	99.60%	99.71%
Recall	99.90%	99.91%
F1-score	99.77%	99.81%
IOU-Background and crop	99.55%	99.61%
IOU-Weeds	79.15%	**81.28%**
MIOU	89.35%	**90.445%**
FWIOU	99.19%	**99.29%**

As per developed methodology, models are trained in a way that crop pixels and background pixels are classified in to one class and weed pixels to other class. This means semantic models should ideally learn shape features of crop and spectral properties of background and club them together into one class while labelling remaining pixels as weeds. It is pertinent to mention that there are no means available to ascertain what model is actually learning except having clues from testing it on various images. If model is learning something close to ideal scenario then it should be able to map new types of weeds which were not included in data at learning stage. To evaluate model performance on new types of weeds, it is tested on images of oat crop containing new weeds. Figure 3a contains a new weed type called Horsetail (highlighted) which is not previously seen by the model. The trained SegNet model successfully detects and maps this weed as shown in Fig. 3b.

There are some points where models confuse weed and crop-background classes. In blurry images oat plants are mapped as weed. Models fail to identify crop plants because of indistinct shapes. So, model labels every vegetation in the image as weed. At image preprocessing stage, training images were made blurry to improve models performance on blurry images. However, when model is confronted with blurry images like Fig. 4, it fails to crop and weed pixels.

(a) Test image with new type of weed namely Horsetail.

(b) Horsetail detected and mapped by model

Fig. 3. SegNet model performance on detecting new types of weeds

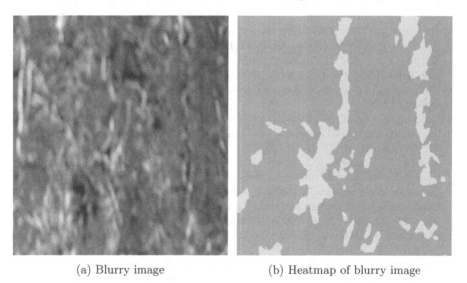

(a) Blurry image

(b) Heatmap of blurry image

Fig. 4. Examples of model confusion on blurry images

5   Conclusion and Future Recommendations

Accurate mapping of weed and crop densities in field provides basis for variable rate herbicide application. Semantic segmentation is a promising technique to estimate these densities. Using two step manual labelling procedure, a relatively bigger set of images can be labelled for model training resulting in better MIOU and accuracy values. As in proposed methodology, trained model eliminates crop pixels along with background pixels, the remaining pixels are labelled as weed pixels. It has advantage of detecting new weeds which are not seen by model during training. In performance comparison of UNET and SegNet, SegNet performs UNET. In future work, we plan to club different density zones to provide basis for variable rate herbicide quantification.

References

1. Oerke, E.: Crop losses to pests. J. Agric. Sci. **144**(1), 31–43 (2006)
2. Guo, L., Qiu, J., Li, L.F., Lu, B., Olsen, K., Fan, L.: Genomic clues for crop-weed interactions and evolution. Trends Plant Sci. **23**, 1102–1115 (2018)
3. Osteen, C.D., Fernandez-Cornejo, J., et al.: Herbicide use trends: a backgrounder. Choices **31**(4), 1–7 (2016)
4. Myers, J.P., et al.: Concerns over use of glyphosate-based herbicides and risks associated with exposures: a consensus statement. Environ. Health **15**(1), 19 (2016)
5. Bah, M.D., Hafiane, A., Canals, R.: Deep learning with unsupervised data labeling for weeds detection on UAV images (2018)
6. Plant, R., Pettygrove, G., Reinert, W., et al.: Precision agriculture can increase profits and limit environmental impacts. Calif. Agric. **54**(4), 66–71 (2000)
7. Slaughter, D., Giles, D.K., Downey, D.: Autonomous robotic weed control systems: a review. Comput. Electron. Agric. **61**(1), 63–78 (2008)
8. Garibay, S.V., et al.: Extent and implications of weed spatial variability in arable crop fields. Plant Prod. Sci. **4**(4), 259–269 (2001)
9. Christensen, S., et al.: Site-specific weed control technologies. Weed Res. **49**(3), 233–241 (2009)
10. Castaldi, F., Pelosi, F., Pascucci, S., Casa, R.: Assessing the potential of images from unmanned aerial vehicles (UAV) to support herbicide patch spraying in maize. Precision Agric. **18**(1), 76–94 (2017)
11. Korres, N., Norsworthy, J., Brye, K., Skinner Jr., V., Mauromoustakos, A.: Relationships between soil properties and the occurrence of the most agronomically important weed species in the field margins of eastern Arkansas-implications for weed management in field margins. Weed Res. **57**(3), 159–171 (2017)
12. Metcalfe, H., Milne, A., Coleman, K., Murdoch, A., Storkey, J.: Modelling the effect of spatially variable soil properties on the distribution of weeds. Ecol. Model. **396**, 1–11 (2019)
13. Oerke, E.C., Gerhards, R., Menz, G., Sikora, R.A.: Precision Crop Protection-the Challenge and Use of Heterogeneity, vol. 5. Springer, Heidelberg (2010). https://doi.org/10.1007/978-90-481-9277-9
14. Saari, H., et al.: Unmanned aerial vehicle (UAV) operated spectral camera system for forest and agriculture applications. In: Remote Sensing for Agriculture, Ecosystems, and Hydrology XIII, vol. 8174. International Society for Optics and Photonics (2011) 81740H
15. Rusu, R.B.: Clustering and segmentation. In: Rusu, R.B. (ed.) Semantic 3D Object Maps for Everyday Robot Manipulation, pp. 75–85. Springer, Heidelberg (2013). https://doi.org/10.1007/978-3-642-35479-3_6

16. Valiente-Gonzalez, J.M., Andreu-García, G., Potter, P., Rodas-Jorda, A.: Automatic corn (Zea mays) kernel inspection system using novelty detection based on principal component analysis. Biosyst. Eng. **117**, 94–103 (2014)
17. Bah, M.D., Hafiane, A., Canals, R.: Deep learning with unsupervised data labeling for weed detection in line crops in UAV images. Remote Sens. **10**(11), 1690 (2018)
18. García-Santillán, I.D., Pajares, G.: On-line crop/weed discrimination through the Mahalanobis distance from images in maize fields. Biosyst. Eng. **166**, 28–43 (2018)
19. Wendel, A., Underwood, J.: Self-supervised weed detection in vegetable crops using ground based hyperspectral imaging. In: 2016 IEEE International Conference on Robotics and Automation (ICRA), pp. 5128–5135. IEEE (2016)
20. Pantazi, X.E., Tamouridou, A.A., Alexandridis, T., Lagopodi, A.L., Kashefi, J., Moshou, D.: Evaluation of hierarchical self-organising maps for weed mapping using uas multispectral imagery. Comput. Electron. Agric. **139**, 224–230 (2017)
21. Greenspan, H., Van Ginneken, B., Summers, R.M.: Guest editorial deep learning in medical imaging: overview and future promise of an exciting new technique. IEEE Trans. Med. Imaging **35**(5), 1153–1159 (2016)
22. Dyrmann, M., Skovsen, S., Laursen, M.S., Jørgensen, R.N.: Using a fully convolutional neural network for detecting locations of weeds in images from cereal fields. In: International Conference on Precision Agriculture. International Society of Precision Agriculture (2018)
23. Yu, J., Sharpe, S.M., Schumann, A.W., Boyd, N.S.: Deep learning for image-based weed detection in turfgrass. Eur. J. Agron. **104**, 78–84 (2019)
24. Dyrmann, M., Mortensen, A.K., Midtiby, H.S., Jørgensen, R.N., et al.: Pixel-wise classification of weeds and crops in images by using a fully convolutional neural network. In: Proceedings of the International Conference on Agricultural Engineering, pp. 26–29, Aarhus, Denmark (2016)
25. Potena, C., Nardi, D., Pretto, A.: Fast and accurate crop and weed identification with summarized train sets for precision agriculture. In: Chen, W., Hosoda, K., Menegatti, E., Shimizu, M., Wang, H. (eds.) IAS 2016. AISC, vol. 531, pp. 105–121. Springer, Cham (2017). https://doi.org/10.1007/978-3-319-48036-7_9
26. Milioto, A., Lottes, P., Stachniss, C.: Real-time semantic segmentation of crop and weed for precision agriculture robots leveraging background knowledge in CNNs. In: 2018 IEEE International Conference on Robotics and Automation (ICRA), pp. 2229–2235. IEEE (2018)
27. Kamilaris, A., Prenafeta-Boldú, F.: A review of the use of convolutional neural networks in agriculture. J. Agric. Sci. **156**(3), 312–322 (2018)
28. Sharma, A., Boroevich, K.A., Shigemizu, D., Kamatani, Y., Kubo, M., Tsunoda, T.: Hierarchical maximum likelihood clustering approach. IEEE Trans. Biomed. Eng. **64**(1), 112–122 (2016)
29. MIT: LabelMe (2019)
30. Ronneberger, O., Fischer, P., Brox, T.: U-Net: convolutional networks for biomedical image segmentation. In: Navab, N., Hornegger, J., Wells, W.M., Frangi, A.F. (eds.) MICCAI 2015. LNCS, vol. 9351, pp. 234–241. Springer, Cham (2015). https://doi.org/10.1007/978-3-319-24574-4_28
31. Badrinarayanan, V., Kendall, A., Cipolla, R.: Segnet: a deep convolutional encoder-decoder architecture for image segmentation. IEEE Trans. Pattern Anal. Mach. Intell. **39**(12), 2481–2495 (2017)
32. Siam, M., Gamal, M., Abdel-Razek, M., Yogamani, S., Jagersand, M.: RTSeg: real-time semantic segmentation comparative study. In: 2018 25th IEEE International Conference on Image Processing (ICIP), pp. 1603–1607. IEEE (2018)

Detecting Global Exam Events in Invigilation Videos Using 3D Convolutional Neural Network

Zichun Dai, Chao Sun[⊠], Xinguo Yu, and Ying Xiang

National Engineering Research Center for E-Learning, Central China Normal University,
Wuhan, China
daizichun@mails.ccnu.edu.cn, {csun,xgyu}@mail.ccnu.edu.cn,
yingxiang333@outlook.com

Abstract. This paper designs a structure of 3D convolutional neural network to detect the global exam events in invigilation videos. Exam events in invigilation videos are defined according to the human activity performed at a certain phase in the entire exam process. Unlike general event detection which involves different scenes, global event detection focuses on differentiating different collective activities in the exam room ambiance. The challenges lie in the great intra-class variations within the same type of events due to various camera angles and different exam room ambiances, as well as inter-class similarities which are challengeable. This paper adopts the 3D convolutional neural network based on its ability in extracting spatio-temporal features and its effectiveness in detecting video events. Experiment results show the designed 3D convolutional neural network achieves an accuracy of its capability of 93.94% in detecting the global exam events, which demonstrates the effectiveness of our model.

Keywords: Exam event detection · Surveillance video · 3D convolutional neural network

1 Introduction

In the modern society the exams are the important activity because they are widely used to evaluate the individual ability. However, the traditional invigilation needs a large number of human resources, which is expensive. Another demerit of invigilating by human being is hardly to get rid of subjective judgment on exam events. The demerits of the traditional invigilation motivate us to develop automatic invigilation systems. An automatic invigilation model is proposed for detecting suspicious activities in exams [1]. Cote *et al.* applies two-state Hidden Markov model to distinguish the abnormal exam events from the normal exam events [2]. However, they take slight attention on global exam event detection. Global event detection is an essential and core part of a complete automatic invigilation system, which can be the prior task of abnormal exam event detection. Besides, the automatic detection of the global exam events benefits the communication between invigilation system and management system, which is convenient for further conducting examination evaluation and analysis. Furthermore, the fairness of exam can be improved by reducing the human subjective judgment.

© Springer Nature Switzerland AG 2020
J. J. Dabrowski et al. (Eds.): PSIVT 2019 Workshops, LNCS 11994, pp. 172–182, 2020.
https://doi.org/10.1007/978-3-030-39770-8_14

One goal of automatic invigilation system is to detect the exam events from the invigilation videos. However, video events detection is still a challenging task due to the background clutter or occlusions. The successful methods in the recent years focuses on extracting spatial-temporal features like STIP [3], HOG3D [4], MBH [5] and dense trajectories [6], and uses bag-of-visual-word histograms or Fisher vectors [7] to represent their distribution in a video for classification. Among these features, improved Dense Trajectories (iDT) perform the best. However, extracting these local features is time-consuming and some discriminative features make difference in finer part of the whole video.

With the breakthrough of image classification brought by convolutional neural network [8], recent researches concentrate on applying convolutional neural network to video events detection. Karpathy *et al.* firstly apply convolutional neural network with different time fusion strategies on Sports-1M video dataset but gain less accuracy than hand-crafted features [9]. Feichtenhofer *et al.* explore the two-stream convolutional network fusion for action recognition in videos. Interestingly, they find that the slow fusion of temporal and spatial network can boost accuracy of classification [10]. Although it is time-consuming by training two networks, it inspired researchers that the temporal information is critical for understanding the video activities. 3D convolutional neural network is then be proposed [11]. It builds an architecture to directly learn the spatial and temporal features by adding temporal dimension to the network. It performs well in extracting compact and discriminative features, which is necessary for efficient video event detection.

Global exam event detection in invigilation videos is a branch of video event detection. Different form detecting abnormal exam behavior like cheating, it aims at detecting the whole status in the exam room. For global exam events detection, one challenge lies in the great intra-class variations. The events take place in different classrooms and the classrooms are invigilated from various angles of cameras, which means the same exam event can occur with different background. Additionally, global exam events detection suffers from inter-class indistinguishability as a result of the finer motion change in different events [12]. It is hard to distinguish the event accurately from one still image. To the best of our knowledge, there is no research targeting at global exam event classification before. After reviewing the technologies in video event detection, we notice the efficiency of 3D convolutional neural network of extracting compact and discriminative features. Therefore, this paper develops the detecting model based on the 3D convolutional neural network to solve the detection problem for global exam events.

2 Proposed 3D Convolutional Neural Network Structure

We detect the global exam events using the 3D convolutional neural network. The proposed method firstly breaks each predefined exam surveillance video into consecutive frames. Then we select N consecutive frames from each video and encapsulate them as a volume to feed the 3D convolutional model. The 3D convolutional model is trained for outputting closer to the predefined category results. Finally, the well-trained model is used for global exam events prediction. The framework is showed in Fig. 1.

Our method adopts 3D convolutional neural network architecture which is developed from C3D model [11, 13]. 2D CNN convolves the spatial dimensions only, whereas 3D

Exam Surveillance Videos (Predefined categories)

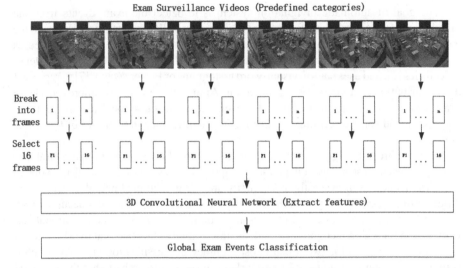

Fig. 1. Framework diagram of detecting global exam events

CNN is different from 2D CNN by adding a temporal dimension to the convolutional kernel. Some behaviors in global exam events take time to finish. The temporal information is required in detecting the events. Therefore, 3D CNN should be considered to be more suitable for implementation on the global exam events scene. Assuming the input is the $F = (c, f, w, h)$ (c: channel, f: frame number, w: width, h: height), 2D CNN or multi-frames 2D CNN only uses the two-dimensional filters (k, k) (k: kernel width, k: kernel height), which results in two dimensions output. As the Fig. 2 shows, 3D CNN does the convolution operation by using filters whose dimension is (d, k, k) (d: kernel temporal depth, k: kernel width, k: kernel height) which convolves the volume (f, w, h) of each channel. Then, add each channel of RGB together to get the output of three-dimensional feature map. Since the 3D CNN kernel convolves the adjacent frames, it reserves temporal information. In this way, 3D CNN model can extract the temporal dimension features of frames, which plays key role in extracting motion features. When the chunks of consecutive frames feed to the 3D CNN architecture, the 3D convolution kernel can encapsulate both temporal and spatial information and output a feature volume map.

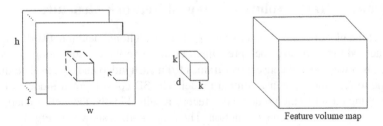

Fig. 2. 3D convolution

The experiment in [10] shows that gradually deeper network which gradually convolves and pools spatial and temporal information can achieve better results. The number of kernels also increase to generate different types of feature map. The pooling operation is max pooling, which reduces the feature map size except that the size of the temporal dimension is not changed in the first pooling layer. After convolution and pooling layers, it comes to fully connective layers to ensemble the features for the six categories of the global exam events. And the softmax function is used for normalizing the results and the cross entropy function is applied for minimizing the gradient loss.

Training: The 3D CNN is trained to extract spatio-temporal features from a given input which is a chunk of consecutive frames. The input dimension is denoted as,

$$x_i \in \mathbb{R}^{b \times f \times w \times h \times c}$$

where b stands for the sample number for a batch, f is the frame number in a chunk. w and h represent the width and height of each frame. c is channel number. Due to the RGB form, the initial input channel is 3.

After convolution and pooling layers, a feature map is produced. Its dimension is denoted as below, where p represents the pooling times, $NumF$ stands for the number of filters in the layer.

$$s_i \in \mathbb{R}^{b \times \frac{f}{p/2} \times \frac{w}{p} \times \frac{h}{p} \times NumF}$$

Our goal is to output vectors of $NumC$ categories, which represent for $NumC$ global exam events.

$$z_j \in \mathbb{R}^{b \times NumC}$$

We use the softmax function to normalize the output components corresponding to each category.

$$y_j = \frac{e^{z_j}}{\sum\limits_{k=1}^{NumC} e^{z_k}} \tag{1}$$

The loss function uses cross entropy function. In order to minimize the gratitude between predefined label and forward propagation result, the parameters in the 3D CNN model is adjusted in the backward propagation phase,

$$loss\left(y_j', y_j\right) = -\sum\limits_{k=1}^{NumC} y_j' \log y_j \tag{2}$$

where y_j' represents the ground true label of the video frames.

3 Experiments and Evaluation

In the experiments, the input is 16 consecutive frames from each predefined video clips. By using the 3D convolution operation, the spatial-temporal information is extracted from the input volume and encapsulated in the output. After the convolutional layer, the pooling layer scales down the spatial sizes and merges the temporal size. Going through two fully connective layers, the output is mapped to six likely outcomes which are six categories of the exam events.

3.1 Dataset

Since there is no available public global exam events dataset, we establish our own dataset. The exam surveillance videos are collected from various exam rooms in primary or secondary schools. Some videos show different perspectives due to camera angles. All videos are in "avi" format with a frame rate of 25FPS. There are 916 videos in total. The global exam events are manually defined into six categories. They are "empty exam room status", "examinees entrance", "distributing papers", "on-exam status", "examinees departure", "collecting papers". Each category includes 153, 162, 148, 180, 113, 160 videos separately. 25% dataset is used for testing. Due to the uneven distribution of samples, the weight for each category will be considered in the following classification result. These six categories can generally classify different phases of exams. Each category is divided into 20 groups with 18 videos of the same behavior contained in one group. The length of each video is generally around 10 s. Some illustrations in each defined exam event category are showed in Fig. 3.

Empty Exam Room Status. Before the exam begins or when the exam ends, there is no one (students or invigilators) in the classroom. This event ends when someone open the door and enters the room.

Examinees Entrance. This event begins when examinees begin to enter the room from the front door. They receive security inspection by the invigilators and walk around the room to find their seat to sit down. This event ends when all the examinees have entered to room and sit down.

Distributing Papers. After all the examinees have entered the room and sit down, invigilators give out papers to examinees. Mostly, they walk to every examinee's seat and hand out the papers to the examinees one by one. Sometimes invigilators choose to give the papers to the first student of each row. This event ends when all papers are handed out to all the examinees.

On-exam Status. When exam begins, examinees begin to do the exam. Mostly, invigilators stay in front or back of the classroom and watch over the examinees. Sometimes, invigilators go around the classroom for inspection. This event ends when exam time is up, every examinee stops to do the exam.

Examinees Departure. After the on-exam status, examinees stand up and walk to the front door of the room for leaving from the room. This event ends when all the examinees leave and there are no examinees in the room.

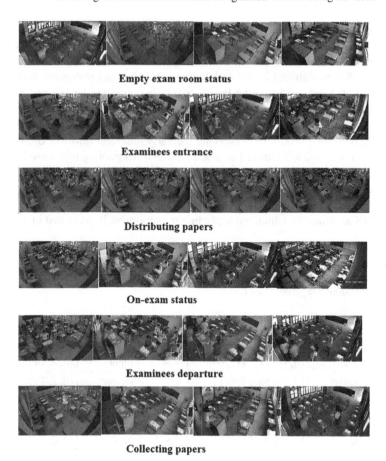

Empty exam room status

Examinees entrance

Distributing papers

On-exam status

Examinees departure

Collecting papers

Fig. 3. Illustrations in six pre-defined global exam events. According to time sequence for an exam, there are phases of Empty exam room, Examinees entrance, Distributing papers, On-exam status, Examinees departure, Collecting papers, separately. These six global exam events depict the whole exam process.

Collecting Papers. After the examinees departure, opposite to distributing papers, invigilators come to each seat to collect the exam papers and sort them together. This event ends when there is no papers on each desk.

3.2 Parameters

We use Tensorflow [14] framework to implement our experiment. We firstly break the predefined videos to clips. Through iteration testing, the optimal value of consecutive frames is 16 which is enough for depicting a completed global exam event. The frames are cropped to 112×112 with channels of 3. The temporal dimension of the 3D kernel is set to 3 this experiment as it has been shown that $3 \times 3 \times 3$ convolution kernel has the best performance [11]. The 16 consecutive frames are treated as a volume and each time we feed the model with 10 volume samples as a batch, thereby our input is of 5 dimensional tensors consisting of $10 \times 16 \times 112 \times 112 \times 3$ (batch-size, frames-per-clip, crop-size, crop-size, channels).

There are 5 convolutional layers with 8 times convolutional operations followed by ReLU activation function, 5 pooling layers, two fully connected layers, and a softmax output layer in total. All 3D convolution kernels are in size of $3 \times 3 \times 3$ with a stride of $1 \times 1 \times 1$. As the network goes deeper, the number of kernels increase from 64, 128, 256 to 512. With the purpose of preserving the early temporal information, the pool1 kernel size is $1 \times 2 \times 2$ with stride $1 \times 2 \times 2$, and all other pooling layers are $2 \times 2 \times 2$ with stride $2 \times 2 \times 2$ to scale down the spatial features and merge the temporal features. The fully connected layer output 4096 units which are then passed to the classification layer for classification. Finally, we get the classification label through the softmax layer. The 3D CNN architecture which we apply in our experiment is presented in Table 1.

Table 1. The architecture of the adopted 3D convolutional neural network. The architecture consists of 5 convolution layers, 5 pooling layers, 2 fully layers and 1 softmax output layer. Detailed descriptions are given in the text.

Conv1	Input:	[10, 16, 112, 112, 3]	Conv4b	Input:	[10, 4, 14, 14, 512]
	Output:	[10, 16, 112, 112, 64]		Output:	[10, 4, 14, 14, 512]
Pool1	Input:	[10, 16, 112, 112, 64]	Pool4	Input:	[10, 4, 14, 14, 512]
	Output:	[10, 16, 56, 56, 64]		Output:	[10, 2, 7, 7, 512]
Conv2	Input:	[10, 16, 56, 56, 64]	Conv5a	Input:	[10, 2, 7, 7, 512]
	Output:	[10, 16, 56, 56, 128]		Output:	[10, 2, 7, 7, 512]
Pool2	Input:	[10, 16, 56, 56, 128]	Conv5b	Input:	[10, 2, 7, 7, 512]
	Output:	[10, 8, 28, 28, 128]		Output:	[10, 2, 7, 7, 512]
Conv3a	Input:	[10, 8, 28, 28, 128]	Pool5	Input:	[10, 2, 7, 7, 512]
	Output:	[10, 8, 28, 28, 256]		Output:	[10, 1, 4, 4, 512]
Conv3b	Input:	[10, 8, 28, 28, 256]	FCNet1	Input:	[10, 1, 4, 4, 512]
	Output:	[10, 8, 28, 28, 256]		Output:	[10, 4096]
Pool3	Input:	[10, 8, 28, 28, 256]	FCNet2	Input:	[10, 4096]
	Output:	[10, 4, 14, 14, 256]		Output:	[10, 4096]
Conv4a	Input:	[10, 4, 14, 14, 256]	Out	Input:	[10,4096]
	Output:	[10, 4, 14, 14, 512]		Output:	[6, 10]

3.3 Results

Eventually, we get a six-category global exam event discrimination of 93.94% by using our method. Due to the pioneer of this work, there are few baselines able to be compared. To the best of our knowledge, our work is the first one to detect the global exam events and the approach in [15] is the most related work. Therefore, we choose [15] as our baseline to demonstrate the performance of our work. Table 2 compares the results using 3D CNN networks with two-classifier using HOG features [15] to demonstrate its superior performance.

Table 2. Comparation with other method

Method	Accuracy
3D CNN	93.94%
[15]	86.1%

Table 3 presents the performance of 3D CNN on classifying the six global exam events and compared with Depth-1 (2D CNN) method. It is worth mentioning that the data in Table 3 is weighted-calculated as a result of the uneven distribution samples. Obviously, empty exam room status event and on-exam status event have the best performance compared to other four events, whereas examinees departure event has the poorest accuracy. This may be due to the short period of time this event takes place, which lead to less training data of this event. A controlling experiment is also carried out by decreasing the temporal depth into 1, which means the whole 16 frames are convolved in 2D way separately. It is interesting to observe from Table 3 that the accuracy of three global exam events decreases when it comes to Depth-1 (2D CNN), they are distributing papers event, on-exam status event as well as collecting papers event. We believe it is due to that these three events are mostly completed through a period of time and are easily-confused from static images. For example, distributing papers is really similar with collecting papers except opposite directions. Reasonably, 3D CNN has higher accuracy on these three events due to its extraction of temporal features, which also demonstrate that 3D CNN functions better under global exam events scenes. Overall, 3D CNN outperforms Depth-1 (2D CNN) method as can be seen weighted average performance in Table 3.

Figure 4 presents the normalized confusion matrix results of the experiment. From the confusion matrix, we can find that the distributing papers event and the examinees departure event have relatively lower accuracy compared with other events, where distributing papers event has chance to be confused with on-exam status, examinees entrance and examinees departure event, examinees departure event tends to confuse with distributing paper event and collecting paper event. It may be caused by the lower discrimination of actions taken in these events and the weakness of this model to classify events when someone or several ones hold the standing position.

To conclude, the experiment result demonstrates that by capturing both spatial and temporal features simultaneously, our model has satisfactory performance for the global exam events recognition.

Table 3. Performance of the two methods. The performance is evaluated in terms of accuracy (Acc.), precision (Pre.), recall and F1 score. The highest value of each case is in bold. Due to the uneven distribution of samples, the weighted average, denoted as W-Mean, is calculated.

Events	3D CNN				Depth-1 (2D CNN)			
Measure	Acc.	Pre.	Recall	F1	Acc.	Pre.	Recall	F1
Empty-exam room	1	1	1	1	1	1	1	1
Examinees entrance	0.8966	**0.9630**	0.8966	**0.9286**	0.8966	0.8387	0.8966	0.8667
Distributing papers	**0.8723**	**0.9111**	**0.8723**	**0.8913**	0.8511	0.8696	0.8511	0.8603
On-exam status	1	0.9020	1	**0.9485**	0.9565	0.9362	0.9565	0.9462
Examinees departure	0.8462	0.9565	0.8462	0.8980	0.8462	0.9565	0.8462	0.8980
Collecting papers	**0.9714**	**0.9189**	**0.9714**	**0.9444**	0.9429	0.9167	0.9429	0.9296
W-Mean	**0.9394**	**0.9406**	**0.9394**	**0.9388**	0.9221	0.9230	0.9221	0.9220

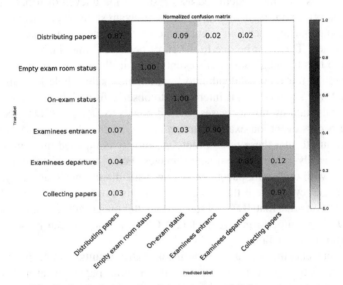

Fig. 4. Confusion matrix of six-category global exam events

4   Conclusions

This paper has proposed a structure of 3D convolutional neural network for the global exam event recognition and gains a promising accuracy result. It firstly built the examination video dataset which includes 916 surveillance videos of different classroom scenes and various camera angles. On the built dataset, it is done to test the proposed structure of 3D convolutional neural network to extract the spatial-temporal features from six kinds of exam events. The proposed algorithm achieved an accuracy of 93.94% to discriminate these six global exam events. Additionally, the superiority of 3D CNN model is evaluated by diminishing the depth kernel into 1.

More works could be explored in the future. For instance, when the accuracy of classifying the exam events is guaranteed, we should try shorter clips to improve its sensitivity and search for the boundary among these different exam events. Besides, examination video event detection is firstly implemented using 3D convolutional neural network, more advanced recognition technology needs to be explored and fused for better result.

Acknowledgement. This work is supported in part by National Natural Science Foundation of China under Grant 61802142, and Fundamental Research Funds for the Central Universities under Grant CCNU19QN031.

References

1. Adil, M., Simon, R., Khatri, S.K.: Automated invigilation system for detection of suspicious activities during examination. In: 2019 Amity International Conference on Artificial Intelligence (AICAI). IEEE (2019)
2. Cote, M., Jean, F., Albu, A.B., Capson, D.W.: Video summarization for remote invigilation of online exams. In: 2016 IEEE Winter Conference on Applications of Computer Vision (WACV), pp. 1–9 (2016)
3. Laptev, I., Marszalek, M., Schmid, C., Rozenfield, B.: Learning realistic human actions from movies. In: 2008 IEEE Conference on Computer Vision and Pattern Recognition, pp. 1–8 (2008)
4. Kläser, A., Marszalek, M., Schmid, C.: A spatio-temporal descriptor based on 3D-gradients. In: British Machine Vision Conference, pp. 995–1004 (2008)
5. Oneata, D., Verbeek, J.J., Schmid, C.: Action and event recognition with fisher vectors on a compact feature set. In: 2013 IEEE International Conference on Computer Vision, pp. 1817–1824 (2013)
6. Wang, H., Kläser, A., Schmid, C., Liu, C.: Action recognition by dense trajectories. In: CVPR 2011, pp. 3169–3176 (2011)
7. Peng, X., Zou, C., Qiao, Y., Peng, Q.: Action recognition with stacked fisher vectors. In: Fleet, D., Pajdla, T., Schiele, B., Tuytelaars, T. (eds.) ECCV 2014. LNCS, vol. 8693, pp. 581–595. Springer, Cham (2014). https://doi.org/10.1007/978-3-319-10602-1_38
8. Krizhevsky, A., Sutskever, I., Hinton, G.E.: Imagenet classification with deep convolutional neural networks. Commun. ACM **60**, 84–90 (2012)
9. Karpathy, A., Toderici, G., Shetty, S., Leung, T., Sukthankar, R., Fei-Fei, L.: Large-scale video classification with convolutional neural networks. In: 2014 IEEE Conference on Computer Vision and Pattern Recognition, pp. 1725–1732 (2014)
10. Feichtenhofer, C., Pinz, A., Zisserman, A.: Convolutional two-stream network fusion for video action recognition. In: 2016 IEEE Conference on Computer Vision and Pattern Recognition (CVPR), pp. 1933–1941 (2016)
11. Tran, D., Bourdev, L.D., Fergus, R., Torresani, L., Paluri, M.: Learning spatiotemporal features with 3D convolutional networks. In: 2015 IEEE International Conference on Computer Vision (ICCV), pp. 4489–4497 (2015)
12. Wang, L., Li, W., Li, W., Gool, L.V.: Appearance-and-relation networks for video classification. In: 2018 IEEE/CVF Conference on Computer Vision and Pattern Recognition, pp. 1430–1439 (2018)
13. Ji, S., Xu, W., Yang, M., Yu, K.: 3D convolutional neural networks for human action recognition. IEEE Trans. Pattern Anal. Mach. Intell. **35**(1), 221–231 (2013)

14. Abadi, M., et al.: TensorFlow: large-scale machine learning on heterogeneous distributed systems. arXiv:abs/1603.04467 (2015)
15. Ding, M., Zhao, J., Hu, F.: Abnormal behavior analysis based on examination surveillance video. In: 2016 9th International Symposium on Computational Intelligence and Design (ISCID), 01, pp. 131–134 (2016)

Spatial Hierarchical Analysis Deep Neural Network for RGB-D Object Recognition

Syed Afaq Ali Shah[✉]

Discipline of Information Technology, Mathematics and Statistics,
Murdoch University, Perth, Australia
afaq.shah@murdoch.edu.au

Abstract. Deep learning based object recognition methods have achieved unprecedented success in the recent years. However, this level of success is yet to be achieved on multimodal RGB-D images. The latter can play an important role in several computer vision and robotics applications. In this paper, we present spatial hierarchical analysis deep neural network, called ShaNet, for RGB-D object recognition. Our network consists of convolutional neural network (CNN) and recurrent neural network (RNNs) to analyse and learn distinctive and translationally invariant features in a hierarchical fashion. Unlike existing methods, which employ pre-trained models or rely on transfer learning, our proposed network is trained from scratch on RGB-D data. The proposed model has been tested on two different publicly available RGB-D datasets including Washington RGB-D and 2D3D object dataset. Our experimental results show that the proposed deep neural network achieves superior performance compared to existing RGB-D object recognition methods.

Keywords: Object recognition · RGB-D images · Deep learning

1 Introduction

Object recognition is a challenging problem in computer vision, deep learning and robotics [24,28]. Automatic recognition of unseen objects in complex scenes is a highly desirable characteristic for intelligent systems [29,31,32]. Development of vision capabilities involves an off-line training, where training data along with the labels is provided and the intelligent object recognition system then predicts the classes for the unseen examples during test time. To achieve high recognition accuracy, few design considerations are required. For instance, a large number of labeled training examples are required ensure good generalization of the deep neural network. In addition, feature descriptors must be descriptive and representative to mitigate the effect of high variation in inter and intra-class. The intelligent system, at test time, is also required be computationally efficient to ensure real-time recognition for robots.

This research is supported by Murdoch University, Australia.

J. J. Dabrowski et al. (Eds.): PSIVT 2019 Workshops, LNCS 11994, pp. 183–193, 2020.
https://doi.org/10.1007/978-3-030-39770-8_15

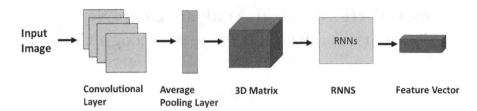

Fig. 1. Block diagram of our proposed network. The input image is given to CNN, which consists of convolutional and average pooling layers. The CNN produces a 3D matrix, which is given as input to RNNs. The latter learn to generate the final feature vector.

Traditional object recognition methods use hand-crafted features extracted from 2D images [13,35]. Recent advances in deep learning methods have shown to achieve good recognition performance for 2D images [16,17,34]. The availability of low-cost depth scanners has enabled the extraction of 2.5D/3D information and more representative features from images, however, RGBD data comes with new challenges [36]. For instance, in contrast to the conventional RGB images, the RGB-D data is noisy and incomplete (because of holes) thus posing additional challenges for recognition systems. Additionally, compared to the traditional RGB images the labeled RGB-D training data is also scarce, which further constrains deployment of powerful deep learning techniques for deep neural network training on the RGB-D images. Recent research works have aimed at addressing these problems [4,18,22,25,26,29,33] with a particular emphasis towards the scarcity of large scale annotated training datasets.

In the recent years, feature representation techniques have also rapidly evolved from hand-crafted features to automatic feature learning [27,37]. The most prevalent methods are based on the deep neural networks which have been shown to achieve the state-of-the-art performance [7,11,12,38]. Deep learning based recognition techniques rely on the features learned by the fully-connected layers, which appear towards the end of the network. Although, fully connected layers contain rich semantic information, they are spatially very coarse [14] and thus need to be complemented by computationally expensive pre-processing steps [7].

In this paper, we address these issues by proposing a deep learning framework, called spatial hierarchical analysis deep neural network (shown in Fig. 1) which consists of a convolutional neural network followed by recurrent neural network applied in hierarchical fashion to extract translationally invariant descriptive features. In contrast to existing deep learning techniques, which rely on transfer learning or pre-trained networks for object recognition, our proposed network is trained from scratch on RGB-D data. The input to our proposed network are RGB-D images captured using Kinect scanner. Initially, the network separately extracts features from each modality. Each image is given as an input to CNN, which extracts the low level features such as edges. The responses of CNN are then given to RNNs. The latter has shown superior performance in text analysis domain such as image captioning and text parsing. In this paper, we explore RNNs for learning high level compositional features from images. Compared to existing RGB-D feature learning methods [4,8], our approach is computationally efficient and does not need additional input channels such as surface normals.

The contribution of this paper can be summarised as follows:

- We propose a novel spatial hierarchical analysis deep learning architecture, which extracts low and high level descriptive features and part interactions in hierarchical fashion.
- The proposed technique is efficient and does not require any additional information channels such surface normals for achieving good performance.
- The proposed deep network achieves superior performance on two publicly available RGB-D datasets.

The rest of this paper has been organised as follow. Related work is presented in the next section. The proposed technique and experimental results are provided in Sect. 3 and 4, respectively. The paper is concluded in Sect. 5.

2   Related Work

Prior works on object recognition relied on hand-crafted features such as SIFT [23], spin images [15] and kernel-based representation [4] for colour, depth and 3D domains. Spin images [15] are popular 3D shape local features, which have been widely applied to 3D meshes and point cloud for object recognition. Some variants of spin images [1,22] have also been proposed to improve the original spin images. Fast point feature histogram [6], is a local feature, which has been shown to outperform spin images in 3D object registration. Normal aligned radial features (NARF) [2] extract object boundary cues to perform recognition. These features, however, fail to capture important cues such as edges and size for object recognition. Kernel descriptors [4] are able to generate rich features by turning any pixel attribute to patch-level features [30].

Despite their simplicity, the aforementioned techniques rely on the prior knowledge of the underlying distribution of data that is not readily available in most applications. Recently, automatic feature learning using machine learning approaches has received significant attention. For instance, deep belief nets [7] learn a hierarchy of features by greedily training each layer separately using a restricted Boltzmann machine. Lee et al. [20] proposed convolutional deep belief networks (CDBN) to learn features from the full sized images. CBDN shares the weights between the hidden and visible layers and uses a small receptive field. Convolutional Neural Networks [16] are feed-forward models that have been successfully applied to object/face recognition, face/object detection, character recognition and pose estimation.

Liu et al. [21] proposed guided cross-layer pooling to extract local features using sub-array of convolutional layers. In [12], the concatenated convolutional layers were used in local regions for feature representations. Schwarz et al. [25] used simple colorization scheme of the depth images to perform transfer learning.

Fig. 2. CNN filters visualization for RGB (left) and Depth (right) images. Only few filters learnt by our model are shown here.

The drawback of their method is that it ignores the significance of earlier convolutional layers and uses the fully connected layers for feature representation. Gupta et al. [11] encoded the depth modality as HHA, which is the combination of horizontal disparity, height above ground and angle with gravity. However, the limitation of their method is that the proposed embedding is geocentric and such information is not always available in recognition tasks, which are object-centric.

To overcome the limitations of the existing methods, we propose spatial hierarchical analysis deep neural network, ShaNet, which does not require a pre-trained model and transfer learning for the task of object recognition. In addition, the proposed method does not require additional information channels for superior recognition performance.

3   Proposed Spatial Hierarchical Analysis Deep Neural Network

In this section, we describe our proposed Spatial Hierarchical Analysis Network (ShaNet), which learns translationally invariant and distinctive features. The lower hierarchy of the network consists of convolutional neural network (CNN) to achieve translational invariance and the upper hierarchy consists of recurrent neural networks (RNN) to learn more distinctive features.

3.1   Network Initialization and Training

Our proposed deep neural network learns distinctive features in a hierarchical fashion, its appropriate intialization is therefore essential. We perform initialization of our proposed network in two stages. In the first stage, we initialize CNN filters in an unsupervised way using [9]. Given a set of input images, we first extract random patches from these images and normalized them. The extracted patches are then clustered in an unsupervised way using the k-means algorithm.

We use k-mean algorithm because its implementation is not complex, its a computationally efficient approach and does not require tuning of any hyperparameters. In the second stage, the weights of RNNs are initialized by using the technique proposed by Le et al. [19]. We observed that compared to random initialization of weights, this approach achieves better optimization.

Since our network learns to extract distinctive features during training, its appropriate initialization is critical. A random initialization of the network can make the variance of its output directly proportional to the number of its incoming connections. To alleviate this problem, we use Xavier initialization [10] and randomly initialize the weights with a variance measure that is dependent on the number of incoming and outgoing connections (k_{f-in} and k_{f-out} respectively) from a neuron:

$$Var(w) = \frac{2}{n_{f-in} + n_{f-out}}, \tag{1}$$

where w are network weights. Note that the fan-out measure is used in the variance above to balance the back-propagated signal as well. Xavier initialization works well in our case and leads to better convergence rates.

To avoid over-fitting, we use batch-normalization as our regularization strategy. Given a set of activations $\{\mathbf{x}^i : i \in [1, a]\}$ (where $\mathbf{x}^i = \{x^i_j : j \in [1, b]\}$ has b dimensions) from a given layer corresponding to a specific input batch with a images, we compute the first and second order statistics (mean and variance respectively) of the batch for each dimension of activations as follows:

$$\mu_{x_j} = \frac{1}{m} \sum_{i=1}^{m} x^i_j \sigma^2_{x_j} = \frac{1}{m} \sum_{i=1}^{m} (x^i_j - \mu_{x_j})^2 \tag{2}$$

μ_{x_j} and $\sigma^2_{x_j}$ represent the mean and variance for the jth activation dimension computed over a batch, respectively. The normalized activation operation is represented as:

$$\hat{x}^i_j = \frac{x^i_j - \mu_{x_j}}{\sqrt{\sigma^2_{x_j} + \epsilon}}. \tag{3}$$

We observe that just the normalization of the activations is not sufficient, because it can alter the activations and disrupt the useful patterns that are learned by the network. Therefore, we rescale and shift the normalized activations to allow them to learn useful discriminative representations:

$$y^i_j = \gamma_j \hat{x}^i_j + \beta_j, \tag{4}$$

where γ_j and β_j are the learnable parameters which are tuned during error back-propagation.

After the initialization of the proposed model, the CNN filters (shown in Fig. 2) are convolved over the input image to extract features in the lower hierarchy of our deep network. Each input image of size $N \times N$ is convolved with L square filter of size $m \times m$, resulting in L filter responses, each of size $(N - m + 1) \times (N - m + 1)$. The CNN applies its nonlinearity as follows. The learned filter responses of size $(N - m + 1) \times (N - m + 1)$ are next average pooled with the square regions of size $l \times l$ and a stride size of s, to obtain a pooled response with the width and height equal to $N - l/s + 1$.

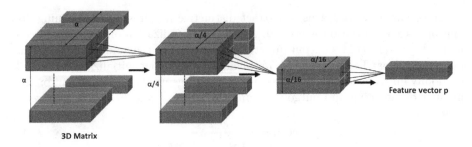

Fig. 3. Spatial hierarchical analysis network feature learning. 3D Matrix X (left most) from the CNN is given to hierarchy of RNNs, which merge 4 adjacent vectors to get the final feature p (right most).

The output of the CNN is a 3D matrix X of size $L \times \alpha \times \alpha$ for each input image. For a given 3D matrix X, a block of size $L \times \beta \times \beta$ consisting of adjacent vectors in the matrix X is defined, as shown in Fig. 3. Note that 4 adjacent vectors are used in the horizontal and vertical directions; β is therefore equal to 4 in this case. As a result, we get a block of size $L \times 4 \times 4$ where L $= 128$. The vectors in 3D matrix are then merged step-wise into the parent vector p (as shown in Fig. 3) by mapping the input $X \in \mathbb{R}^{128 \times 64 \times 64}$ to a representation $p \in \mathbb{R}^{128}$, as follows:

$$p^{(1)} = f(W^{(1)})X + b^{(1)} \tag{5}$$

$$p^{(2)} = f(W^{(2)})X + b^{(2)} \tag{6}$$

$$p = f(W^{(3)})X + b^{(3)} \tag{7}$$

where $W^{(i)}$, $i = 1,2,3,...$ is the parameter matrix, $f(.)$ is a non-linear activation function (*sigmoid* in this case), b is the bias vector, and $p^{(1)}$, $p^{(2)}$ and $p^{(3)}$ are matrices of dimension $\mathbb{R}^{L \times \alpha/4 \times \alpha/4}$, $\mathbb{R}^{L \times \alpha/16 \times \alpha/16}$ and $\mathbb{R}^{L}$, respectively. In our implementation, vector p is used as the feature vector to a softmax classifier. The input, output sizes and the parameters of our proposed network are reported in Table 1.

4   Experimental Results

The proposed deep neural network is evaluated on the publicly available Washington RGB-D [18] and 2D3D [6] datasets, which are widely used for benchmarking RGB-D object recognition techniques. In the following, we will briefly describe the datasets and compare our method against several state-of-the-art algorithms.

Table 1. Input, Output (feature sizes) and parameters of the proposed Spatial Hierarchical Analysis Deep Neural Network.

Description	Value/size
Input image	20×20
CNN filter bank size	128
Filter (width × height)	3×3
Pooling region size	10
Stride size	5
3D matrix (CNN feature)	$128 \times 64 \times 64$
RNN output (Feature vector)	128

4.1   Washington RGB-D Object Dataset

Washington RGB-D dataset contains 300 household object instances which are organized into 51 categories. Each instance is captured using Kinetic scanner on a revolving turntable from three elevation angles ($30°$, $45°$ and $60°$). We follow the experimental setup of Lai et al. [18] in our evaluation and use the same training/ testing splits and the cropped images as suggested by Lai et al. [18]. We then compute LBP features for each image and pass the image to the network for feature learning. Our object recognition results and comparison with state-of-the-art is reported in Table 2. Our proposed technique achieves object recognition accuracy of 89.8% on RGB-D images, the second best performance is achieved by CNN-colourized. Note that our approach achieves superior performance for all the modalities compared to existing RGB-D object recognition methods.

4.2   2D3D Object Dataset

2D3D object dataset contains 16 different categories of highly textured common objects (e.g. drink cartons, computer monitors). We follow the experimental protocol of Browatzki et al. [6] for a fair comparison. Due to the small number of examples, we specifically combine the spoon, knife and fork classes into a joint class of silverware and exclude phone and perforator. This makes a final dataset of 156 instances and 14 classes for category recognition. Our experimental results are reported in Table 3. The proposed approach achieves better performance compared to state-of-the-art methods.

The superior performance of the proposed network can be attributed to the hierarchical architecture of the deep neural network, which learns translationally invariant and distinctive features in the lower and higher levels of the architecture, respectively.

Table 2. Performance comparison in terms of recognition accuracy (in %) of the proposed technique with state-of-the-art methods on Washington RGB-D object dataset. The reported accuracy is an average over 10 trials.

Techniques	RGB	Depth	RGB-D
EMK-SIFT [18]	74.5 ± 3.1	64.7 ± 2.2	83.8 ± 3.5
Depth Kernel [4]	77.7 ± 1.9	78.8 ± 2.7	86.2 ± 2.1
CKM [3]	-	-	86.4 ± 2.3
HMP [5]	82.4 ± 2.1	81.2 ± 2.3	87.5 ± 2.9
SSL [8]	81.8 ± 1.9	77.7 ± 1.4	87.2 ± 1.1
Subset-RNN [2]	82.8 ± 3.4	81.8 ± 2.6	88.5 ± 3.1
CNN-colourized [25]	83.1 ± 2.0	-	89.4 ± 1.3
CaRF [1]	-	-	88.1 ± 2.4
LDELM [39]	78.6 ± 1.8	81.6 ± 0.7	88.3 ± 1.6
Proposed technique	84.2 ± 3.8	82.4 ± 1.2	89.8 ± 1.7

Table 3. Performance comparison in terms of recognition accuracy (in %) of the proposed technique with state-of-the-art methods on 2D3D Object Dataset.

Techniques	RGB	Depth	RGB-D
2D+3D [6]	66.6	74.6	82.8
HMP [5]	86.3	87.6	91.0
R^2ICA [14]	87.9	89.2	92.7
Subset-RNN [2]	88.0	90.2	92.8
Proposed technique	89.2	91.1	93.2

4.3   Computation/Implementation Details

These experiments were run on high performance computing devices with NVIDIA Titan V GPU and 128 GB RAM. Our code was implemented in MAT-LAB.

5   Conclusion and Future Directions

In this paper, we proposed a spatial hierarchical analysis deep neural network for RGB-D object recognition. The proposed network consists of CNN and RNNs to learn distinctive features in a hierarchical fashion. The tanslationally invariant features of CNN are analyzed and merged systematically using RNNs to get the most representative and descriptive feature for a given input image. The proposed technique has been tested on two publicly available RGB-D datasets for the task of object recognition. Our proposed deep neural network achieves state-of-the-art performance on these datasets.

In our implementation, our CNN generates a 3D matrix of size $128 \times 64 \times 64$, which is merged to get a final feature vector of size 128×1. As a future work, we intend to test a 3D matrix of higher dimensions and instead of merging 4 adjacent vectors (as done in this work), we intend to choose a bigger neighbourhood for combining these vectors. This will require more RNNs in the architecture and computational resources. In our technique, we have used sigmoid activation function, however, we believe that recognition performance can be further increased by using ReLU activation function.

Acknowledgment. The author would like to thank NVIDIA for their Titan-V GPU donation.

References

1. Asif, U., Bennamoun, M., Sohel, F.: Efficient RGB-D object categorization using cascaded ensembles of randomized decision trees. In: 2015 IEEE International Conference on Robotics and Automation (ICRA), pp. 1295–1302. IEEE (2015)
2. Bai, J., Wu, Y., Zhang, J., Chen, F.: Subset based deep learning for RGB-D object recognition. Neurocomputing **165**, 280–292 (2015)
3. Blum, M., Springenberg, J.T., Wülfing, J., Riedmiller, M.: A learned feature descriptor for object recognition in RGB-D data. In: 2012 IEEE International Conference on Robotics and Automation, pp. 1298–1303. IEEE (2012)
4. Bo, L., Ren, X., Fox, D.: Depth kernel descriptors for object recognition. In: 2011 IEEE/RSJ International Conference on Intelligent Robots and Systems, pp. 821–826. IEEE (2011)
5. Bo, L., Ren, X., Fox, D.: Unsupervised feature learning for RGB-D based object recognition. In: Desai, J., Dudek, G., Khatib, O., Kumar, V. (eds.) Experimental Robotics. Springer Tracts in Advanced Robotics, vol. 88, pp. 387–402. Springer, Heidelberg (2013). https://doi.org/10.1007/978-3-319-00065-7_27
6. Browatzki, B., Fischer, J., Graf, B., Bülthoff, H.H., Wallraven, C.: Going into depth: evaluating 2D and 3D cues for object classification on a new, large-scale object dataset. In: 2011 IEEE International Conference on Computer Vision Workshops (ICCV Workshops), pp. 1189–1195. IEEE (2011)
7. Chatfield, K., Simonyan, K., Vedaldi, A., Zisserman, A.: Return of the devil in the details: Delving deep into convolutional nets. arXiv preprint arXiv:1405.3531 (2014)
8. Cheng, Y., Zhao, X., Huang, K., Tan, T.: Semi-supervised learning for RGB-D object recognition. In: 2014 22nd International Conference on Pattern Recognition, pp. 2377–2382. IEEE (2014)
9. Coates, A., Ng, A., Lee, H.: An analysis of single-layer networks in unsupervised feature learning. In: Proceedings of the Fourteenth International Conference on Artificial Intelligence and Statistics, pp. 215–223 (2011)
10. Glorot, X., Bengio, Y.: Understanding the difficulty of training deep feedforward neural networks. In: Proceedings of the Thirteenth International Conference on Artificial Intelligence and Statistics, pp. 249–256 (2010)
11. Gupta, S., Girshick, R., Arbeláez, P., Malik, J.: Learning rich features from RGB-D images for object detection and segmentation. In: Fleet, D., Pajdla, T., Schiele, B., Tuytelaars, T. (eds.) ECCV 2014. LNCS, vol. 8695, pp. 345–360. Springer, Cham (2014). https://doi.org/10.1007/978-3-319-10584-0_23

12. Hariharan, B., Arbeláez, P., Girshick, R., Malik, J.: Hypercolumns for object segmentation and fine-grained localization. In: Proceedings of the IEEE Conference on Computer Vision and Pattern Recognition, pp. 447–456 (2015)
13. Hu, H., Shah, S.A.A., Bennamoun, M., Molton, M.: 2D and 3D face recognition using convolutional neural network. In: TENCON 2017–2017 IEEE Region 10 Conference, pp. 133–132. IEEE (2017)
14. Jhuo, I.-H., Gao, S., Zhuang, L., Lee, D.T., Ma, Y.: Unsupervised feature learning for RGB-D image classification. In: Cremers, D., Reid, I., Saito, H., Yang, M.-H. (eds.) ACCV 2014. LNCS, vol. 9003, pp. 276–289. Springer, Cham (2015). https://doi.org/10.1007/978-3-319-16865-4_18
15. Johnson, A.E., Hebert, M.: Using spin images for efficient object recognition in cluttered 3D scenes. IEEE Trans. Pattern Anal. Mach. Intell. **21**(5), 433–449 (1999)
16. Khan, S., Rahmani, H., Shah, S.A.A., Bennamoun, M.: A guide to convolutional neural networks for computer vision. Synth. Lect. Comput. Vis. **8**(1), 1–207 (2018)
17. Krizhevsky, A., Sutskever, I., Hinton, G.E.: Imagenet classification with deep convolutional neural networks. In: Advances in Neural Information Processing Systems, pp. 1097–1105 (2012)
18. Lai, K., Bo, L., Ren, X., Fox, D.: A large-scale hierarchical multi-view RGB-D object dataset. In: 2011 IEEE International Conference on Robotics and Automation, pp. 1817–1824. IEEE (2011)
19. Le, Q.V., Jaitly, N., Hinton, G.E.: A simple way to initialize recurrent networks of rectified linear units. arXiv preprint arXiv:1504.00941 (2015)
20. Lee, H., Pham, P., Largman, Y., Ng, A.Y.: Unsupervised feature learning for audio classification using convolutional deep belief networks. In: Advances in Neural Information Processing Systems, pp. 1096–1104 (2009)
21. Liu, L., Shen, C., van den Hengel, A.: The treasure beneath convolutional layers: cross-convolutional-layer pooling for image classification. In: Proceedings of the IEEE Conference on Computer Vision and Pattern Recognition, pp. 4749–4757 (2015)
22. Liu, W., Ji, R., Li, S.: Towards 3D object detection with bimodal deep Boltzmann machines over RGBD imagery. In: Proceedings of the IEEE Conference on Computer Vision and Pattern Recognition, pp. 3013–3021 (2015)
23. Lowe, D.G.: Distinctive image features from scale-invariant keypoints. Int. J. Comput. Vis. **60**(2), 91–110 (2004)
24. Nadeem, U., Shah, S.A.A., Bennamoun, M., Togneri, R., Sohel, F.: Image set classification for low resolution surveillance. arXiv preprint arXiv:1803.09470 (2018)
25. Schwarz, M., Schulz, H., Behnke, S.: RGB-D object recognition and pose estimation based on pre-trained convolutional neural network features. In: 2015 IEEE International Conference on Robotics and Automation (ICRA), pp. 1329–1335. IEEE (2015)
26. Shah, S., Bennamoun, M., Boussaid, F., El-Sallam, A.: A novel local surface description for automatic 3D object recognition in low resolution cluttered scenes. In: Proceedings of the IEEE International Conference on Computer Vision Workshops, pp. 638–643 (2013)
27. Shah, S.A., Nadeem, U., Bennamoun, M., Sohel, F., Togneri, R.: Efficient image set classification using linear regression based image reconstruction. In: Proceedings of the IEEE Conference on Computer Vision and Pattern Recognition Workshops, pp. 99–108 (2017)

28. Shah, S.A.A., Bennamoun, M., Boussaid, F.: Performance evaluation of 3D local surface descriptors for low and high resolution range image registration. In: 2014 International Conference on Digital Image Computing: Techniques and Applications (DICTA), pp. 1–7. IEEE (2014)
29. Shah, S.A.A., Bennamoun, M., Boussaid, F.: A novel 3D vorticity based approach for automatic registration of low resolution range images. Pattern Recogn. **48**(9), 2859–2871 (2015)
30. Shah, S.A.A., Bennamoun, M., Boussaid, F.: Iterative deep learning for image set based face and object recognition. Neurocomputing **174**, 866–874 (2016)
31. Shah, S.A.A., Bennamoun, M., Boussaid, F.: A novel feature representation for automatic 3D object recognition in cluttered scenes. Neurocomputing **205**, 1–15 (2016)
32. Shah, S.A.A., Bennamoun, M., Boussaid, F.: Keypoints-based surface representation for 3D modeling and 3D object recognition. Pattern Recogn. **64**, 29–38 (2017)
33. Shah, S.A.A., Bennamoun, M., Boussaid, F., El-Sallam, A.A.: 3D-div: a novel local surface descriptor for feature matching and pairwise range image registration. In: 2013 IEEE International Conference on Image Processing, pp. 2934–2938. IEEE (2013)
34. Shah, S.A.A., Bennamoun, M., Boussaid, F., El-Sallam, A.A.: Automatic object detection using objectness measure. In: 2013 1st International Conference on Communications, Signal Processing, and Their Applications (ICCSPA), pp. 1–6. IEEE (2013)
35. Shah, S.A.A., Bennamoun, M., Boussaid, F., While, L.: Evolutionary feature learning for 3-D object recognition. IEEE Access **6**, 2434–2444 (2017)
36. Shah, S.A.A., Bennamoun, M., Molton, M.: A fully automatic framework for prediction of 3D facial rejuvenation. In: 2018 International Conference on Image and Vision Computing New Zealand (IVCNZ), pp. 1–6. IEEE (2018)
37. Shah, S.A.A., Bennamoun, M., Molton, M.K.: Machine learning approaches for prediction of facial rejuvenation using real and synthetic data. IEEE Access **7**, 23779–23787 (2019)
38. Sharif Razavian, A., Azizpour, H., Sullivan, J., Carlsson, S.: CNN features off-the-shelf: an astounding baseline for recognition. In: Proceedings of the IEEE Conference on Computer Vision and Pattern Recognition Workshops, pp. 806–813 (2014)
39. Zaki, H.F., Shafait, F., Mian, A.: Localized deep extreme learning machines for efficient RGB-D object recognition. In: 2015 International Conference on Digital Image Computing: Techniques and Applications (DICTA), pp. 1–8. IEEE (2015)

Reading Digital Video Clocks by Two Phases of Connected Deep Networks

Xinguo Yu$^{(\boxtimes)}$, Zhiping Chen$^{(\boxtimes)}$, and Hao Meng$^{(\boxtimes)}$

National Engineering Research Center for E-Learning,
Central China Normal University, Wuhan 430079, China
xgyu@mail.ccnu.edu.cn, {zpchen,menghao}@mails.ccnu.edu.cn

Abstract. This paper presents an algorithm for reading digital video clocks by using two phases of connected deep networks to avoid the demerits of existing heuristic algorithms. The problem of reading digital video clocks can divided into two phases: locating the clock area and reading the clock digits. First, a phase of connected deep networks is a chain of neural networks to localize the clock area. Each of these neural networks takes use the properties of the working digital video clocks to work on one task. Its key step is to localize the place of second place by using the constancy and the periodicity of the pixels belong to second place. Second, the other phase of deep networks is a batch of custom digit recognizers that are designed based on deep networks and the properties of the working digital video clocks. The proposed method gets rid of the tedious heuristic procedure to find the accurate locations of all digits. Thus this paper forms the first algorithm that key tasks are taken by different neural networks. The experimental results show that the proposed algorithm can achieve a high accuracy in localizing and reading all the digits of clocks.

Keywords: Clock area localization · Digits recognition · YOLO · Text localization

1 Introduction

Reading digital video clocks (or called time recognition) is an active research problem because the clock time plays a critical role in video event detection and event inference [1,2,7,8,13–17]. This paper considers the common case in which a digital video clock has been superimposed on video. Although current videos already have a text channel that can be used to store the encoded clock or timestamp information, the algorithm presented in this paper does not need to use these encoded clocks or timestamps. Most sports and surveillance videos have superimposed digital video clocks or timestamps for various reasons – such as to show game-related time in sports videos or to show the time of the recording in surveillance videos. For, example, the video clock in a soccer video indicates the game time lapsed at the current frame, whereas the reversely-running video clock

© Springer Nature Switzerland AG 2020
J. J. Dabrowski et al. (Eds.): PSIVT 2019 Workshops, LNCS 11994, pp. 194–205, 2020.
https://doi.org/10.1007/978-3-030-39770-8_16

in a basketball video indicates the remaining game time at the current frame. In surveillance videos and sports videos recorded from TV programs by digital recorders, superimposed digital video clock or timestamps is one method guard against malicious tampering of the encoded timestamp information stored in the text channel [1, 2, 7, 8, 13–17]. Hence, it is highly desired to develop the algorithms for reading the superimposed digital video clocks, independently of the clock or timestamp encoded in the text channel.

Reading digital video clocks is a special case of reading text from videos that is a very challenging problem [3, 9, 11]. The recent algorithms for reading text based on the sliding window scanning and deep networks, being a kind of region-based method [4–6, 10–12]. This region-based method reaches the best performance (accuracy in 83.3%) for object detection [12]. The flow of this method includes the steps of generating candidate regions and then detecting the object within the candidate regions. The detection accuracy of this method depends on the recall of identifying candidate regions. Although region-based methods employs inexpensive features to do the selective search of candidate regions. It still requires much running time for detection task. YOLO (You Only Look Once) [12] was proposed in 2016 to predicts bounding boxes and class probabilities directly from full images in one evaluation. It is quickly applied to solve the various problems due to that it is simple, fast, and high performance [12]. However, YOLO has not applied to the problem of reading digital video clocks.

The researchers have been designing custom algorithms for reading clocks since no general algorithms can have a satisfactory performance for reading text from images or videos [1, 2, 7, 8, 14–17]. The problem of reading digital video clocks can be divided into two sub-problems: clock-area localization and clock-digit recognition. The first sub-problem is a special case of the general text (character) localization problem. The second sub-problem is a special case of the text recognition problem within the text area. This problem appears after the text area is localized. The researchers have proposed a batch of methods designed custom methods for these two problems [1, 2, 7, 8, 14–17]. In the early years, multiple algorithms adopted image processing approach to localize clock digits in video [1, 2]. These algorithms only have a low accuracy. Then, some improved algorithms were proposed [7, 8]. They use the method based on clock digit periodicity to verify the localized characters, but they still use image processing approach to localize the candidates of clock digits. Particularly, they find the character candidates by doing character segmentation and the connected component analysis (CCA) on the detected clock board. Then they monitor all character candidates to find the one whose color change is approximately of secondly periodicity, called region periodicity. They are tedious yet not as robust due to they use error-prone process of character segmentation and CCA.

In 2012 a pixel periodicity method was proposed and a custom algorithm based on this method was proposed to localize clock digits that discarded the tedious image processing components in [14]. This paper designed a set of functions to describe the second pixel periodicity and the heuristic algorithm of using those functions achieved 100% of accuracy on the second-digit place localization.

However, the algorithm is a custom one but it is not a neural network algorithm and the thresholds in those functions were set manually but not through a learning process. The periodicity of the value change of the s-digit pixel disclosed in [14,15] can be used to design the algorithm for reading clocks, but it is difficult in designing the features to represent this periodicity. Hence, a batch of mathematical functions is designed to describe this periodicity. Additionally, the algorithm in [14,15] only uses the periodicity of second-digit place pixels but the constancy of neighbouring second-digit place pixels.

With the advance of deep network and the high performance of YOLO this paper is to use a batch of neural networks, particularly YOLO, to replace the heuristic components in the algorithm presented in [14,15], aiming to eliminate the demerits of the algorithm. The general idea is to use the properties of working digital video clocks to customize the deep networks to form the deep networks or the connected deep works to conduct the tasks of reading digital video clocks. The convolutional neural networks (CNNs) is first used to identify the relatively constancy pixels. Then based on [14,15], a frame-aligned pixel recognition network (PRN) is proposed to identify the s-digit pixels that their color values change periodically within the neighbour pixels of the identified constancy pixels. Compared to the functions it gets rid of the job of setting thresholds for functions. More importantly, deep networks parameters have potential to take use of the properties of digital video clocks better than the heuristic functions. After the second-digit place is localized, the area that contains all the digits of the clock can be decided. The remaining task is to localize and recognize all the digits in this area. This paper proposes two YOLO based procedures that mainly take YOLO framework with the customized deep networks. Thus, two heuristic procedures of finding the bounding boxes of digits and recognizing the clock digits in [14,15] were done by the neural networks.

The rest of the paper is organized as follows. Section 2 presents the technical details of the proposed algorithm for reading digital video clocks. Experimental results are presented in Sect. 3. Section 4 concludes the paper.

2   Two Phases of Deep Networks for Reading Clocks

2.1   Notations and Overview of the Proposed Algorithm

This paper divides the problem of reading digital video clock into two tasks: clock area localization and clock digit recognition. The task of clock area localization is to find the area that contains all the digits of a clock; and the task of clock digit recognition is to identify each digit and recognize it. For the first task, a phase of customized deep networks are proposed. It first uses a CNN based procedure to identify the constancy pixels; then it is to localize s-digit place by pixel recognition network (PRN) and YOLO [12] with Clock-Digit Recognition Network (CDRN) as its first several layers. The CDRN is an clock digit classifier network which based on the deep network proposed by LeCunn in paper [4]. In our paper, CDRN is the base of YOLO, which is used for feature extraction of digit in video clock. The CDRN only trained for 11 classes, which contains the digit classes of from 0 to 9 and the clock area of none-digit. The YOLO localizes the bounding box of s-digit. Then we localizes clock area based on the bounding box of s-digit. Finally in this clock area, sliding the bounding box of s-digit with YOLO to do the localization and recognition of other digits.

Definition 1: (s-digit, x-digit) In video clock, a digit on the second place of the clock is called as an s-digit; any digit representing ten second, minute, and ten minute in video clock are called as an x-digit.

An algorithm for reading video clocks is described in Algorithm 1. The proposed algorithm for detecting digital video clocks has two main phases: clock area localization and clock digit recognition.

Algorithm 1: Reading working digital video digit clocks

Input: A video with a working digital video clock
Output: The time representing by four digits and the frame number of appearing this time

1 *Phase 1: localizing the clock area by a phase of connected neural networks*
2 *1.1: Find constancy pixels from the video by a CNN*
3 *1.2: Find s-digit pixel around pixel by PRN*
4 Then we can use Sliding-CDRN to do the localization and recongnition of other digit in clock area
5 *1.3: Use CDRN and YOLO to get s-digit bounding box*
6 *1.4: Get clock area based on s-digit bounding box*
7 *Phase 2: Reading the four clock digits by another phase of connected neural networks*
8 *Use 3-digit sequence with CDRN to read s-digits in the bounding box of s-digit*
9 *Use Sliding-CDRN to read x-digits within the clock area*

2.2   A Phase of Deep Networks for Localizing the Clock Area

This section presents a phase of neural networks for localizing the clock area by taking use of the properties of digital clocks.

Some Properties of S-Digit Pixels. Some properties of s-digit pixels are presented so that the proposed methods can be understood. Figure 2 shows the flow of this pixel periodicity on the s-digit place. Refer paper [15] for some notations and concepts used in this paper, and relevant formulae for computing the s-digit bounding box are presented.

Let W and H be the width and the height of the images of a given video. Let B be the set of all pixels within an image. Let F_i be the considered frame. Then $F_{i-R}, F_{i-R+1}, ..., F_{i-1}$ and $F_i, F_{i+1}, ..., F_{i+R-1}$ are the R frames in the preceding second and the succeeding second, respectively. Let $c(k, p)$ be the grey value of pixel p in frame F_k. Then we have following definitions.

Definition 2: (Constancy Pixel) Let F_k for $k = 1$ to be L frames including at least 3 second consecutive frames. Pixel p is called as a constancy pixel if it meets the following condition.

$$|c(k,p) - C_1| < \beta_1 \text{ for } k = i \text{ to } L, \text{ where } C_1 = \frac{1}{L}\sum_{k=1}^{L} c(k,p); \text{ where } \beta_1 \text{ is a}$$

threshold.

Definition 3: (Constancy Adjacency Pixel) A non-constancy pixel (NCP) is called as a constancy adjacency pixel (CAP) if it is a neighbour pixel of a constancy pixel (CP), i.e. $dist(NCP, CP_i) < \beta_2$.

We design a CNN based procedure to identify the constancy pixels according to Definition 2. It uses the mean of pixel values and the variances of pixel values to identify the constancy pixels. After getting constancy pixels, all of the constancy adjacency pixels can be found according to Definition 3. Next, PRN is used to find s-digit pixel in the constancy adjacency pixels .

Finding the S-Digit Pixels with the Periodicity of S-Digit Pixels. We localize the pixels belong to s-digit place by finding the pixel pairs of a constancy pixel and a pixel with the periodicity. A sample of the periodic variation of the gray value of the second pixel is shown in Fig. 2.

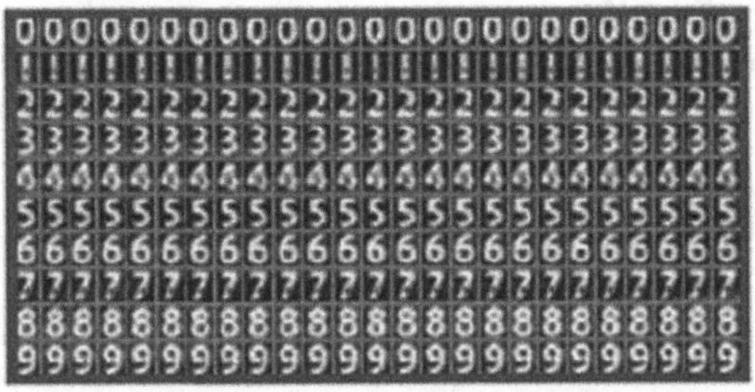

Fig. 1. The number of digits in the digital box changes continuously for 10 s (the video frame rate is 25 fps), and the red dot indicates one of the second pixels. (Color figure online)

As shown in Fig. 1, during frame conversion of s-digit pixels, the change of second pixel gray value is significantly larger than other time periods. Thus, we proposed an efficient pixel recognition network based on frame-align. We convert the $n\_seconds * 25$ length frame sequence into a $n\_seconds * 25$ two-dimensional matrix, so that their transit-frames are aligned just as Fig. 3. the structure of CDRN showed in Fig. 4.

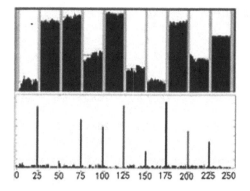

Fig. 2. The upper figure shows the gray value map of the second pixel point (red dot) for 10 consecutive seconds, and the lower one shows the gray value map of the frame difference for 10 consecutive seconds. (Color figure online)

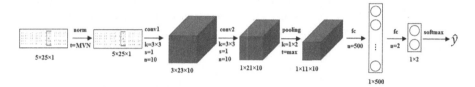

Fig. 3. The structure of PRN, its data input is shown, k indicates kernel size, s indicates stride and n indicates the number of conv layer.

The reason why the PRN could recognize s-digit pixel well. During the frame conversion, the difference of gray-values is obvious. However, the values in other conditions are constant. Through the frame alignment, the pixel data stream would be transferred into two-dimensional, and regarding the pixel data stream as a gray image. In the gray image, the change of second-pixel gray value is periodic. Which causes larger gray values existing in adjacent columns. Thus, gray image features can be seen as some vertical stripes, and the pixel recognition network (Based CNN) can learn these features. The experiment results shows that the pixel recognition network is generalized to detect certain periodic problems and contains better learning performance.

S-Digit Localization: CNNs [4] and YOLO [12] are customized to get the bounding box of s-digit. The CDRN is used for clock digit feature extraction inside of the area identified by YOLO. As shown in Fig. 4, the structure of CDRN is designed more simpler than ResNet-50 and DarkNet-19 because the CDRN only recognizes clock digits.

Deciding the Clock Area: A procedure is designed to decide the clock area based on the preceding outcomes such as the found s-digit place and the following

```
layer           filters    size      input              ouput
  0 conv          32       5×5/1     52×52×1      ->    52×52×32
  1 conv          32       5×5/1     52×52×32     ->    52×52×32
  2 max                    2×2/2     52×52×32     ->    26×26×32
  3 conv          64       3×3/1     26×26×32     ->    26×26×64
  4 conv          64       3×3/1     26×26×64     ->    26×26×64
  5 max                    2×2/2     26×26×64     ->    13×13×64
  6 route 2
  7 conv          64       1×1/1     26×26×32     ->    26×26×64
  8 reorg                  /2        26×26×64     ->    13×13×256
  9 route 8 5
 10 conv          256      3×3/1     13×13×320    ->    13×13×256
 11 conv          80       1×1/1     13×13×256    ->    13×13×80
 12 detection
```

Fig. 4. The structure of YOLO with CDRN. the structure of 0–5 layers is CDRN, and the structure of layers of 6–12 is the rest of YOLO. The 9th layer is the combination of the output of 5th layer and 8th layer, In the 11th layer, the number of filters is 80, because each grid in YOLO predicts 5 boxes and each boxe has 16 parameters. which contains 11 classes probabilities, 4 coordinate parameters for each box and 1 confidence.

two facts: (1) digits in clock area usually are the same in color and bounding box size. (2) the pixels around clock area are background, which are constant. Based on this two facts, we can localize clock area by s-digit bounding box.

2.3 Reading Clock Digits by a Phase of Deep Networks

A CDRN based procedure is proposed to localize and recognize s-digits in the found clock area because the traditional OCR can not achieve a satisfactory performance for this task.

Custom Networks for Localizing and Recognizing Clock Digits. After finding the bounding box of s-digit by YOLO with CDRN. We use digit sequence to recognize s-digit by CDRN. This procedure is built based on the following facts. Frames from $t + k * R + 1$ to $t + (k + 1) * R$ have the same s-digit if frame t is s-digit transit frame because the s-digit transits every R frames. Thus, the s-digit in the frames $t + k * R + 1$ to $t + (k + 1) * R$ is number k if the s-digit in the frames from t to $t + R$ is "0". In other words, the s-digits in the frames from t to $t + v * R$ form a digit periodic increasing sequence according to the clock knowledge, supposed that the input clip is v second long ($v < 10$). Based on these facts, we use 3-digit sequence CNN recognition procedure for finding both s-digit transit frames and recognizing s-digits, denoted as Procedure I.

Procedure I: The digit sequence Clock-Digit Recognition Network recognition procedure

---

Input: A 4 second long clip with single clock and the bounding box of each
       s-digit

Output: The first frame number that all the s-digits are correctly recognized
       and the recognized s-digits on each frame for each clock

1   Let $s = 0$, $e = R$, and $m = [(s + e)/2]$;

2   **while** $e \mathrel{!}= s$ **do**

3   Sequence $1 = F_s$, F_{s+R}, F_{s+2R}, Sequence $2 = F_m$, F_{m+R}, F_{m+2R}, Sequence
       $3 = F_e$, F_{e+R}, F_{e+2R};

4   Use the trained Clock-Digit Recognition Network to recognize these three
       3-digit sequences;

5   **if** *all the recognized results of Sequence 1 to 3 are the same or different* **then**

6 | return the clock is not a proper running clock;

7   **end**

8   **if** *the recognized results of Sequence 1 and 2 are the same* **then**

9 | $s = m$, $m = [(s + e)/2]$;

10   **end**

11   **if** *the recognized results of Sequence 2 and 3 are the same* **then**

12 | $e = m$, $m = [(s + e)/2]$;

13   **end**

14   **if** $s = e$ **then**

15   return frame s is the s-digit transit frame and the number on frame s,
        terminate the procedure;

16   **end**

17 **end**

Procedure II: The sliding-Clock-Digit Recognition Network recognition
and localization procedure

Input: A 4 second long clip of clock-area with running clocks

Output: The localization and recognition x-digits on each frame for each
      clock

1   An odd number v is the parameter of this procedure, indicating how
    many instances are recognized at the same time;

2   Denote the first s-digit transit frame as s, then each x-digit place has the
    same digit in frame s to frame $s + 75$;

3 **for** *Sliding s-digit box in clock area* **do**

4 | use CDRN to get label and probabilities for this box;

5 | save (label, probabilities, localization) for this box;

6 **end**

7 delete none-digit box;

8 use Non-Maximum Suppression(NMS)[9] to get all x-digits include box
    and label;

Once s-digit transit frames are known by Procedure I, all the transit frames for all x-digits are known. Thus, we can take at least 50 frames with the same digit for any x-digit from a 4 second long clip (Notice that our video is 25 frames per second). Hence an odd number of frames from these 50 frames can be selected to recognize an x-digit in Procedure II.

3   Experimental Results

The algorithm for reading digital video clocks is implemented in C++. To evaluate the proposed algorithm of dataset is built. This dataset comprises of 300 broadcast soccer videos and 300 broadcast basketball videos, where each clip is 15 second long. Each of 300 broadcast soccer videos has a single clock; each of 300 broadcast basketball videos has two clocks. All clocks in the clips are working clocks. These clips vary in digit color, digit background color, size, and font.

By setting different threshold parameters, the CPP method [15] can achieve good results, but these threshold parameters are difficult to set. Our experimental data was collected based on CPP method and the threshold parameters provided.

3.1   Experiments on the S-Digit Pixel Identification

In order to verify the effectiveness of Pixel Recognition Network (PRN), this paper compares it with several commonly used methods, namely SVM, FCN (fully connected network). PRN is implemented by caffe(c++) and its detail described in Sect. 2. We use libraries of libsvm(c++, svm_type=c_svc, kernel_type=rbf) and FCN(layer=[125, 10, 2], activation=sigmoid) implemented by caffe(c++). The results are presented in Table 1.
Train: 20162 positive samples, 21003 negative samples
Test: 20143 positive samples, 20925 negative samples

Table 1. Comparison with SVM, and FCN for recognizing s-digit pixel in Test

Algorithm	PRN	SVM	FCN
Accuracy in %	99.6	96.2	82.8
Precision in %	99.4	95.2	81.0
Recall in %	99.7	97.2	87.3
F1 score in %	99.5	96.2	84.0
Time (s)	1.28	1.15	0.89

According to Table 1 we draw the following conclusions. First, the recall value of the proposed method is generally higher than the precise value, due to the amount of none-s-digit pixel larger than the s-digit pixel around the stable pixel. Second, during the periodicity of the s-digit pixel, the result of Pixel Recognition Network (PRN) is relatively best with a little time consumption. In addition, the PRN can be generalized to detect certain periodic problems.

3.2   Experiments on Finding the S-Digit Bounding Box

According to the s-digit pixel detected in Sect. 2, we can generate the s-digit region, and then we use the Clock-Digit Recognition Network (CDRN) and YOLO to get s-digit bounding box. Unlike general YOLO detection framework, we use Clock-Digit Recognition Network as the backbone instead of the commonly used as VGG, ResNet, and DarkNet. The Clock-Digit Recognition Network structure is simpler as shown in Table 2 and is more suitable for feature extraction of video clock digit. The Clock-Digit Recognition Network is improved on the basis of LeNet-5. The experiments show that the Clock-Digit Recognition Network extracts the digital features of the video clock better.

In this step, we use the algorithm presented in [14, 15] to collect a variety of s-digit region images amounted 2w+ by setting best threshold parameters. The training set contains 10435 and the test set is 10779. Then we convert dataset to a gray image and resize 8 times larger, which makes s-digit region's resolution higher. The result of localizing s-digit bounding box showed in Table 2.

Table 2. The result of the localizing s-digit bounding box in Test

Backbone	IOU	Time (s)
ResNet-50	0.79	0.53
DarkNet-19	0.77	0.33
Clock-Digit Recognition Network	0.79	0.25

From the Table 2 we can draw following conclusions. First, our method locates the bounding box of s-digit more accurately and with minimal time. Second, compared with ResNet-50, the structure of Clock-Digit Recognition Network (CDRN) is simpler in structure, and the effect of localizing s-digit is the same. Third, it can be proved that CDRN is more suitable for extracting clock digital features.

3.3   Experiments on Clock Digit Localization and Recognition in Clock Area

In this step, we use the algorithms in [14, 15] by setting best threshold parameters to collect a variety of clock area images amounted 2w+. Next, we use sliding-CRDN to locate and recognize digits in clock area showed in Sect. 3 Procedure II. The library is caffe(c++), and the result showed in Table 3. The accuracy indicates ratio of digits recognized correctly account for all digits in total clock areas.

Table 3. The result of the recognition in clock area

Algorithm	Time (s)	Accuracy
Sliding-CDRN	0.42	0.94

4   Conclusions and Future Work

This paper has presented an algorithm for reading digital video clocks to eliminate the demerits of existing heuristic algorithms by using two phases of connected neural networks. The first phase of neural networks is used to localize the clock area. This phase of neural networks takes the approach that first find the s-digit place and then expands to obtain the clock area. The second phase of neural networks adopts YOLO as framework and uses the deep networks customized by making use of properties of digital clocks to work as the bases of YOLO. The experimental results has showed that the proposed algorithm can achieve a high accuracy in second digit localization and reading all the digits of clocks. This paper has the following contributions. First, a pixel recognition network (based on frame alignment) to identify the periodic s-digit pixels. This is the first neural network that can identify individual pixels by taking use of the periodicity of pixel values. Second, it proposed the first algorithm constituted by a batch of neural networks to localize and recognize s-digit and x-digits. Compared to the method that uses a batch of functions to localize s-digit place, it gets rid of the job of setting thresholds for functions. And the trained deep networks have potential to take use of the properties of digital video clocks better than the heuristic functions.

The two future jobs can be done to enhance the proposed algorithm. First, it is to improve the algorithm design to achieve an accuracy of 100% to reach the accuracy level of the existing heuristic algorithms. Second, it is to further integrate the connected deep networks into one whole deep network as YOLO localizes and recognize object in one pipe.

References

1. Bu, F., Sun, L.-F., Ding, X.-F., Miao, Y.-J., Yang, S.-Q.: Detect and recognize clock time in sports video. In: Huang, Y.-M.R., et al. (eds.) PCM 2008. LNCS, vol. 5353, pp. 306–316. Springer, Heidelberg (2008). https://doi.org/10.1007/978-3-540-89796-5_32
2. Covavisaruch, N., Saengpanit, C.: Time stamp detection and recognition in video frames. In: CISST, pp. 173–178 (2004)
3. Hanif, S.M., Prevost, L.: Text detection and localization in complex scene images using constrained Adaboost algorithm. In: 10th International Conference on Document Analysis and Recognition, ICDAR 2009, pp. 1–5. IEEE (2009)
4. LeCun, Y., Bottou, L., Bengio, Y., Haffner, P., et al.: Gradient-based learning applied to document recognition. Proc. IEEE 86(11), 2278–2324 (1998)

5. Lee, J.J., Lee, P.H., Lee, S.W., Yuille, A., Koch, C.: Adaboost for text detection in natural scene. In: 2011 International Conference on Document Analysis and Recognition, pp. 429–434. IEEE (2011)
6. Li, Y., He, K., Sun, J., et al.: R-FCN: object detection via region-based fully convolutional networks. In: Advances in Neural Information Processing Systems, pp. 379–387 (2016)
7. Li, Y., Wan, K., Yan, X., Yu, X., Xu, C.: Video clock time recognition based on temporal periodic pattern change of the digit characters. In: 2006 IEEE International Conference on Acoustics Speech and Signal Processing Proceedings, vol. 2, p. II. IEEE (2006)
8. Li, Y., Xu, C., Wan, K.W., Yan, X., Yu, X.: Reliable video clock time recognition. In: 18th International Conference on Pattern Recognition, ICPR 2006, vol. 4, pp. 128–131. IEEE (2006)
9. Neubeck, A., Van Gool, L.: Efficient non-maximum suppression. In: 18th International Conference on Pattern Recognition, ICPR 2006, vol. 3, pp. 850–855, August 2006
10. Ren, S., He, K., Girshick, R., Sun, J.: Faster R-CNN: towards real-time object detection with region proposal networks. In: Advances in Neural Information Processing Systems, pp. 91–99 (2015)
11. Shahab, A., Shafait, F., Dengel, A.: ICDAR 2011 robust reading competition challenge 2: reading text in scene images. In: 2011 International Conference on Document Analysis and Recognition, pp. 1491–1496. IEEE (2011)
12. Shi, C., Wang, C., Xiao, B., Zhang, Y., Gao, S.: Scene text detection using graph model built upon maximally stable extremal regions. Pattern Recogn. Lett. **34**(2), 107–116 (2013)
13. Xu, C., Wang, J., Wan, K., Li, Y., Duan, L.: Live sports event detection based on broadcast video and web-casting text. In: ACM International Conference on Multimedia, Santa Barbara, CA, USA, pp. 221–230, October 2006
14. Yu, X.: Localization and extraction of the four clock-digits using the knowledge of the digital video clock. In: 2012 21st International Conference on Pattern Recognition (ICPR), pp. 1217–1220. IEEE (2012)
15. Yu, X., Ding, W., Zeng, Z., Leong, H.W.: Reading digital video clocks. Int. J. Pattern Recogn. Artif. Intell. **29**(04), 1555006 (2015)
16. Yu, X., Li, L., Leong, H.W.: Interactive broadcast services for live soccer video based on instant semantics acquisition. J. Vis. Commun. Image Represent. **20**(2), 117–130 (2009)
17. Yu, X., Li, Y., San Lee, W.: Robust time recognition of video clock based on digit transition detection and digit-sequence recognition. In: 2008 19th International Conference on Pattern Recognition, pp. 1–4. IEEE (2008)

Author Index

Printed in the United States
By Bookmasters

Lecture Notes
in Business Information Processing 405

More information about this series at http://www.springer.com/series/7911

Adiel Teixeira de Almeida ·
Danielle Costa Morais (Eds.)

Innovation for Systems Information and Decision

Second International Meeting, INSID 2020
Recife, Brazil, December 2–4, 2020
Proceedings

 Springer

Editors
Adiel Teixeira de Almeida (iD)
Federal Univ of Pernambuco
Recife, Pernambuco, Brazil

Danielle Costa Morais (iD)
Departamento de Engenharia de Producao
Universidade Federal de Pernambuco
Recife, Pernambuco, Brazil

ISSN 1865-1348   ISSN 1865-1356   (electronic)
Lecture Notes in Business Information Processing
ISBN 978-3-030-64398-0   ISBN 978-3-030-64399-7   (eBook)
https://doi.org/10.1007/978-3-030-64399-7

This Springer imprint is published by the registered company Springer Nature Switzerland AG
The registered company address is: Gewerbestrasse 11, 6330 Cham, Switzerland

Preface

The INnovation for Systems Information and Decision meeting (INSID) is an event (http://insid.events) linked to the international network INCT-INSID (http://insid.org.br). This network involves academics and practitioners from different countries, bringing together outstanding researchers from around the world in the field of Information Systems and Decision.

The INSID meetings have provided a stimulating environment for the dissemination of state-of-the-art knowledge about innovation for systems, information, and decision. This broad theme is transversely related to many areas, particularly to operational research, management engineering (or production engineering), including also, system engineering (and engineering in general), management science, computer science, and their interdisciplinary related areas. These meetings have allowed discussions among participants as well as the exchange of ideas and critical comments for further improvement since 2008, under the acronym SIDS.

INSID 2020 should have been held at the Federal University of Pernambuco, in Recife-Pernambuco, Brazil, during December 2–4, 2020. However, due to the COVID-19 pandemic, it took place virtually. This was the first time that the event happened in an online format since 2008. However, this was not the only reason it was a historic meeting. This is the first volume of the INSID meeting included in the *Lecture Notes in Business Information Processing* (LNBIP) series.

In total, 84 papers were approved for presentation covering the main topics related to themes and areas of interest of the meeting as follows: Methodological advances in decision making and aid; decision models in the environmental context; decision models in the energy context; decision models in the service systems; and, potential applications of decision and negotiation models. After a thorough review process, 8 of these papers were selected for inclusion in this volume entitled *INnovation for Systems Information and Decision: Models and Applications*.

These selected papers reflect methodological improvements and advances in Multicriteria Decision-Making/Multicriteria Decision-Aid (MCDM/MCDA) oriented toward real-world applications, contributing to the understanding of relevant developments of current research on, and future trends of, innovation for systems, information, and decision.

The first paper by Danielson and Ekenberg explores and tests a robust multicriteria weight generating method under uncertainty covering a wide set of decision situations and exemplify its application with a problem of selecting strategies for combatting COVID-19. Then, a paper by von Nitzsch, Tönsfeuerborn, and Siebert introduces the ENTSCHEIDUNGSNAVI, a multi-criteria decision support system, which besides the basic functionalities of a decision support system, provides training to improve the user's decision-making skills. The third paper by Angelo and Lins deals with a combination of Soft and Hard Operational Research (OR) presenting a multimethodology named Complex Holographic Assessment of Paradoxical Problems (CHAP^2) applied to a complex health system.

Zaraté presents the results of multicultural experiments in order to see whether decision-makers feel comfortable with shared preferences and how the need to use private preferences could be seen using a multicriteria Group Decision Support System (GDSS) called GRUS. Eufrazio and Costa propose a synthetic index of quality life for OECD countries called Synthetic Better Life Index (SBLI). It follows a study by Xu, Liu, Kilgour, and Hipel, which presents a new algebraic definition to facilitate calculating of Stackelberg stability in a graph model for conflict resolution with two decision-makers, and a superpower military confrontation is used to illustrate how Stackelberg stability can be applied to a real-world problem.

Fossile, Costa, and Lima deal with a study on the development of a sustainable measurement model of renewable energy sources, aiming to identify the most adequate energy source to be used in Brazilian ports. Finally, the eighth paper by Cunha, Mota, de Almeida, Frej, and Roselli presents an application related to security in the Brazilian Federal Police, applying Value Focused Thinking with the FITradeoff method for the assignment of priorities regarding special operations.

The preparation of this volume required the efforts and collaboration of many people. In particular, we would like to thank the Steering Committee and Program Committee for their contributions to the INSID 2020. Special thanks also go to all members of the INCT-INSID network. We are also very grateful to the following reviewers for their timely and informative additional reviews: Marc Kilgour, Liping Fang, Ana Paula Gusmão, Mischel Carmen Belderrain, Eduarda Frej, Leandro Rego, Maisa M. Silva, Carolina Lino, Luciana Hazin, and Ana Paula Cabral.

We would also like to thank Ralf Gerstner, Alfred Hofmann, Christine Reiss, Guido Zosimo-Landolfo, and Anna Kramer at Springer for the excellent collaboration.

Finally, we hope readers will find the content of this book useful and stimulating for further developments and applications of innovation for systems, information, and decision.

December 2020   Adiel Teixeira de Almeida
                                                                  Danielle Costa Morais

Organization

Program Chair

Danielle Costa Morais   Universidade Federal de Pernambuco, Brazil

Steering Committee

Adiel Teixeira de Almeida	Universidade Federal de Pernambuco, Brazil
Keith Hipel	University of Waterloo, Canada
Love Ekenberg	Stockholm University,Sweden
Marc Kilgour	Wilfrid Laurier University, Canada
Pascale Zarate	Université Toulouse 1 Capitole, France
Ralph Keeney	Duke University and University of Southern California, USA
Roman Slowinski	Poznań University of Technology, Poland
Rudolf Vetschera	University of Vienna, Austria
Petr Ekel	Pontifícia Universidade Católica do Minas Gerais, Brazil
Marcos Pereira Estellita Lins	Universidade Federal do Rio de Janeiro, Brazil
Helder Gomes Costa	Universidade Federal Fluminense, Brazil
Mischel Carmen Neyra Belderrain	Instituto Tecnológico de Aeronáutica, Brazil
Danielle Costa Morais	Universidade Federal de Pernambuco, Brazil

Program Committee

Alexandre Bevilacquea Leoneti	Universidade de São Paulo, Brazil
Ana Paula Cabral Seixas Costa	Universidade Federal de Pernambuco, Brazil
Ana Paula Henriques de Gusmã	Universidade Federal de Sergipe, Brazil
Annibal Parracho Sant'Anna	Universidade Federal Fluminense, Brazil
Carlos Francisco Simões Gomes	Universidade Federal Fluminense, Brazil
Caroline Maria de Miranda Mota	Universidade Federal de Pernambuco, Brazil
Cristiano Alexandre V. Cavalcante	Universidade Federal de Pernambuco, Brazil
Cristiano Torezzan	Universidade Estadual de Campinas, Brazil

Daniel Aloise	Polytechnique Montréal, Canada
Haiyan Xu	Nanjing University of Aeronautics and Astronautics, China
Hannu Nurmi	University of Turku, Finland
João Carlos Correia Baptista Soares de Mello	Universidade Federal Fluminense, Brazil
Johannes Siebert	MCI Management Center Innsbruck, Austria
José Rui Figueira	Technical University of Lisbon, Portugal
Leandro Chaves Rêgo	Universidade Federal do Ceará, Brazil
Liping Fang	Ryerson University, Canada
Luciana Hazin Alencar	Universidade Federal de Pernambuco, Brazil
Luiz Bueno da Silva	Universidade Federal da Paraíba, Brazil
Luiz César Ribeiro Carpinetti	Universidade de São Paulo, Brazil
Maria Teresinha Arns Steiner	Pontifícia Universidade Católica Paraná, Brazil
Mariana Rodrigues de Almeida	Universidade Federal do Rio Grande do Norte, Brazil
Salvatore Greco	University of Catania, Italy
Sérgio Eduardo Gouvêa da Costa	Pontifícia Universidade Católica Paraná, Brazil
Vanessa Batista de Sousa Silva	Universidade Federal de Campina Grande, Brazil

Contents

Automatic Criteria Weight Generation for Multi-criteria Decision Making Under Uncertainty

Mats Danielson[1,2] and Love Ekenberg[2,1](✉)

[1] Department of Computer and Systems Sciences, Stockholm University, PO Box 7003,
SE-164 07 Kista, Sweden
mats.danielson@su.se
[2] International Institute for Applied Systems Analysis, IIASA, Schlossplatz 1,
A-2361 Laxenburg, Austria
ekenberg@iiasa.ac.at

Abstract. Real-life decision situations almost invariably involve large uncertainties. In particular, there are several difficulties connected with the elicitation of probabilities, utilities, and criteria weights. In this article, we explore and test a robust multi-criteria weight generating method covering a broad set of decision situations, but which still is reasonably simple to use. We cover an important class of methods for criteria weight elicitation and propose the use of a reinterpretation of an efficient family (rank exponent) of methods for modelling and evaluating multi-criteria decision problems under uncertainty. We find that the rank exponent (RX) family generates the most efficient and robust weighs and works very well under different assumptions. Furthermore, it is stable under varying assumptions regarding the decision-makers' mindset and internal modelling. We also provide an example to show how the algorithm can be used in a decision-making context. It is exemplified with a problem of selecting strategies for combatting COVID-19.

Keywords: Multi-criteria decision analysis · Uncertain reasoning · Criteria weights · Criteria ranking · Rank order · Automatic weight generation · COVID-19

1 Introduction

A problem with many Multi-Criteria Decision Making (MCDM) models is that there is a lack of numerically precise information available in real life and it is hence difficult for a decision-maker to enter realistic input data into a model. There is, therefore, a perceived need for relaxing the demand for precise judgments to more realistically model decision problems. See, for instance, (Park 2004; Larsson et al. 2014) among others. Solutions to such problems are sometimes significantly hard to find and the results can be difficult to interpret. Quite well-known methods for approaching this problem are based on, e.g., sets of probability measures, upper and lower probabilities as well as interval probabilities and utilities (Coolen and Utkin 2008), fuzzy measures (Aven and Zio 2011; Shapiro

© Springer Nature Switzerland AG 2020
A. T. de Almeida and D. C. Morais (Eds.): INSID 2020, LNBIP 405, pp. 1–14, 2020.
https://doi.org/10.1007/978-3-030-64399-7_1

and Koissi 2015; Tang et al. 2018) as well as evidence and possibility theory, cf., e.g., (Dubois 2010; Dutta et al. 2018; Rohmer and Baudrit 2010) just to mention a few of them. Other approaches include second-order methods (Ekenberg et al. 2014; Danielson et al. 2007, 2019) and modifications of classical decision rules, cf., (Ahn and Park 2008; Sarabando and Dias 2009; Aguayo et al. 2014; Mateos et al. 2014). Regarding MCDM problems, Salo, Hämäläinen, and others have suggested methods for handling imprecise information, for instance, the PRIME method (Salo and Hämäläinen 2001) with various implementations thereof, see e.g. (Mustajoki et al. 2005b). Several other models are focussing on preference intensities, such as the MACBETH method (Bana e Costa et al. 2002), a variety of ROC approaches, such as (Sarabando and Dias 2010), or the Simos's method and variants thereof (Figueira and Roy 2002). Furthermore, there are smart swaps methods, such as (Mustajoki and Hämäläinen 2005a). Mixes of the above techniques are also common, as in Jiménez et al. (2006).

A major problem is combining interval and qualitative estimates without introducing evaluation measures like Γ-maximin or (Levi's) E-admissibility, cf., e.g., (Augustin et al. 2014). Greco et al. (2008) suggest the UTA^{GMS} methodology for purposes similar to ours. By using an ordinal regression technique, they can form a representation based on a set of pairwise comparisons. This is generalised in Figueira et al. (2009) by introducing cardinalities for obtaining a class of total preference functions compatible with user assessments. However, this is less suitable for our purposes since it is unclear how interval constraints can be handled in combination with the extracted preference functions without encountering the computational difficulties discussed in, e.g., (Danielson and Ekenberg 2007). Also, structural constraints should be taken into consideration as discussed already in, e.g., (Ekenberg et al. 2005).

This paper will, more particularly, discuss a method for criteria weight elicitation that can be generally applied to any case where automatic weight generation is considered and with the property that weight functions can be elicited while preserving efficiency and correctness. Below we will provide a brief discussion of so-called surrogate weight methods and then propose a reinterpretation of the rank exponential method. Herein, we focus on ordinal information. In many circumstances, there is only ordinal information available which merits the investigation into ordinal weights. In (Danielson and Ekenberg 2017), it is investigated how much contribution cardinality brings over ordinality, where it is demonstrated that weights are much more insensitive to cardinality than values, which has implications for all ranking methods. We also provide experimental simulations and investigate some properties of the method. Thereafter, a problem of selecting a national strategy for handling the COVID-19 pandemic is discussed. The conclusion is that the method seems to be a very competitive candidate for weight elicitation and evaluations.

2 Rank Ordering Methods

Ordinal methods for generating weights, sometimes with some kind of further discrimination mechanism, constitute a quite commonly used approach to handle the difficulties in eliciting precise criteria weights from decision-makers, c.f., e.g., (Stewart 1993; Arbel and Vargas 1993; Barron and Barrett 1996a, 1996b; Katsikopoulos and Fasolo 2006). The decision-maker supplies ordinal information on importance, which subsequently is converted into numerical weights following the ordinal information. There have in the literature been several suggestions of such methods, e.g., rank sum weights (RS), rank reciprocal weights (RR) (Stillwell et al. 1981), and centroid (ROC) weights (Barron 1992). Based on simulation experiments, Barron and Barrett (1996b) found ROC weights superior to RS and RR. Danielson and Ekenberg (2014 2016a, 2016b), applied in large-scale contexts, such as (Fasth et al. 2020, Komendantova et al. 2018, 2020), have also suggested a spectrum of methods and suggested some that are more robust than the earlier suggestions. In these experiments, surrogate weights as well as "true" reference weights are sampled from some underlying distribution. Then it is investigated how well the surrogate number results match the result of using the "true" results. The method is however dependent on the distribution used for generating the weight vectors.

RS is based on the idea that the rank order should be reflected directly in the weights. Given a simplex S_w generated by $w_1 > w_2 > \ldots > w_N$, where $\Sigma w_i = 1$ and $0 \leq w_i$, assign an ordinal number to each item in the ranking, starting with the highest-ranked item as number 1. Let i be the ranking number among N items to rank. RS then becomes

$$w_i^{RS} = \frac{N + 1 - i}{\sum_{j=1}^{N}(N + 1 - j)} = \frac{2(N + 1 - i)}{N(N + 1)}$$

for all $i = 1,\ldots,N$.

RR has a similar design as RS but is based on the reciprocals (inverted numbers) of the rank order items. Assign an ordinal number to each item ranked, starting with the highest-ranked item (receiving number 1). Then assign the number i to the i:th item in the ranking to obtain

$$w_i^{RR} = \frac{1/i}{\sum_{j=1}^{N} \frac{1}{j}}$$

ROC is a function based on the average of the corners in the polytope defined by the same simplex $S_w = w_1 > w_2 > \ldots > w_N$, $\Sigma w_i = 1$, and $0 \leq w_i$, where w_i are variables representing the criteria weights. The ROC weights are given by

$$w_i^{ROC} = 1/N \sum_{j=i}^{N} \frac{1}{j}$$

for the ranking number i among N items to rank.

As a generalization to the RS method previously discussed, a rank exponent weight method was introduced by (Stillwell et al. 1981). In the original RS formula, they introduced the exponent $z < 1$ to yield the rank exponent (RX) weights given by

$$w_i^{RX(z)} = \frac{(N + 1 - i)^z}{\sum_{j=1}^{N}(N + 1 - j)^z}.$$

For $0 \leq z \leq 1$ the parameter z mediates between the case of equal weights (no discrimination between the importance of criteria) and RS weights such that for $z = 0$ it in effect becomes equal weights and for $z = 1$ it instead becomes RS weights. Thus, for these values of the parameter z the RX(z) formula is the (exponential) combination of equal and RS weights. In this paper, we suggest a reinterpretation of RX.[1] This has, to our knowledge, not been investigated before. Beyond $z = 1$ it becomes something else, a novel weighting scheme in its own right. Earlier, before the accessibility and use of simulations to evaluate different weights, parameters such as the z parameter of RX was considered hard to estimate and thus less suitable for real-life decisions. In this work, we examine the potential of $RX(z)$ in detail and compare it to established state-of-the-art weights such as RS, RR, and ROC.

3   Assessing Automatically Generated Weights

There are basically two categories of elicitation models that are in use depending on the degrees of freedom (DoF) present when decision-makers assign their weights. In point allocation (PA), decision-makers are given point sums, e.g. 100, to distribute among N criteria and there are consequently $N-1$ degrees of freedom. In the Direct Rating (DR) way of assigning weights, on the other hand, the decision-makers have no limitation on the point sum they are allowed to use, and thus a decision-maker may allocate as many points as desired. Only thereafter, the points are normalized, i.e., in DR there are N degrees of freedom. Consequently, when generating weight vectors in an $N-1$ DoF model, they must sum to 100%, and when generating vectors for an N DoF model, a vector is generated keeping components within [0%, 100%] which is thereafter normalised. Other distributions would of course at least theoretically be possible, but it is important to remember that the validation methods are strongly dependent on these assumptions and affect the validations. Different decision-makers use different mental strategies and models when weighting criteria. Thus, a reasonable weighting scheme must be able to perform well in both PA and DR cases, i.e. regardless of the degrees of freedom being $N-1$ or N (Danielson and Ekenberg 2019).

3.1   Experimental Setup

The experiments below for an $N-1$ DoF model was based on a homogenous N-variate Dirichlet distribution generator, and a standard round-robin normalised random weight generator was used for the N DoF experiments. We call the $N-1$ DoF model type of generator an $N-1$-generator and the N DoF model type an N-generator. Details of the simulation generators are given in (Danielson and Ekenberg 2014).

The simulation experiment consisted of four numbers of criteria $N = \{3, 6, 9, 12\}$ and five numbers of alternatives $M = \{3, 6, 9, 12, 15\}$, i.e. a total of 20 simulation scenarios. These simulation sets were selected to cover the most common sizes of decision problems. The behaviour with large decision problems is not within the scope of this article. Each scenario was run 10 times with 10,000 trials for each of them yielding a total of 2,000,000 decision situations. Unscaled value vectors were generated uniformly, and no significant differences were observed with other value distributions. The results

---

[1] Stillwell et al. prescribed a very different use of the z parameter, $0 < z < 1$, in which z is the decision-maker's estimate of the largest weight. In their original version, z is thus a required extra input parameter. In our reinterpretation, z is a configuration parameter that can be determined beforehand and not required user input. We still chose to keep the RX name despite that.

of the simulations are shown in the tables below, where we show a subset of the results with chosen pairs (N, M).

The "winner frequency" in the tables refers to the fraction of cases where the best alternative was correctly predicted. Other measurements include "podium frequency" where the three best alternatives are correctly predicted and "total frequency" where the positions of all alternatives are correctly predicted. The latter two measurements showed the same pattern across the weighting methods as the winners, and are thus not presented here since they would not add to the discussion [2].

The first set of tables shows the winner frequency for the $RX(z)$ family of methods and the second set of tables shows the winner frequency for the older ROC, RR, RS methods together with selected $RX(z)$ methods. Both sets of tables utilise the simulation methods $N-1$ DoF, N DoF, and an equal combination of $N-1$ and N DoF. All hit ratios in all tables are given in percent and are mean values of the 10 scenario runs. With hit ratios is meant the fraction of times that the correct winner is predicted.

The first set of studies concern the parameter z of the $RX(z)$ method. Recall that $z = 1$ is the same as the RS method studied previously and which is used as one of the comparisons in the next set of tables. For values $0 \leq z \leq 1$, which is a combination of RS and equal weights, the algorithm underperforms compared to already known algorithms. This is easily understood since equal weights is a very weak weighting scheme as it does not take any information on the decision situation into account. Thus, this study focuses on parameters $z > 1$.

3.2 Results

In Table 1, using an $N-1$-generator, it can be seen that higher parameter values tend to outperform the others when looking at the winner. In Table 2, the frequencies have changed according to expectation since we employ a model with N degrees of freedom. Now lower parameter values outperform higher (lower being closer to RS), but not at all by as much. In Table 3, the N and $N-1$ DoF models are combined with equal emphasis on both. Now, we can see that in total medium-sized parameters generally perform the best. While (Stillwell et al. 1981) discussed $z < 1$, it is evident by examining the formula that it cannot outperform RS (which is $z = 1$) since it is the linear combination of RS and equal weights, the latter being the worst performer since it does not take any information into account. Thus, we did in this experiment vary z from 1 (RS) and up in steps of 0.1 until the performance declined. The best performances for the different sizes were always found in the interval $[1.1, 1.6]$. Thus, it gives guidance to select the best z given the problem size.

It is clear from the table that parameters $z \in [1.3, 1.5]$ are the best performers but that all of the range $[1.2, 1.6]$ are performing well. Since we do not know exactly what goes on inside a particular decision-maker's head when giving input to a decision situation, it is not wise to rely on a weight function to perform well on only one side of the dimensionality spectrum above. Instead, we consider the mix of N and $N-1$ dimensions to constitute the most valid measurement of a viable automatically generated weighting scheme.

---

[2] In a choice problem, which we discuss here, it is better to use "winner frequency" while in an ordering problem it would be more appropriate to use "total frequency".

Table 1. Hit ratio for predicting winners using an $N-1$-generator

$N-1$ DoF	$z =$	1.1	1.2	1.3	1.4	1.5	1.6
3 criteria	3 alternatives	89.1	89.5	89.9	90.0	90.1	90.1
3 criteria	15 alternatives	77.0	77.4	77.8	78.3	78.5	78.6
6 criteria	6 alternatives	80.9	81.7	82.5	83.2	83.6	83.8
6 criteria	12 alternatives	76.7	77.7	78.8	79.4	79.8	80.2
9 criteria	9 alternatives	77.4	78.6	79.6	80.4	81.3	81.9
12 criteria	6 alternatives	79.1	80.1	81.2	82.3	83.0	83.6
12 criteria	12 alternatives	75.5	76.9	77.9	79.1	79.9	80.4

Table 2. Hit ratio for predicting winners using an N-generator

N DoF	$z =$	1.1	1.2	1.3	1.4	1.5	1.6
3 criteria	3 alternatives	89.2	89.0	88.8	88.5	88.3	87.9
3 criteria	15 alternatives	81.0	80.8	80.4	79.8	79.4	78.6
6 criteria	6 alternatives	87.0	86.7	86.3	85.7	84.9	84.1
6 criteria	12 alternatives	83.9	83.7	83.0	82.1	81.3	80.4
9 criteria	9 alternatives	86.9	86.5	85.7	84.9	83.7	82.6
12 criteria	6 alternatives	90.1	89.6	89.0	88.2	87.3	86.6
12 criteria	12 alternatives	87.2	86.8	86.1	85.1	83.8	82.6

Table 3. Hit ratio for predicting winners using N and $N-1$ DoF generators combined

Combined	$z =$	1.1	1.2	1.3	1.4	1.5	1.6
3 criteria	3 alternatives	89.2	89.3	89.4	89.3	89.2	89.0
3 criteria	15 alternatives	79.0	79.1	79.1	79.1	79.0	78.6
6 criteria	6 alternatives	84.0	84.2	84.4	84.5	84.3	84.0
6 criteria	12 alternatives	80.3	80.7	80.9	80.8	80.6	80.3
9 criteria	9 alternatives	82.2	82.6	82.7	82.7	82.5	82.3
12 criteria	6 alternatives	84.6	84.9	85.1	85.3	85.2	85.1
12 criteria	12 alternatives	81.4	81.9	82.0	82.1	81.9	81.5

But in line with that reasoning, we would also like to minimise the spread between the dimensions, i.e. having a generating function that differs less between both end-points of the input dimensionality scale is preferred to one that has a larger spread. To that effect, in addition to studying the overall hit ratio, we also studied the spread of the results from different dimensionalities. This is shown in Table 4 for the different z parameters of RX(z). Now a quite different picture emerges. While all parameters z $\in [1.2, 1.6]$ perform well overall, it is clear that higher z keeps the spread down, especially for problems of larger size. Since this is a highly desirable property given that we don't know the thinking process of a particular decision-maker, we tend to favour higher z parameters for their robustness as long as they do perform well overall. For comparisons with current well-known weight functions, we select both RX(1.5) and RX(1.6).

Table 4. Spread between hit ratio for predicting winners using N and $N-1$ DoF generators

Spread	$z =$	1.1	1.2	1.3	1.4	1.5	1.6
3 criteria	3 alternatives	0.1	0.5	1.1	1.5	1.8	2.2
3 criteria	15 alternatives	4.0	3.4	2.6	1.5	0.9	0.0
6 criteria	6 alternatives	6.1	5.0	3.8	2.5	1.3	0.3
6 criteria	12 alternatives	7.2	6.0	4.2	2.7	1.5	0.2
9 criteria	9 alternatives	9.5	7.9	6.1	4.5	2.4	0.7
12 criteria	6 alternatives	11.0	9.5	7.8	5.9	4.3	3.0
12 criteria	12 alternatives	11.7	9.9	8.2	6.0	3.9	2.2

3.3 Comparing with Earlier State-of-the-Art Weights

In (Danielson and Ekenberg 2014), previous classic weighting functions were compared. Here, these results are repeated together with the new results for RX. The latter is represented by RX(1.5) and RX(1.6) which achieved the best results above. In Table 5, using an $N-1$-generator, it can be seen that ROC outperforms the other classical ones when looking at the winner. RR is better than RS (which is RX(1.0)). In Table 6, the frequencies have changed according to expectation since we employ a model with N degrees of freedom. Now RS outperforms the others including RX while ROC and RR are far behind. In Table 7, the N and $N-1$ DoF models are combined with equal emphasis on both. Now, we can see that in total RX generally performs the best.

It is clear from studying the resulting tables that the RX family of automatic weight functions easily outperform the more well-known functions, provided that it is possible to select the z parameter in an informed manner. The picture becomes even clearer once the spread between different decision-maker ways of thinking is being taken into consideration.

None of the other studied state-of-the-art functions perform well under varying conditions, while the RX(z) family is able to do so. Especially somewhat higher z parameters perform very well, making parameter selection a trade-off between pure performance and robustness. Our suggestion is to use $z \in [1.5, 1.6]$ as the optimal compromise for the parameter. As was seen in Table 4, lower z-values lead to less robustness with respect to decision-maker styles of reasoning. With a higher parameter, the RX(z) family by far outperforms the earlier known ROC, RS, and RR weighting schemes.

Table 5. Hit ratio for predicting winners using an $N-1$-generator

$N-1$ DoF		ROC	RS	RR	RX(1.5)	RX(1.6)
3 criteria	3 alternatives	90.2	88.2	89.5	90.1	90.1
3 criteria	15 alternatives	79.1	76.6	76.5	78.5	78.6
6 criteria	6 alternatives	84.8	79.9	82.7	83.6	83.8
6 criteria	12 alternatives	81.3	75.6	78.2	79.8	80.2
9 criteria	9 alternatives	83.5	75.6	79.5	81.3	81.9
12 criteria	6 alternatives	86.4	77.8	80.8	83.0	83.6
12 criteria	12 alternatives	83.4	72.9	76.8	79.9	80.4

Table 6. Hit ratio for predicting winners using an N-generator

N DoF		ROC	RS	RR	RX(1.5)	RX(1.6)
3 criteria	3 alternatives	87.3	89.3	88.3	88.3	87.9
3 criteria	15 alternatives	77.9	81.1	79.1	79.4	78.6
6 criteria	6 alternatives	80.1	87.3	78.1	84.9	84.1
6 criteria	12 alternatives	76.4	84.3	74.3	81.3	80.4
9 criteria	9 alternatives	76.3	87.2	69.8	83.7	82.6
12 criteria	6 alternatives	77.5	90.3	67.8	87.3	86.6
12 criteria	12 alternatives	73.4	87.6	63.1	83.8	82.6

Table 7. Hit ratio for predicting winners using N and $N-1$ DoF generators combined

Combined		ROC	RS	RR	RX(1.5)	RX(1.6)
3 criteria	3 alternatives	88.8	88.8	88.9	89.2	89.0
3 criteria	15 alternatives	78.5	78.9	77.8	79.0	78.6
6 criteria	6 alternatives	82.5	83.6	80.4	84.3	84.0
6 criteria	12 alternatives	78.9	80.0	76.3	80.6	80.3
9 criteria	9 alternatives	79.9	81.4	74.7	82.5	82.3
12 criteria	6 alternatives	82.0	84.1	74.3	85.2	85.1
12 criteria	12 alternatives	78.4	80.3	70.0	81.9	81.5
Mean		81.3	82.4	77.4	83.2	83.0

Table 8. Spread between hit ratio for predicting winners using N and $N-1$ DoF generators

Spread		ROC	RS	RR	RX(1.5)	RX(1.6)
3 criteria	3 alternatives	2.9	1.1	1.2	1.8	2.2
3 criteria	15 alternatives	1.2	4.5	2.6	0.9	0.0
6 criteria	6 alternatives	4.7	7.4	4.6	1.3	0.3
6 criteria	12 alternatives	4.9	8.7	3.9	1.5	0.2
9 criteria	9 alternatives	7.2	11.6	9.7	2.4	0.7
12 criteria	6 alternatives	8.9	12.5	13.0	4.3	3.0
12 criteria	12 alternatives	10.0	14.7	13.7	3.9	2.2
Mean		5.7	8.6	7.0	2.3	1.2

4 Example

In the current outbreak of the COVID-19 pandemic, several nation-states seem to have been less than fully prepared. Where strategic plans existed, they were often either not complete or not followed. In some cases, the supply of resources was not sufficient to sustain the outbreak over time. Further, cognitive and behavioural biases seem to have played a significant role in the decision-making processes regarding which risk mitigation and management measures to implement. Many countries were to a large extent unprepared for a similar scenario to arise, despite the fact that predictions about a significant probability for a pandemic to occur in a foreseeable future, and national governments of several countries often acted in an uncoordinated manner, which have resulted in suboptimal responses from national bodies. The current discourse has had a strong emphasis on the number of direct fatalities, while there still is a multitude of relevant aspects of the current crisis. In this example, we briefly discuss how a more general framework, including epidemiological and socio-economic factors, could look like using a model for evaluating the qualitative and quantitative aspects involved.

A detailed account of all the relevant aspects is beyond the scope of this article and for demonstrational purposes only, we just use a few possible options and criteria for a national policy with four levels of restrictions suggested to be imposed on the population of a country affected by COVID-19.[3]

Some examples of possible mitigation strategies could then be:

1. An unmitigated response
2. Response by pharmaceutical measures and case isolation, public communication encouraging increased hygiene and personal protection.
3. 2 + additional personal protective measures and mild social distancing measures.

---

[3] A more complete discussion of possibilities for how to contain the virus spread from a policy point of view, while considering different societal and policy factors in a multi-stakeholder-multi-criteria context, as well as preferences amongst relevant stakeholder groups, is, without any mathematical details, provided in (Ekenberg et al. 2020).

4. 3 + self-selected social distancing and comprehensive contact tracing and publicly disclosed detailed location information of individuals that tested positive for COVID-19.

We use the following four criteria:

1. Number of cases (including critical, severe and mild)
2. Economic aspects
3. Human rights violations
4. Effects on education

The estimates (for demonstrational purpose only) on the values of each response level under each criterion are shown in Table 9 below.

Table 9. The valuation of strategies under the respective criteria

Criterion/Measure	Cases (in 10s of thousands)[a]	Economy (GDP decline in %)	Human rights	Education (% of students having no access to online or any other schooling)
Strategy 1	1415–1729	1–3	Better than Str.2	0
Strategy 2	1412–1725	1–4	Better than Str.3	1–5
Strategy 3	1334–1630	5–7	Better than Str.4	10–20
Strategy 4	1217–1487	5–10		10–30

[a]Epidemiological simulations and other estimates are from (Ekenberg et al. 2020). The estimates are based on the effects of various measures, which are sometimes overlapping due to the significant uncertainties involved and some significant similarities between them.

We need to calibrate the different scales since they are of very different characters and in this example, we assume that:

- The maximum difference between Str.1 and Str.4 in Cases is more important than the maximum difference of Str.1 and Str.4 in Economy.
- The maximum difference between Str.1 and Str.4 in Economy is more important than the maximum difference of Str.1 and Str.4 in Human rights.
- The maximum difference between Str.1 and Str.4 in Human rights is more important than the maximum difference between Str.1 and Str.4 in Education.

The resulting criteria ranking then becomes the following: The importance of Cases is higher than that of Economy, which in turn is more important than Human rights. Further,

Human rights is more important than Education. This ranking is then represented by the RX(1.5) weight generating algorithm. The weights (using the enumeration above) then become w(1) = 0.470, w(2) = 0.305, w(3) = 0.166, and w(4) = 0.059 respectively.

The generated weights together with estimates on the values of each response strategy can then be evaluated by solving successive optimisation problems using the program DecideIT which employs the RX weights together with algorithms from (Danielson et al. 2019). For the evaluation, belief distributions are generated from the input data (both weights and values) using the algorithms in the program. The value $V(S_i)$ for each strategy is then assessed as $V(S_i) = \sum w_i \cdot v_{ij}$ for all weight and value variables involved. The result can be seen in Fig. 1, where Str.1 is found to be the best option for a policy given the background information used herein. The strategy values $V(S_i)$ are seen at the top of the evaluation bars. The coloured parts are the contributions from each criterion.

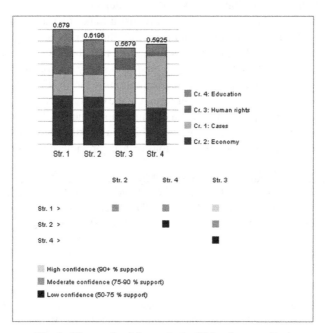

Fig. 1. The result of the analysis. (Color figure online)

Without going into the details, Fig. 1 shows that, given the background information, the higher the bars representing the strategies, the better the respective strategies are. We can also see the result's robustness by the colour markings. A green square means that there is a significant difference between the strategies and that there must be large changes in the input data for it to change. A yellow square means that there is still a significant difference, but that the result is more sensitive to input data. A black square means that there is no significant difference between the strategies. An extended explanation of the semantics regarding the bars and the colour markings are provided in (Danielson et al.

2019). Str.1 is thus the best option in this example. Furthermore, this result is quite robust. It is followed by Str.2, which is quite similar to Str.4, but better than Str.3.[4]

5 Conclusions

This paper aims to define and test a robust multi-criteria weight generating method covering a broad set of decision situations, but which still is reasonably simple to use. In the analyses, we have investigated the average hit rate in percent over the pairs (N, M) of number of criteria and alternatives. From Tables 7 and 8 concerning generated weight performances, RX(1.5) and RX(1.6) are found to be the best candidates for representing weights when searching an optimal alternative. The other weight generation methods are clearly inferior. In particular, ROC is heavily biased by an assumption that decision-makers have a decision process with $N-1$ degrees of freedom considering N criteria, while a reasonable requirement on a robust a rank ordering method is that it should provide adequate alternative rankings under the varying assumptions that we have little real-life knowledge about. It is thus clear that the RX family of methods generates the most efficient and robust weighs and works very well on different problem sizes. Furthermore, it is stable under varying assumptions regarding the decision-makers' mindset and internal modelling. As further research, the obvious next step and extension to the observations in this paper is to find a configuration function that asserts different parameter values to problems of different sizes. This would further increase the efficiency of the RX family of automatic weight functions over its previous competitors.

Acknowledgements. This research was supported by the EU-project Co-Inform (Co-Creating Misinformation-Resilient Societies H2020-SC6-CO-CREATION-2017) as well as the EU-project Open-Science Evidence-Based Methodologies for the Development of Epidemic Combating Policies, European Open Science Cloud EOSC, Covid-19 Fast Track Funding.

References

Aguayo, E.A., Mateos, A., Jiménez-Martín, A.: A new dominance intensity method to deal with ordinal information about a DM's preferences within MAVT. Knowl. Based Syst. **69**, 159–169 (2014)

Ahn, B.S., Park, K.S.: Comparing methods for multiattribute decision making with ordinal weights. Comput. Oper. Res. **35**(5), 1660–1670 (2008)

Arbel, A., Vargas, L.G.: Preference simulation and preference programming: robustness issues in priority derivation. Eur. J. Oper. Res. **69**, 200–209 (1993)

Augustin, T., Coolen, F.P., De Cooman, G., Troffaes, M.C. (eds.) Introduction to Imprecise Probabilities. Wiley Series in Probability and Statistics. Wiley, Hoboken (2014)

Aven, T., Zio, E.: Some considerations on the treatment of uncertainties in risk assessment for practical decision making. Reliabil. Eng. Syst. Saf. **96**, 64–74 (2011)

Bana e Costa, C.A., Correa, E.C., De Corte, J.M., Vansnick, J.C.: Facilitating bid evaluation in public call for tenders: a socio-technical approach. Omega **30**, 227–242 (2002)

---

[4] The result depends largely on the values in Table 9. These will not be discussed further here since the main purpose of the article is to showcase the weights.

Barron, F.H.: Selecting a best multiattribute alternative with partial information about attribute weights. Acta Physiol. (Oxf) **80**(1–3), 91–103 (1992)

Barron, F., Barrett, B.: The efficacy of SMARTER: simple multi-attribute rating technique extended to ranking. Acta Physiol. (Oxf) **93**(1–3), 23–36 (1996a)

Barron, F., Barrett, B.: Decision quality using ranked attribute weights. Manag. Sci. **42**(11), 1515–1523 (1996b)

Coolen, F.P., Utkin, L.V.: Imprecise reliability. In: Melnick, E.L., Everitt, B.S. (eds.) Encyclopedia of Quantitative Risk Analysis and Assessment (2008)

Danielson, M., Ekenberg, L.: Computing upper and lower bounds in interval decision trees. Eur. J. Oper. Res. **181**(2), 808–816 (2007)

Danielson, M., Ekenberg, L.: Rank ordering methods for multi-criteria decisions. In: Zaraté, P., Kersten, G.E., Hernández, J.E. (eds.) GDN 2014. LNBIP, vol. 180, pp. 128–135. Springer, Cham (2014). https://doi.org/10.1007/978-3-319-07179-4_14

Danielson, M., Ekenberg, L.: A robustness study of state-of-the-art surrogate weights for MCDM. Group Decis. Negot. **7** (2016a)

Danielson, M., Ekenberg, L.: The CAR method for using preference strength in multi-criteria decision making. Group Decis. Negot. **25**(4), 775–797 (2016b)

Danielson, M., Ekenberg, L.: Simplifying cardinal ranking in MCDM methods. In: Schoop, M., Kilgour, D.M. (eds.) Proceedings of the 17th International Conference on Group Decision and Negotiation, University of Hohenheim, Stuttgart (2017)

Danielson, M., Ekenberg, L.: An improvement to swing techniques for elicitation in MCDM methods. Knowl.-Based Syst. **168**, 70–79 (2019)

Danielson, M., Ekenberg, L., Larsson, A.: Distribution of belief in decision trees. Int. J. Approx. Reason. **46**(2), 387–407 (2007)

Danielson, M., Ekenberg, L., Larsson, A.: A second-order-based decision tool for evaluating decisions under conditions of severe uncertainty. Knowl.-Based Syst. **191** (2019)

Dubois, D.: Representation, propagation, and decision issues in risk analysis under incomplete probabilistic information. Risk Anal. **30**(3), 361–368 (2010)

Dutta, P.: Human health risk assessment under uncertain environment and its SWOT analysis. Open Publ. Health J. **11** (2018)

Ekenberg, L., Danielson, M., Larsson, A., Sundgren, D.: Second-order risk constraints in decision analysis. Axioms **3**, 31–45 (2014)

Ekenberg, L., Mihai, A., Fasth, T., Komendantova, N., Danielson, M.: Mitigating cognitive and behavioural biases during pandemics responses. Under review (2020)

Ekenberg, L., Thorbiörnson, J., Baidya, T.: Value differences using second order distributions. Int. J. Approx. Reason. **38**(1), 81–97 (2005)

Fasth, T., Bohman, S., Larsson, A., Ekenberg, L., Danielson, M.: Portfolio decision analysis for evaluating stakeholder conflicts in land use planning. Group Decis. Negot. **29**(2), 321–343 (2020)

Figueira, J.R., Greco, S., Słowiński, R.: Building a set of additive value functions representing a reference preorder and intensities of preference: GRIP method. Eur. J. Oper. Res. **195**(2), 460–486 (2009)

Figueira, J., Roy, B.: Determining the weights of criteria in the ELECTRE type methods with a revised Simos' procedure. Eur. J. Oper. Res. **139**, 317–326 (2002)

Greco, S., Mousseau, V., Słowiński, R.: Ordinal regression revisited: multiple criteria ranking using a set of additive value functions. Eur. J. Oper. Res. **191**(2), 416–436 (2008)

Jiménez, A., Ríos-Insua, S., Mateos, A.: A generic multi-attribute analysis system. Comput. Oper. Res. **33**, 1081–1101 (2006)

Katsikopoulos, K., Fasolo, B.: New tools for decision analysis. IEEE Trans. Syst. Man Cybern. – Part A: Syst. Hum. **36**(5), 960–967 (2006)

Komendantova, N., Ekenberg, L., Marashdeh, L., Al Salaymeh, A., Danielson, M., Linnerooth-Bayer, J.: Are energy security concerns dominating environmental concerns? Evidence from stakeholder participation processes on energy transition in Jordan. Climate 6(4) (2018)

Komendantova, N., et al.: Water-energy nexus: addressing stakeholders' preferences in Jordan. Sustainability (2020)

Larsson, A., Riabacke, M., Danielson M., Ekenberg, L.: Cardinal and rank ordering of criteria – addressing prescription within weight elicitation. Int. J. Inf. Technol. Decis. Mak. 13 (2014)

Mateos, A., Jiménez-Martín, A., Aguayo, E.A., Sabio, P.: Dominance intensity measuring methods in MCDM with ordinal relations regarding weights. Knowl. Based Syst. 70, 26–32 (2014)

Mustajoki, J., Hämäläinen, R.: A preference programming approach to make the even swaps method even easier. Decis. Anal. 2, 110–123 (2005)

Mustajoki, J., Hämäläinen, R., Salo, A.: Decision support by interval SMART/SWING - incorporating imprecision in the SMART and SWING methods. Decis. Sci. 36(2), 317–339 (2005)

Park, K.S.: Mathematical programming models for characterizing dominance and potential optimality when multicriteria alternative values and weights are simultaneously incomplete. IEEE Trans. Syst. Man Cybern. - Part A: Syst. Hum. 34(5), 601–614 (2004)

Rohmer, J., Baudrit, C.: The use of the possibility theory to investigate the epistemic uncertainties within scenario-based earthquake risk assessments. Nat. Hazards 56, 613–632 (2010). Springer

Salo, A.A., Hämäläinen, R.P.: Preference Ratios in Multiattribute Evaluation (PRIME)—elicitation and decision procedures under incomplete information. IEEE Trans. Syst. Man Cybern. Part A Syst. Hum. 31, 533–545 (2001)

Sarabando, P., Dias, L.: Multi-attribute choice with ordinal information: a comparison of different decision rules. IEEE Trans. Syst. Man Cybern. Part A 39, 545–554 (2009)

Sarabando, P., Dias, L.: Simple procedures of choice in multicriteria problems without precise information about the alternatives' values. Comput. Oper. Res. 37, 2239–2247 (2010)

Shapiro, A.F., Koissi, M.C.: Risk Assessment Applications of Fuzzy Logic. Casualty Actuarial Society, Canadian Institute of Actuaries, Society of Actuaries (2015)

Stewart, T.J.: Use of piecewise linear value functions in interactive multicriteria decision support: a Monte Carlo study. Manag. Sci. 39(11), 1369–1381 (1993)

Stillwell, W., Seaver, D., Edwards, W.: A comparison of weight approximation techniques in multiattribute utility decision making. Org. Behav. Hum. Perform. 28(1), 62–77 (1981)

Tang, M., Liao, H., Li, Z., Xu, Z.: Nature disaster risk evaluation with a group decision making method based on incomplete hesitant fuzzy linguistic preference relations. Int. J. Environ. Res. Publ. Health (2018)

Decision Skill Training
with the ENTSCHEIDUNGSNAVI

Rüdiger von Nitzsch[1]([✉]), Mendy Tönsfeuerborn[1], and Johannes Ulrich Siebert[2]

[1] Decision Theory and Financial Services Group, RWTH Aachen University,
52062 Aachen, Germany
{nitzsch,toensfeuerborn}@efi.rwth-aachen.de
[2] Department Business and Management, Management Center Innsbruck,
6020 Innsbruck, Austria
Johannes.Siebert@mci.edu

Abstract. Decisions with multiple objectives are challenging for many individuals. The decision problem has to be structured appropriately (decision frontend) and the decision makers' preferences have to be elicited and aggregated (decision backend). There are dozens of decision support systems helping decision makers to deal with their decision problems and thereby promote the quality of one concrete decision. However, most of them require expertise in decision making. Furthermore, they neglect the improvement of decision-making skills, which lead to better and higher quality decisions in general, for decision makers with little expertise and experience. In this paper, we introduce the ENTSCHEIDUNGSNAVI, a freely available decision support system for multi-criteria decision making, which combines the basic functionalities of a decision support system with a training to improve the user's decision-making skills. Based on the concepts of value-focused thinking, multi-attribute utility theory and various debiasing techniques, the decision maker can practice his proactive decision-making skills by going through three main phases: structuring the decision situation, developing the consequence table, evaluating the alternatives. Moreover, we report on the experience gained so far from using the ENTSCHEIDUNGSNAVI and what conclusions can be drawn from it.

Keywords: Decision support system · Multi-criteria decision making ·
Value-focused-thinking · Decision skill training

1 Decision Skill Training and Decision Support Tools

Individuals often struggle with decisions with multiple objectives. Researchers found out that they are for example not able to define all relevant objectives [1] or alternatives [2, 3] and thus, to structure their decision problem. This leads to a low quality of the decision. Decision support systems (DSS) are developed to support the decision-maker (DM)[1] solving unstructured problems [4] and promoting the quality of one concrete

---

[1] The male form chosen in this paper always refers to both female and male persons.

© Springer Nature Switzerland AG 2020
A. T. de Almeida and D. C. Morais (Eds.): INSID 2020, LNBIP 405, pp. 15–30, 2020.
https://doi.org/10.1007/978-3-030-64399-7_2

decision. However, the improvement of decision-making skills, especially for DMs with little expertise and experience, which may lead to better and higher quality decisions in the future is often neglected. Researcher Ralph Keeney makes clear in his approach of Value-Focused Thinking (VFT) [5] as well as in his latest book "Give yourself a nudge" [6] that decision-making is a skill that must be learned.

According to our research, the contribution of DSS to this skill improvement is rarely addressed in literature. Therefore, we follow the approach of combining the basic functionalities of a DSS with a training to improve decision-making skills in the design of our new multi-criteria DSS called ENTSCHEIDUNGSNAVI (www.entscheidungsnavi. de/en). To the best of our knowledge, the tool is the only one that follows this approach explicitly. With the help of this DSS the DM can run through a self-chosen decision problem on the basis of a detailed step-by-step guide in order to improve his skills with the concept 'learning by doing'.

To make a high quality decision, skills must be learned in the whole decision-making process. This process can be roughly divided into three phases: (1) Structuring of the decision situation, (2) Development of the consequences table and (3) Evaluation of the alternatives and the decision [7, 8] [2]. In the conception of the ENTSCHEIDUNGSNAVI, we have formulated our aims for each phase as follows:

1. With regard to the structuring of a decision-making situation, studies show that there are major deficits in this area. The decision statement is often formulated too narrowly [9], the objectives are incompletely [1] or not formulated fundamentally, and likewise good options are often not identified when the alternatives are specified [2, 3]. Therefore, the user of the tool should learn which methods can be used to specifically address these deficits. The concept of VFT provides a framework for structuring the decision (decision frontend) that has been tested in many case studies [10]. Therefore, methods suggested by Keeney's VFT should be implemented in a DSS consistently. In his new book, Ralph Keeney has already cited the ENTSCHEIDUNGSNAVI as the only adequate DSS to support this structuring phase with the help of his VFT-approach.

2. There are various decision making biases that can occur when assessing consequences or articulating preferences. Montibeller and von Winterfeldt provide a comprehensive overview about motivational and cognitive biases in decision and risk analysis [11, 12]. Therefore, the user of the tool should improve his decision-making skills by being informed about the essential biases. Additionally, appropriate debiasing methods should be given to him in order to avoid distortions. With these skills he is then in a position to assess the consequences with far fewer biases than without this mediation.

3. In the evaluation and decision phase (decision backend) it is essential that the user of the tool should trust the result, which is naturally derived in a DSS in an analytical way, in order to implement the decision. Otherwise, the whole effort was in

---

[2] Keeney and Raiffa divide the process into four phases ((1) structuring the decision problem, (2) determining the performance of alternatives, (3) assessing the preferences of decision-makers, and (4) evaluating the alternatives). In this paper we combine the third and fourth into one step (Evaluation of the alternatives and the decision).

vain. Therefore, the DM has to feel comfortable with the result, i.e. his gut feeling should support the decision. Thus, the tool should be designed in such a way that the user learns to understand intuitive and analytical decision paths not as opponents but as synergetic paths. This should be made possible by explicitly addressing discrepancies between intuition and analytics and a very transparent determination of the decision parameters (e.g. objectives, alternatives, consequences prognoses, preference statements, ...), which at the same time support learning effects about the DM's own preferences.

In this article, we present the DSS ENTSCHEIDUNGSNAVI in its basic features. Furthermore, we report on the experience gained so far from using this tool and what conclusions can be drawn from it. Section 2 introduces the basic structuring procedure, Sect. 3 deals with the developing of the consequences table, and Sect. 4 with the evaluation procedure. Section 5 then presents the experiences and conclusions.

2   Structuring the Decision Situation with the Entscheidungsnavi

In order to improve decision making skills for structuring decision situations it is very useful when the DM completely run through a self-chosen decision problem on the basis of a detailed step-by-step guide. Regardless of whether the decision problem in question is worth the effort or not, all relevant methodologies should be run through once to acquire the skills. Accordingly, the ENTSCHEIDUNGSNAVI contains a guideline in the first phase (structuring the decision situation), which guides the user with a total of 16 sub-steps through the three relevant steps: formulating the decision statement, identifying the objectives and determining the alternatives. These steps are roughly sketched out in the following.

2.1   Formulating the Decision Statement

It is important to formulate the decision statement in order to make it clear to which context the following decision steps refer. Especially when several people are involved in a group decision, this definition and coordination is a fundamental component of a high-quality decision [13]. Therefore, the DM must learn to consider all relevant decision aspects which include determining who is the DM, who can choose between alternatives, and what is to be achieved with the decision. At the same time, the assumptions made must be explicitly formulated and it must be stated what is not decided now or what is to be decided at a later date [6].

An at least equally important point in the formulation of the decision statement is the correction of a typical narrow thinking phenomenon, namely that people usually formulate the decision statement too narrowly [9]. As a consequence, relevant alternatives or objectives are overlooked and not included in the decision. Therefore, the DM has to learn that the decision statement is formulated for the right context. Good decision quality requires that this bias is broken down and that the decision statement is approached more broadly. This has the effect that even better and more attractive alternatives for action can be found that have not been thought of before. Thus, a reactive approach to a decision statement should be turned into a proactive decision opportunity.

In the ENTSCHEIDUNGSNAVI, firstly, the DM can make a first attempt to formulate the decision statement. Our experience has shown that this statement is not be chosen very broadly at this stage. Therefore, the DM is then consciously led into a very broad thinking process. It is his task to reflect on his basic life goals and to identify the five most important aims. He will be assisted by a list of about 20 aims that are known from relevant research [14, 15] or have often been chosen by other DMs. He is then asked to think about and take notes on four impulse questions. These impulse questions help him concretely to question assumptions made and to think the decision situation more fundamentally and broadly. Based on this preliminary work, the DM can then reformulate his decision statement. So that he chooses the right frame for his decision situation, the five most important life goals and all notes are presented to him again collectedly.

At the end of this step, the DM should have formulated a proactive, right-framed decision statement in order to ensure an appropriate basis for the following steps.

2.2 Identifying the Objectives

In the concept of VFT, it is intended that once the decision statement has been formulated, in the first step the objectives are identified and used as prompt in the second step to create alternatives [5, 6, 16]. This is to ensure that the DM does not limit himself hastily to a selection of seemingly obvious alternatives, but that the formulated objectives enable him to proactively and creatively find new alternatives [2].

For this to be possible, the objectives must be well reflected. In particular, VFT requires the DM to state his so-called fundamental objectives. These are exactly the aspects that are of core interest and that are associated with an independent value for the DM. Means objectives, which only advance fundamental objectives, should be avoided. In this step, the DM learns to distinguish fundamental objectives from means objectives how to identify his decision-relevant fundamental objectives.

The identification and formulation of fundamental objectives places high demands on a DM. This process is best accomplished with the support of an experienced decision analyst, who, together with the DM, collects all decision-relevant aspects in a brainstorming session first. These are then structured in an objective hierarchy. The decision analyst insists that the DM tells him why he considers each objective important. In this way, all relations between means and end become transparent and it becomes clear what is important at the core. At the end of the process, the superior objective is at the top of the hierarchy and the fundamental objectives are directly on the first following hierarchy level. In all other levels, mainly means-end relations are clarified, i.e. means objectives or, sometimes, fundamental aspects that are further differentiated in terms of content are located there.

This process is simulated as far as possible equivalently in the ENTSCHEIDUNGSNAVI. The DM starts with a brainstorming session, in which he is only supported by creativity-promoting impulse questions, but otherwise can specify all decision-relevant aspects in an unstructured way. He is then presented with a master list of about 70 objectives from which he can add aspects that have been overlooked so far. The subsequent structuring of

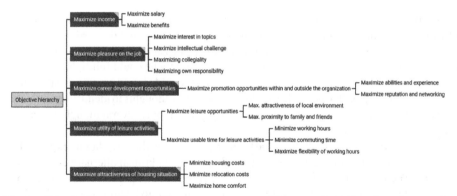

Fig. 1. Objective hierarchy in the ENTSCHEIDUNGSNAVI (The example is taken from the paper by Siebert and von Nitzsch [17].)

the objectives is technically supported in the tool by an easy-to-use graphical interface, but in terms of content the DM is required to recognize the means-end relations himself and to classify them accordingly in the hierarchy (Fig. 1). When creating the hierarchy possible redundancies between the objectives can be detected and avoided. Furthermore, the ENTSCHEIDUNGSNAVI supports the DM like a decision analyst by presenting more questions which should question the fundamentality of the objectives, e.g. 'What exactly do you understand by this aspect? Could you possibly specify this further?' or 'Why is this aspect important to you? Is there a fundamental objective behind it?'. Moreover, the ENTSCHEIDUNGSNAVI points out that the DM should check whether the relevance of a fundamental objective depends on how well another objective is fulfilled. If this is the case, there is a preference dependency, which reduces the validity of the recommendation. This should be avoided. On top of that, the ENTSCHEIDUNGSNAVI provides a lot of examples and finished decision situations that have already been analyzed with the ENTSCHEIDUNGSNAVI by other DMs.

At the end of this step, the DM should have ideally identified four to six fundamental objectives for the previously defined decision statement.

2.3 Determining the Alternatives

With the now defined objective hierarchy, the foundation stone has been laid to support a creative identification of new action alternatives. The ENTSCHEIDUNGSNAVI focuses on the idea of using objectives by VFT to identify new alternatives. First of all, the DM can specify the alternatives known to him anyway in the ENTSCHEIDUNGSNAVI. Then he goes through four sub-steps to find new alternatives. The aim of this step is, that the DM learns to be creative and open-minded in order to determine all possible alternatives for the decision situation.

In the first step, the DM should identify the greatest weaknesses of the alternatives already defined and try to find new, related alternatives with creative considerations that no longer have these weaknesses or hardly have any. Therefore, all previously defined objectives are presented to him and the DM can think about in which objective the respective alternative would have the greatest weakness. The weaknesses should be obviously recognizable for the DM and should not require a more detailed analysis.

In the second step, the DM should forget the previous alternatives for a moment and consider for each of the objectives in isolation how exactly he could fulfill this objective very well. The ENTSCHEIDUNGSNAVI indicates that the DM should be very creative and think as openly as possible here. He should try to use these thoughts to identify completely new action alternatives and it may also be possible to combine several thoughts creating one new alternative.

In the third step, the DM should ask other people. For this, he should explain the decision situation to suitable people and ask them what additional alternatives they can imagine. These people should either know the DM well or be familiar with the decision situation. Moreover, the ENTSCHEIDUNGSNAVI recommends to imagine people who have completely different views in order to find new alternatives.

In the fourth step, the DM must try to identify the two or three key design parameters (KDP) in which all possible alternatives differ. On the one hand, he can use this KDP to find new, previously overlooked alternatives in a combinatorial approach. On the other hand, these KDP also serve as valuable support for reducing the number of alternatives, which may have increased too much, to a manageable number by combining them accordingly.

Finally, it is the DM's task to arrange the formulated alternatives according to his gut feeling. This order serves as a basis to uncover possible discrepancies between head and gut in the later steps after the analytical evaluation.

At the end of this step, the DM should determine all relevant alternatives for the decision situation.

3 Developing the Consequences Table

After structuring the decision problem, the DM is confronted with a still empty consequences table. The task now is to fill the table with the performance evaluation of each alternative to each objective. The difficulty is here to create a consequences table as undistorted as possible.

Researchers point out, that there are various biases [11, 12, 18] that can occur when performance evaluations are given in the consequences table. DMs are often influenced by them especially if they have little experience and expertise in decision making. Objective consequences are not affected by this, but subjective estimates, e.g. probability estimates, can be biased and this leads to a distorted consequences table. For this reason, it is important to inform the DM about the essential biases and teach him how to prevent them. The following biases and hints are explained in the ENTSCHEIDUNGSNAVI:

- *Only observing the future:* The DM is advised not to take into account past, unchangeable results in the consequences but only measure results that he can influence in the future by choosing an action alternative. Otherwise, the result can be falsified if these past results are only taken into account for some alternatives and not for others.
- *Not relying on the intuition:* If the DM has a lot of relevant experience, intuition might be very helpful. However, he should be careful stating probabilities simply based on

any 'gut feeling', particularly when there is a danger of falling back on pre-conceived thought patterns (see Linda example by Tversky and Kahneman [19]). The DM is advised to think objective and to consider the factual situation rather than hastily assuming something probable just because it currently seems feasible.

- *Avoiding overreaction:* Readily available information or events can cause the DM to overreact and misjudge the estimations (availability heuristic [20]). The DM should check whether he is unduly influenced by a certain event or by current media reports while stating his estimations.

- *Not drawing general conclusions from things only heard about:* The so-called 'narrative bias' occurs when the DM is influenced by selected narratives or individual life stories [21]. The more conclusive the story itself is - or the more vivid a specific individual life story is - the greater the risk that a person will draw general conclusions from it. To avoid this bias, the DM should rather use statistics or data sources as basis for his probability estimations.

- *Not underestimating marginal events:* 'Narrow thinking' hinders people from being able to conceive large deviations from the norm. This is why DM in general tend to rate the probabilities of the average state/extremely marginal events too high/low. Studies show that with the help of 'time unpacking' [22], in which estimation forecasts are made step by step and not in one go, the range of variation that results are wider and more realistic than without such steps.

- *Not let themselves be manipulated:* If the DM additionally incorporate information from outside parties than he should bear in mind that in some publications the data and the results might have been modified in such a way that they imply a stronger effect than is actually the case. For this reason, the DM should be consciously aware of what interested parties are involved and how reliable any source is.

- *Not being too hasty with the estimations:* The 'confirmation bias' [18] occurs when the DM prefers a specific alternative and state too positive values for this particular alternative. In this case, he often tends to limit his search of information which will support his preferences. To avoid this bias, the DM should make sure that this information does not favor his favorite alternative(s).

- *Watching out for a potential commitment:* The Sunk-Costs Effect [23] as well as emotional involvement can lead to the fact that the DM evaluates the results of a certain alternative too positively. The DM should not be influenced by the fact that efforts have already been wasted but consciously set his estimation of results for the alternatives with potential commitment at a slightly more conservative level.

- *Thinking not only in the success scenario:* If the DM develops an alternative himself, the so-called Inside View can occur. That means that the DM estimate this alternative too positively because he believes in the success of the alter-native and only little thought is given to failure. The prospective hindsight method can help the DM to choose the estimations more realistic [24].

- *Improving estimations through Dialectical Bootstrapping:* The 'Wisdom of the Crowd'-method is one option to improve the values. The DM can ask many people and make the average of their opinions in order to get more realistic values. With the help of Dialectical Bootstrapping [25] the DM is not dependent on other people but can statistically prove better values as well.

With these skills the DM is in a position to make his consequences prognoses with far fewer biases than without this mediation.

In order to measure the objectives, the DM has to define the attributes with which he can measure his objectives and therefore, also the scales of measurement. This step is also not entirely trivial for DMs without experience and expertise in decision making. Therefore, the DM is provided various hints to facilitate the choice of attributes and scales for the individual objectives. The ENTSCHEIDUNGSNAVI follows the approach of VFT which differentiates between natural, constructed and proxy attributes [5]. Objectives that can be measured unambiguously on a certain natural-numerical scale can usually be recognized by their formulation (e.g. purely monetary objectives should logically be measured in the respective currency, objectives referring to a distance should be measured accordingly with a measure of length). If there is no natural-numerical scale for an objective the DM can measure his objectives with the help of constructed scales. One option would be to use a numerical scale with an artificial unit like points or grades. This scale is relatively general but can basically always be used. To make it less vulnerable it is important that the DM think about the degree of fulfillment of every number given in the scale. Another option is to define a verbal scale (e.g. 'bad' to 'good' or with additions like 'very low' to 'very high') with a small amount of possible result states, like 3 to 7. Also with this scale it makes sense to describe the verbal statements to make them less vulnerable and general. As a third option, the DM can create an indicator scale based on proxy attributes. These proxy attributes can consist of fundamental partial aspects, means objectives or correlated scales. The DM can choose how the attributes should be considered in the measurement of the objective: either he can determine weights for every proxy attribute or he defines an own formula which allows great design possibilities. The ENTSCHEIDUNGSNAVI provides a template for the scales mentioned above, allowing the decision maker to select a suitable scale for each objective.

In addition to the above-mentioned information and learning skills, the ENTSCHEIDUNGSNAVI offers further technical functionality to make it easier for the decision maker to fill out the table and to get an overview of the results.

To consider uncertainties, the DM can define a specific, additional influence factor in each table field, which is defined with a discrete number of states. Probabilities for each state are then to be indicated. Moreover, the results are to be specified state dependent. To facilitate the specification of the probabilities, the ENTSCHEIDUNGSNAVI uses the concept of imprecise information. Therefore, the DM can link his specification with a certain degree of precision.

The moment the consequences table is completely filled in for the first time, all fields of the table are automatically colored. The worst (best) possible values according to the defined bandwidths get a red (green) background, intermediate values are adapted in color accordingly. This visualization serves as a first, at this point still rough view of the advantages and disadvantages of the individual alternatives. Dominated alternatives are highlighted and can be excluded by the DM from further analysis.

4 Evaluation

In order to implement the decision, a fundamental point in this evaluation and decision phase is that the DM trust the result, i.e. analytical result and gut feeling should match.

Otherwise, the whole effort was in vain. The merging of head decision and gut feeling is also a good validation for the result of the analytical DSS calculation. The DM has to understand intuitive and analytical decision paths not as competition but as synergetic paths. In case of discrepancies between intuition and analytics the gut feeling can contain some more information that may have been left out in the analytical model. For example, objectives may have been completely neglected or may not have been formulated fundamentally enough. For this reason, it is important that the DM takes his gut feeling seriously.

The ENTSCHEIDUNGSNAVI already asks the DM for his gut feeling after the structuring phase. There, the DM must rank his defined alternatives according to his gut feeling in a general way and without any analytical calculations. The aim of this ranking is that the DM can identify and investigate any discrepancies between intuition and analytics. These discrepancies could either indicate that the intuition is already influenced by a bias or that important decision parameters have been forgotten in the analytical model. This is to be found out in the evaluation phase.

The calculation basis of the ENTSCHEIDUNGSNAVI is the multi-attribute utility theory (MAUT) [26] which enables a DM to map several objectives within a decision situation in a preference model. Furthermore, this preference model offers the possibility of a transparent determination of the decision parameters which makes the decision making process and the calculation of the best alternative more comprehensible for the DM. However, the MAUT is not very simple, especially the attribute weighting causes problems for many DM, but it offers the possibility to understand and analyze the preference statements given by the DM. In the ENTSCHEIDUNGSNAVI, the DM is supported in the development of his preferences by providing explanations and several preference statements for the selected parameters, so that the DM can always understand what exactly he is doing. Furthermore, he has the possibility at any point to return to a previous step and adjust or add parameters to the decision situation since preferences often develop after a closer examination of the decision problem.

In the evaluation and decision phase, the ENTSCHEIDUNGSNAVI offers different variants of evaluation to provide a detailed and transparent view to the calculated results. Additionally, the DM can take a critical look at the result and identify possible reasons for discrepancies between intuition and analytics.

4.1 Utility Functions

The MAUT requires that the DM indicates utilities. Therefore, he has to define his preferences and determine utility functions for each objective. DMs who are not familiar with this or who find it difficult to formulate their preferences will also receive various hints by the ENTSCHEIDUNGSNAVI in this step. Firstly, the basic understanding of a utility scale is explained followed by an explanation of linear and non-linear utility functions. If the DM is risk neutral, he can choose linear utility functions and does not need to concern himself with this step any further. If there is a decreasing or increasing marginal value, he should choose a non-linear utility function.

Figure 2 shows an example of how the utility function of the objective 'Income' can be analyzed in the ENTSCHEIDUNGSNAVI.

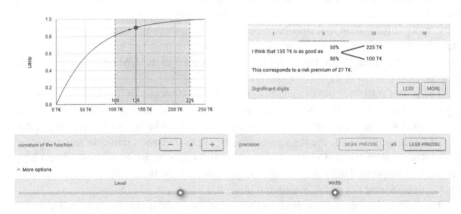

⑤ Utility function

Continue to change the form of the utility function for the **objective "Maximize income"** until your preferences are as precise as possible. (Example)

Fig. 2. Determine utility functions in the ENTSCHEIDUNGSNAVI

In order to analyze the non-linear utility functions more closely the ENTSCHEIDUNGSNAVI supports the DM with the help of graphical representations (Fig. 2 left) and different interpretations (Fig. 2 right). Thus, the DM can check his statements and adjust them if necessary. The curvature of the utility function should be chosen in such a way that the DM can identify with the preference statements presented in all explanation variants.

In the first variant, which is suitable for objectives under certainty, risk preferences are not taken into account, so that the utility function can be interpreted as a measurable value function. The second variant as shown in Fig. 2 compares a sure option (135 T€) with a lottery with fixed probabilities (50% chance of 225 T€; 50% chance of 100 T€) based on the bisection method. The third variant is structured like the second one with the difference that the probabilities of the lottery are variable. The fourth variant presents the parameter responsible for the curvature of the utility function.

If the DM is not sure about his preferences and the shown preference statements are too detailed, he can make use of the option 'precision' which offers the DM to use an interval for potential utility functions. The DM should select the interval only wide enough to reflect his uncertain preferences as well as possible.

4.2 Attribute Weights

After determining the utility functions, the DM need to indicate the attribute weights which represent the scale constants of the multi-attribute utility theory. Determining the attribute weights, the ENTSCHEIDUNGSNAVI basically follows the trade-off procedure by Keeney and Raiffa [26]. Figure 3 shows an example of a trade-off in the ENTSCHEIDUNGSNAVI.

In order to determine the attribute weights of n objectives, the DM has to make n-1 trade-off statements. Therefore, he chooses a reference objective which is compared

⑥ Weight of objectives

Change the indifference curve for the pair of objectives "Maximize usable time for leisure activities" and "Maximize income" until your preferences are precisely denoted. Assume that the alternatives considered do not differ in the other objectives (Example).

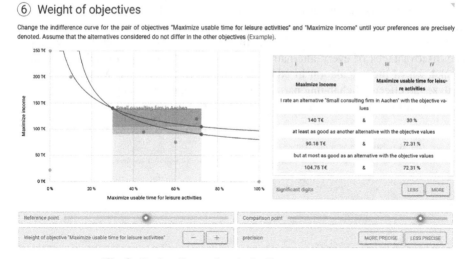

Fig. 3. Trade-off procedure in the ENTSCHEIDUNGSNAVI

with all other defined objectives in a trade-off. In the ENTSCHEIDUNGSNAVI, one real alternative is compared to a fictitious alternative. These only differ in the results of two objectives. The DM must specify how deteriorations in one objective can be compensated for by improvements in the other objective. So that the appropriate trade-off statements can be found faster it is possible to give flat-rate estimations of the attribute weights. The ENTSCHEIDUNGSNAVI then displays the trade-offs as they result from the blanket weights of objectives the DM has specified. With the help of explanation variant I (in table form) and II (in verbal form) on the right-hand side the DM can check the preference statements and modify the trade-offs by changing the relative weight of the comparison objective. He should do this until he can identify with the statements. Furthermore, the DM also has the possibility in the explanation variant III to formulate and enter a new, own trade-off without regard to already entered weights. In this case, the ratio of the weights is automatically adjusted accordingly. (Explanation variant IV presents the calculated weights for both objectives.)

The ENTSCHEIDUNGSNAVI recommends to check each trade-off even with different reference and comparison points, to see whether the resulting statements are suitable for the DM or not. If he has difficulties in determining the exact trade-off, he can set the degree of precision to an interval that allows him to identify with each of the resulting preference statements even with different parameter constellations.

4.3 Evaluation of Alternatives

As soon as all relevant parameters (decision statement, objectives, alternatives, consequences table, utility function, attribute weights) have been entered into the tool by the DM, the ENTSCHEIDUNGSNAVI calculates the expected utility for every defined alternative and presents the results in a ranking.

In order to take a critical look at the result and to identify possible reasons for discrepancies between intuition and analytics, the ENTSCHEIDUNGSNAVI offers different evaluation methods. The Pros and Cons overview (Fig. 4) points out the advantages and disadvantages of every alternative. Furthermore, the DM can display a detailed breakdown of the calculation in addition to the overall overview. Moreover, he can analyze the effects of changing parameters on the ranking in a sensitivity analysis and have a robustness test performed if imprecise parameters are used (Fig. 5).

⑦ Evaluation: Pros and Cons

The following histogram displays for each objective your evaluation of the utility differences in relation to the average of all selected alternatives.

		Objective 1 Maximize income	Objective 2 Maximize pleasure on the job	Objective 3 Maximize career development opportunities	Objective 4 Maximize leisure opportunities	Objective 5 Maximize usable time for leisure activities	Objective 6 Maximize attractiveness of housing situation
☑ 1.	*Alternative 4* Research assistant (upgraded position)	75 bis 125 T€	very much	very good	B	30 bis 60 %	medium
☑ 2.	*Alternative 1* Research assistant (half position)	75 T€	very much	very good	B	60 %	medium
☑ 3.	*Alternative 5* Trainee position in a company in the Eif	140 T€	much	good	C	30 %	high
☑ 4.	*Alternative 6* Small consulting firm in Aachen	140 T€	much	medium	D	30 %	medium
☑ 5.	*Alternative 3* Big consulting firm down south	200 T€	none bis much	excellent	0	10 %	extremely bad
☑ 6.	*Alternative 2* Department office in a company in the Eif	120 T€	little	very bad	A	70 %	high
☐ 7.	*Alternative 7* Start-up						

Fig. 4. Pros and Cons in the ENTSCHEIDUNGSNAVI

⑦ Evaluation: robustness check

In this robustness check, simulation runs were performed to determine how often an alternative was the best one (rank 1), how often it was the second best one (rank 2), and so on. The ranking score calculates the average rank on this basis.

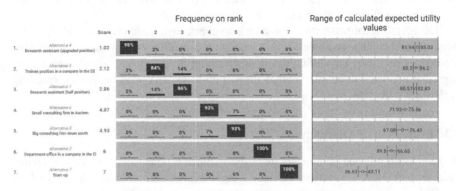

Fig. 5. Robustness check in the ENTSCHEIDUNGSNAVI

The Pros and Cons overview offers the DM a clear overview of the calculated results in an easy and understandable way. The DM can decide which alternatives he wants to compare with and then, the ENTSCHEIDUNGSNAVI displays for each objective the utility differences in relation to the average of all selected alternatives. The bars pointing upwards (down) show the relative advantages (disadvantages) over the other alternatives in the respective objective considering the attribute weight in the height of the bar. The DM can see directly which weaknesses and strengths the individual alternatives have.

A detailed breakdown of the calculation shows how the expected utility for every alternative is composed. With the help of this evaluation variant, the DM can see how large the utility is in each objective category for the respective alternatives.

In the sensitivity analysis, the DM is able to change previously set parameters. The ENTSCHEIDUNGSNAVI calculates the new utility of the alternatives and presents the possible new ranking to the decision maker. This sort of playful approach enables the DM to identify sensitive parameters and examine his results even more closely.

In case the DM has allowed imprecision for any of his parameters, he has the opportunity to do an additional robustness test (Fig. 5). This test checks how robust the ranking is with regard to changes in the parameters (utility functions, objective weights and probabilities) that he has not defined precisely with the help of a Monte-Carlo Simulation.

The results of the robustness check visualize the number of ranked positions (frequency on rank) and the ranges of possible expected utilities of all alternatives (range of calculated expected utility values). Furthermore, an average score for every alternative is given which is calculated as the expected rank.

5 Experiences and Conclusions

The development of the tool was started in 2016. Since the first launch, the tool has been in a continuous development process, in which the functionalities are constantly being expanded and the extensive feedback from users is incorporated. At the time of printing this article, version 5.3 is available. It is a freely accessible software, which is available in both German and English. The decision problems analyzed by the user can be stored locally on the user's own computer if desired. There is also the possibility of registration and storage on the ENTSCHEIDUNGSNAVI-server. The decision problems there are then used in anonymized form for research purposes.

There are now over 1,300 students at RWTH Aachen University, who have analyzed their own real decision problem as part of a voluntary project within the course "Decision Theory". If the students successfully complete the project, they are rewarded with a grade bonus for their careful work. Furthermore, more than 300 students at the Management Center Innsbruck used the ENTSCHEIDUNGSNAVI to structure an important professional or personal decision situation in groups of 4–5 students. Their grade was based on their detailed report and the ENTSCHEIDUNGSNAVI-file.

We have also requested and received detailed feedback by the students. The gut feeling of many students coincided with the analytically calculated decision, which increases the chance that the decision will actually be implemented. Determining the utility functions and attributed weights are the most difficult steps, which shows that students find it difficult to indicate their preferences and support is necessary especially in these steps. Overall, the user-friendliness is rated very positively. Both the structure of the tool and the comprehensibility of the instructions were rated by most students with the best school grade 1.

In the meantime, the ENTSCHEIDUNGSNAVI is already being used at several universities in appropriate courses, including in Austria and Switzerland. Examples of use are decision analyses that students carry out in project modules in order to develop creative solutions for federal or regional political issues, or use in courses for personal career development.

In addition, the ENTSCHEIDUNGSNAVI was part of an intervention in a study on the trainability of proactive cognitive skills in decision making [27]. The proactive decision-making scale measures proactive cognitive skills and proactive traits in decision situations [28]. The more proactive decision makers are, the more satisfied they are with their decisions and ultimately with their lives [29]. In a quasi-experimental field study based on a repeated measures design Siebert et al. found out that decision training helps to promote individuals' effective decision making. In two of three decision trainings, the participants also dealt intensely with a decision situation using the ENT-SCHEIDUNGSNAVI. For these two groups, the training effect was higher than without using the ENTSCHEIDUNGSNAVI. Therefore, we assume that using intensely the ENT-SCHEIDUNGSNAVI positively influences proactive cognitive skills in decision making.

The ENTSCHEIDUNGSNAVI is also used as a supporting tool in professional consulting projects. One example is the Kopernikus-project ENSURE, which pursues the objective of researching new energy network structures for energy system transformation and comprehensively evaluating them with regard to their social acceptability with the participation of several stakeholder groups [30]. Moreover, the tool was also used in a consulting project carried out by the Strategic Decision Group (SDG) for the pharmaceutical division of global company to evaluate early-stage development projects [31].

The experience gained so far can be summarized as follows: Basically there are no restrictions in the field of application for the ENTSCHEIDUNGSNAVI, the methodology is independent of a context. Only the basic motives used in step 1 (formulating the decision statement) and the master list of fundamental objectives used in step 2 (identifying objectives) only make sense in a suitable context. Therefore, we have adapted the two sub-steps for three fields of application, i.e. the user must now choose one of the three categories: (1) Private Life and Career, (2) Politics and Society and (3) Organizations.

Regardless of the field of application, it is seen as positive that just by dealing with the objectives one can gain knowledge in the analysis of the decision problem. Especially in group decisions, a coordinated objective system provides a high transparency and improves the coordination. However, it is also difficult. A typical comment from a user: 'I would not have thought that it is so difficult to formulate objectives.'

As a great challenge, especially for professional or complex applications, we have experienced the appropriate development of scales in addition to the formulation of objectives. This is often associated with a similar effort as the formulation of objectives.

In professional applications, in which several stakeholders are taken into account, the ENTSCHEIDUNGSNAVI serves only as a supporting tool. The evaluation part is particularly valuable here. The structuring part as well as the setting up of scales should better be carried out in workshops with a decision analysis expert.

According to the feedback from previous users, the tool has proven its worth as skill training. For the application area 'Private Life and Career', users need an average of about 8 h for a complete analysis, but consider the time well invested, since 84% would either probably or in any case recommend the tool to others. Furthermore, the functionality of the steps 2) Developing the consequences table and 3) Evaluation of the alternatives and the decision have proven particularly useful for professional use in group decisions in companies. Regarding the first step 'Structuring of the decision situation', we found that the methodologies used in the tool are exactly the right ones, but that they can be carried out even better in moderated workshops. Therefore, we will continue to develop the ENTSCHEIDUNGSNAVI in the coming years in order to be able to support the structuring part especially for group decisions even better.

References

1. Bond, S.D., Carlson, K.A., Keeney, R.L.: Generating objectives: can decision makers articulate what they want? Manag. Sci. **54**(1), 56–70 (2008)
2. Siebert, J.U., Keeney, R.L.: Creating more and better alternatives for decisions using objectives. Oper. Res. **63**(5), 1144–1158 (2015)
3. Siebert, J.U.: Can novices create alternatives of the same quality as experts? Decis. Anal. **13**(4), 278–291 (2016)
4. Sprague, R.H.: A framework for the development of decision support systems. MIS Q. **4**(4), 1–26 (1980)
5. Keeney, R.L.: Value-Focused Thinking: A Path to Creative Decisionmaking. Harvard University Press, Cambridge (1992)
6. Keeney, R.L.: Give Yourself a Nudge: Helping Smart People Make Smarter Personal and Business Decisions. Cambridge University Press, Cambridge (2020)
7. Keeney, R.L.: Decision analysis: an overview. Oper. Res. **30**(5), 803–838 (1982)
8. Raiffa, H.: Decision Analysis Introductory Lectures on Choices Under Uncertainty. Wesley Publishing Company, Boston (1970)
9. Maule, J., Villejoubert, G.: What lies beneath: reframing framing effects. Think. Reason. **13**(1), 25–44 (2007)
10. Parnell, G.S., et al.: Invited review—survey of value-focused thinking: applications, research developments and areas for future research. J. Multi-criteria Decis. Anal. **20**(1–2), 49–60 (2013)
11. Montibeller, G., von Winterfeldt, D.: Cognitive and motivational biases in decision and risk analysis. Risk Anal. **35**(7), 1230–1251 (2015)
12. Kahneman, D.: Thinking, Fast and Slow. Farrar, Straus and Giroux, New York (2011)
13. Baer, M., Dirks, K.T., Nickerson, J.A.: Microfoundations of strategic problem formulation. Strateg. Manag. J. **34**(2), 197–214 (2013)
14. Maslow, A.H.: Motivation and Personality, 3rd edn. Longman, New York (1981)
15. Reiss, S.: The Normal Personality: A New Way of Thinking about People. Cambridge University Press, Cambridge (2008)
16. Siebert, J.U., Keeney, R.L.: Decisions: problems or opportunities? WiSt - Wirtschaftswissenschaftliches Studium **49**(6), E4–E9 (2020)
17. Siebert, J.U., von Nitzsch, R.: The job selection problem for career starters: a decision-theoretical application. Part 1: structuring the problem into objectives, alternatives and uncertainties. Sci. Contrib. Wirtschaftswissenschaftliches Studium. (accepted)

18. Gilovich, T., Griffin, D., Kahneman, D.: Heuristics and Biases: The Psychology of Intuitive Judgment. Cambridge University Press, Cambridge (2002)
19. Tversky, A., Kahneman, D.: Extensional versus intuitive reasoning: the conjunction fallacy in probability judgment. Psychol. Rev. **90**(4), 293 (1983)
20. Tversky, A., Kahneman, D.: Availability: a heuristic for judging frequency and probability. Cogn. Psychol. **5**(2), 207–232 (1973)
21. Winterbottom, A., et al.: Does narrative information bias individual's decision making? A systematic review. Soc. Sci. Med. **67**(12), 2079–2088 (2008)
22. Tversky, A., Koehler, D.J.: Support theory: aA nonextensional representation of subjective probability. Psychol. Rev. **101**(4), 547 (1994)
23. Arkes, H.R., Blumer, C.: The psychology of sunk cost. Organ. Behav. Hum. Decis. Process. **35**(1), 124–140 (1985)
24. Klein, G.: Performing a project premortem. Harvard Bus. Rev. **85**(9), 18–19 (2007)
25. Herzog, S.M., Hertwig, R.: The wisdom of many in one mind: improving individual judgments with dialectical bootstrapping. Psychol. Sci. **20**(2), 231–237 (2009)
26. Keeney, R.L., Raiffa, H.: Decisions with Multiple Objectives: Preferences and Value Trade-Offs. Cambridge University Press, Cambridge & New York (1976)
27. Siebert, J.U., Kunz, R., Rolf, P.: Effects of decision training on individuals' decision-making proactivity (submitted)
28. Siebert, J.U., Kunz, R.: Developing and validating the multidimensional proactive decision-making scale. Eur. J. Oper. Res. **249**(3), 864–877 (2016)
29. Siebert, J.U., Kunz, R., Rolf, P.: Effects of proactive decision making on life satisfaction. Eur. J. Oper. Res. **280**(1), 1171–1187 (2020)
30. Höfer, T., von Nitzsch, R., Madlener, R.: Using value-focused thinking and multicriteria decision making to evaluate energy transition alternatives. Decis. Anal. (2020). (accepted)
31. SDG. https://europe.sdg.com/2020/08/17/cutting-edge-prioritization-model-enables-consistent-evaluation-of-early-stage-drugs-across-pharma-portfolio/. Accessed 01 Oct 2020

Multimethodology Applied to a Complex Health System

Simone Aldrey Angelo[1]([✉]) [ID] and Marcos Pereira Estellita Lins[1,2] [ID]

[1] COPPE/Federal University of Rio de Janeiro, Rio de Janeiro, RJ, Brazil
`simonealdrey@gmail.com`
[2] Federal University of State of Rio de Janeiro, Rio de Janeiro, RJ, Brazil

Abstract. This study aims to support a complex health problem, referring to a large public hospital, which works only with elective surgeries and stands out as a center of excellence in the treatment of orthopedic diseases and trauma. For this purpose, the $CHAP^2$ was used, which consists of a systemic methodology to structure and facilitate the integration between qualitative and quantitative aspects of complex social problems. This method provided a broad qualitative context for the problems, in particular the excessive size of patient in the admission queue and the huge number of exams with expired validity. The qualitative approach also supported the choice and application of quantitative simulation by mediating the selection of decision variables, their sensitivity analysis and the validation of results from simulation. The quantitative approach used scenarios and indicators in order to provide guidance for management to solve hospital management.

Keywords: Health · $CHAP^2$ · Simulation

1 Introduction

Papageorgiou (1978), Cardoen et al. (2010), Rais and Viana (2011) provide a vast survey of the applications and contributions of Operational Research (OR) to healthcare, which shows the considerable development of the use of OR in healthcare over the years. According to Brailsfordand and Vissers (2011), the application of OR in the health sector differs from the application in other areas, because of the special characteristics of healthcare, such as the lack of a direct command line, the fact that decision making is carried out by stakeholders with different interests, the difficult in standardizing products and process and the absence of a charge to the customer for the process as a whole.

According to Heyer (2004), Soft OR predominantly employs qualitative, rational, interpretive and structured techniques to deal, define and explore various perspectives of problems in detail. In a different way, Hard OR is characterized by the use of strict mathematical, quantitative and optimization techniques applied to a reduced scope a priori.

As OR aims to solve real and everyday organizational problems, one must consider human behavior with its impacts on the problem, since OR mathematical and technical

A. T. de Almeida and D. C. Morais (Eds.): INSID 2020, LNBIP 405, pp. 31–46, 2020.
https://doi.org/10.1007/978-3-030-64399-7_3

optimization models alone do not take into account critical perspectives and missing qualitative factors, when solving the problem. In this sense, the Soft OR complements Hard OR (Reisman and Oral 2005; Kotiadis and Mingers 2006). And this complement occurs in multiple ways according to the problem posed, giving rise to a multimethodological view of OR.

The combination of Soft OR and Hard OR will be used through the multimethodology named Complex Holographic Assessment of Paradoxical Problems (CHAP[2]), which, according to Lins (2018), consists of a systemic methodology to structure and facilitate the integration between qualitative and quantitative aspects of complex social problems. This methodology is based on metacognitive maps to assist in the resolution of poorly structured and overly complex problems, which involve interactions between human, technological, organizational and environmental components.

This research had formerly the original objective of finding a case study to which a preselected stochastic methodology could be applied. However, as we became aware later, the health sector problem in hands showed important non-stochastic events, which would make the initial approach unsuitable. It was necessary to carry out a comprehensive analysis of the various aspects related to the problem at hand in advance to understand the problem in its entirety and only then identify one or more methods that could contribute to the systematic treatment and the proposition of solutions.

This approach was then applied through the use of a multi methodology that performs a qualitative analysis to contextualize the entire process of patients in the queues, and through the understanding that some variables were neither independent nor stochastic, but deterministic. Therefore, it was decided to use Simulation to seek the most appropriate solution to the problem.

2 The Hospital

The hospital under study is large, works only with elective surgeries and stands out as a center of excellence in the treatment of orthopedic diseases and trauma, of medium and high complexity. It serves exclusively patients from the Unified Health System (UHS), which is one of the largest public health systems in the world.

High demands for surgery have incurred in a long waiting list, comprising 14 specialties that correspond to the following Specialized Care Centers (SCCs): Spine, Knee, Hip, Shoulder, Hand, Foot, Infant, Skull, Maxillofacial, Microsurgery, Tumor, Adult Trauma Center, Elderly Trauma Center, External Fixative, Sports Trauma.

2.1 Flow and Process

At the time of confirmation of surgery, indicated by the hospital's orthopedist, the patient is placed on the waiting list of one of the SCC, in a specific sub-queue. The orthopedist fills in the form "Surgical Planning" with the patient's data and the proposed procedure, detailing the sub-line in which he will be inserted. If the patient has two pathologies in different areas of the body, he needs to be inserted in two different sub-lines, in different centers and with different positions in the lists. This results in different waiting times as well.

Thus, after the patient is placed on the waiting list, the patient goes through several stages until he is operated on. In this study, such stages are called patient status. According to official hospital documents, there are nine status.

The map in Fig. 1 follows the methodology known as concept maps, where different kinds of relations between concepts are allowed and represented by arrows, using the CmapTools software, version 6.01, free license. It is based on patient status, as depicted and the arrows connect them to explanatory concepts. It is important to highlight that Inactive Status can occur at four different stages of the process, which follow different paths, so they were characterized by Inactive1, Inactive 2, Inactive 3, and Inactive 4 by facilitators and decision makers.

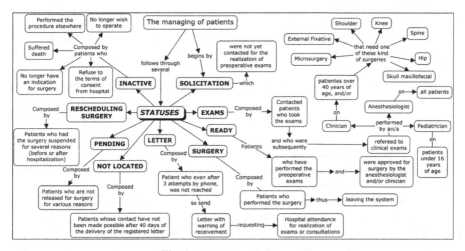

Fig. 1. Status description map

When there is no problem in the process, the patient follows the **ideal flow** through the several statuses, in the following order: **Solicitation, Exams, Ready, Surgery**. However, failing of requirements imply in a **deviation** from the ideal flow and the patient goes through some other statuses, such as: **Letter, Not Located, Inactive 1, Pending, Inactive 2, Inactive 3, Rescheduling surgery, Inactive 4.** Such deviations cause delays and disturbances in the flow, because when leaving the ideal flow, the patient will go through an additional status and then return to the ideal flow in the position following the one he left earlier.

The call for exams is made according to a First In First Out (FIFO) criterion based on the date of entry in the patient list. The calculation of the number of patients to be called for exams is based on the expectation of performing the surgeries due to historical productivity of the Centers. It is increased by a spare percentage on account of cancelled or delayed surgeries. The hospital currently applies a rule of thumb that specifies that the number of patients to be called for exams (Exam Call Rate – ECR) must be 1.5 times the number of procedures performed.

2.2 Data

For data collection, 12071 medical records and 13054 reservation codes were analyzed, both referring to the period from 11/01/2016 to 11/01/2017. From these medical records, a spreadsheet was prepared with the following information: Reservation code, Number of the medical records, Date of arrival of patients, Age of the patient, Specialty, Date of change of status, Current status, Previous status, Motive for change of status and Date of surgery.

With the information in this spreadsheet it was extracted: the Matrix of transition probabilities of the states, the Times of each status, the percentage of patients who left the flow from the Inactive status 1,2, 3,4 and Not Located, the Rate of arrival of patients/day and the Rate of surgery/day.

Also, when considering only the patients who completed the complete flow (Solicitation until surgery), it is observed that they represent 64% of all cases, while the other 36% go through deviations.

After identifying the Times of each status, the Rates of patient arrival/day and the Rate of surgery/day, the distribution for such variables was adjusted using Stat Fit.

3 Methodology

Soft Operations Research methodology was proposed to help structuring issues, problems and situations before solving them properly. According to Rosenhead and Mingers (2001) there are many methods that help groups make progress with their problems, and some of them use formal models to deal with problematic situations. Amongst these, they present Soft Systems Methodology – SSM (Checkland 1972), Strategic Options Development and Analysis – SODA (Eden 1998), Strategic Choice (Friend and Hickling 2005) as well as Drama Theory (Bryant 1997), Robustness Analysis (Rosenhead and Mingers 2001) and Viable Systems Model (Beer 1981). These and many other methodologies present contrasting and converging characteristics regarding products, processes and complexity (Rosenhead and Mingers 2001).

The most widely used method for structuring problems is the SSM, developed by Peter Checkland (Checkland 1972, 1981; Checkland and Poulter 1994; Checkland and Scholes 1999). In short, the SSM is a general method for system redesign. Participants build ideal-type conceptual models (CMs), one for each relevant world view. They compare them with perceptions of the existing system in order to generate debate about what changes are culturally feasible and systemically desirable. SODA method was developed by Eden (1998), as a general problem identification method that uses cognitive mapping as a modelling device for eliciting and recording individuals' views of a problem situation. The merged individual cognitive maps (or a joint map developed within a workshop session) provide the framework for group discussions, and a facilitator guides participants towards commitment to a portfolio of actions. The SCA method was developed by Friend and Hickling (2005) and is an interactive planning approach centered on managing uncertainty in strategic situations through a process of communication and collaboration between people with different backgrounds and skills. SCA is carried out to support a group of decision-makers in through four modes: shaping, designing, comparing and choosing. Lins (2018) explains that, unlike the hard OR that starts modeling problems by exploring databases with different mathematical models, soft OR starts in a step backwards when characterizing the concrete problem to be studied. That's because the qualitative representation of the context allows to structure the problems, and only then to identify the necessary data and to adopt an integrated set of methodologies (multimethodologies) in order to support the decision in structured problems.

The methodology proposed here in, named Complex Holographic Assessment of Paradoxical Problems (CHAP^2) (Lins 2018) presents some striking differences in relation to the previous ones, mainly in terms of its cognitive foundations, which make explicit some aspects hitherto implicit. Firstly, it is characterized as a multimethodology, since it provides a mapping interface between Soft and Hard approaches, that accounts for both present and missing issues. This greatly enhances the metacognitive function of concept maps, and is supported by recent developments in the integration between individual and social groups concerning theory of mind (Malle and Hodges 2005), metacognition, organizational paradoxes and dialogical self (Hermans and Dimaggio 2004; Lins 2018). Both Habermas' emancipatory freedom (Midgley 2000) and cultural change as an invisible product (Rosenhead and Mingers 2001) require an improved understanding and awareness towards mental operations research, i.e. the applied management of our own minds. Another remarkable property of the proposed methodology is the emphasis on a double approach: one search for a consensus or accommodation of proposals and the other recognizes the need to preserve divergent and still irreconcilable aspects. These two approaches were called respectively conceptual and paradoxical models.

CHAP^2 comprises six phases, which are, in synthesis:

I.   Facilitators prepare knowledge maps assumed as characterization of the real system, based on literature research and/or interviews with privileged specialists/generalists. An expanded group of agents is identified.
II.   Training/guidance of agents is carried out through seminars to present the CHAP^2 methodology, evaluations and dynamics with techniques that facilitate the development of metacognition.
III. Characterization of agents' perspectives towards problematic situations are made through interviews, their transcription and representation in concept maps, where possible conflicting perspectives are preserved and even emphasized, under a metacognitive cultural setting.
IV.   Workshop for discussing the thematic maps are organized, resulting in the conceptual (explaining convergences) and paradoxical (explaining divergences) models that represent the organizational context and priority problems.
V.   Development of quantitative models and indicators to support decision making in the selected problems.
VI.   Implementation of viable actions. Monitoring.

Therefore, the modeling of the problem was performed through the multimethodology CHAP^2, which comprises both qualitative (phases I to IV) and quantitative (phase V) approaches, with an explicit interface between them. We describe these phases as they are applied in this work. Notice that the application steps correspond to the phases of the methodology, as explained in Fig. 3.

Phase I - In this phase, we selected hospital's board of directors, as the privileged agent to start the problem identification. Meetings were held where they reported that the maximum period of validity of the exams is 6 months and that many of the patients, after undergoing the exams, are not submitted to surgery within their validity, causing the repetition of preoperative exams.

Afterwards, we organized information, raising the available documents concerning the queue, the history and the norms, and initiated the identification of the agents to be interviewed, who would be capable of contributing to the understanding and mapping of the flow and the process.

The selected interviewees were the ones in charge of:

a) Informatics to provide the indicative data of a previous context;
b) The Sector that manages the queue and deals directly with the flow of patients;
c) Diverse activities in the process (doctors, nurses, biochemists, etc.).

With the discussions and information from the meeting, the expert created a map that expresses his general view about the "real" problem, that is, a metacognitive map, since it represents the expert's perceptions about the problem situation.

Phase II - The available documents were analyzed to outline a draft for the flow of the process. Then, a previous contact with the interviewees was made to schedule the respective interviews. In this contact there was a brief explanation as to: the Method used, the Problem Situation, the Initial Flow of the process and the Metacognitive Map of the "real" problem. The latter two were subsequently made available to agents. In addition, we requested the information technology sector to provide the necessary data for the study. Thus, training, interaction, contribution of agents and their perspectives on the system, the problem and the process/flow were sought.

Phase III - The data made available by information technology were processed, interviews were conducted with the sector that manages the queues and agents in charge of each part of the process.

We asked the agents to elaborate on the assessment of the hospital, the understanding and contextualization of the process and to contribute to the modeling of flow based on the initial draft. They then acknowledged the inaccuracy of the ECR that causes several problems, including the increase in the cost of the surgical procedure and the social cost, and disruption to the flow of the hospital.

Thus, in this phase, the flow of the process previously built was discussed, changed and validated by the agents of the focus. In this way, after the first three phases, the problem situation was deeply explored, and it was possible to better understand the characteristics of the Hospital, map its process and consolidate the flow of patients according to the need of the model.

Phase IV - This phase is intended to provide a qualitative dialogue and integrate agents' perspectives, regarding the broader social context, the relevant process factors and the simulation modeling purposes, marked by the respective following 3 stages, described in chronological order of completion:

a) The first stage comprised the identification of issues that should be considered to perform desirable changes. Further interviews were carried out with the agents, aiming at making explicit cultural and behavioral factors that can contribute or hinder initiatives for improvement. In the latter case it is worth noticing that several barriers, disclosed in synthetic metacognitive map in Fig. 2, result from conflicts between cultural values or worldviews that cannot be resolved, but only managed, therefore composing a paradoxical model.

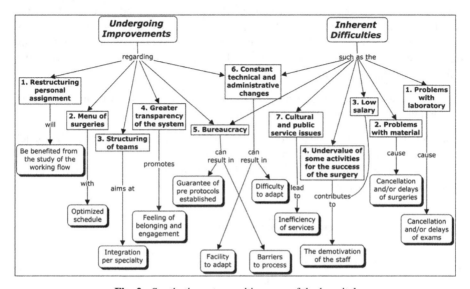

Fig. 2. Synthetic metacognitive map of the hospital

The synthetic metacognitive map in Fig. 2 represents some concepts related to improvements and difficulties in managing changes in the hospital. One can observe, for example, the importance of granting greater transparency to the system, thus promoting the feeling of integration between agents and groups. This proposition faces some difficulties, shown in this map, such as cultural and personal barriers. Among them, the undervalue some activities in the success of the surgery. The CHAP[2] method, due to its systemic nature, facilitates the emergence of attitudes favorable to integration between the parties, with the mutual perception of the agents' points of view and the relationships between their activities.

b) In the second stage a workshop was held, in which the data processing was presented and validated by the agents. This workshop presented and discussed:

– A General Spreadsheet of the data requested from information technology
– A matrix of states transition probabilities regarding the status of patients
– The Patient Arrival Rate, Examination Call Rate and Surgery Call Rate

- Average times of each status covered by the patients
- Percentage of patients leaving/returning to the flow

After presenting each item, the agents contrasted the collected data with the observed organizational knowledge. Afterwards, outliers and data were discussed and identified in order to obtain a sample as representative of the "real" observed system.

c) A third stage also consisted of a workshop, where we simulated the model and presented its results, which were discussed and validated by the agents. Faced with the simulated model, the agents highlighted the wealth of details of the flow and recommended that more information could be extracted, proposing to study the system from the perspectives of both reducing the number of Expired Exams and increasing the number of surgeries. Thus, we composed scenarios that could also account for uncertainties regarding both increase and decrease in the Capacity of Surgery, the first due to plans for expanding the hospital, the second due to the occurrence of problems that reduce the Capacity of Surgery, such as lack of surgical materials.

Phase V - Articulates with the quantitative method, which in this study is Discrete Events Simulation and will be presented in detail in Sect. 4.

Phase VI - Understanding and approval by the board of directors and technical personnel to enforce the recommendations obtained from this research.

In a general way, the application of the 6 phases of CHAP^2, as reported above, are presented in Fig. 3 below.

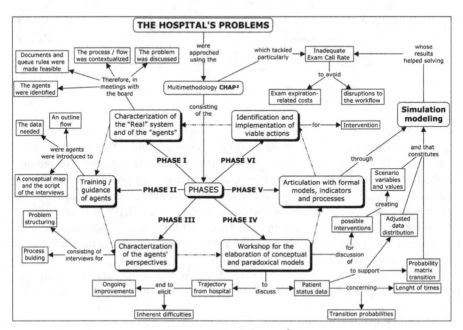

Fig. 3. Phases of CHAP^2

4   Simulation

"Simulation is the imitation of the operation of a real-world process or system over time. It involves the generation of an artificial history of the system, and the observation of that artificial history to draw inferences concerning the operating characteristics of the real system that is represented" (Banks et al. 2000).

Simulation is a powerful tool of traditional OR and has been successfully employed in several areas, mainly in the health sector, applied by Milne and Whitty (1995), Harper and Shahani (2002), Rhodes et al. (2012), Zhu et al. (2012), among others. Simulation has also been used in conjunction with soft OR. Kotiadis et al. (2014) describe the participation and integration of stakeholders during the structuring of conceptual modeling for a study of simulation of discrete events, which was tested in a real case related to obesity care. Pessôa et al. (2015) used Simulation together with concept maps to propose alternatives to increase the number of surgeries performed in a university hospital in Rio de Janeiro.

This study will also combine qualitative and quantitative methods, namely the Discrete Event Simulation as a phase in a multimethodological approach named CHAP[2].

4.1   The Simulation Model

We aim at simulating the status of the surgical hospital system based on estimative or assumed distributions for the patients' solicitation and the provision of resources for exams and surgery. These are characterized as the service rate, the status average times and the percentage of patients leaving/returning to the flow, as presented in Table 1. The Transition Probability Matrix that feeds the model with the probabilities of going from one status to another is shown in Table 2. The simulation model was built in the Simul8 software according to the flow in Fig. 4.

The relevant characteristics in the flow model in Fig. 4 are the large queue of 11000 patients at the beginning of the flow and the limiting validity of the exams, which is 180 days. Thus, in the model it was defined that from the exam status, the maximum period of time until performing the surgery will be 180 days, if this time expired, the patient would be directed to Expired Exams (EE) and then forwarded to Exams again. Thus, the number of patients with Expired Exams becomes an important measure to be controlled in the model is and the controlling variable is the Rate for Exams Calling (REC).

4.2   Model Settings

Warm-Up
To calculate the warm-up length, a model variable was selected, which in this case was the Solicitation queue time, successive simulations were performed with relatively short duration times compared to the original time. In each simulation, the times in the Solicitation queue were noted and, through a graph, it was possible to identify from which day, approximately, the rates showed stability.

Table 1. Service rate, average times, percentage patients leaving/returning to the flow

Service rate			Status average times			Percentage of patients leaving/ returning to the flow		
STATUS	AVERAGE patients/ day	DISTRIBUTION	STATUS	AVERAGE TIME IN STAGES (Days)	DISTRIBUTION	STATUS	LEAVE THE FLOW	RETURN TO FLOW
Solicitation	28	Pearson 6 (8.36, 1.59, 0.0025)	Exams	49	Pearson 5 (3.45, 159)	Not Located	43%	57%
Exams	40	Beta (1.59, 101, 0.0159, 0.667)	Inactive	51	Weibull (0.612, 36.5)	Inactive 1	32%	68%
Surgery	27	Beta (1.61, 101, 0.0238, 1)	Letter	34	Lognormal (28.8/21.7)	Inactive 2	99,9%	0,1%
			Not Located	30	Lognormal (37.3, 125)	Inactive 3	97%	3%
			Pending	66	Pearson 6 (1.65/4.12/129)	Inactive 4	100%	0%
			Rescheduling Surgery	26	Pearson 5 (1.11, 13.7)			

Table 2. Transition probability matrix

	Solicitation	Letter	Not Located	Inactive 1	Exams	Pending	Inactive 2	Ready	Inactive 3	Resch. surgery	Inactive 4	Surgery
Solicitation		14%		3%	83%							
Letter	8%		39%	5%	48%							
Not Located	21%			27%	52%							
Inactive 1					100%							
Exams		5%				5%	5%	85%				
Pending		18%			44%			29%	7%	1%		1%
Inactive 2						100%						
Ready		1%				5%			5%	12%		77%
Inactive 3										100%		
Resch. surgery					3%	8%					12%	77%
Inactive 4												
Surgery												

Thus, through the graph in Fig. 5, it is observed that around 350 days, Solicitation queue time started to stabilize, so the warm-up chosen for the simulations was 350 days.

Replications

Asimulated sample with 20 replications of the total number of expired exams resulted in a standard deviation (s) of 664. The minimum number of replications needed (n^*) can be estimated using the following formula $n^* = (\frac{zs}{h^*})^2$, where z is the level of significance corresponding to the desired confidence interval and h^* represents the desired accuracy. We assumed a confidence interval of 95%, corresponding to $z = 2.09$, a desired accuracy (h^*) of 200 and $s = 664$, which resulted in $n^* = 48,15$. Thus, the minimum number of replications adopted as a sample size was 49.

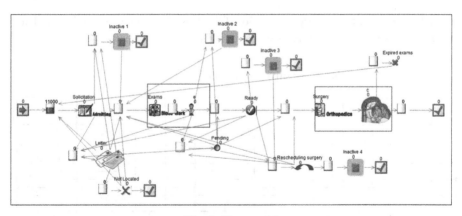

Fig. 4. Flow model

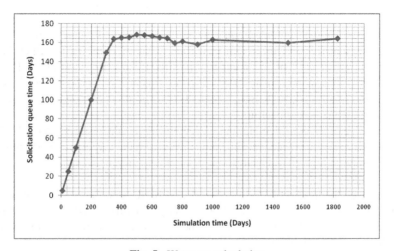

Fig. 5. Warm-up calculation

5 Resulting Simulated Scenarios

We used data from the period November 2016 to November 2017 to simulate a base current scenario and adopted the two varying scenario variables: the Exam Call Rate (ECR) and Surgery Capacity (SC), as recommended in the phase IV workshops of CHAP[2]. We created several scenarios and assumed that the Total Number of Arrival of Patients(AP) is constant in all of them.

5.1 Sensitivity of Performance to Variation in Exams Call Rate

The first proposed scenario variable in the workshop was the Exams Call Rate. ECR is the rate of patients called to exams as a percentage of the number of patients called for surgery. That is, currently the number of patients called for exams is 150% that of the available vacancies for surgery. We explored the feasible range using eight simulated scenarios together with the current, shown in Table 3.

Table 3. Sensitivity to alteration of exam call rate

	Rate	Total number	Average time of patients	Number of patients who left in					Average number of patients	Utilization rate	Total number		Ratio	
Scenarios	Exam call (ECR)	Arrival of patients (AP)	Solicitation queue (TSQ)	Not found	Inative 1	Inative 2	Inative 3	Inative 4	Surgery queue (NSQ)	Surgery (SUR)	Expired exams (EE)	Surgeries performed (SP)	Expired exams/ Performed exams (Ee/Pe)	Expired Exams simulated/ current (EEs/EEc)
1	1,00	31737	506	1031	494	2207	1197	379	1	78	875	21401	3,9%	-91%
2	1,20	31737	342	1211	570	2689	1422	442	6	93	1045	25599	3,9%	-90%
3	1,30	31737	268	1300	631	2936	1552	479	136	100	1213	27502	4,2%	-88%
4	1,35	31737	236	1354	640	3045	1597	496	650	100	1691	27543	5,8%	-83%
5	1,40	31737	203	1410	660	3146	1654	505	1315	100	2801	27539	9,2%	-72%
6	1,45	31737	177	1462	684	3268	1731	516	1997	100	5226	27536	16,0%	-48%
Current	1,50	31737	158	1527	709	3388	1805	531	2764	100	10138	27536	26,9%	0%
7	1,60	31737	142	1624	759	3608	1918	560	4114	100	15909	27537	36,6%	57%
8	2,00	31737	50	2033	929	4605	2368	688	10216	100	23891	27548	46,4%	136%

The results for the simulated and current scenarios shows that Expired Exams presents high sensitivity to the Exam Call Rate. That is, if the ECR, which is currently 1.50, is reduced to 1.00, the number of Expired Exams (EE) varies from 10138 to 875, equivalent to an approximate 91% reduction. It is also observed that its reduction is more expressive for the ECR from 1.50 to 1.30, from this point on, the reduction in the number of EE is less impactful.

However, another considerable and extremely important resulting variable is the Surgery Utilization Rate. Since all apparatus involved in the surgery must be optimized and not left idle, a high SUR ensures that when the apparatus is available, a patient is ready for surgery.

Considering the impact of ECR in both EE and SUR, we observe that, if the current Exam Call Rate is reduced from 1.50 to 1.30, the Surgery Utilization Rate is not impacted, as it remains at 100%. However, a reduction below 1.30 has a significant impact on the SUR, which is not desirable.

Regarding the Expired Simulated/Current Exams ratio, it is also possible to observe this expressive impact up to 1.30. For example, we observe if we reduce the Current ECR from 1.50 to 1.30, there is a 88% reduction in Expired Exams, in relation to the current value, but if it further reduces to 1.00 the additional impact on EE is much smaller, of 3%, with a total of 91%.

Therefore, the ideal operation point for the ECR is 1.30, since the Surgery Utilization Rate remains at 100%, the Expired Exams/Performed Exams Ratio goes from 26.9% to 4.2%, the Total Number of Expired Exams goes from 10138 to 1213.

Other performance results are:

– Average time of patients in the Solicitation queue (TSQ) - Increases as ECR decreases, that is, the fewer patients are called for exams, the longer the average time in the Solicitation queue, since this last status is anterior to the call for exams.
– Number of patients left in Not Located, Inactive 1, Inactive 2, Inactive 3 and Inactive 4 - increases as ECR increases, that is, if more patients enter, consequently more patients will leave, even though these exits are in the middle of the process.

– Average number of patients in the surgery queue (NSQ) - Increases as ECR increases, that is, if more patients enter, consequently there will be more patients for surgery queue.
– Total number of surgeries performed (SP) - When ECR goes from 1,00 to 1,30%, the total number of surgeries performed has a more significant increase, but after 1,30% the SP is practically constant. When SUR reaches the maximum limit of 100%, the number of surgeries performed tends to become almost constant.
– Ratio of Expired Exams/Performed Exams (Ee/Pe) - This ratio refers to the percentage of expired exams over those performed. It increases as the ECR increases and vice versa.

5.2   Sensitivity of Performance to Variation in Surgery Capacity

The second scenario variable proposed by the agents in the workshop was the Surgery Capacity. Thus, after definition the new Exam Call Rate to 1.30%, scenarios that alter the capacity of the surgery were simulated, exploring the range of possibilities, both for increasing and reducing the surgical capacity. And so, the results of the model were observed, especially the behavior of the Solicitation queue, which is of great concern to the hospital. These scenarios are shown in Table 4 below.

Table 4. Results of alteration of surgery capacity

Scenarios	Alteration Surgery capacity (SC)	Total number Arrival of patients (AP)	Number of patients Solicitation queue (after 3 years)	Average number of patients Solicitation queue (ASQ)	Average time of patients Solicitation queue (TSQ)	Number of patients who left in Not found	Inative 1	Inative 2	Inative 3	Inative 4	Average number of patients Surgery queue (NSQ)	Utilization rate Surgery (SUR)	Total number Expired exams (EE)	Surgeries performed (SP)	Ratio Expired exams/ Performed exams (Ee/Pe)
1	-50%	31737	30589	21924	734	674	321	1429	758	275	74	100%	620	13859	4,3%
2	-20%	31737	16914	13542	458	1066	503	2294	1233	385	98	100%	967	22069	4,2%
3	-10%	31737	12278	10683	361	1185	556	2627	1395	431	136	100%	1110	24823	4,3%
4	-5%	31737	10118	-9331	314	1243	598	2780	1468	457	142	100%	1162	26144	4,3%
5	Current	31737	7828	7581	268	1300	631	2936	1552	479	136	100%	1213	27502	4,2%
6	5%	31737	5601	6620	222	1366	644	3074	1611	496	107	100%	1254	28887	4,2%
7	10%	31737	3130	5111	171	1442	681	3226	1712	512	147	100%	1337	30296	4,2%
8	20%	31737	2	2716	97	1564	722	3487	1857	545	136	99%	1432	31834	4,3%
9	50%	31737	1	1479	57	1462	688	3390	1777	525	12	74%	1348	29835	4,3%

From Table 4, the following results were highlighted:

– When simulating the current model for a period of 3 years, a total of 7828 patients are observed in the Solicitation Queue, but if the SC is increased by 20% this queue practically disappears.
– The average number of patients in the Solicitation Queue (ASQ) decreases as the SC increases and vice versa. A small variation in the capacity of the surgery has a great impact on the average number of patients in the Solicitation queue, for example, the 20% increase in SC reduces the ASQ from 7581 to 2716 (reduction of approximately 64%).
– Like the ASQ, the average time of patients in the Solicitation queue (TSQ) increases as the capacity of the surgery increases. A small variation in the SC also has a great impact on the TSQ.

- As expected, the Ratio of Expired Exams/Performed Exams, hardly changed. This is due to the fact that the same RCT = 1.30% is used for all scenarios.
- When comparing the increase in SC from 20% to 50%, it is observed that, differently from what was expected, the number of surgeries performed decreased. This is because when calling more patients, bottlenecks are formed in stages prior to surgery, that is, some patients are stuck in previous stages and take longer to arrive at surgery. Consequently, the Surgery Utilization Rate reduces, considering that it went from 99% to 74%.

Thus, from the analysis of the Alteration of the Surgery Capacity together with the other performance measures, it is observed that a 20% increase in the SC is an optimal solution to the problems of the Solicitation queue, since after a period of 3 years the existing queue will practically disappear, the average number of patients in the Solicitation queue reduces approximately 64%, the Surgery Utilization Rate remains above 99% and the average number of people in the Solicitation queue reduces 64%.

It was also possible to analyze that any reduction in the Surgery Capacity has a negative impact on the Solicitation queue, since the reduction in SC reflects significantly in the increase in the number of patients and in their queue time.

6 Conclusion

The present study proposes the use of a multimethodology to improve the performance of a hospital that performs surgeries for orthopedic diseases and trauma. This approach provided a qualitative context for the problem and supported the identification of the quantitative model and its role to decision aiding. It also mediates the choosing of decision variables, their analysis of sensitivity validation of results from simulation.

The two decision variables: rate of calling to exams and hospital capacity, led to final recommendations that allowed a remarkable reduction of the mismatch between the call for exams and the call for surgery, with a corresponding decrease in expired exams. Changing the current exam call rate (RCT) to 1.30, the percentage of expired exams is reduced from 36,8% to 4,4%. Notice that its useless to further reducing RCT, since, even when RCT = 1.00, that is, Call Rate for Exams = Call Rate for Surgery, the percentage of expired exams is still 4.2%, due to time spent in previous status such as: Pending, Inactive, Rescheduling of Surgery, etc.

The results of the models that alter the Surgery Capacity were also useful for the Hospital, since there are plans to increase the Capacity of Surgery and with the changes in scenarios, it was possible to visualize its impact on various performance measures, especially in the Solicitation queue, which is considered a serious problem at the Hospital. In addition, this change in SC also made it possible to visualize the impact of a fact that occurred in the hospital. This fact refers to a significant increase in the Solicitation queue, which occurred after a period of shortage of some surgical materials and consequently a reduction in the Capacity of Surgery.

Moreover, it is emphasized that the results of this study allow us to go beyond the objective recommendations, as it has been shown to be an inclusive modeling process providing a wealth of information capable of supporting improvements in hospital management.

References

Banks, J., et al.: Discrete Event System Simulation, 3rd edn. Prentice Hall, Upper Saddle River (2000)

Beer, S.: Brain of the Firm. Wiley, Chichester (1981)

Brailsford, S., Vissers, J.: OR in healthcare: a European perspective. Eur. J. Oper. Res. **212**(2), 223–234 (2011)

Bryant, J.: The plot thickens: understanding interaction through the metaphor of Drama (1997)

Cardoen, B., Demeulemeester, E., Beliën, J.: Operating room planning and scheduling: a literature view. Eur. J. Oper. Res. **201**(3), 921–932 (2010)

Checkland, P.: Towards a systems based methodology for real-world problem solving. J. Syst. Eng. **3**(2), 87–116 (1972)

Checkland, P.: Systems Thinking, Systems Practice. Wiley, Chichester (1981)

Checkland, P., Poulter, J.: Towards varieties of systems thinking: the case os soft systems methodology. Syst. Dyn. Rev. **10**, 189–197 (1994)

Checkland, P., Scholes, J.: Soft Systems Methodology in Action. Wiley, Chichester (1999)

Eden, C.: Cognitive mapping: a review. Eur. J. Oper. Res. **36**, 1–13 (1998)

Friend, J.K., Hickling, A.: Planning Under Pressure: The Strategic Choice Approach. Butterworth-Heineman, Oxford (2005)

Harper, P.R., Shahani, A.K.: Modelling for the planning and management of bed capacities in hospitals. J. Oper. Res. Soc. **53**(1), 11–18 (2002)

Hermans, H., Dimaggio, G. (ed.): The Dialogical Self in Psychotherapy. Brunner-Routledge, Abingdon (2004)

Heyer, R.: Understanding soft operations research: the methods, their application and its future in defense setting. Defense Science and Technology Organization, Department of Defense Australian Government, DSTO-GD-0411 (2004)

Kotiadis, K., Mingers, J.: Combining PSMs with hard OR methods: the philosophical and practical challenges. J. Oper. Res. Soc. **57**(7), 856–867 (2006)

Kotiadis, K., Tako, A.A., Vasilakis, C.: A participative and facilitative conceptual modelling framework for discrete event simulation studies in healthcare. J. Oper. Res. Soc. **65**(2), 197–213 (2014)

Lins, M.P.E.: Avaliação Complexa Holográfica de Problemas Paradoxais in Estruturação de problemas sociais complexos. Interciência, Rio de Janeiro (2018)

Malle, B.F., Hodges, S.D.: Other Minds - How Humans Bridge the Divide Between Self and Others (2005)

Midgley, G.: Systemic Intervention: Philosophy, Methodology and Practice. Kluwer Academic, Alphen upon Rhine (2000)

Milne, E., Whitty, P.: Calculation of the need for pediatric intensive care beds. Arch. Disease Childh. **73**(6), 505–507 (1995)

Papageorgiou, J.C.: Some operations research applications to problems of healtcare systems (a survey). Int. J. Biomed. Comput. **9**(2), 101–104 (1978)

Pessôa, L., Lins, M., Silva, A., Fiszman, R.: Integrating soft and hard operational research to improve surgical centre management at a university hospital. Eur. J. Oper. Res. **245**, 851–861 (2015)

Rais, A., Viana, A.: Operations research in healthcare: a survey. Int. Trans. Oper. Res. **18**(1), 1–31 (2011)

Reisman, A.M., Oral, S.G.: Soft systems methodology: a context within a 50-year retrospective of OR/MS. Interfaces **35**(2), 164–178 (2005)

Rhodes, A., Ferdinande, P., Flaatten, H., Guidet, B., Metnitz, P.G., Moreno, R.P.: The variability of critical care bed numbers in Europe. Intensive Care Med. **38**(10), 1647–1653 (2012)

Rosenhead, J., Mingers, J.: Rational Analysis for a Problematic World: Problem Structuring Methods for Complexity, Uncertainty and Conflict. Wiley, Hoboken (2001)

Zhu, Z., et al.: Estimating ICU bed capacity using discrete event simulation. Int. J. Health Care Qual. Assur. **25**(2), 134–144 (2012)

Multi-criteria Group Decision Support System: Multi Cultural Experiments

Pascale Zaraté[(⊠)] [iD]

Toulouse University - IRIT, Toulouse, France
pascale.zarate@irit.fr

Abstract. In this paper we discuss comparative results about three experiments that have been conducted using a Multi-Criteria Group Decision Support Systems. The three experiments were conducted in France, in Canada and in Brazil. The two first experiments are already published in references [8] and [9]. We report in this paper, the experiment conducted in Brazil and we compare the results in the three countries. Master students in Brazil, used the developed system called GRUS, in order to see how the participants to a group decision making process feel comfortable using shared criteria but also private criteria. The used methodology was the following: three hypothesis are proposed which are: 1) there is a need to use private and common criteria in a collaborative decision making process; 2) the number of private and common criteria should be the same; 3) the use of GDSS remains difficult without a human facilitator. After each experiment the participants answered to a semi-directed questionnaire. The results are then analyzed to see if the three hypothesis are verified in each country. As main result of this study we can assume than two of the three hypothesis are verified but the third one is not or partially verified.

Keywords: GDSS · Multi-criteria group decision making · Private criteria · Public criteria

1 Introduction

In large organizations, the vast majority of decisions are taken after intensive consultations involving numerous people rather than by individual decision makers [1]. According to [2] the use of Information and Communication Technologies to support the increasing complexity of organizations implies a modification of decision processes becoming more complex and involving more actors. These modifications are present at two levels; at the organizational level, the processes involve more actors at various degrees of responsibilities but also for the cognitive processes of decision makers that are more demanding in terms of effort and investment. Decision Makers face with a big amount of information and must operate an ultra-rapid sorting out of information.

According to [7], the big investment at the cognitive level is particularly intense in group decision processes, in which two main kinds of process may be considered: (1) aggregation of DMs' initial preferences and (2) aggregation of DMs' individual choices,

© Springer Nature Switzerland AG 2020
A. T. de Almeida and D. C. Morais (Eds.): INSID 2020, LNBIP 405, pp. 47–61, 2020.
https://doi.org/10.1007/978-3-030-64399-7_4

which means the ranking of alternatives by each DM's. In this study, we only consider the first kind of process, a cardinal evaluation for each alternative is given by decision makers.

Nevertheless, in a collective decision making framework, the difficulty for each stakeholder is to balance their own preferences with the building of common preferences within the group. The purpose of the paper is to conduct an experiment in order to see whether decision makers feel comfortable with shared preferences and how the need to use private preferences could be seen. This experiment is based on a MultiCriteria approach using a Group Decision Support System (GDSS) called GRoUp System (GRUS). The motivation of this research was to observe how participants perceive the advantages of making decisions in Group MultiCriteria approach. Another objective of this research is also to evaluate how the stakeholders need to be supported using such GDSS.

This paper is structured as follows. In the Sect. 2, we describe the used GRUS system. In the Sect. 3, we present the experiment conducted in Brazil, as well as the hypothesis of this work. In the Sect. 4, the results of the conducted experiment are analyzed. The fifth section consists in a discussion comparing the hypothesis with the obtained results but also the results obtained for the two other experiments conducted in France and in Canada. Finally, in the Sect. 6, concluding remarks and perspectives of this work are given.

2 The GRoUp System: GRUS

GRoUp Support (GRUS) is a free web platform available at http://www.irit.fr/GRUS. This platform is accessible by a login and a password available upon request to the author.

The system can be used in several kinds of situations: synchronous, asynchronous, distributed or face to face meetings. In case of a distributed/asynchronous situation, the decision making process is managed by the facilitator as a classical project, introducing deadlines etc.

On a technical point of view, GRUS is a toolbox and is implemented in the framework Grails. This framework is based on the Groovy language, a very high level language like Python or Ruby. Groovy can be compiled to Java Virtual Machine bytecode and can interoperate with others java codes or libraries (for more details about these tools see [3]).

On a functional point of view, it can be used by different types of users: designers of collaborative tools, designers of collaborative process, sessions facilitators, decision Makers. GRUS offers the basic services commonly available in GDSS. The first set of functionalities is devoted to a facilitator and is composed by:

– definition or design of a group decision process in a static as well as dynamic way. For the static way the process is designed and then used. For the dynamic way, it means that the facilitator can modify the process during the Decision Making session and it implies to use the following set of functionalities;

- management (add, modify, delete, etc.) of collaborative tools,
- management of automatic reporting in PDF files form.

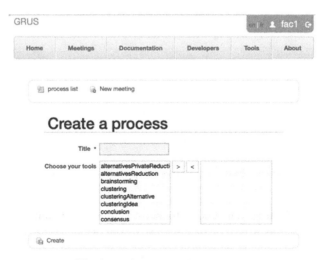

Fig. 1. Facilitator creating a process

The second set of functionalities can be used by the facilitator but also by the decision makers. It is composed by the following elements:

- Brainstorming tool: the end-users define here the several potential solutions to the problem to solve but they also can define the several criteria that would be used.
- Clustering tool: this functionality is sometimes mandatory in order to simplify or reduce the decision making process. It allows end-users to group several similar ideas in categories that will be used in the rest of the process. These categories can be those for the alternatives but also for the criteria.
- MultiCriteria Analyis: in the previous tools, the users have the possibility to define several criteria, several alternatives. Here the end-users give their own preferences of each alternative on each criterion, called preferences matrix. Each preference is marked on a scale from 0 to 20. The decision makers have also the possibility to give their own preference on each weight of each criterion.
- Voting tool: this tool is developed to allow the decision makers to vote. The Borda [10] and Condorcet [11] procedures are implemented.
- Consensus tool: during this step, the facilitator has the hand but not the decision makers. After seeing the aggregation of the individual preferences, i.e. the group result, and after a discussion the facilitator selects the final solution.
- Direct vote: this tool allows the facilitator to nominate the selected alternative after aggregation of all individual preferences.

All these tools can be used to compose a decision making process. Sometimes, simple decision making process can be composed by only one-step and one tool like

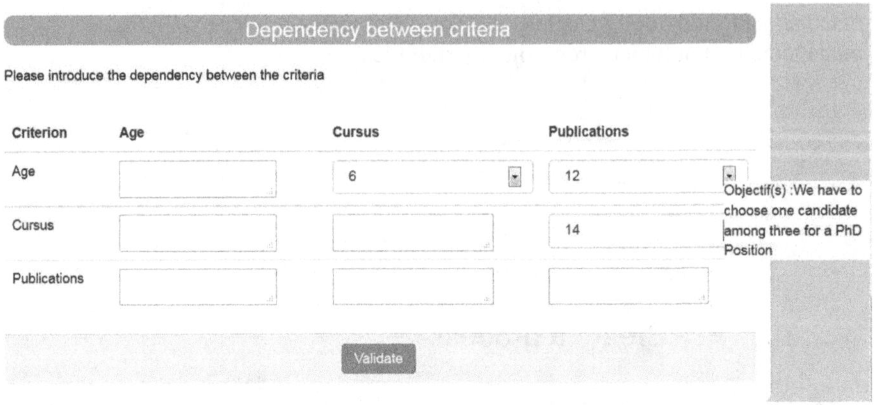

Fig. 2. Multi-criteria process: preferences matrix

for example Brainstorming. The GRUS framework allows designing decision making process in a flexible way using one or several steps and one or several tools.

3 About the Experiment

The experiment was conducted in the Postgraduate Program of Management Engineering at Universidade Federal de Pernambuco, Recife, Brazil (http://ppgep.org.br/). A group of Master students attending a course on MCDA was selected to participate in the experiment. 15 persons were selected to be part of the experiment.

3.1 Experiment Description

A case-study decision making problem was proposed. The problem was a simulation of an administrative committee of a company. This committee, during its previous meeting decided to buy one cell phone for each person in the company. The company is developing software games and includes 150 collaborators, from three categories of employees: Computer Science Engineers (80%), Business Staff (15%), and Administrative Staff (5%). The needs from each category of employees are not the same; as an example the computer scientists need to test the games on the cell phones on different operating systems, the business staff needs to have a large screen in order to demonstrate the games. A list of five models of cell phones is given to each participant.

The 15 students are divided in four groups. Each group must simulate the decision making for 90 min.
Using the GRUS system the following process was selected to be applied:

– Brainstorming for generating Criteria and Alternatives in electronic way. Each decision maker expresses himself in an anonymous way. In order to satisfy all requirements an alternative can be a combination of several cell phones.

- Clustering: It consists in a reduction of number of Criteria to 4–5 Criteria and Alternatives to 4–5 alternatives. This step is conducted by the facilitator in an oral way. Each decision maker can express himself in order to categorize all the ideas. The facilitator then assigns each criterion to one category of criteria and each alternative to one category of alternative.
- Mutlicriteria Evaluation: the participants have to give their own preferences for each alternatives on each criteria, it is called preference matrix, and also give their own weights of each criteria which represent the individual importance of criteria.

Then the system aggregated the individual preferences giving the order of alternatives for the whole group.

- Direct Vote: here is the nomination of the best alternative in an oral way. This step is normally done by the facilitator. Finally, the facilitator have to conclude giving the best alternative
- Reporting: a report of the session is generated.

Unfortunately, the clustering step took a long time and it was not possible to finish totally the process. The report was generated based on the alternatives and criteria generation and alternatives and criteria reduction/clustering.

Finally, after this meeting, the participants fill out a questionnaire evaluating their feeling about the way to find criteria. This questionnaire was composed of ten questions, five about the common/private criteria, two about the facilitation and three about the system usability. The questionnaire is given in the Appendix A.

3.2 Hypothesis of the Experiment

A benefit of a group decision-making process is sharing information that supports the participants' preferences. Whether participants announce their preferred alternative without providing each other arguments about the appropriateness of this alternative to solve the problem at hand, the decision process does not contribute to a deeper understanding of the problem, a better knowledge of the alternatives and the possible matches between the two, so that the decision does not benefit from being taken by a group [4]. However, this way of doing is seldom practicable, first because participants have personal information or considerations that they will not (strategic reasons) or may not (privacy reasons) to be public and second because some reasons for their own preference may not be crystal clear to themselves.

Thus, the result of a group decision-making process is a mix of objective and subjective reasons. To meet this requirement, we proposed to evaluate how decision makers feel comfortable using common and private criteria. Common criteria means that the criteria are discussed and shared by the group.

According to [5] collective and individual criteria are defined as follows:

- A criterion is collective if the group participants agree on the relevance of this criterion and on the score of each alternative for this criterion;

- A criterion is individual if it is considered by one (or several, but not all) participant or if the participants do not agree on the scoring of alternatives regarding this criterion.

Collective criteria contribute to the objective part of the group's assessment while individual ones contribute to its subjective part.

We describe hereafter the adopted hypothesis of the experiment.

Hypothesis 1: *In collaborative decision making process, there is a need to allow participants to use private criteria as well as common criteria.*

In order to guarantee cohesion in the group and the consistency in the group decision, it is necessary to find a balance between the individual part of the problem, i.e. the private criteria, and the collective part, i.e. the common criteria.

Hypothesis 2: *In collaborative decision making process, the number of private criteria must be equal to the number of common criteria.*

Collaborative decision making processes are generally supported by Group Decision Support Systems. The use of GDSS implies a group facilitation that is defined as a process in which a person who is acceptable to all members of the group intervenes to help improving the way the group identifies and solves problems, and makes decisions [6]. Facilitation, on the other hand, is a dynamic process that involves managing relationships between people, tasks, and technology, as well as structuring tasks and contributing to the effective accomplishment of the intended outcomes.

Nevertheless, it seems difficult for decision makers to use GDSS without a human facilitator.

Hypothesis 3: *GDSS use remains difficult without a human facilitator.*

The facilitation of GDSS is a complex task. We assume that using such systems like GDSS is difficult for non-expert decision makers. Some researchers aim to facilitate these decision making processes in an automatic way. We wat to check if an automatic facilitation should be possible.

4   The Results

4.1   Common/Private Criteria Results

Five questions about whether the decision makers feel comfortable using only common criteria were asked in the questionnaire. The participants answer on a scale including 4 degrees and one level for those who have no opinion: Completely agree, Rather agree, Rather not agree, Not at all agree, Without opinion.

The first question was: Do you think it is difficult for the group to find a set of shared criteria?

No participant answered that they don't have any opinion or they completely agree. The result is that we have a small majority (60% including completely not agree and rather not agree) thinks that it is not difficult to find shared criteria in a group as shown in Fig. 1.

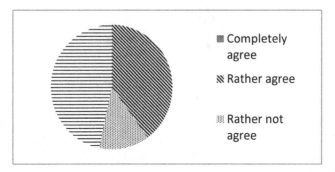

Fig. 3. Difficult to find shared criteria.

The second question was: Do you think that group size makes it difficult for the group to find the shared criteria?

One participant answered that he doesn't have any opinion. The result is that a majority (60% including completely not agree) thinks that the group size does not influence reaching to find shared criteria as shown in Fig. 2.

The third question was: Do you think it should be mandatory for all group members to use the same criteria?

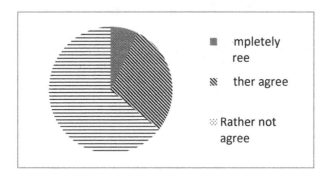

Fig. 4. Size of the group influences reaching to find shared criteria.

One participant answered that he doesn't have any opinion. The result is that a small majority (53% including rather agree and completely agree) thinks that it is mandatory that the group works with the same criteria as shown in Fig. 3.

The fourth question was: Would you like to work with shared criteria in addition to private criteria for individual decision makers?

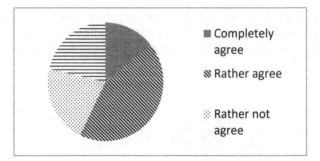

Fig. 5. Group members use the same criteria.

Two participants answered that they don't have any opinion. The result is that a small majority (52% including completely agree and rather agree) thinks that they would like to work with private criteria in addition to shared criteria; 40% think the contrary. The result is quite balanced. Figure 4.

The fifth question was: Do you think that the number of private criteria for each decision maker should at least as great as the number of shared criteria?

No participant answered that they don't have any opinion. The result is that 46% thinks that the number of private criteria must be lower than the shared criteria as shown in Fig. 5.

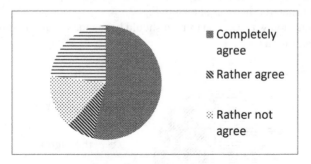

Fig. 6. Use private criteria.

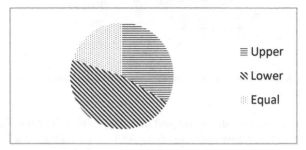

Fig. 7. Number of private criteria equal to number of shared criteria.

4.2 Facilitation Results

Two questions about the facilitation process were asked to the stakeholders. The participants answer on a scale including four degrees and one level for those who have no opinion: Completely agree, Rather agree, Rather not agree, Not at all agree, Without opinion.

The first question was: Do you think that GRUS could be used without facilitator?

No participant answered that they don't have any opinion. The result is that a small majority (60% including completely agree and rather agree) thinks that the system could be used without facilitator as shown in Fig. 8.

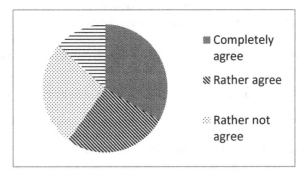

Fig. 8. Use of the system without facilitator.

The second question was: Do you think that a decision process using the GRUS system is enough to support a Group decision meeting?

Two participants have no opinion. The result is that a large majority (73% including completely agree and rather agree) thinks that the system could be used with a work process introduced in the GRUS system as shown in Fig. 9.

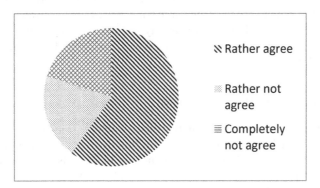

Fig. 9. Use of the system with a work process.

5   Discussion

5.1   Brazil Experiment

The hypotheses were analyzed according to the results obtained in the experiment.

Hypothesis 1: In collaborative decision making process, there is a need to allow participants to use private criteria as well as common criteria.

Most (60%) of the participants did not find it difficult to define shared criteria (see Fig. 1) and a small majority (60%) thinks that the size of the group does not influence its ability to find common criteria (see Fig. 2). If we refer to Figs. 3 and 4, a small majority (53%) of the participants thinks that the group must use shared criteria and that each participant could use private criteria (52%). Following these results we conclude that the Hypothesis 1 is satisfied.

Following this first hypothesis, the question is to determine the number of criteria to be used and the proportion of private and common criteria.

Hypothesis 2: In collaborative decision making process, the number of private criteria should be equal to the number of common criteria.

The results given in Fig. 5 show that 46% of participants also estimate that the number of private criteria must be less than the number of common criteria. So, we conclude that the hypothesis 2 is not verified and we can assume that the number of private criteria must be less than the number of common criteria.

The GDSS use is generally conducted by a facilitator who should be replaced by a computer system. The next hypothesis aims to see how the participants feel with or without a human facilitator.

Hypothesis 3: GDSS use remains difficult without a human facilitator.

For Fig. 6 the results are balanced. 40% of the participants think that a human facilitator could help and 40% that a human facilitator is not mandatory. With the result of the Fig. 7 we can see that a large majority (74%) thinks that an automated process implemented in the system could facilitate the decision making process. So, we cannot assume that the hypothesis 3 is satisfied in a large majority. We only can say, that if an automated process is implemented to support the group, it could help, but that a human facilitator may also be helpful.

5.2   Comparison with Other Experiments

The same experiment was conducted in two other countries: Canada and France.

The first time that the experiment was done at Toulouse Capitole 1 University, France. One Master-level computer science class comprising 14 students was selected to participate. Three groups were created, including 4, 4 and 6 participants respectively. Each group worked independently, in a one-session meeting of 90 min (for more details see [8]). It was also conducted at Wilfrid Laurier University and the University of Waterloo in Waterloo, Canada. A group of 15 persons, mostly PhD students and visiting researchers, was selected to participate (for more details see [9]). The same questions were asked than in Brazil.

The hypothesis were also the same. We have the following results in the other countries.

For the first hypothesis, in France, most participants find it difficult to identify common criteria and agree that the size of the group influences its ability to find common criteria. Thus, the participants were aware that it is difficult for everyone to define the problem in the same way. A small majority of the participants agree that the group may use only shared criteria, but that a large majority sees some private criteria as appropriate. In Canada, most participants did not find it difficult to define shared criteria and a small majority thought that the size of the group influences its ability to find common criteria. A large majority believed that the group should not use only shared criteria and that the system worked better when participants could use private criteria. Based on these results, we conclude that Hypothesis 1 is confirmed in the three countries.

For the second hypothesis, in France, half of the respondents feel that the number of private criteria should equal the number of common criteria. But the remaining respondents split almost equally between larger and smaller. The survey results suggest that the participants are comfortable with both common and private criteria, when they are in roughly the same proportions. We conclude that the hypothesis 2 is weakly verified in France. In Canada, the majority thought that the number of private criteria should at least equal the number of common criteria. Forty percent of participants also indicated that the number of private criteria should be less than the number of common criteria. We conclude that hypothesis 2 is partially confirmed. In Brazil, we assumed that we conclude that the hypothesis 2 is not verified and we can assume that the number of private criteria must be less than the number of common criteria.

For the third hypothesis, in France we saw that the participants appreciate the contribution of a human facilitator, but believe that an automated system can help too. So we cannot draw any conclusions from our survey about the status of Research Question 3. We can only say that if an automated process is implemented to support the group, it could help, but that a human facilitator may also be helpful. In Canada, the results are balanced. Forty percent of the participants thought that a human facilitator would help, but forty percent felt that a human facilitator is not mandatory. We also saw that a large majority (74%) believed that an auto-mated process implemented in the system could facilitate the decision making process. Therefore, we cannot interpret Hypothesis 3 as confirmed. We only can say that an automated process implemented to support the group could be helpful, but that a human facilitator may be at least equally effective. In Brazil, the results are balanced. 40% of the participants think that a human facilitator could help and 40% that a human facilitator is not mandatory. We also saw that a large majority (74%) thinks that an automated process implemented in the system could facilitate the decision making process. So, we cannot assume that the hypothesis 3 is satisfied in a large majority. We only can say, that if an automated process is implemented to support the group, it could help, but that a human facilitator may also be helpful.

In order to summarize the three experiments we prepared the following table:

	France	Canada	Brazil
Hypothesis 1	Verified	Verified	Verified
Hypothesis 2	Weakly verified	Partially verified	Not verified
Hypothesis 3	Human facilitation needed but automated process could be helpful	Human facilitation needed but automated process could be helpful	Human facilitation needed but automated process could be helpful

We can see that no differences are found in the three countries for the hypothesis 1 and 3. For the hypothesis 2, it seems that it is too strong and is not generally verified but only partially in one country.

6 Conclusion

Group decisions can be complex and conflicting. Participants may feel dissatisfied and unmotivated, and they may not feel that their wishes and views have been properly considered. We have shown that using private and common criteria in Multi-Criteria Group Decision making can improve the participants feeling and satisfying.

This study aimed to conduct a descriptive analysis about the hypothesis and mainly see the effects of using private and common criteria in group decisions.

Nevertheless, the facilitation process stays a difficult point in Group Decision Making and some studies must be conducted in order to find the best way to facilitate Group Decision Making Process.

It should be observed that the participants were at the very beginning of the course on MCDA and did not have already conceptual knowledge about group decision and negotiation, which is another course expected to the following term. So, for future studies we may wonder if this kind of knowledge would make difference in the results. Similarly, we may conduct future evaluation considering participants with no knowledge on MCDM neither on Group Decision concepts. Maybe they should agree with Hypothesis 3 and be inclined to require a facilitator in the process. Other investigation must be conducted about the hypothesis 2 assuming that the number of private and common criteria must be equal. We should conduct experiments with more private criteria and also other experiments with more private criteria.

As the experiments were conducted in several countries, some cultural effects should probably influence the found results. Nevertheless, the proposed questionnaire was not enough precise on this issue. Some more experiments should be conducted taking into account the cultural aspect.

Acknowledgment. The author would like to thank the CIMI Excellence Laboratory, Toulouse, France, for allowing to Pascale Zaraté a funding as visiting Professor at Universidade Federal de Pernambuco – Recife - Brazil during the period March – April 2016.

Appendix A

Questionnaire

We aim at understanding how you perceive the Group Multi-Criteria decision making and this questionnaire will support us to better understand this kind of process. The questionnaire is anonymous, is approximately fulfilled in 2 min. There are 5 questions with only ONE answer by question. The results will help us to improve the GRUS system in a future version. As soon as you have finished you can give me back the questionnaire.

Thank you for your participation!

Question 1: Do you think difficult for the group to find a set of shared criteria?

☐ Completely agree
☐ Rather agree
☐ Rather not agree
☐ Not at all agree
☐ Without Opinion

Question 2: Do you think that group size makes it difficult for the group to find the shared criteria by the group?

☐ Completely agree
☐ Rather agree
☐ Rather not agree
☐ Not at all agree
☐ Without Opinion

Question 3: Do you think it should be mandatory for all group members to use the same?

☐ Completely agree
☐ Rather agree
☐ Rather not agree
☐ Not at all agree
☐ Without Opinion

Question 4: Would you like work with shared criteria in addition to private criteria for individual decision maker?

☐ Completely agree
☐ Rather agree
☐ Rather not agree
☐ Not at all agree
☐ Without Opinion

Question 5: Do you think that the number of private criteria for each decision maker should be at least as great as the number of shared criteria?

☐ Upper
☐ Lower
☐ Equal

This questionnaire aims to have a feedback of the GRUS system use. The questionnaire is anonymous, is approximately fulfilled in 2 min. There are 5 questions with only ONE answer by question. The results will help us to improve the GRUS system in a future version. As soon as you have finished you can give me back the questionnaire.

Thank you for your participation!

Question 1: Do you think difficult to use GRUS?

☐ Completely agree
☐ Rather agree
☐ Rather not agree
☐ Not at all agree
☐ Without Opinion

Question 2: Do you think that GRUS could be used without facilitator?

☐ Completely agree
☐ Rather agree
☐ Rather not agree
☐ Not at all agree
☐ Without Opinion

Question 3: Do you think that a decision using the GRUS system is enough to support Group decision meeting?

☐ Completely agree
☐ Rather agree
☐ Rather not agree
☐ Not at all agree
☐ Without Opinion

Question 4: What are the functionalities difficult to use?

Question 5: Which improvement could be done for the GRUS system?

References

1. Gorry, G., Morton, M.S.: A framework for management information systems. Sloan Manag. Rev. **13**(1), 50–70 (1971)
2. Zaraté, P.: Tools for Collaborative Decision-Making. Wiley, Hoboken (2013)
3. Camilleri, G., Zaraté, P.: EasyMeeting: a group decision support system (Release 1). Rapport de recherche IRIT/RR–2014–10–FR (2014)
4. Schmidt, K., Bannon, L.: Taking CSCW seriously: supporting articulation work. Comput. Support. Coop. Work (CSCW) **1**(1), 7–40 (1992)
5. Sibertin-Blanc, C., Zaraté, P.: A flexible multi-criteria methodology for collective decision making preferences. Group Decis. Negot. J. (2016). (submitted)
6. Schwarz, R.: The Skilled Facilitator. Jossey-Bass Publishers, San Francisco (1994)
7. de Almeida, A.T., Cavalcante, C.A.V., Alencar, M.H., Ferreira, R.J.P., de Almeida-Filho, A.T., Garcez, T.V.: Multicriteria and Multiobjective Models for Risk Reliability and Maintenance Decision Analysis. International Series in Operations Research & Management Science, vol. 231, pp. 1–416. Springer, New York (2015). https://doi.org/10.1007/978-3-319-17969-8
8. Zaraté, P., Camilleri, G., Kilgour, D.M.: Multi-criteria group decision making with private and shared criteria: an experiment. In: Bajwa, D., Koeszegi, S.T., Vetschera, R. (eds.) GDN 2016. LNBIP, vol. 274, pp. 31–42. Springer, Cham (2017). https://doi.org/10.1007/978-3-319-52624-9_3
9. Zaraté, P., Kilgour, D.M., Hipel, K.: Private or common criteria in a multi-criteria group decision support system: an experiment. In: Yuizono, T., Ogata, H., Hoppe, U., Vassileva, J. (eds.) CRIWG 2016. LNCS, vol. 9848, pp. 1–12. Springer, Cham (2016). https://doi.org/10.1007/978-3-319-44799-5_1
10. Zahid, M.A., De Swart, H.: The borda majority count. Inf. Sci. (Ny) (2015). https://doi.org/10.1016/j.ins.2014.10.044
11. Gehrlein, W.V.: Condorcet's paradox and the Condorcet efficiency of voting rules. Mathematica Japonica. **45**, 173–199 (1997)

A Proposed Synthetic Index of Quality Life for OECD Countries

Edilvando Pereira Eufrazio$^{(\boxtimes)}$ (iD) and Helder Gomes Costa (iD)

Universidade Federal Fluminense, Niterói, RJ 24210-240, Brazil
{edilvandopereira,heldergc}@id.uff.br

Abstract. OECD has maintained the Better Life initiative, that was proposed the Life Index (BLI) composed by 11 dimensions. The weighting of the BLI is done through the user perception, considering that it is difficult to have a single number that synthesizes the perception of quality of life. Thus, the work aims to weight the variables of BLI to obtain the Synthetic Better Life Index (SBLI). Based on a literature review, gaps in weighting the variables and dimensions were identified. The article presents a factor analysis modeling to weight and reorganize the BLI variables in 3 dimensions (factors), that were weighted by the explained variance of each factor. A cluster analysis based on the SBLI was also proposed, by comparing the grouping differences regarding the original set of variables. It was not observed significant loss in terms of country grouping when using SBLI in comparison with the use of the original set of variables. The SBLI could assist in making public policy decisions for the development of quality of life issues.

Keywords: OECD · Better Life Index · Synthetic index

1 Introduction

According to the OECD [1], the Better Life Index (BLI) is a web-based interactive tool designed to engage people in the debate about well-being and quality of life. The tool enables the user to compare welfare across countries through a portal (http://www.OECDbetterlifeindex.org) and according to the importance given to 11 topics: community, education, environment, civic engagement, health, housing, income, jobs, personal satisfaction, safety and life/work (balance between personal and professional life). Once one has created here own index, you can see how the average achievements of countries compare based on their priorities, as well as the differences in welfare between men and women in each country. One can also compare and share the index created with others, as well as with the OECD. Viewing the number of user responses by country, age and gender is also available, and which topics people think are most important for a better life. The BLI is updated annually. Currently the index is calculated for the following countries: Australia; Austria; Belgium; Brazil; Canada; Chile; Czech Republic; Denmark; Estonia; Finland; France; Germany; Greece; Hungary; Iceland; Ireland; Israel; Italy; Japan; Korea; Latvia; Luxembourg; Mexico; Netherlands; New Zealand; Norway; Poland; Portugal; Russia; Slovakia; Slovenia; South Africa; Spain; Sweden; Switzerland; U.S; UK.

© Springer Nature Switzerland AG 2020
A. T. de Almeida and D. C. Morais (Eds.): INSID 2020, LNBIP 405, pp. 62–76, 2020.
https://doi.org/10.1007/978-3-030-64399-7_5

Considering the difficult to organize a complex concept as quality life and wellbeing the use of a composite indicators could be useful. The composite indicators can be summarize complex or multi-dimensional issues, in view of supporting decision-makers [2]. They can be easier to interpret than trying to find a trend in many separate indicators [3]. They facilitate the task of ranking countries on complex issues. They can help attracting public interest by providing a summary figure with which to compare the performance across countries and their progress over time.

As described in the next section, despite of advances already reached in this subject there is still a gap: to build Synthetic Better Life Index (SBLI), that generates a reduction in the number of criteria. The objective of this paper is to fulfill this gap.

2   Previous Related Works

After a review on the theme in the Scopus and Web of Science bases – as reported in [4], the use of such databases in justified for reducing the possibility of taking gray and predatory literature into account. And, considering a query that listed terms related to quality of life and wellbeing concatenated to the BLI. Thus, after the proper filters and overlays, we obtained a set of 42 articles that were analyzed, from which the data shown in the Table 1 bring the main applications in methodological terms. We sought methods that brought some aggregation of variables and some form of weighting. The most frequent methods found out to weight or aggregate BLI dimensions were methods based on Data Envelopment Analysis (DEA) with 5 occurrences. The Principal Component Analysis (PCA), Correlation Analysis and Arithmetic/Weighted mean were highlighted with 4 evidence for each. With 3 articles comes right after the multicriteria based methods and Benefit of the Doubt (BOD) method. And finally, we have the cluster analysis and Generalized mean aggregation both with two occurrences. Some articles are counted in more than one line because they apply more than one technique.

Hence, in the literature it was observed that there are studies that seek to report the difficulty in weighting the dimensions and criticize the weighting only by the user [5–9].

There are also works that consider the dimensions of the BLI using different methodologies from the proposal in the present work (e.g. [9, 10]) and that do not use a new reading in terms of new dimensions.

Therefore, a gap was identified in the literature regarding the weighting of the dimensions of the BLI using factor analysis with factors that can be aggregated in a synthetic index and the possibility of reduction in terms of the 11 dimensions originally proposed.

In this context, we structured the following research objectives to serve as guidelines for the performed study:

- Create a synthetic index by considering the variables that make up the BLI.
- Rank countries according to synthetic index and analyze clusters.

Table 1. Methodology summary.

Method	Articles	Frequency
Literature review	[11–16]	6
DEA	[10, 17–19]	5
Correlation Analysis	[20–23]	4
Principal Component Analysis	[18, 24–26]	4
Arithmetic mean/Weighted arithmetic mean	[21, 27–29]	4
Benefit of the Doubt (BOD)	[10, 19, 30]	3
Multicriteria	[10, 31, 32]	3
Cluster analysis	[10, 33]	2
Generalized mean aggregation	[34, 35]	2

3 Method and Results

This section is intended to describe the methodological steps and results obtained, as well as the synthetic index considering the dimensions of BLI. And yet as after the index's withdrawal the countries were grouped into clusters. Thus, to facilitate the reader's understanding, the work is organized in the follow steps: standardization and exploratory analysis; factor analysis model application; Factor calculation and index weighting; cluster analysis (k-means). For each step, a subsection will be dedicated that will bring the steps followed and the results obtained in each step and the theoretical framework used.

3.1 Standardization and Exploratory Analysis

To access the data and variables, we used the OECD STATS portal available at https://stats.OCDE.org/ which was accessed in June 2020. This site is a repository of statistics maintained by the OECD. Variables that make up the 11 dimensions of the BLI publicly and for free. The available data were from 2013 to 2017, as 2017 is the last year compiled, although more current data already exist, these are not yet consolidated and not all variables are available. Given this, this paper bases its analysis on the latest consolidated edition of the Better Life Index, which is How's Life? For the year 2017 [36]. Data are available for download from the portal in csv format. This approach was adopted because the OECD repository itself warns against comparisons between the years of the research, although the methodological steps presented here may be replicated in other years.

With data, these were standardized using two types of standardization. The first one based on the z-score method that makes normal variables with mean 0 and variance 1. The second form of standardization to be applied consists in the standardization of the variables between 0 and 1. This technique will be used to present the results of the synthetic index calculation.

To facilitate the writing and the elaboration of the graphics, the coding of the variables was used according to the Table 2.

Table 2. Variable coding

Dimension	Variable	Units	Coding
Housing	Dwellings without basic facilities	Percentage	V1
	Housing expenditure	Percentage	V2
	Rooms per person	Ratio	V3
Income	Household net adjusted disposable income	US Dollar	V4
	Household net financial wealth	US Dollar	V5
Jobs	Labor market insecurity	Percentage	V6
	Employment rate	Percentage	V7
	Long-term unemployment rate	Percentage	V8
	Personal earnings	US Dollar	V9
Community	Quality of support network	Percentage	V10
Education	Educational attainment	Percentage	V11
	Student skills	Average score	V12
	Years in education	Years	V13
Environment	Air pollution	Micrograms per cubic meter	V14
	Water quality	Percentage	V15
Civic engagement	Stakeholder engagement for developing regulations	Average score	V16
	Voter turnout	Percentage	V17
Health	Life expectancy	Years	V18
	Self-reported health	Percentage	19
Life Satisfaction	Life satisfaction	Average score	V20
Safety	Feeling safe walking alone at night	Percentage	V21
	Homicide rate	Ratio	V22
Work-Life Balance	Employees working very long hours	Percentage	V23
	Time devoted to leisure and personal care	Hours	V24

Figure 1 graphically shows the hypothesis tests that evaluate the significance of correlation to the pairs of variables at a level of 5%. What according to Hair et al. [37] is indicative of the use of factor analysis. The figure shows that if the correlation is significant it will be painted, and once again the color indicates whether the correlation between the variables is positive or negative. This time, it is possible to notice that most of the pairs are statistically correlated.

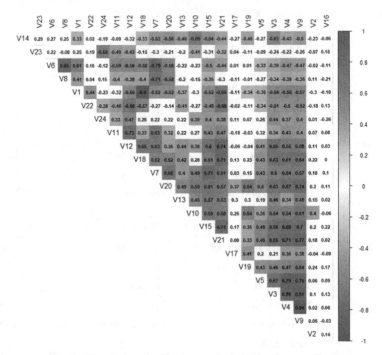

Fig. 1. Correlation significance analysis (Color figure online)

3.2 Factor Analysis

Factor analysis was introduced by Spearman [38]. Another relevant contribution was made by Thurstone [39] in developing the idea of multiple factor analysis.

As the principal component analysis Mingoti [40] mentions that, factor analysis aims to describe the original variability of the random variables that make up the vector X, in a smaller number of random variables, called common factors that are related. With the original vector X through a linear model. According to Hair et al. [37] factor is the linear combination of the original variables. Once the factors are identified, their numerical values, called scores, can be obtained for each sample element. In turn, these scores can be used in other analyzes involving other statistical techniques.

Initially the variables were standardized and all subsequent analyzes were performed with the variables standardized by the Z-score.

Regarding the assumptions, it was found that all variables are continuous [37]. It was found that according to the correlation analysis performed in the descriptive statistics section that most variables correlate with correlation coefficient greater than 0.3. Also, according to Table 3, the KMO (Kaiser-Meyer-Olkin) statistic was verified, which is an indicator that compares the magnitude of the correlation coefficients observed with the magnitudes of the partial correlation coefficients and ranges from 0 to 1. A KMO greater than 0.5 shows suitability for factor analysis. Finally, the Bartlett Test of Sphericity (BTS) should be statistically significant ($p < 0.05$), although this is not appropriate when not all data are normal. Therefore, interpretation under the KMO prevails [37].

Table 3. KMO and Bartlett tests.

Kaiser-Meyer-Olkin adequacy measure		0,729
Bartlett Test of Sphericity	Aprox. Chi-square	1232,438
	df	276
	Sig.	0,000

For factor extraction there are some possible methods such as maximum likelihood, least squares and principal components. In the present work, it was decided to use extraction by principal components. This is due to the objective of giving weight to the factors, which has easy interpretation in the use of principal components. And according to Hair et al. [37] normality is not required for this extraction to be used.

From the original p-variables up to p main components can be obtained. However, it is desired that there be a reduction of the original p-variables, to facilitate the interpretation of the main components. Thus, the information contained in the original p-variables is replaced by the information of the uncorrelated k ($k < p$) main components. However, the quality of this approach will depend on the number of components.

In this work we use to determining the number of factors the two criteria:

Criteria 1: Analysis of the proportion of the total variance related to each estimated eigenvalue ωi, given by $\omega i = \omega i/p$, $i = 1, 2, ..., p$. Those eigenvalues that represent the largest proportions of the total variance remain and, therefore, the value of m will be equal to the number of eigenvalues retained [40];
Criteria 2: Observation of the screen-plot graph, which arranges the values of ωi ordered in ascending order. By this Criteria, the graph seeks a "jump point", which would represent a decrease in importance in relation to the total variance. The value of m would then be equal to the number of eigenvalues prior to the "jump point". This Criteria is equivalent to Criteria 1.

Consideration should be given to the choice of m value, number of factors, interpretability, and parsimony principle, i.e. to describe the variability structure of the normalized random vector Z with the fewest possible factors.

Looking at the graph in Fig. 2 and according to the criteria in question, it is possible to perceive a jump point between the numbers 5 and 6. This is an indicative graph of working with a maximum of 6 components.

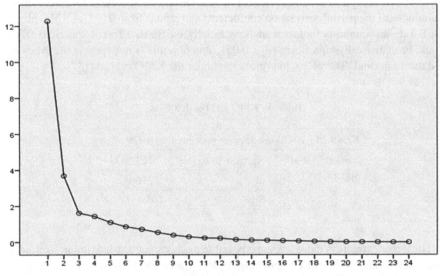

Fig. 2. Scree plot.

Table 4 shows the percentage of variance explained for the first tree components and the cumulative to measured variance that are added components. A 60% threshold as acceptable [37]. Thus, the extraction of factors should continue until this level is reached. In the present case, it is observed that this level is already reached with two components, but to have a robust analysis that satisfactorily explains the data set, we chose to use 3 factors that together explain 73.266% of the variance.

Table 4. Obtaining factors and percentage of variance explained.

Component	Initial eigen values			Sums of squared loads extraction		
	Total	% variance	% cumulative	Total	% variance	% cumulative
1	12,280	51,165	51,165	12,280	51,165	51,165
2	3,690	15,375	66,541	3,690	15,375	66,541
3	1,614	6,725	73,266	1,614	6,725	73,266

Interpreting the original factors F1, F2, ..., Fm may not be quite easy. In this situation, an orthogonal transformation of the original factors can be used to achieve a simpler structure to be interpreted. There are two main types of rotation: orthogonal and oblique [41]. Also, the two forms of rotation produce similar results, especially when there is a clear correlation pattern between the variables used [37]. The Varimax orthogonal rotation type is the most used (this method seeks to minimize the number of variables that have high loads in each factor). Considering that, this work uses this rotation to better analyze the data [42].

3.3 Factors Interpretation

In this subsection, we will analyze the factors based on the loadings found after rotation. Each factor will be interpreted individually for the subsequent composition of the synthetic index.

For the identification and naming of the factors was used the criteria of a factor load with at least 0.7 in modulus of the variable in relation to the factor. It was also observed what advocate Hair et al. [37] which suggest that one of the assumptions of factor analysis is the simple structure of its components.

For each factor its name will be presented, as well as the variables that name it (i.e., they have a factor load in modulus greater than 0.7) and in parentheses will be presented the factor load of the variable within the factor. After this analysis will be presented the factor scores for each factor.

- Factor 1 (Personal Development and Support Factors): For factor 1 according to the adopted criteria the following variables have significant weight: V12 - Student Skills (0.969); V24 - Time devoted to leisure and personal care (0.952); V18 - Life expectancy (0.95); V10 - Quality of Support Network (0.949); V13 - Years in Education (0.921); V7 - Employment rate (0.883); V15 - Water quality (0.859); V20 - Life satisfaction (0.845); V2 - Housing expenditure (0.839); V11 - Educational attainment (0.772); V21 - Feeling safe alone at night (0.762). The variables presented relate to issues of the individual's development regarding educational variables. The factor also brings the variable how much free time there is for reading and personal care (V24) with the second highest loading, indicating a preponderance of the variable in the factor. Finally, there are variables that address the conditions of support and support to the individual. Such as the quality of the support network (V10), the issue of feeling safe when going out alone at night (V21) and water quality (V15).
- Factor 2 (Financial Balance): For the second factor the following variables have significant weight: V9 - Personal earnings (0.774); V5 - Household net financial wealth (0.724); V4 - Household net adjusted disposable income (0.72). In this factor you can see that it deals with the individual's income (V9) and how is the family balance between income and expenses (V5, V4).
- Factor 3 (Labor Market Insecurity): For the third and last factor the following variables have significant weights: V6 - Labor Market insecurity (0.936); V8 - Long term unemployment rate (0.915). In this factor only these two variables were relevant, which gave a well-defined meaning to the factor. That is, the first variable (V6) is associated with the expected loss of income due to unemployment and the second variable (V8) associates the time that the person is unemployed. These two variables show the feeling and fragility of losing one's job and eventually not getting it back.

3.4   Synthetic Better Life Index (SBLI)

In response to one of the objectives of this article, we present in this section the composition of the Synthetic Better Life Index. We describe the methodology for calculating the index. And finally, a ranking by country considering the SBLI was presented.

SBLI Weighting

The weighting chosen is based on the weighted average of the factors by the percentage of variance explained by each factor. Still for this analysis was observed the "meaning" of the factor in terms of perception of quality of life. That is, this qualitative analysis was adopted to define the sign of the factor scores. In the case of Factor 1 scores (Personal Development and Support Factors), it was adopted as a positive sign, since it is understood that high scores of this factor indicate a perception of a good quality of life. Regarding Factor 2 (Financial Equilibrium), a positive sign in the equation is also understood, indicating that as this factor is closer to 1 there is an increase in quality of life. Factor 3 (Insecurity with the labor market) will be weighted associated with a negative sign, because in this case it is understood that the higher the insecurity score with the labor market, the worse the country is in terms of quality of life.

Thus, the equation that defines the SBLI as a function of the qualitative analysis made and also as a function of the weighting given for the explained variance is:

$$SBLI = \frac{F_{1x} * ve_{F1} + F_{2x} * ve_{F2} - F_{3x} * ve_{F3}}{ve_{F1} + ve_{F2} + ve_{F3}} \tag{1}$$

Where:

$SBLI$ = Synthetic Better Life Index – Represent the index vector for each country
F_{ix} = Ith factor scores, i = 1, 2, 3; for each country
ve_{Fi} = percentage of variance explained by the ith factor, i = 1, 2, 3
ve_{F1} = 51,165%; ve_{F2} = 15,375%; ve_{F3} = 6,725%.

Country Comparison Based on SBLI

Here countries will be ranked according to each factor and according to the SBLI. It will also be presented a table with the values of each factor and the SBLI, all of them standardized between 0 and 1.

Table 5 shows the ranking of the four first countries and the last four countries according to the scores of the three factors and the values of the SBLI. It is noteworthy that the factor 3 ordering is reversed, that is, the former has a lower value, which has already discussed represents a better quality of life considering the negative association of the factor. In this context it is possible to see that ranking differs between factors, so that some countries excel in some dimensions of quality of life and in others not. In relation to SBLI, the first four countries are equal to factor 1, due to the higher weight given to this factor, but due to the weight of the other factors this is not repeated throughout the list. Here is a highlight, already identified in the analysis of outliers, which is South Africa, which ranks in all ranks in the worst position. This is explained

Table 5. Ranking of countries according to factors and SBLI.

Factor 1 (51,17%)	Factor 2 (15,38%)	Factor 3 (6,73%)	SBLI
The first four countries			
Denmark	United States	Switzerland	Denmark
Iceland	Australia	United States	Iceland
Switzerland	Iceland	Canada	Switzerland
Australia	Switzerland	Iceland	Australia
The last four countries			
Brazil	Brazil	Turkey	Brazil
Turkey	Mexico	Spain	Turkey
Mexico	Russia	Greece	Mexico
South Africa	South Africa	South Africa	South Africa

by the socio-demographic situation of the country and in numerical terms, as this case is in most cases a negative outlier in most of the base variables.

K-means Comparison

In this subsection some clusters will be compared in order to understand the difference obtained between them. Clustering will be done using K-means. The K-means method basically allocates each sample element to the cluster whose centroid (sample mean vector) is closest to the observed value vector for the respective element [40]. The cluster number will be checked by elbow method which according to Ketchen et al. [43] is a cluster analysis consistency interpretation and validation method designed to help find the appropriate number of clusters in a dataset.

This method examines the percentage of variation explained as a function of the number of clusters: you must choose a number of clusters so that adding another cluster does not provide much better modeling of the data. More precisely, if one plots the percentage of variance explained by clusters in relation to the number of clusters, the first clusters will add a lot of information (explain a lot of variation), but at some point, the marginal gain will drop, giving the graph an angle. The number of clusters is chosen at this point, hence the method name "elbow method".

Figure 3 shows the countries grouped according to 3 clusters considering the 24 variables that make up the base. It can be seen that cluster 1 includes Brazil, Mexico, South Africa and Turkey, of which Brazil and South Africa are non-OECD countries. But by analyzing this cluster it is possible to perceive in terms of economic and social development the similarity between countries, which by descriptive statistical analysis indicates that this is the worst group in terms of quality of life and economic development. Cluster 2 is basically made up of medium-developed nations in terms of the variables that make up the base, but the countries in this cluster are closer to Cluster 3, which brings the countries with the highest indexes than those in cluster 1 that brings the worst performances. In cluster 2 it is possible to see non-European countries such as Japan and Korea, as well as a South American country that is Chile. The cluster 3 has as countries with the highest values in the study variables, which is a strong indicator of a high perception of quality of life.

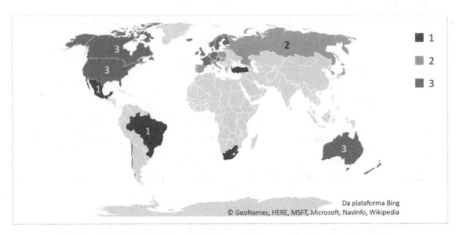

Fig. 3. Spatial distribution of cluster analysis considering the 24 variables.

Figure 4 shows the cluster analysis distribution considering the 3 factors. In order to investigate clusters without the presence of an extreme outlier such as South Africa, the cluster model was run eliminating the presence of that country. It is possible to see a much closer grouping of the first one that considered all the variables of the base. Here the variables are close, but it is possible to see the group of poorer and less developed countries that belong to cluster 1. Cluster 2 mixes middle level countries in some variables and high in others, but in general have a good quality of life. Cluster 3 brings the countries with the highest score in each factor and therefore a higher perception of quality of life.

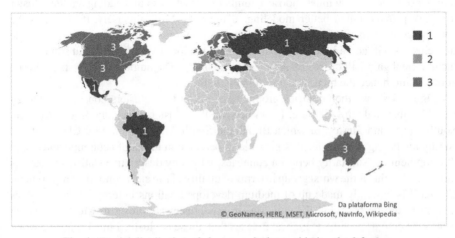

Fig. 4. Spatial distribution of cluster analysis considering the 3 factors.

In Fig. 5 it is possible to identify that cluster 1 brings the countries with the worst performance in terms of SBLI, which include South Africa, which was outlier in the other analyzes and Brazil. In cluster 1 we can see the presence of non-member countries and European countries with less expressiveness in terms of income and living conditions. Cluster 2 brings together countries that have high average values in terms of SBLI and therefore due to the discrimination made by the index a reasonable quality of life. Finally, cluster 3 brings the best performing countries in terms of SBLI, among them Denmark, which has the highest relative value among the countries studied the third cluster.

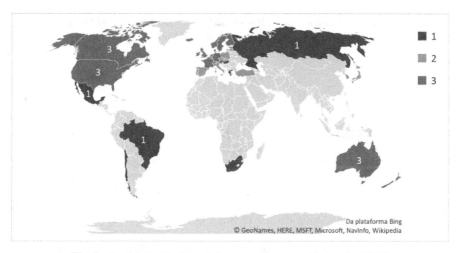

Fig. 5. Spatial distribution of cluster analysis considering the SBLI.

4 Conclusion

The work was aimed at achieving the following objectives: to rank the countries according to the synthetic index and finally to analyze possible clusters and groupings. Using factor analysis was observed the explained variance of the factors obtained according to the variables of the base and still considering the principle of partiality, we obtained the number of 3 factors that together explain 73.26% of the variance of the data set. After the extraction of the factors, the factors were interpreted by means of factorial loads.

Therefore, when pursuing the goal of ranking countries according to the synthetic index SBLI and still analyze the possible clusters and groupings. A cluster analysis was performed by means of K-means. The conclusions of this analysis showed that there is similar behavior in terms of aggregation and that the fact of using a synthetic index does not cause loss for the grouping at term of countries.

In terms of academic contribution, a form of aggregation is proposed that removes part of the subjectivity of the BLI aggregation that is originally done by the user. Using a weighting form not identified in the literature that is a weighting proportional to the explained variance. This approach is also a workflow that can be applied to other sets of variables both for aggregation in index, as well as for pre-processing seeking to reduce the size of the original data set.

As work limitations, it is identified that a benchmarking can be made between the aggregation techniques present in the literature, seeking to demonstrate the efficiency of the proposed approach in comparison to others. For future work, we intend to use the variable aggregation approach in factors such as pre-processing for multicriteria techniques.

Acknowledgments. Conselho Nacional de Desenvolvimento Científico e Tecnológico - Award Number: 314352/2018-0.

Coordenação de Aperfeiçoamento de Pessoal de Ensino Superior - Award Number: 001.

Ministério da Ciência, Tecnologia e Inovações – Award Number: 001.

References

1. How's Life? OECD (2011)
2. Saltelli, A., Tarantola, S., Campolongo, F., Ratto, M.: Sensitivity Analysis in Practice: A Guide to Assessing Scientific Models. Wiley, Hoboken (2004)
3. do Carvalhal Monteiro, R.L., Pereira, V., Costa, H.G.: Dependence analysis between childhood social indicators and human development index through canonical correlation analysis. Child Indic. Res. **13**(1), 337–362 (2020). https://doi.org/10.1007/s12187-019-09715-6
4. da Silva, G.B., Costa, H.G.: Mapeamento de um núcleo de partida de referências em Data Mining a partir de periódicos publicados no Brasil. Gestao e Producao **22**(1), 107–118 (2015). https://doi.org/10.1590/0104-530X792-13
5. Hetschko, C., von Reumont, L., Schöb, R.: Embedding as a pitfall for survey-based welfare indicators: evidence from an experiment. J. R. Stat. Soc. Ser. A: Stat. Soc. **182**(2), 517–539 (2019). https://doi.org/10.1111/rssa.12410
6. Koronakos, G., Smirlis, Y., Sotiros, D., Despotis, D.K.: Assessment of OECD Better Life Index by incorporating public opinion. Socio-Econ. Plan. Sci. **70** (2020). https://doi.org/10.1016/j.seps.2019.03.005
7. Resce, G., Maynard, D.: What matters most to people around the world? Retrieving Better Life Index priorities on Twitter. Technol. Forecast. Soc. Change **137**, 61–75 (2018). https://doi.org/10.1016/j.techfore.2018.06.044
8. Balestra, C., Boarini, R., Tosetto, E.: What matters most to people? Evidence from the OECD Better Life Index users' responses. Soc. Indic. Res. **136**(3), 907–930 (2017). https://doi.org/10.1007/s11205-016-1538-4
9. Lorenz, J., Brauer, C., Lorenz, D.: Rank-optimal weighting or "how to be best in the OECD Better Life Index?". Soc. Indic. Res. **134**(1), 75–92 (2016). https://doi.org/10.1007/s11205-016-1416-0
10. Peiró-Palomino, J., Picazo-Tadeo, A.J.: OECD: one or many? Ranking countries with a composite well-being indicator. Soc. Indic. Res. **139**(3), 847–869 (2017). https://doi.org/10.1007/s11205-017-1747-5
11. Oehler-Şincai, I.M.: Looking for a genuine indicator welfare—În căutarea unui indicator veritabil al bunăstării. Calitatea Vietii **1**, 62–81 (2014)
12. Nikolaev, B.: Economic freedom and quality of life: evidence from the OECD's your better life index. J. Priv. Enterp. **29**(3), 61–96 (2014)
13. Boarini, R., D'Ercole, M.M.: Going beyond GDP: an OECD Perspective*. Fisc. Stud. **34**(3), 289–314 (2013). https://doi.org/10.1111/j.1475-5890.2013.12007.x

14. Kasparian, J., Rolland, A.: OECD's 'Better Life Index': can any country be well ranked? J. Appl. Stat. **39**(10), 2223–2230 (2012). https://doi.org/10.1080/02664763.2012.706265
15. Hagerty, M.R., Land, K.C.: Constructing summary indices of quality of life. Sociol. Methods Res. **35**(4), 455–496 (2007). https://doi.org/10.1177/0049124106292354
16. Marsella, A.J., Levi, L., Ekblad, S.: The importance of including quality-of-life indices in international social and economic development activities. Appl. Prev. Psychol. **6**(2), 55–67 (1997). https://doi.org/10.1016/S0962-1849(05)80011-3
17. Tsurumi, T., Managi, S.: Monetary valuations of life conditions in a consistent framework: the life satisfaction approach. J. Happiness Stud. **18**(5), 1275–1303 (2016). https://doi.org/10.1007/s10902-016-9775-4
18. Patrizii, V., Pettini, A., Resce, G.: The cost of well-being. Soc. Indic. Res. **133**(3), 985–1010 (2016). https://doi.org/10.1007/s11205-016-1394-2
19. Mizobuchi, H.: Measuring world better life frontier: a composite indicator for OECD Better Life Index. Soc. Indic. Res. **118**(3), 987–1007 (2013). https://doi.org/10.1007/s11205-013-0457-x
20. Michalos, A.C., Hatch, P.M.: Good societies, financial inequality and secrecy, and a good life: from Aristotle to Piketty. Appl. Res. Qual. Life **15**(4), 1005–1054 (2019). https://doi.org/10.1007/s11482-019-09717-0
21. Chaaban, J., Irani, A., Khoury, A.: The Composite Global Well-Being Index (CGWBI): a new multi-dimensional measure of human development. Soc. Indic. Res. **129**(1), 465–487 (2015). https://doi.org/10.1007/s11205-015-1112-5
22. Mazumdar, K.: Measuring the well-beings of the developing countries: achievement and improvement indices. Soc. Indic. Res. **47**(1), 1–60 (1999). https://doi.org/10.1023/A:1006895213769
23. Diener, E.D.: A value based index for measuring national quality of life. Soc. Indic. Res. **36**(2), 107–127 (1995). https://doi.org/10.1007/BF01079721
24. Greyling, T., Tregenna, F.: Construction and analysis of a composite quality of life index for a region of South Africa. Soc. Indic. Res. **131**(3), 887–930 (2016). https://doi.org/10.1007/s11205-016-1294-5
25. Delhey, J., Steckermeier, L.C.: The good life, affluence, and self-reported happiness: introducing the good life index and debunking two popular myths. World Dev. **88**, 50–66 (2016). https://doi.org/10.1016/j.worlddev.2016.07.007
26. Ali, H., Rashid, N.H.A., Lukman, Z.M., Awang, A.: Socioeconomic well-being and the quality of life between regions: a case of Malaysia. Int. Bus. Manag. **4**(4), 250–254 (2010). https://doi.org/10.3923/ibm.2010.250.254
27. Anderson, J., Gerber, J.: A human development index for the United States-Mexico border. J. Borderl. Stud. **19**(2), 1–26 (2004). https://doi.org/10.1080/08865655.2004.9695624
28. Chan, Y.K., Kwan, C.C.A., Shek, T.L.D.: Quality of life in Hong Kong: the CUHK Hong Kong quality of life index. Soc. Indic. Res. **71**(1), 259–289 (2005). https://doi.org/10.1007/s11205-004-8020-4
29. Bobbitt, L., Green, S., Candura, L., Morgan, G.A.: The development of a county level index of well-being. Soc. Indic. Res. **73**(1), 19–42 (2005). https://doi.org/10.1007/s11205-004-6165-9
30. Mizobuchi, H.: Measuring socio-economic factors and sensitivity of happiness. J. Happiness Stud. **18**(2), 463–504 (2016). https://doi.org/10.1007/s10902-016-9733-1
31. Kaklauskas, A., et al.: Multiple criteria analysis of environmental sustainability and quality of life in post-Soviet states. Ecol. Indic. **89**, 781–807 (2018). https://doi.org/10.1016/j.ecolind.2017.12.070
32. Rahman, T.: Measuring the well-being across countries. Appl. Econ. Lett. **14**(11), 779–783 (2007). https://doi.org/10.1080/13504850600605952

33. do Carvalhal Monteiro, R.L., Pereira, V., Costa, H.G.: Analysis of the Better Life Index trough a cluster algorithm. Soc. Indic. Res. **142**(2), 477–506 (2018). https://doi.org/10.1007/s11205-018-1902-7

34. Pinar, M.: Multidimensional well-being and inequality across the European regions with alternative interactions between the well-being dimensions. Soc. Indic. Res. **144**(1), 31–72 (2018). https://doi.org/10.1007/s11205-018-2047-4

35. Aroca, P., Gonzalez, P.A., Valdebenito, R.: The heterogeneous level of life quality across Chilean regions * (2017). https://doi.org/10.1016/j.habitatint.2017.06.010

36. How's Life? 2017. OECD (2017)

37. Hair, J.: Multivariate Data Analysis. Pearson Education Limited, Harlow (2014)

38. Spearman, C.: General intelligence, objectively determined and measured. Am. J. Psychol. **15**, 201–293 (1904)

39. Thurstone, L.L.: The Vectors of Mind. University of Chicago Press, Chicago (1935)

40. Mingoti, S.A.: Análise de dados através de métodos de Estatística Multivariada: Uma abordagem aplicada, p. 297 (2005)

41. Tabachnick, B.G., Fidell, L.S.: Using Multivariate Statistics, 5th edn. Pearson Education Limited, London (2007)

42. Pallant, J.: SPSS Survival Manual. Allen & Unwin, Crows Nest (2001)

43. Ketchen, D.J., Shook, C.L.: The application of cluster analysis in strategic management research: an analysis and critique. Strateg. Manag. J. **17**(6), 441–458 (1996). https://doi.org/10.1002/(sici)1097-0266(199606)17:6%3c441:aid-smj819%3e3.0.co;2-g

Stackelberg Stability in the Graph Model for Conflict Resolution: Definition and Implementation

Haiyan Xu[1](✉), Guixian Liu[1,2], D. Marc Kilgour[3], and Keith W. Hipel[4]

[1] College of Economics and Management,
Nanjing University of Aeronautics and Astronautics, Nanjing, Jiangsu, China
`xuhaiyan@nuaa.edu.cn`
[2] School of Mathematics and Information Science, Henan polytechnic University,
Jiaozuo, China
[3] Department of Mathematics, Wilfrid Laurier University,
Waterloo, Ontario N2L 3C5, Canada
[4] Department of Systems Design Engineering, University of Waterloo, Waterloo,
Ontario N2L 3G1, Canada

Abstract. This paper proposes a new algebraic definition that facilities calculating of Stackelberg stability in a graph model for conflict resolution with two decision makers. Most stability definitions used in the graph model methodology place decision makers at the same level, in the sense that their roles are symmetric. In practice, however, one decision maker may join by forcing the other to respond to his or her decision. So, to be applied, a model must specify the leader and the follower. Stackelberg stability can be defined logically, but an algorithm to implement it has not been developed until now, due to its complicated recursive formula. To permit Stackelberg stability to be calculated efficiently and encoded conveniently, within a decision support system, an algebraic test for the stability is developed. This algebraic representation of Stackelberg stability is easy to implement and interpret. A superpower military confrontation is used to illustrate how Stackelberg stability can be employed to a real-world application using the new approach.

Keywords: Conflict analysis · Decision maker · Algebraic expressions · Stackelberg stability · Graph model · Ordinal preferences

1 Introduction

Strategic conflict inevitably occurs on a daily basis in life. It may involve two or more persons or organizations with different power, and can happen throughout society [17,27,31]. Therefore, studies of how to resolve these conflicts are of great importance. Many kinds of Stackelberg Solutions [30] have been formulated [1,13,22,29] with their features. Among the formal methodologies that handle strategic conflict, the graph model for conflict resolution (GMCR) [6,7,20,21,28]

© Springer Nature Switzerland AG 2020
A. T. de Almeida and D. C. Morais (Eds.): INSID 2020, LNBIP 405, pp. 77–92, 2020.
https://doi.org/10.1007/978-3-030-64399-7_6

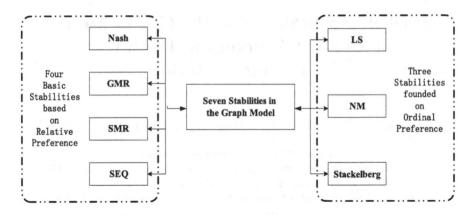

Fig. 1. Seven stabilities in the graph model for conflict resolution.

provides a remarkable combination of simplicity and flexibility. A range of solution concepts for GMCR have been defined, including Nash stability [25,26], general metarationality (GMR) and symmetric metarationality (SMR) [16], sequential stability (SEQ) [12], limited-move stability (LS) [6,19,39], non-myopic stability (NM) [2,3,18], and Stackelberg equilibrium (ST) [30]. The seven solution concepts shown in Fig. 1 as defined within the GMCR framework can be divided into the four basic stabilities, Nash stability, GMR, SMR, and SEQ, which require only relative pairwise preference information, and the three stabilities of LS stability, NM stability, and ST stability that require ordinal preferences. To assess the stability of a state from the viewpoint of a particular decision maker (DM), the consequences the DM expects, should he or she unilaterally move from the status quo (initial state), must be considered. Studies on the four basic stabilities displayed on the left in Fig. 1 in which the roles of the DMs are symmetric have developed rapidly. The concept of anticipation is related to the latter three stabilities shown on the right in Fig. 1.

For the stabilities, LS, NM, and ST, Stackelberg stability is very important and is related to Limited-move and Nonmyopic stabilities [6]. Consider a two-DM game in which one DM is called the leader and the other is the follower. For Stackelberg stability, the DM who holds the more powerful position is called the leader, and the other, who reacts to the leader, is called the follower. Conflict models that include this feature, in which a DM can force his opponent to react to his decision, can be very useful in practical situations.

Stackelberg stability in the graph model for two DMs was defined using a complicated recursive formula in terms of the underlying graphs and an ordinal preference relation [6]. Preference information plays a pivotal role in decision analysis [10,11,14,15,23,24]. Each DM has preference among the possible states that can take place. The four basic stabilities require only relative preference information for each DM and, therefore, can handle both intransitive and transitive preferences. Stackelberg stability assumes ordinal preference which consists of two cases. For strict ordinal preferences, states are ranked from most to least preferred for a DM. When the preferences are weak ordinal or non-strict, the DM has at least one set of equally preferred states among which he or she is indifferent. In other words, ties are allowed. Clearly, ordinal preferences are transitive. DMs in the four basic stabilities are at the same level in the sense that their roles are symmetric—that is to say, each DM's stability concept could be the same. But, it can often be seen in the practice that one DM has the ability to force his or her decision on another. We believe that Stackelberg stability can play an important role in decision analysis because of its occurrence in practice. However, as was noted in the development of the decision support system (DSS) GMCR II [8,9], the nature of recursive representations in a logically-defined structure makes coding difficult. The DSS GMCR II is programmed for employment with the four basic stability definitions, but is difficult to modify or adapt to other analysis techniques, such as Stackelberg stability. Table 1 lists the Current status of analysis stage in the graph model. An innovative matrix system to efficiently calculate the four basic stabilities in the graph model was proposed by [32–38]. The matrix representation effectively converts stability analysis from a logical to a matrix structure, which has been done for the four stabilities on the left in Fig. 1.

Table 1. Current status of analysis stage in the graph model

Model	Analysis	Algorithms?	In GMCR II?
Graph model with certain preference	Individual stability	Yes	Yes
	Coalition stability analysis	Yes	Yes
	Status quo analysis	Yes	No
	Policy stability	No	No
Graph model with uncertain preference	Individual stability	No	No
	Status quo analysis	Yes	No
Graph model with strength of preference	Individual stability	No	No

The objective of this research is to devise an algebraic approach to determine Stackelberg stability. The idea of Stackelberg stability was first defined logically [6]. However, due to its complicated recursive formula, an algorithm to implement it has never been developed well. Accordingly, an algebraic method is proposed to permit Stackelberg stability to be efficiently calculated and conveniently encoded within a decision support system in a graph model with two DMs having strict or non-strict ordinal preference. The proposed algebraic representation of Stackelberg stability simplifies the coding of logically-defined stability definitions and is designed for easy implementation.

Several important concepts corresponding to the latter three stabilities are defined and the recursive formula of Stackelberg stability is presented in Sect. 2.

Next, the algebraic representation of Stackelberg stability in the graph model for two DMs is developed in Sect. 3. Within Sect. 4, a superpower military confrontation (SMC) conflict in which a DM is a leader and the other is the follower, is used to demonstrate the unique features of the proposed algebraic method. Finally, some conclusions and ideas for future work are provided in Sect. 5.

2 Recursive Formula of Stackelberg Stability

In the first subsection, basic definitions for GMCR are introduced, including the types of moves that DMs can take. This is followed by defining Stackelberg stability using a logical or recursive representation.

2.1 Graph Model for Conflict Resolution

A *graph model* is a structure $G = \langle N, S, \{\succeq_i, A_i, i \in N\}\rangle$, where

- N is a non-empty, finite set, called the set of DMs.
- S is a non-empty, finite set, called the set of feasible states.
- $\succeq_i$ denotes the preference relation for DM i defined below. If preference between two states is indifferent for all DMs, the two states are treated as the same state in a game.
- For each DM i, $A_i \subseteq S \times S$ is DM i's set of oriented arcs, which contains the movements in one step controlled by DM i.

Here, $G_i = (S, A_i)$ is DM i's directed graph in which S denotes the vertex set and each oriented arc in $A_i \subseteq S \times S$ indicates that DM i can make a one-step unilateral move (UM) from the initial state of the arc to its terminal state. For simple models, sometimes it is informative to combine all of the DMs' directed graphs, $\{G_i : i \in N\}$, along with their preferences, to create what is called an integrated graph model. The simple preference of DM i is coded by a pair of relations $\{\succ_i, \sim_i\}$ on S, where $s \succ_i q$ indicates that DM i prefers state s to q and $s \sim_i q$ means that DM i is indifferent between s and q (or equally prefers s and q). Note that the preferred relation "$\succ$" is assumed to be transitive for Stackelberg stability in this paper. The formal definition of the transitive preference is given as follow.

Definition 1. *Let $s, q, k \in S$ and R be a relation between two states in a graph model. If kRs and sRq imply kRq, then R is transitive. Otherwise, R is intransitive.*

For example, $k \succ s$ and $s \succ q$ imply $k \succ q$, then the preference $\succ$ is transitive. Note that the assumption of transitivity of preferences is not required in the four basic stability definitions on the left in Fig. 1.

One advantage of the graph model is its innate capability to systematically keep track of state transitions. State transition is the process by which a conflict model moves from one state to another. If a DM can cause a state transition on his or her own, then this transition is called a unilateral move (UM) for that DM. Let $R_i(s)$ denote DM i's reachable list from state s by UMs. This set contains all states to which DM i can move from state s in one step, and, hence, $R_i(s) = \{q \in S : (s, q) \in A_i\}$, where S is the set of feasible states and A_i is the set of arcs connecting two states which are controlled by DM i.

2.2 Recursive Representation of Stackelberg Stability

A recursive representation is a formula that is used to determine the next term of a sequence using one or more of the preceding terms.

For Stackelberg stability, DM i's anticipation vector is an important concept. The vector amounts to a specification of DM i's beliefs about the results of all possible future plays that i could start. Let $N = \{i, j\}$ denote the set of DMs and $m = |S|$ be the number of states. The formal definition of the anticipation vector is given as follows (adapted from [6]):

Definition 2. *Let $i \in N$, $s_k \in S$, and h be a fixed positive integer. $L_h(i, s_k) \in S$ is DM i's anticipated final state for a sequence of moves from initial state s_k, with horizon h. Specifically, $L_h(i, s_k)$ denotes the final state of a game of length h beginning at state s_k with the initial move controlled by DM i. $L_h(i)$, DM i's anticipation vector, has dimension m, with $L_h(i, s_k)$ as its kth element.*

Based on Definition 2, the limited-move stability at length h is defined as follows.

Definition 3. *Let $i \in N$ and $s \in S$. State s is limited-move stable (LS) at horizon h denoted L_h for DM i iff $L_h(i, s) = s$.*

The three stabilities on the right in Fig. 1 require ordinal preference information, and therefore require more information than the four stabilities on the left in Fig. 1. To keep track of ordinal preference information, each state can be associated with a cardinal number such that the higher the number, the more preferred the state. One may define DM i's ordinal preference for $s \in S$ by

$$P_i(s) = |\{x \in S : s \succeq_i x\}|, \; for \; \forall s \in S \; and \; i \in N, \tag{1}$$

where x is a dummy variable and $|U|$ denotes the cardinality of the set $U = \{x \in S : s \succeq_i x\}$. Based on the preference function, the concept of a preference vector in a graph model can be defined as follows.

Definition 4. *Let $i \in N$ and $s_k \in S$. DM i's preference row vector is the m-dimensional vector with $P_i(s_k)$ as its kth element, where $P_i(s_k)$ is i's preference for state s_k.*

Before presenting the recursive formula of Stackelberg stability, some important notations are introduced. Let $i, j \in N$, $s \in S$, $R_i(s)$ denote DM i's reachable list from state s by UMs, and h be a fixed positive integer. The subset of states, $M_h(i, s)$, and the maximum preference value at level h, $P_h^*(i, s)$, are described as follows (adapted from [6]).

- If $R_i(s) = \emptyset$, set $M_h(i, s) = s$.
- If $R_i(s) \neq \emptyset$, let

$$\phi_i(s) = \{q^* \in R_i(s) : P_i(L_{h-1}(j, q^*)) = max\{P_i(L_{h-1}(j, q)) : q \in R_i(s)\}\}$$

be the set of the solution q^*, where P_i is DM i's m-dimensional preference vector and j is DM i's opponent.

(i) If $|\phi_i(s)| = 1$, set

$$M_h(i, s) = \phi_i(s); \qquad (2)$$

(ii) If $|\phi_i(s)| > 1$, set

$$M_h(i, s) = \{\tilde{q} \in \phi_i(s) : P_j(L_{h-1}(j, \tilde{q})) = min\{P_j(L_{h-1}(j, q^*)) : q^* \in \phi_i(s)\}\}. \qquad (3)$$

If $\tilde{q}$ is not uniquely defined, then there exist states s and q satisfying $P_i(s) = P_i(q)$ and $P_j(s) = P_j(q)$. According to the definition of the graph model, $s = q$.

- $P_h^*(i, s)$, the maximum preference value at level h that DM i anticipates can be achieved at level h by moving from state s, is

$$P_h^*(i, s) = P_i(L_{h-1}(j, M_h(i, s))). \qquad (4)$$

Based on the definition for the maximum preference value, the concept of a maximum preference values vector at level h in a graph model can be defined as follows.

Definition 5. *Let $i \in N$, $s \in S$, and h be a fixed positive integer. DM i's maximum preference values vector at level h, $P_h^*(i)$, is the m-dimensional row vector with $P_h^*(i, s)$ as its sth element.*

With the notation, the anticipation vector can be defined recursively as follows (adapted from [6]).

Definition 6. *Let $i, j \in N$, $s \in S$, and h be a fixed positive integer. Let $L_h(i, s)$ denote the sth element of DM i's anticipation vector $L_h(i)$. Then $L_h(i, s)$ must satisfy*

$$L_h(i, s) = \begin{cases} s & if\ R_i(s) = \emptyset\ or\ P_i(s) \geq P_h^*(i, s) \\ L_{h-1}(j, M_h(i, s)) & otherwise, \end{cases} \qquad (5)$$

with $L_0(i, s) = s$.

Based on Definitions 3 and 6, the next result is obvious.

Corollary 1. *Let $i \in N$ and $s \in S$. State s is L_1 stable for DM i iff s is Nash stable for DM i.*

Proof: Based on Definition 6 for $h = 1$,

$$L_1(i, s) = \begin{cases} s & if\ R_i(s) = \emptyset\ or\ P_i(s) \geq P_1^*(i, s) \\ L_0(j, M_1(i, s)) & otherwise, \end{cases}$$

$$= \begin{cases} s & if\ R_i(s) = \emptyset\ or\ P_i(s) \geq P_i(M_1(i,s)) \\ M_1(i,s) & otherwise. \end{cases} \tag{6}$$

(i) If $R_i(s) = \emptyset$, then $M_1(i,s) = s$ and $L_1(i,s) = s$ from (6). Hence, s is L_1 stable for DM i according to Definition 3. Let $R_i^+(s) = \{q \in R_i(s) : P_i(q) > P_i(s)\}$. According to the definition of Nash (Fang et al., [6]), s is Nash stable for DM i when $R_i^+(s) = \emptyset$. Accordingly, if $R_i(s) = \emptyset$, s is L_1 stable and Nash stable for DM i.

(ii) If $R_i(s) \neq \emptyset$, then $L_1(i,s) = s$ iff $P_i(s) \geq P_i(M_1(i,s))$. According to (2) in notation definition, $P_i(s) \geq P_i(M_1(i,s))$ iff $R_i^+(s) = \emptyset$. Accordingly, if $R_i(s) \neq \emptyset$, s is L_1 stable iff s is Nash stable for DM i. □

Based on the definitions of the limited-move, horizon $h = 1$ and $h = 2$, stabilities, Stackelberg stability can be defined from [6].

Definition 7. *Let $i \in N$. State $s \in S$ is Stackelberg stable for i as leader iff s is L_2 stable for DM i and Nash stable for DM j.*

From Definition 7, if s is Stacklberg stability with DM i as leader, then DM i prefers to stay at s, assuming that the follower, DM j would respond to any move in his or her own interest. In addition, DM j prefers state s to any state that he or she can reach from s. To apply Definition 7, the key point is to determine the element $L_2(i,s)$.

3   Algebraic Representation of Stackelberg Stability

Some important definitions related to the proposed algebraic method and two algebraic representations for strict ordinal preference and non-strict ordinal preference are introduced, respectively, in this section.

3.1   Important Definitions

Some important matrices and concepts are introduced as follows.

Definition 8. *Let M and Q be two $m \times m$ matrices. **The Hadamard product** "$\circ$" for M and Q is an $m \times m$ matrix W with the $W(s,q)$ entry as $W(s,q) = M(s,q) \cdot Q(s,q)$.*

Definition 9. ***The sign function***, *$sign(\cdot)$, maps an $m \times m$ matrix M with (s,q) entry $M(s,q)$ to the $m \times m$ matrix*

$$sign[M(s,q)] = \begin{cases} 1 & M(s,q) > 0, \\ 0 & M(s,q) = 0, \\ -1 & M(s,q) < 0. \end{cases}$$

The adjacency matrix equivalent to the reachable list $R_i(s)$ is defined as follows.

Definition 10. *DM i's adjacency matrix is the $m \times m$ 0–1 matrix J_i with (s, q) entry*

$$J_i(s, q) = \begin{cases} 1 & if \ (s, q) \in A_i, \\ 0 & otherwise, \end{cases}$$

in which A_i is DM i's set of oriented arcs.

DM i's reachable list from state s, $R_i(s)$, and DM i's adjacency matrix J_i have the relation: $R_i(s) = \{q : J_i(s, q) = 1\}$. It contains all states to which DM i can move from state s in one step. To define Stackelberg stability, two new functions are required.

Definition 11. *The functions "$\arg \max f(x)$" and "$\arg \min f(x)$" are the nonempty sets of values of x where $f(x)$ attains its largest and smallest values, respectively. If "$\arg \max f(x)$" is uniquely defined, then the function "$\arg \max$" is used to map an $m \times m$ matrix Q to an m–dimensional vector H by defining the sth element $H(s)$ using $H(s) = \arg \max(e_s^T \cdot Q)$ in which e_s is the unit vector with s^{th} element 1 and others 0. Then $H(s)$ is the maximum entry in row s of Q.*

Note that when "$\arg \max$" is used for a matrix, "$\arg \max$" can be understood as "$\arg row \max$", that is the function "$\arg \max$" applied to the matrix, row by row.

Based on these definitions, the algebraic representation of Stackelberg Stability for strict ordinal preference can be introduced first.

3.2 Stackelberg Stability with Strict Ordinal Preference

From Definition 7 for Stackelberg stability, the key step in determining whether state s is Stackelberg stable for DM i as the leader is to find the element $L_2(i, s)$. An algebraic expression of $L_2(i, s)$ can be provided in this section. The relationship between the limited move preference matrix at $h = 1$ and the anticipation vector $L_1(i)$ is described in the following lemma.

Lemma 1. *Let $i \in N$, $s \in S$, and $m = |S|$. P_i denotes DM i's preference vector with dimension m. Let $A_{1i} = (J_i + I) \circ (e \cdot P_i)$. DM i's anticipation vector at $h = 1$ is $L_1(i)$, the m–dimensional vector*

$$L_1(i) = \arg \max\{A_{1i}\}, \tag{7}$$

in which e is the m–dimensional column vector with each element 1, I is the $m \times m$ identity matrix, and "$\circ$" denotes the Hadamard product.

Proof: Let $V = \arg \max(A_{1i})$. Then, $V(s) = \arg \max[e_s^T \cdot ((J_i + I) \circ (e \cdot P_i))]$.

(i) If $V(s) = s$, then $R_i(s) = \emptyset$ or $P_i(s) \geq \max_{q \in R_i(s)} \{P_i(q)\}$. Because of strict ordinal preference, $P_i(s) > \max_{q \in R_i(s)} \{P_i(q)\} = P_1^*(i, s)$. Hence, $V(s) = L_1(i, s)$ by Definition 6;

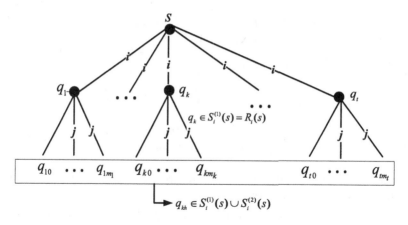

Fig. 2. The terminal states reachable from s in one or two steps by the first DM i.

(ii) If $V(s) = k \neq s$, then $P_i(k) > P_i(s)$ and $P_i(k) = \max\limits_{q \in R_i(s)} \{P_i(q)\}$. Hence, $k = M_1(i, s)$. From (4), we have $P_i(k) = P_1^*(i, s)$. Based on Definition 6, $V(s) = L_1(i, s)$.

Therefore, $V(s) = L_1(i, s)$, i.e., $L_1(i) = \arg\max((J_i + I) \circ (e \cdot P_i))$.   □

Definition 12. *Let $i \in N$, $s \in S$, and $m = |S|$. $L_1(i)$ is DM i's anticipation vector at $h = 1$. Then, the limited-move matrix at $h = 1$ for DM i is the $m \times m$ 0–1 matrix Q_i with (s, q) entry*

$$Q_i(s, q) = \begin{cases} 1 \ if \ L_1(i, s) = q, \\ 0 \ otherwise. \end{cases}$$

Theorem 1. *Let $i, j \in N$ and $s \in S$. P_i denotes DM i's preference vector with dimension m. Let $A_{2i} = sign(J_i \cdot Q_j + I) \circ (e \cdot P_i)$. The anticipation vector $L_2(i)$ can be expressed as an m–dimensional vector*

$$L_2(i) = \arg\max\{A_{2i}\}, \tag{8}$$

in which "sign" denotes the sign function that reflects each positive entry to 1, each negative entry to -1, and otherwise with 0.

Proof: Let $S_i^{(1)}(s)(= R_i(s))$ and $S_i^{(2)}(s)$ denote states reachable from s in one and two legal moves with first mover DM i, respectively. Let $V = sign(J_i \cdot Q_j)$. If $V(s, q) = 1$ for $q \neq s$ iff there exists $q_k \in S_i^{(1)}(s)$ as shown in Fig. 2, such that $Q_j(q_k, q) = 1$ in which $L_1(j, q_k) = q$ for $q_k \in R_i(s)$ by Definition 12. Let $q_k = q_{k0}$ and m_k be the number of states reachable from q_k in one step by DM j, i.e., $m_k = |R_j(q_k)|$. Therefore, $q \in S_i^{(2)}(s) \cup S_i^{(1)}(s)$ and $q = q_{kh^*} = \arg\max\limits_{0 \leq h \leq m_k} \{P_i(q_{kh}) : q_{kh} \in R_j(q_k) \cup \{q_k\}\}$ from Definition 6. Assume that t is the number of states reachable from s in one step by DM i, i.e., $t = |R_i(s)|$.

Let $A_{2i} = sign(J_i \cdot Q_j + I) \circ (e \cdot P_i)$. Since $e_s^T \cdot A_{2i} = (e_s^T \cdot (V + I)) \circ P_i$, hence, (1) if $A_{2i}(s,s) = \max\{e_s^T \cdot A_{2i}\}$, then $\arg\max\{e_s^T \cdot A_{2i}\} = s$; (2) if $A_{2i}(s,q^*) = \max\{e_s^T \cdot A_{2i}\}$ for $q^* \neq s$, then $\arg\max\{e_s^T \cdot A_{2i}\} = q^*$. From (4), $P_2^*(i,s) = P_i(L_1(j, M_2(i,s))) = \max\{P_i(L_1(j,q_k)) : q_k \in R_i(s)\}$. From the discussion above, $q^* \in S_i^{(1)}(s) \cup S_i^{(2)}(s)$ and $P_2^*(i,s) = P_i(q^*)$.

Conclude the discussions in (1) and (2),

$$\arg\max\{e_s^T \cdot A_{2i}\} = \begin{cases} s & if\, R_i(s) = \emptyset \text{ or } P_i(s) \geq P_2^*(i,s) \\ L_1(j, M_2(i,s)) & otherwise. \end{cases}$$

It is identical with $L_2(i,s)$ defined in (5). Accordingly, (8) holds for each element s so the proof of (8) is completed. □

The discussions above assumed strict ordinal preference. For the case of non-strict ordinal preference, the algebraic formula to calculate Stackelberg stability is presented next.

3.3   Stackelberg Stability with Non-strict Ordinal Preference

When DM i wants to choose among two or more states, each of which maximizes her or his own anticipated preference values, but among which DM j is not indifferent. Specifically, when DM i moves unilaterally, he or she wants to maximize his or her own and to minimize the preference value he or she anticipates his or her opponent, DM j will receive.

Lemma 2. Let $i,j \in N$ and $s \in S$. P_i denotes DM i's preference vector. If the game is strict ordinal, the sth element of DM i's anticipation vector $L_2(i)$ must satisfy

$$L_2(i,s) = \arg\max[(e_s^T \cdot sign(J_i \cdot Q_j + I)) \circ P_i].$$

Proof: If the game is strict ordinal, $|\phi_i(s)| = 1$. $L_2(i) = \arg\max\{sign(J_i \cdot Q_j + I) \circ (e \cdot P_i)\}$ from Theorem 1. Therefore, $L_2(i,s) = \arg\max\{e_s^T \cdot [sign(J_i \cdot Q_j + I) \circ (e \cdot P_i)]\} = \arg\max[(e_s^T \cdot sign(J_i \cdot Q_j + I)) \circ P_i]$. □

Theorem 2. Let $i,j \in N$ and $s \in S$. P_j denotes DM j's preference vector. If the game is non-strict ordinal, there are two cases: (i) $|\phi_i(s)| = 1$, the sth element of DM i's anticipation vector $\widetilde{L_2(i)}$ is identical to $L_2(i,s)$. (ii) $|\phi_i(s)| > 1$, The anticipation vector $\widetilde{L_2(i)}$ can be expressed as an m–dimensional vector with s^{th} element

$$\widetilde{L_2(i,s)} = \{\tilde{s} \in L_2(i,s) : P_j(\tilde{s}) = min\{P_j(L_2(i,s))\}\}. \tag{9}$$

Proof: If the game is non-strict ordinal, (i) If $|\phi_i(s)| = 1$, the conclusion is obviously from Lemma 2.

(ii) If $|\phi_i(s)| > 1$, by formula (3), Definition 6 and Lemma 2, $\widetilde{L_2(i,s)} = \{\tilde{s} \in L_2(i,s) : P_j(\tilde{s}) = min\{P_j(L_2(i,s))\}\}$. □

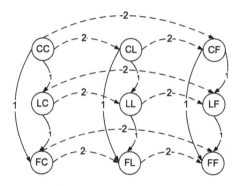

Fig. 3. Graph model for the Superpower Military Confrontation.

4   Application: Superpower Military Confrontation

A model of a superpower military confrontation (SMC) is employed to illustrate the proposed algebraic formulation of Stackelberg stability. A SMC might have arisen in Europe in the 1960s. The two main DMs were USA and USSR, each with three strategies: a conventional attack, labeled C; a limited nuclear strike below the total war threshold, labeled L; and a full nuclear attack on the home countries, labeled F. The details were presented in [6]. The graph model, with DMs USA and USSR, is presented in Fig. 3. Reachable lists and preferences for the two DMs are shown in Table 2. In this model, preference is strictly ordinal.

Table 2. Reachable lists and preference ranks for SMC

State	USA		USSR	
	Reachable list R_1	Preference P_1	Reachable list R_2	Preference P_2
s_1: CC	s_4, s_7	5	s_2, s_3	8
s_2: CL	s_5, s_8	4	s_3	9
s_3: CF	s_6, s_9	1		7
s_4: LC	s_7	9	s_5, s_6	4
s_5: LL	s_8	6	s_6	6
s_6: LF	s_9	2		5
s_7: FC		8	s_8, s_9	1
s_8: FL		7	s_9	2
s_9: FF		3		3

To apply the algebraic representation of the Stackelberg stability with strictly ordinal preference, one can apply to the following steps:

- Construct adjacency matrices, J_i and J_j, using the information given in Table 2;

Table 3. SMC limited-move preference matrices at $h = 1$.

Matrix	$A_{11} = (I + J_1) \circ (e \cdot P_1)$									$A_{12} = (I + J_2) \circ (e \cdot P_2)$								
State	s_1	s_2	s_3	s_4	s_5	s_6	s_7	s_8	s_9	s_1	s_2	s_3	s_4	s_5	s_6	s_7	s_8	s_9
s_1	5	0	0	9	0	0	8	0	0	8	9	7	0	0	0	0	0	0
s_2	0	4	0	0	6	0	0	7	0	0	9	7	0	0	0	0	0	0
s_3	0	0	1	0	0	2	0	0	3	0	0	7	0	0	0	0	0	0
s_4	0	0	0	9	0	0	8	0	0	0	0	0	4	6	5	0	0	0
s_5	0	0	0	0	6	0	0	7	0	0	0	0	0	6	5	0	0	0
s_6	0	0	0	0	0	2	0	0	3	0	0	0	0	0	5	0	0	0
s_7	0	0	0	0	0	0	8	0	0	0	0	0	0	0	0	1	2	3
s_8	0	0	0	0	0	0	0	7	0	0	0	0	0	0	0	0	2	3
s_9	0	0	0	0	0	0	0	0	3	0	0	0	0	0	0	0	0	3

- Obtain preferences, P_i for $i = 1, 2$, using information provided by Table 2;
- Calculate the limited-move preference matrices, A_{hi} at $h = 1$, for $i = 1, 2$, using $A_{1i} = (I + J_i) \circ (e \cdot P_i)$. The two preference matrices are presented in Table 3;
- Construct the limited-move matrices, Q_i, for $i = 1, 2$, using Definition 12. The results are shown in Table 4;
- Calculate limited-move preference matrices, A_{hi} at $h = 2$, for $i = 1, 2$, using $A_{2i} = sign(I + J_i \cdot Q_j) \circ (e \cdot P_i)$. The results are given in Table 5;
- Calculate the anticipation vectors, $L_2(i)$ for $i = 1, 2$, using $L_2(i) = \arg\max\{A_{2i}\}$;
- Analyze the results: If $L_2(i, s) = s$, then s is L_2 stable for DM i;
- Identify Stackelberg stability using Definition 7: If s is L_2 stable for DM i and L_1 stable for DM j, then s is Stackelberg stable for i as leader.

In fact, the anticipation vectors at $h = 1$, $L_1(i)$, can be obtained from Table 3. For example, if we want to calculate $L_1(1, s_4)$, then identify $\arg\max\{e_4^T \cdot A_{11}\} = s_4$ from Table 3. Therefore, $L_1(1, s_4) = s_4$, i.e., s_4 is L_1 stable for DM 1. If we calculate $L_1(2, s_4)$, then obtain $\arg\max\{e_4^T \cdot A_{12}\} = s_5$ from Table 3. Hence, $L_1(2, s_4) = s_5$, so, s_4 is L_1 unstable for DM 2. Accordingly, $L_1(1) = (s_4, s_8, s_9, s_4, s_8, s_9, s_7, s_8, s_9)$ and $L_1(2) = (s_2, s_2, s_3, s_5, s_5, s_6, s_9, s_9, s_9)$. Clearly, s_4, s_7, s_8, s_9 is L_1 stable for DM 1; s_2, s_3, s_5, s_6, s_9 is L_1 stable for DM 2.

The anticipation vectors $L_2(i)$ for $i = 1, 2$ can be calculated by results presented in Tables 4 and 5. $L_2(1) = \arg\max\{A_{21}\} = (s_5, s_5, s_9, s_4, s_5, s_9, s_7, s_8, s_9)$ and $L_2(2) = \arg\max\{A_{22}\} = (s_1, s_2, s_3, s_4, s_5, s_6, s_9, s_9, s_9)$. Therefore, s_4, s_5, s_7, s_8, and s_9 are L_2 stable for DM 1; $s_1, s_2, s_3, s_4, s_5, s_6$, and s_9 are L_2 stable for DM 2.

From Definition 7 for the Stackelberg stability, if DM 1 is selected as a leader, since s_4, s_5, s_7, s_8, s_9 are L_2 stable for DM 1 and s_2, s_3, s_5, s_6, s_9 are L_1 stable for DM 2, then there are two Stackelberg equilibria, $s_5 = (LL)$ and $s_9 = (FF)$; similarly, when USSR is the leader, there are two Stackelberg equilibria, $s_4 = (LC)$

Table 4. SMC limited-move matrices.

Matrix	Q_1									Q_2								
State	s_1	s_2	s_3	s_4	s_5	s_6	s_7	s_8	s_9	s_1	s_2	s_3	s_4	s_5	s_6	s_7	s_8	s_9
s_1	0	0	0	1	0	0	0	0	0	0	1	0	0	0	0	01	0	0
s_2	0	0	0	0	0	0	0	1	0	0	1	0	0	0	0	0	0	0
s_3	0	0	0	0	0	0	0	0	1	0	0	1	0	0	0	0	0	0
s_4	0	0	0	1	0	0	0	0	0	0	0	0	0	1	0	0	0	0
s_5	0	0	0	0	0	0	0	1	0	0	0	0	0	1	0	0	0	0
s_6	0	0	0	0	0	0	0	0	1	0	0	0	0	0	1	0	0	0
s_7	0	0	0	0	0	0	1	0	0	0	0	0	0	0	0	0	0	1
s_8	0	0	0	0	0	0	0	1	0	0	0	0	0	0	0	0	0	1
s_9	0	0	0	0	0	0	0	0	1	0	0	0	0	0	0	0	0	1

Table 5. SMC limited-move preference matrices at $h = 2$.

Matrix	$A_{21} = sign(I + J_1 \cdot Q_2) \circ (e \cdot P_1)$									$A_{22} = sign(I + J_2 \cdot Q_1) \circ (e \cdot P_2)$								
State	s_1	s_2	s_3	s_4	s_5	s_6	s_7	s_8	s_9	s_1	s_2	s_3	s_4	s_5	s_6	s_7	s_8	s_9
s_1	5	0	0	0	6	0	0	0	3	8	0	0	0	0	0	0	2	3
s_2	0	4	0	0	6	0	0	0	3	0	9	0	0	0	0	0	0	3
s_3	0	0	1	0	0	2	0	0	3	0	0	7	0	0	0	0	0	0
s_4	0	0	0	9	0	0	0	0	3	0	0	0	4	0	0	0	2	3
s_5	0	0	0	0	6	0	0	0	3	0	0	0	0	6	0	0	0	3
s_6	0	0	0	0	0	2	0	0	3	0	0	0	0	0	5	0	0	0
s_7	0	0	0	0	0	0	8	0	0	0	0	0	0	0	0	1	2	3
s_8	0	0	0	0	0	0	0	7	0	0	0	0	0	0	0	0	2	3
s_9	0	0	0	0	0	0	0	0	3	0	0	0	0	0	0	0	0	3

and $s_9 = (FF)$. Specifically, if USA selects L, USSR also performs L. If USA takes F, the most preferred choice for the USSR is also F. Therefore, (LL) and (FF) are most preferred for the USA, and they constitute the Stackelberg equilibria with the USA as a leader. Similarly, (LC) and (FF) are Stackelberg equilibria with the USSR as a leader. To see why (LL) is a Stackelberg equilibrium when DM 1 (USA) is the leader, it is clear from Fig. 3 that DM 1 can move only from (LL) to (FL). In this case, the follower, DM 2, can move to (FF) and prefer to do so. Anticipating since $P_1(LL) > P_1(FF)$. In fact, it is not surprising that (FF) is an equilibrium, since neither DM can move away from it. Therefore, once (FF) forms, it will endure. Therefore, state (FF) is a Stackelberg equilibrium regardless of which DM is the leader, (FF) is called a dual Stackelberg equilibrium.

The above Stackelberg stabilities are identical with the results presented in [6] using the recursive approach presented (5). Clearly, comparing with the recursive formula, the algebraic presentation is more efficient for calculating and analyzing Stackelberg stabilities [4,5].

5   Conclusion and Future Work

In this paper, the matrix representation of four basic stabilities is extended to Stackelberg stability, which includes DMs with different power levels. Stackelberg stability is easiest to implement using the proposed algebraic representation, which eases the coding of the recursive definition. With the algebraic method, Stackelberg stability can be integrated easily into a decision support system (DSS). Another benefit of the algebraic form is that it facilitates modification and extension of the definitions.

This paper concerns only conflict models with two DMs, a leader and a follower. Most of the time, there are more than two DMs, so in order to demonstrate the efficiency of the new representations, it would be worthwhile to extend the algebraic method to general n-DM cases. Also, to implement the limited-move stability (LS) and non-myopic stability (NM) easily, it would be valuable to extend the algebraic form to include the two stabilities, but this project will require much additional study.

Acknowledgement. The authors appreciate financial support from the National Natural Science Foundation of China (71971115, 71471087) and National Social Science Foundation of China (12AZD102).

References

1. Averboukh, Y., Baklanov, A.: Stackelberg solutions of differential games in the class of nonanticipative strategies. Dyn. Games Appl. **4**(1), 1–9 (2013). https://doi.org/10.1007/s13235-013-0077-8
2. Brams, S.J., Wittman, D.: Nonmyopic equilibria in 2×2 games. Conflict Manage. Peace Sci. **6**(1), 39–62 (1981)
3. Brams, S.J.: Theory of Moves. Combridge University Press, Cambridge (1993)
4. Cohn, H., Kleinberg, R., Szegedy, B., Umans, C.: Group-theoretic algorithms for matrix multiplication. In: Proceedings of the 46th Annual Symposium on Foundations of Computer Science, pp. 379–388 (2005)
5. Coppersmith, D., Winograd, S.: Matrix multiplication via arithmetic programming. J. Symb. Comput. **9**, 251–280 (1990)
6. Fang, L., Hipel, K.W., Kilgour, D.M.: Interactive Decision Making: The Graph Model for Conflict Resolution. Wiley, New York (1993)
7. Fang, L., Hipel, K.W., Wang, L.: Gisborne water export conflict study. In: Proceedings of 3rd International Conference on Water Resources Environment Research, vol. 1, pp. 432–436 (2002)
8. Fang, L., Hipel, K.W., Kilgour, D.M., Peng, X.: A decision support system for interactive decision making, part 1: model formulation. IEEE Trans. Syst. Man Cybern. Part C Appl. Rev. **33**(1), 42–55 (2003)

9. Fang, L., Hipel, K.W., Kilgour, D.M., Peng, X.: A decision support system for inter-active decision making, part 2: analysis and output interpretation. IEEE Trans. Syst. Man Cybern. Part C Appl. Rev. **33**(1), 56–66 (2003)

10. Fischer, G.W., Jia, J., Luce, M.F.: Attribute conflict and preference uncertainty: the randMAU model. Manage. Sci. **46**(5), 669–684 (2000)

11. Fischer, G.W., Luce, M.F., Jia, J.: Attribute conflict and preference uncertainty: effects on judgment time and error. Manage. Sci. **46**(1), 88–103 (2000)

12. Fraser, N.M., Hipel, K.W.: Solving complex conflicts. IEEE Trans. Syst. Man Cybern. **9**, 805–817 (1979)

13. Fraser, N.M., Hipel, K.W.: Conflict Analysis: Models and Resolution. Wiley, New York (1984)

14. Hamouda, L., Kilgour, D.M., Hipel, K.W.: Strength of preference in the graph model for conflict resolution. Group Decis. Negot. **13**, 449–462 (2004)

15. Hamouda, L., Kilgour, D.M., Hipel, K.W.: Strength of preference in graph models for multiple-decision-maker conflicts. Appl. Math. Comput. **179**, 314–327 (2006)

16. Howard, N.: Paradoxes of Rationality: Theory of Metagames and Political Behavior. MIT press, Cambridge (1971)

17. Julien, L.A.: A note on Stackelberg competition. J. Econ. **103**, 171–187 (2011)

18. Kilgour, D.M.: Equilibria for far-sighted players. Theor. Decis. **16**, 135–157 (1984)

19. Kilgour, D.M.: Anticipation and stability in two-person noncooperative games. In: Dynamic Model of International Conflict, pp. 26–51. Lynne Rienner Press, Boulder (1985)

20. Kilgour, D.M., Hipel, K.W., Fang, L.: The graph model for conflicts. Automatica **23**, 41–55 (1987)

21. Kilgour, D.M., Hipel, K.W.: The graph model for conflict resolution: past, present, and future. Group Decis. Negot. **14**, 441–460 (2005)

22. Lafay, T.: A linear generalization of Stackelberg's model. Theor. Decis. **69**, 317–326 (2010)

23. Li, K.W., Hipel, K.W., Kilgour, D.M., Fang, L.: Preference uncertainty in the graph model for conflict resolution. IEEE Trans. Syst. Man Cybern. Part A Syst. Hum. **34**, 507–520 (2004)

24. Li, K.W., Kilgour, D.M., Hipel, K.W.: Status quo analysis in the graph model for conflict resolution. J. Oper. Res. Soc. **56**, 699–707 (2005)

25. Nash, J.F.: Equilibrium points in n-person games. Proc. Natl. Acad. Sci. **36**, 48–49 (1950)

26. Nash, J.F.: Noncooperative games. Ann. Math. **54**(2), 286–295 (1951)

27. von Neumann, J., Morgenstern, O.: Theory of Games and Economic Behavior. Princeton University Press, Princeton (1944)

28. Noakes, D.J., Fang, L., Hipel, K.W., Kilgour, D.M.: An examination of the salmon aquaculture conflict in British Columbia using the graph model for conflict reso-lution. Fish. Manage. Ecol. **10**, 123–137 (2003)

29. Pensavalle, C.A., Pieri, G.: Stackelberg problems with followers in the grand coali-tion of a Tu-game. Decisions Econ. Finan. **36**, 89–98 (2013)

30. von Stackelberg, H.: Marktform und Gleichgewicht. Springer, Vienna (1934)

31. Wowak, K.D.: Supply chain knowledge and performance: a meta-analysis. Decis. Sci. **44**(5), 843–875 (2013)

32. Xu, H., Hipel, K.W., Kilgour, D.M.: Matrix representation of solution concepts in multiple decision maker graph models. IEEE Trans. Syst. Man Cybern. Part A Syst. Hum. **39**(1), 96–108 (2009)

33. Xu, H., Hipel, K.W., Kilgour, D.M., Chen, Y.: Combining strength and uncertainty for preferences in the graph model for conflict resolution with multiple decision makers. Theor. Decis. **69**(4), 497–521 (2010)
34. Xu, H., Kilgour, D.M., Hipel, K.W.: An integrated algebraic approach to conflict resolution with three-level preference. Appl. Math. Comput. **216**, 693–707 (2010)
35. Xu, H., Kilgour, D.M., Hipel, K.W., Kemkes, G.: Using matrices to link conflict evolution and resolution in a graph model. Eur. J. Oper. Res. **207**, 318–329 (2010)
36. Xu, H., Kilgour, D.M., Hipel, K.W.: Matrix representation of conflict resolution in multiple-decision-maker graph models with preference uncertainty. Group Decis. Negot. **20**(6), 755–779 (2011)
37. Xu, H., Kilgour, D.M., Hipel, K.W., McBean, E.A.: Theory and application of conflict resolution with hybrid preference in colored graphs. Appl. Math. Model. **37**, 989–1003 (2013)
38. Xu, H., Kilgour, D.M., Hipel, K.W., McBean, E.A.: Theory and implementation of coalitional analysis in cooperative decision making. Theor. Decis. **76**(2), 147–171 (2013). https://doi.org/10.1007/s11238-013-9363-6
39. Zagare, F.C.: Limited-move equilibria in games 2×2 games. Theor. Decis. **16**, 1–19 (1984)

Sustainable Measurement Model of Renewable Energy Sources: An Application in Port Located in the South Region of Brazil

Dayla Karolina Fossile[1](✉), Sergio E. Gouvea da Costa[1,2](✉), and Edson Pinheiro de Lima[1,2](✉)

[1] Pontifícia Universidade Católica do Paraná, Rua Imaculada Conceição, 1155, Curitiba 80215-901, Brazil
daylafossile@gmail.com, {s.gouve,e.pinheiro}@pucpr.br
[2] Universidade Tecnológica Federal do Paraná, Avenida Sete de Setembro, 3165, Curitiba 80230-901, Brazil

Abstract. Several ports worldwide use renewable energy sources such as: wind, photovoltaic and wave energy. Rotterdam in the Netherlands, Genoa in Italy, Hartlepool in the United Kingdom, Kitakyushu in Japan, Port Kembla in Australia, Gothenburg in Sweden, ports in Spain, San Diego, Tokyo and Los Angeles can be cited. Regarding Brazilian ports, the Pecém Port in Ceará implemented wave energy; however, due to the need for adjustments and further investments, it is no longer operational. The main goal behind the study is to propose and test a sustainability measurement model for renewable energy sources for Brazilian ports, identifying the most appropriate clean energy. In order to define the evaluation criteria for the model, information from literature, legislation and rulings (environmental, social, economic and national energy policies) were considered alongside an evaluation by 10 experts through the Lawshe method. The criteria were classified through the Phrase Completion scale; the scale presents 11 points, where zero indicates the absence of the attribute (excellence) and 10 indicates the presence of all possible levels of excellence. Finally, the Renewable Energy Sustainability Partial Score, Renewable Energy Sustainability Score and Renewable Energy Corporate Sustainability Grid were applied. This model was applied in a port enterprise located in the South Region of Brazil and indicated that the photovoltaic energy is regarded as the most appropriate to be used, matching the environmental, social and economic criteria. The model is applicable to companies with different characteristics, regardless of industrial sector and geographic location of the company.

Keywords: Renewable energy · Ports · Lawshe · Phrase completion

1 Introduction

The energy efficiency has an important role in the political agenda of many coun-tries, since it is connected with industrial competitiveness and environmental benefits such as reduction of CO_2 emissions.

© Springer Nature Switzerland AG 2020
A. T. de Almeida and D. C. Morais (Eds.): INSID 2020, LNBIP 405, pp. 93–109, 2020.
https://doi.org/10.1007/978-3-030-64399-7_7

The need to establish operational indicators to measure energy efficiency, measurement methodologies are still not unified and overlooked by many [1]. The energy efficiency indicators seek to capture the dynamics in a network of interconnected processes revealing short/long-term [2].

The energy generation is the main contributing factor to the emission of greenhouse effect gases, thus, in order to reduce CO2 emissions, improvements have to be implemented, using energy conservation processes [3]. The port industry is regarded as a sector that presents one of the highest pollution levels [4]. Mainly, because this activity requires high consumption of energy in their operations [5]. It is important to remember that studies on the port industry and renewable energy are still scarce [3].

Prevention initiatives, according to the European Union, have focused on creating scarcity prevention mechanisms and control of productive energy. The Eco-Ports can be cited as example of these initiatives. They represent a foundation integrated into the European port structure, which can conduct studies on how to address issues: water quality, solid waste management and port energy efficiency [6]. It is also important to point out that the Brazilian National Waterway Transportation Agency (ANTAQ, in Brazilian Portuguese) (2017) [7] has demanded energy management from Brazilian ports, aiming to reduce consumption, clean energy sources utilization, reduction of CO2 emissions and provision of energy to ships.

This study is divided in five sections including the Introduction. The second section deals with methodological procedures. The third section describes the development of the model. The fourth section discusses the application of the model in a port located in the South region of Brazil. Finally, the conclusions related to the study are presented and future research.

2 Methodology

In order to develop a sustainability measurement model for renewable energy sources, sustainability dimensions and information presented in the systematic literature review on energy efficiency management and port sustainability [8] were considered. The latter identified that the majority of European ports use clean energy sources to reduce CO2 emissions and improve the efficiency related to sustainability. That study concluded that the most used renewable energy sources worldwide are: wind, photovoltaic and wave energy. These will be the three sources to be evaluated in the present study. Furthermore, the information presented in legislation and Brazilian rulings, regarding the topic, were taken into consideration along with data generated in the multicriteria analysis of the studies by Fossile et al. (2020) [9].

To define the model criteria, 10 experts with knowledge on management, strategy and sustainability applied to renewable energy sources were selected. The process of expert selection used the intentional non-probability sampling. This method involves the selection of a group from the population provided that it contains representative information on the whole. The first interview aims to identify the criteria that the experts consider pertinent to compose a sustainability measurement model for renewable energy sources. Moreover, the criteria defined in the study by Fossile et al. (2020) [9] were used.

In that study, four experts of a Brazilian port enterprise determined, through brainstorming, 20 criteria for the environment, social and economic dimensions. Table 1 presents the criteria.

Table 1. Criteria defined in the brainstorming process.

Environmental Dimension	Social Dimension	Economic Dimension
Land extensions ownership and suppression of vegetation	Displacement and compensation of the local community	Energy source efficiency
Marine extensions ownership and suppression of fluvial-marine vegetation	Noise generation	Enterprise low initial investment
Contamination level	Limitation and interference in the navigation and fishing	Tax incentives
The utilization of extremely toxic and pollutant products	Deforestation and green area decline for the local community	Low level of yearly enterprise maintenance costs vs. initial investment
Materials recycling	Work health and safety	Financing period for the enterprise
Building access routes	Employability level	Annual equipment depreciation rate or useful life
Public/Licenses interference and bureaucracy	–	Equipment installation schedule

It was necessary to identify which other criteria the 10 experts regarded as relevant to be included in the model proposed in the study.

Six personal interviews, in the first interview, four other criteria were identified and included in the study: natural resources availability, physical space availability, payback period and percentage of enterprise financing.

After the first interview, a second questionnaire was applied with the 10 experts. This aimed to evaluate all 24 criteria, considering a scale of importance between 1 (one) and 3 (three): 1 – essential; 2 – important, but not essential, 3 – not important.

The analysis of the results of the second questionnaire was conducted through the Lawshe method. This is a procedure used to validate the content in several areas [10]. And vital to validate questionnaires with experts, who should evaluate the items according to three categories: a) essential; b) important, but not essential; c) not important, nevertheless, the answers are gathered into two groups: essential and non-essential [11]. The Lawshe method is a simple mathematical model, robust and easy to understand, which can be obtained through the following mathematical formula [10]:

$$VR = ne - \frac{\left(\frac{N}{2}\right)}{\left(\frac{N}{2}\right)} \tag{1}$$

Where, CVR = Content Validity Ratio; ne = number of experts that classified the criteria as essential; N = number of experts. CVR values range between -1 (perfect disagreement) and $+1$ (perfect agreement) [12]. Whenever more than 50% of the experts indicate that the criterion is essential, the CVR is positive. Thus, when the CVR is negative it means that 50% of the experts considered the criterion as non-essential [11]. To evaluate the criteria that will be included in the final model indicates that CVR Values under the critical limit (CVR_critical) can be excluded from the final model. The calculation for the CVR_critical considers the approximation to the binominal distribution (discrete distribution) by the normal distribution (continuous distribution). This approach considers the parameters as average, variance and standard deviation [11]:

$$\mu = n.p \tag{2}$$

$$\sigma^2 = n.p.(1-p) \tag{3}$$

$$\sigma = \sqrt{n.p.(1-p)} \tag{4}$$

Where, n: represents the number of experts that responded the questionnaire; p: the probability of designating the criterion as essential $\left(p = \frac{1}{2} = 0,5\right)$. The levels between 1% and 5% of significance or error (probability) are the most commonly used. The level of significance of 5% is assumed for the standard normal distribution, setting the value of the z-score = 1.96, considering that $ne_{critical} = \mu + z.\sigma$, which corresponds to the minimum of experts that is required so that the item regarded as essential is considered valid. The calculation of the $CVR_{critical}$ is obtained through the formula:

$$CVR_{critical} = ne_{critical} - \frac{\left(\frac{N}{2}\right)}{\left(\frac{N}{2}\right)} \tag{5}$$

According to this information, in the study, an average for the normal distribution = 5 and variance = 2.5 (standard deviation = 1.5811).

Considering the critical value is $\mu + z . \sigma$, the critical value is 5 + (1.96 . 1.5811) = 8, which corresponds to the minimum of experts that should consider the criterion as essential so that it is valid. For the criterion to remain valid, the $CVR_{calculated}$ should be equal or higher than the $CVR_{critical}$ as presented in Table 2.

Only one was regarded as not important, hence, it will not be a part of the sustainability measurement model for renewable energy sources.

The model also used as reference and information the structure of the Sustainability Partial Scores and Corporate Sustainability Score calculations and the Corporate Sustainability Grid, proposed in the studies by Callado and Fensterseifer in 2011 [13]; and, Lapinskaite and Radikaite in 2015 [14].

Table 2. Results of the Lawshe method according to the perception of the experts.

Environmental Aspects

Criteria	ne	N	$ne_{critical}$	$CVR_{calculated}$	$CVR_{critical}$	Decision
Availability of natural resources	10	10	8.0	1.00	0.60	Keep
Physical space availability	10	10	8.0	1.00	0.60	Keep
Land extensions ownership and suppression	8	10	8.0	0.60	0.60	Keep
Marine/fluvial-marine extensions ownership	8	10	8.0	0.60	0.60	Keep
Building access routes	9	10	8.0	0.80	0.60	Keep
Potential area contamination	8	10	8.0	0.60	0.60	Keep
Utilization of toxic and pollutant products	8	10	8.0	0.60	0.60	Keep
Materials and equipment recycling	10	10	8.0	1.00	0.60	Keep
Environmental public/licenses interf. and bureaucracy	10	10	8.0	1.00	0.60	Keep

Social Aspects

Criteria	ne	N	$ne_{critical}$	$CVR_{calculated}$	$CVR_{critical}$	Decision
Green area decline	8	10	8.0	0.60	0.60	Keep
Limitation of navigation and fishing	9	10	8.0	0.80	0.60	Keep
People displacement and compensation	9	10	8.0	0.80	0.60	Keep
Noise generation	10	10	8.0	1.00	0.60	Keep
Risks of the workplace	10	10	8.0	1.00	0.60	Keep
Employability and income levels	9	10	8.0	0.80	0.60	Keep

Economic Aspects

Criteria	ne	N	$ne_{critical}$	$CVR_{calculated}$	$CVR_{critical}$	Decision
Source efficiency level	10	10	8.0	1.00	0.60	Keep
Low initial investment	7	10	8.0	0.40	0.60	Exclude
Payback period	10	10	8.0	1.00	0.60	Keep
Yearly maintenance costs vs. initial investment	10	10	8.0	1.00	0.60	Keep
Percentage of enterprise financing	8	10	8.0	0.60	0.60	Keep
Enterprise financing period	8	10	8.0	0.60	0.60	Keep
Enterprise installation schedule	9	10	8.0	0.80	0.60	Keep
Average useful life for assets	9	10	8.0	0.80	0.60	Keep
Federal and state tax incentives	10	10	8.0	1.00	0.60	Keep

3   Model Development

Initially, each criterion will be described and classified according to the classification of the environmental, social and economic dimensions, using Phrase Completion. This scale presents 11 points, where zero (0) does not address any degree of excellence and 10 addresses all the possible excellence levels [15], as per Table 3.

Table 3. Phrase Completion Scale.

Intensity level										
Very small			Moderate					Very high		
0	1	2	3	4	5	6	7	8	9	10

Source: Hodge and Gillespie (2003) [15]

Regarding the evaluation of the environmental dimension, initially, the energy generation power to be installed should be identified. After that, it is necessary to evaluate the enterprise location with the purpose of checking the characteristics of the natural resources in that region, since the characterization of the potential and installation are essential to the project [16]. The Table 4 below presents a brief description of the social and economic environmental criteria.

Table 4. Description of the social and economic environmental criteria.

Criteria	Description
CA 1 – Natural resources	Availability of natural resources
CA 2 – Physical space availability	It is necessary to identify the available physical space for a renewable energy project
CA 3 – Land extensions	Evaluate the need for land extensions and vegetation suppression
CA 4 – Marine extensions	Evaluate the need for marine extensions and suppression of river-marine vegetation
CA 5 – Contaminations	Evaluate the possibility of terrestrial pollution the navy
CA 6 – Toxic and polluting	Evaluate the use of toxic products and pollutants in the production process used in renewable energy enterprises
CA7 – Recycling	Evaluate the constant need for recycling of materials from renewable energy sources
CA8 – Environmental licenses	Evaluate the bureaucracy of the expeditions of environmental licenses for each renewable energy enterprises
CA9 – Access routes	Evaluate the need to build access roads for renewable energy enterprises

(continued)

Table 4. (*continued*)

Criteria	Description
CS 10 – Displacement	Evaluate the need for displacement of the local community with the installation of renewable energy sources
CS 11 – Noises	Evaluate the noise level of renewable energy sources
CS 12 – Navegation/fishing	Evaluate the limitation of navigation and fishing
CS 13 – Deforestation	Evaluate the need for displacement of the local community with the installation of renewable energy sources
CS 14 – Health and safety	Evaluate the risks and safety of workers in a renewable energy enterprises
CS 15 – Employability	Evaluate the level of employability of renewable energy sources
CE 16 – Efficiency	Evaluate the efficiency of renewable energy projects.
CE 17 –Payback period	It is also vital to check the period for the return on the investment
CE 18 – Percentage of enterprise financing	It is necessary to verify the type of resource fundraising for the enterprise, which can be through equity capital or third-party capital
CE 19 – Incentives	Evaluate the volume of tax incentives offered by the Government of Brazil
CE 20 – Cost	Evaluate the annual maintenance costs of renewable energy enterprises
CE 21 – Enterprise financing period	Evaluate the term of the financing offered by Brazilian Development Bank
CE 22 – Average useful life for assets	Evaluate the depreciation rates of equipment from renewable energy source
CE 23 – Installation Enterprise installation period	Evaluate the installation time of renewable energy enterprises

Note: CA - Environmental Criterion; CS - Social Criterion; CE - Economic criterion.

3.1   Evaluation of the Most Viable Renewable Energy Soucers

Initially, it is necessary to evaluate the model 23 criteria, placing in the scale from 0 (zero) to 10 (ten) each project. Three performance levels were proposed for the each dimension: 1° - Inferior performance: the performance is insufficient for the company; 2° - Intermediate performance: the performance is average for the company; 3° - Superior performance: the performance exceeds the average for the company.

It is important to evaluate the results of the real performance scores and corresponding average for each dimension. The dimension which presents a performance below the intermediate performance value set by the company will score 0 (zero), i.e., the performance is considered unsatisfactory. When the total dimension performance is higher or equal to the intermediate performance will score 1 (one).

After verifying the satisfactory and unsatisfactory performances, the Renewable Energy Sustainability Score is calculated and evaluated through the equation:

$$RESS = PSS_E + PSS_S + PSS_{EC}$$

Where,

RESS = Renewable Energy Sustainability Score
PSS_E = Partial Score of Environmental Sustainability
PSS_S = Partial Score of Social Sustainability
PSS_{EC} = Partial Score of Economic Sustainability

After identifying the results of the Renewable Energy Sustainability Score, the level of sustainability for each source is evaluated. The proposed model classifies the renewable energy sources in four levels, as per Table 5.

Table 5. Renewable Energy Sustainability Score Results.

Score	Level	Description
SRESL = 3	Satisfactory Renewable Energy Source Level	The renewable energy source presents good performance in every dimension
MRESL = 2	Moderate Renewable Energy Source Level	The renewable energy source presents good performance in two of the dimensions
LRESL = 1	Low Renewable Energy Source Level	The renewable energy source presents good performance in only one of the dimensions
NRESL = 0	Non-existent Renewable Energy Source Level	The renewable energy does not present good performance in any of the dimensions

Source: Adapted from Callado and Fensterseifer (2011) [13]

The different result levels for the Renewable Energy Sustainability Score in the model should be used as a general reference for the project. The main objective behind its use is to guide managers in the enterprise decision-making and implementation.

After analyzing the Renewable Energy Sustainability Score, the Renewable Energy Corporate Sustainability Grid is evaluated. It integrates the environmental, social and economic dimensions; it is able to identify the energy source positioning through eight positions [13] These types are described next:

- Position I represents companies with low economic performance which do not have good social interactions and are not committed to environmental issues;
- Position II represents companies with low economic performance that have good social interactions but are not committed to environmental issues;
- Position III represents companies with good economic performance that but do not have good social interactions and are not committed to environmental issues;
- Position IV represents companies with low economic performance that do not have good social interactions but are committed to environmental issues;
- Position V represents companies with good economic performance and good social interactions but are not committed to environmental issues;
- Position VI represents companies with low economic performance but those have good social interactions and are committed to environmental issues;
- Position VII represents companies with good economic performance that do not have good social interactions but are committed to environmental issues;
- Position VIII represents companies with good economic performance, good social interactions and committed to environmental aspects; this is the position that corresponds to sustainable companies.

Through the identification of the Renewable Energy Sustainability Partial Scores and four levels of the Renewable Energy Sustainability Score, it is possible to identify the Renewable Energy Corporate Sustainability Grid for the wind, photovoltaic and wave energy sources.

4   Model Application

This section presents an application of the model for the measurement of the renewable energy sources sustainability in a port located in the South region of Brazil. Initially, the scale of the criterion of natural resources availability was identified through the RETScreen software and Wave App which present weather information from NASA (National Aeronautics and Space Administration). After this step, the data on the firm characteristics and information on the following criteria were collected: physical space availability, land extensions appropriation and vegetation suppression, fluvial-marine extensions appropriation, building and paving needs, green area decrease, navigation and fishing limitations, people displacement and compensation, enterprise financing percentage, and, enterprise financing period.

After checking this information, one of experts on renewable energy sources that participated in the application of the Lawshe method was contacted. This contact aimed to identify the average investment by m^2 for each of the energy sources and the criteria scales: potential area contamination, toxic and pollutant products use, materials and equipment recycling, workplace risk and employability level.

Other criteria such as environmental reports and licenses and public interference, noise generation, energy source efficiency, payback period, enterprise installation period, yearly maintenance costs vs. initial investment, average useful life of assets, and, tax incentives at federal and state level were defined according to rules, regulations, legislation and information presented in literature on the topic.

4.1 Environmental Criteria Analysis

The first aspect to be considered was the environmental dimension performance. Nine criteria were evaluated; they were defined through the Lawshe method. The criteria were described in the previous section. The results of the company analyzed in the study are summarized in Table 6.

Table 6. Environmental criteria scale.

Environmental criteria	Port Alpha Scale		
Energy sources	W	P	W'
Natural resources availability	5	5	4
Physical space availability	0	4	1
Land extensions appropriation and suppression	0	10	9
Marine/fluvial-marine extensions appropriation	0	10	9
Paving and building needs	0	10	8
Potential contamination	0	9	7
Utilization of toxic and pollutant products	0	5	6
Equipment and materials recycling	0	4	6
Environmental reports/licenses and public interference	0	5	1
TOTAL	**5**	**62**	**51**
AVERAGE	**1**	**7**	**6**

Note: W = Wind; P = Photovoltaic; W' = Wave

For the wind energy, the area available is non-existent, since this is one of the bottlenecks for this port, the lack of physical space for its operations. This lack of space prevents the installation of the energy source. Thus, it is considered inadequate and not feasible as per all the other model criteria.

It is important to point out that physical space in ports is extremely important, since it requires large land extensions to allow the movement of their operations [17].

The availability of natural resources has favored the photovoltaic energy, which has a yearly average solar radiation of 3.95 kWh m^2/day. The wave energy natural resources have 10 s with only 0.5 m in height. Evaluating the availability of the physical space, the photovoltaic energy is indicated as the most favorable. Nonetheless, the area available of 3,000 m^2 does not match the energy demand for the company. The daily average energy demand is around 6,360 kWh, the average solar radiation per year is 3.95 kWh/m^2/day.

The evaluation of the physical space available for wave energy, it is shown to be unfavorable, since the daily average of energy demand is around 6,360 kWh, wave level is 10 m/s and 0.5 m in height. These characteristics of the natural resources are not considered high in potential.

The company made available an area of approximately 6,000 m^2 for the installation of wage energy. Because of this information, the installation of two pieces of equipment would generate around 192 kW/h daily.

The photovoltaic energy has been shown to be adequate for the following criteria: land extensions appropriation and vegetation suppression, marine/fluvial-marine extensions appropriation and building and paving needs. The area made available by the company does not require modifications or deforestation for the land or marine/fluvial-marine vegetation. The wave energy, however, requires suppression of approximately 10% of land vegetation, 10% of marine/fluvial-marine vegetation and around 20% for building and paving access routes, according to information presented by the company.

Regarding the area contamination for the photovoltaic energy, it is important to emphasize that the waste generated in the work site can contaminate the area. This occurs because of chemical products handling and storage.

Pollutant emissions such as lubricants and oil come from the utilization of heavy machinery and vehicles. According to the authors, a project with an adequate prevention plan presents a low probability of contamination [18]. The risk of contamination of the area destined for the installation was estimated as 10% (maximum).

Regarding the risk of contamination of wave energy, being regarded as an offshore energy, it is vital to consider that the equipment is installed in the water. Thus, some level of contamination is to be expected [19]. In case of an accident with an offshore energy, the environmental impact becomes higher, since oil spills or chemical products can run long distances, affecting coral reefs, mangroves, contaminating mammals, shellfish, seaweed, fish and sea birds, and, in consequence, human health [20]. The probability of contamination for the wave energy was estimated as 30% of the area destined for the enterprise.

Comparing the photovoltaic and wave energy, regarding the utilization of toxic and pollutants products, materials and equipment recycling, the former energy source was shown to be less favorable than the latter. Photovoltaic panels are composed by blocks of silicon with high degree of purity, ethyl vinyl acetate, epoxy resin, thermoset polymers and glass fibers, which are toxic pollutants. Moreover, there is no legislation in Brazil for the recycling of these materials, which are regarded as extremely pollutants. In comparison, wave energy equipment is regarded as less harmful.

The photovoltaic energy was considered more advantageous than the wave energy for environmental reports/licenses. Wave energy is installed in marine waters, that is, it is regarded as high impact. It requires an Environmental Impact Study, Environ-mental Impact Report and public interference. A simplified environmental study is required for the photovoltaic energy for this enterprise, with no public interference, since it is regarded as a large-scale enterprise by presenting more than 30 WM in power [21].

4.2 Social Criteria Analysis

The second aspect to be considered is the performance in the social dimension. Six criteria were analyzed as per Table 7.

Table 7. Table captions should be placed above the tables.

Social criteria	Scale Port Alpha		
Energy Sources	W	P	W'
Green area decrease	0	10	9
Navigation and fishing limitation	0	10	3
People displacement and compensation	0	10	10
Noise generation	0	10	9
Workplace risk	0	7	6
Employability and income level	0	10	7
TOTAL	**0**	**57**	**44**
AVERAGE	**0**	**9**	**7**

Nota: W = Wind; P = Photovoltaic W' = Wave

The photovoltaic energy is more advantageous than the wave energy. The criteria green area decrease, navigation and energy limitations, people compensation and displacement, noise generation and employability level were evaluated as reaching maximum excellence. Only the criterion, workplace environment risks, was under evaluated, since the employees of a photovoltaic energy enterprise are subject to light and frequent severity.

The criterion navigation and fishing limitation related to a wave energy enterprise presents a hurdle related to 70% of the available area, which is considered high impact, according to the information presented by the port company.

Because the wage energy is undeveloped in Brazil, there is a scarcity of labor. Thus, the expert indicates that approximately 30% of the employees to be hired will not belong to local and regional community.

4.3 Economic Criteria Analysis

The third aspect to be considered is the economic performance. Eight criteria were analyzed. The results of the port are summarized in Table 8.

Table 8. Table captions should be placed above the tables.

Economic criteria	Scale Port Alpha		
Energy Sources	W	P	W'
Enterprise efficiency	0	5	7
Payback period	0	4	0
Enterprise installation period	0	9	4

(*continued*)

Table 8. (*continued*)

Economic criteria	Scale Port Alpha		
Energy Sources	W	P	W'
Yearly maintenance cost × initial investment	0	10	4
Percentage of enterprise financing	0	8	8
Enterprise financing period	0	9	5
Assets average useful life	0	5	10
Federal and state tax incentives	0	8	3
TOTAL	**0**	**58**	**41**
AVERAGE	**0**	**7**	**5**

The wave energy stands out in the efficiency criterion and average useful life of the assets, its average efficiency is around 70% [22]. The photovoltaic energy presents an efficiency of approximately 50% [23]. It is important to point out that the efficiency can in-crease according to the equipment technological advances.

Evaluating the investment payback period, both energy sources present disadvantages. According to information from the expert on renewable energy sources, the investment in square meters related to the photovoltaic energy is approximately 197 dollars. Considering the company made available an area of 3,000 m^2, the total investment will be 590 thousand dollars. The investment corresponds to only 35% of the yearly energy demand for the company. Considering that, the maintenance costs are 1% per year on the investment [24]. Thus, the payback period is approximately 22 years.

The investment of the wave energy per square meters is around 615 dollars as informed by the expert. The company made available an area of approximately 6,000 m^2; the total investment would be 3.7M. Furthermore, it is necessary to consider the yearly maintenance cost, which can reach 14% per year [25]. Because of the data, the wave enterprise presents a loss and the payback period is 36 years.

The yearly maintenance costs versus initial investment for the photovoltaic presents the maximum scale of excellence. The wave energy indicates an elevated yearly cost. This occurs because the operations are performed at sea with high degree of marine aggressiveness [25].

Next, the enterprise installation period was evaluated. According to the expert, the photovoltaic enterprise can be installed in one year. The wave energy requires significant bureaucracy; the installation period can be more than three years. In terms of the financing percentage and period, Port Alpha considered the data presented by the National Bank for Economic and Social Development. However, both energy sources presented the same percentage, since the company is middle-sized. The bank finances 80% of the project. The bank also grants 20 years of financing for a photovoltaic energy enterprise and 10 years for wave energy. It is possible to identify the useful life of the wind energy equipment as 21 years, for the photovoltaic is nine years and wave energy 25 years [26, 27].

For the photovoltaic energy, there is specific legislation dealing with tax incentives at federal and state level. There are reductions, suspensions or exemptions of the Tax on the Circulation of Goods and Services, Industrialized Products, Corporate Income Tax, Social Contribution on Net Profit, Financial Operations, Import Tax, Contribution for the Social Integration Programmed and the Social Security Financing Contribution.

4.4 Evaluation of Most Viable Energy Source for Company

Value intervals associated with corresponding Renewable Energy Sustainability Partial Scores were proposed for each dimension. These intervals have three relevant reference points, which are: minimum, average and maximum performances. The port company defined them.

The minimum performance represents the minimum possible values for the performance indicators of a given dimension. The average performance represents average possible values and maximum represents the maximum values assumed by the criteria of a specific dimension. Table 9 indicates the minimum, average and maximum performances defined by the company on a scale from 0 (zero) to 10 (ten).

Table 9. Minimum, average and maximum performance.

Dimension	Port Alpha		
	Minimum Performance	Average Performance	Maximum Performance
Environmental	5	6	7
Social	3	5	6
Economic	6	8	10

After evaluating the average of each dimension and the minimum, average and maximum performance, the classification of the energy sources was analyzed. The performance is considered satisfactory (1) when the scale of dimension criteria is equal to or higher than the average score; when the average is less, the dimension is regarded as unsatisfactory (0). The results of the evaluation are summarized in Table 10.

Considering the integration and performance of the renewable energy partial scores and renewable energy sustainability levels, it is possible to categories eight positions that compose the renewable energy corporate sustainability grid. Nevertheless, the interactions that defined the renewable energy sources positions in the study are presented in Table 11

The wind energy is ranked in the Position I, which is the energy source with low economic performance, no good social interaction, not committed to social aspects. The photovoltaic energy is in Position VIII. This means that it has a good economic performance, good social interaction and commitment to environmental aspects. Wave energy is in Position VI, i.e., this energy source presents low economic performance, good social interaction and commitment to environmental aspects.

Table 10. Classification of the sustainability dimension scores.

Environmental Criteria	Energy Sources		
Company	Wind	Photovoltaic	Wave
Port Alpha $\geq$ 6	0	1	1
Social Criteria	Energy Sources		
Company	Wind	Photovoltaic	Wave
Port Alpha $\geq$ 5	0	1	1
Economic Criteria	Energy Sources		
Company	Wind	Photovoltaic	Wave
Port Alpha $\geq$ 8	0	1	0
Renewable Energy Sustainability Score	$\Sigma 0$	$\Sigma 3$	$\Sigma 2$

Table 11. Interaction among the Sustainability Partial Scores, Renewable Energy Sustainability Scores and Renewable Energy Corporate Sustainability Grid.

Sources	Renewable Energy Sustainability Partial Scores (E)	Renewable Energy Sustainability Partial Scores (S)	Renewable Energy Sustainability Partial Scores (EC)	Renewable Energy Sustainability Score	Renewable Energy Corporate Sustainability Grid
W	0	0	0	0	I
P	1	1	3	3	VIII
W'	1	1	0	2	VI

5 Conclusion

The research approaches the development and simulation of a model for the measurement of the sustainability of renewable energy sources, which has innovation as its economic efficiency, with social and environmental responsibility. It aims to identify the most adequate energy source to be used in Brazilian ports. Given the growth of the competition of port companies at a global level, it is important to pay special attention to the main decisions that can improve the results of the companies' sustainable performance.

This model was developed by using 23 criteria with participation of 10 experts on management, strategy and sustainability focusing on renewable energy sources through the application of the Lawshe method.

After defining the model criteria, they were evaluated through the Phrase Completion 11 points. The main goal behind this evaluation was to identify the degree of criteria excellence regarding the renewable energy source. By observing the criteria classification, a port company located in the South of Brazil was analyzed along with information from 10 experts and data collected from studies, laws and rulings on the research topic.

The port company also identified the minimum, average and maximum score for each sustainability dimension. It was possible to indicate the renewable energy source sustainability score through the criteria definition, classification of the each criterion on the scale and identification of the average score for each dimension. After this process, it was possible to verify the renewable energy corporate sustainability grid for each energy source addressed in the research.

It was clear, nonetheless, that the company that participated in the model simulation does not encompass the adequate physical space for the installation of the wind energy. Thus, it is considered inadequate and unfeasible.

The photovoltaic energy presented a satisfactory level of sustainability, that is, the environmental, social and economic dimensions reached the average performance desired by the company. The renewable energy corporate sustainability grid presents good economic performance, good social interaction and commitment to the environmental dimension.

Unlike the wave energy, which showed a moderate sustainability level, that is, the energy presented a good performance in the environmental and social dimensions. Therefore, the most viable renewable energy to be ports is the photovoltaic energy source.

References

1. Patterson, M.G.: What is energy efficiency? Energy Policy **24**, 377–390 (1996)
2. Perroni, M.G., Gouvea da Costa, S.E., Pinheiro de Lima, E., Silva. W.V., Tortato, U.: Measuring energy performance: a process based approach. Appl. Energy, **222**, 540–553 (2018)
3. Beer, J., Worrell, E., Blok, K.: Long term energy efficiency improvement in the paper and board industry. Energy **23**(1), 21–41 (1998)
4. Acciaro, M., Ghiara, H., Cusano, M.I.: Energy management in seaports: a new role for port authorities. Energy Policy **71**, 4–12 (2014)
5. Martinsons, M.G., Tseng, C.S.: High-technology management in China: a case study of the Shanghai success stories. J. Eng. Technol. Manage. **12**, 111–137 (1995)
6. Tichavska, M., Tovar, B.: Environmental cost and eco-efficiency from vessel emissions in Las Palmas Port. Transport. Res. **83**, 126–140 (2015)
7. Brazilian Waterway Transportation Agency, Environmental performance index (2017). http://antaq.gov.br/Portal/MeioAmbiente_IDA.asp. Accessed 02 Mar 2017
8. Fossile, D.K., Gouvea da Costa, S.E., Pinheiro de Lima, E.: The Evolution of Scientific Production on Ports Energy Efficiency Management. III CIDESPORT-Congresso Internacional de Desempenho Portuário. Florianópolis/SC (2016)
9. Fossile, D.K., Frej, E.A., Gouvea da Costa, S.E., Pinheiro de Lima, E., Almeida, T.A.: Selecting the most viable renewable energy source for Brazilian ports using the FITradeoff method. J. Cleaner Prod. 121107 (2020)
10. Wilson, F.R., Pan, W., Schumsky, D.A.: Recalculation of the critical values for Lawshe's contentvalidity ratio. Measure. Eval. Counsel. Dev. Londres, Inglaterra **45**(3), 197–210 (2012)

11. Lawshe, C.H.A.: Quantitative approach to content validity. Personnel Psychol. Nova Jersey, EUA **28**(4), 563–575 (1975)
12. Ayre, C.; Scally, A.J.: Critical values for Lawshe's content validity ratio. Measure. Eval. Counsel. Dev. **47**(1), 79–86 (2014)
13. Callado, A.L., Fensterseifer, J.E.: Corporate sustainability measure from an integrated perspective: the corporate sustainability grid. Int. J. Bus. Insights Transformation **3**, 44–53 (2011)
14. Lapinskaite, I., Radikaite, G.: Analysis of measurement ofsustainable development in the insurance company. Euro. Sci. J. **11**(13), 446–464 (2015)
15. Hodge, D.R., Gillespie, D.F.: Phrase completion: an alternative to Likert scales. Social Work Res. **27**(1), 45–55 (2003)
16. Grah, V.F., Ponciano, I.M., Botrel, T.A.: Potential for wind energy generation in Piracicaba, SP, Brazil. Revista Brasileira de Engenharia Agrícola e Ambiental **18**(5), 559–564 (2014)
17. Rocha, M.J.: A conflagração do espaço: a tensa relação porto-cidade no planejamento urbano. Estudos Avançados **33**(95), 91–112 (2019)
18. Gunerhan, H., Hepbasli, A., Giresunlu, U.: Environmental impacts from the solar energy systems. Energy Sources **31**, 131–138 (2009)
19. Guimarães, L.N.M.R.: Parques eólicos offshore en el derecho ambiental marinho. Veredas do Direito **16**(34), 156–173 (2019)
20. Pi, Y., Xu, N., Bao, M., Li, Y., LV, D., Sun, P. Bioremediation of the oil spill polluted marine intertidal zone and its toxicity effect on microalgae. Environ. Sci. Processes Impacts, **17**(4), 877–885 (2015)
21. State Council of The Environment Nº 98/2017. Aprova, nos termos do inciso XIII, do art. 12, da Lei nº 14.675, de 13 de abril de 2009, a listagem das atividades sujeitas ao licenciamento ambiental, define os estudos ambientais necessários e estabelece outras providências. http://www.pmf.sc.gov.br/arquivos/arquivos/pdf/RES%20CONSEMA%2098%202017%20comp ilada%20-%20SDS%2014fev18%20-%20inclui%20consema%20112-2017.pdf.   Accessed 11 Feb 2018
22. Polinder, H., Mueller, M.A., Scuotto, M., Goden de Sousa Prado, M.: Linear generator systems for wave energy conversion. In: 7th European Wave and Tidal Energy Conference, Porto, Portugal (2007)
23. Lee, J., Park, J., Jung, H., Park, J.: Renewable energy potential by the application of a building integrated photovoltaic and wind turbine system in global urban areas. Energies **10**(12), 3–20 (2017)
24. Energy Research Company, Nota técnica. Análise da inserção da energia solar na matriz elétrica brasileira 2012. http://www.epe.gov.br/geracao/Documents/Estudos_23/NT_Energi aSolar_2012.pdf. Accessed 05 Apr 2017
25. Astariz, S., Vasques, A., Iglesias, G.: Evaluation and comparison of the levelized cost of tidal, wave, and offshore wind energy. J. Renew. Sustain. Energy, **7**, 5 (2015)
26. Manual of Energy Asset Control, (2017). Energy Sector Asset Control Manual. http://www.aneel.gov.br/documents/656815/14887121/MANUAL+DE+CONTROLE+PATRIM ONIAL+DO+SETOR+EL%C3%89TRICO+-+MCPSE/3308b7e2-649e-4cf3-8fff-3e78dd eba98b. Accessed 12 May 2017
27. Tolmasquim, M.T.: Energia renovável hidráulica eólica solar e oceânica. Empresa de Pesquisa Energética (2016). http://www.epe.gov.br/acessoainformacao/Paginas/acoesepro gramas.aspx. Accessed 12 May 2017

Applying the FITradeoff Method for Aiding Prioritization of Special Operations of Brazilian Federal Police

Carla Patrícia Cintra Barros da Cunha[1], Caroline Maria de Miranda Mota[2],
Adiel Teixeira de Almeida[2,3], Eduarda Asfora Frej[2,3(✉)],
and Lucia Reis Peixoto Roselli[2,3]

[1] Policia Federal, Superintendência Regional de Pernambuco, Cais do Apolo, 321,
Recife, PE 50030-907, Brazil
`carla.cpcbc@pf.gov.br`
[2] Departamento de Engenharia de Produção, Universidade Federal de Pernambuco,
Av. da Arquitetura - Cidade Universitária, Recife, PE, Brazil
`caroline.mota@ufpe.br, {almeida,eafrej,lrpr}@cdsid.org.br`
[3] Center for Decision Systems and Information Development – CDSID, Universidade Federal
de Pernambuco, Av. da Arquitetura - Cidade Universitária, Recife, PE, Brazil

Abstract. This paper presents a broader view of the Flexible and Interactive
Tradeoff (FITradeoff) multicriteria method and its practical applicability in a problem of prioritization of resources for special operations in Brazilian Federal Police.
The FITradeoff method works based on partial information of decision makers
(DMs), but keeps the whole axiomatic structure of the classical tradeoff procedure. Due to the reduction of the level of difficulty in the elicitation process for
obtaining information from the DM, this tool has a great potential for application
in practical real world decision situations. This paper brings up a decision-making
problem in which the aim is to rank ten special police operations, which are evaluated with respect to fourteen criteria, with the main goal of prioritizing scarce
resources allocation of the Brazilian Federal Police. The decision process is aided
by graphical tools presented in FITradeoff Decision Support System (DSS), which
enables the elicitation process to be shortened with a view to the flexibility of the
method.

Keywords: FITradeoff · Multicriteria decision making · Brazilian federal
police · Special police operations

1 Introduction

According to the Brazilian Constitution, the Federal Police must have to combat several
illicit acts (Brazil 2017). In this context, several investigations are performed by the
Federal Police. These investigations present different characteristics. For instance, some
investigations are named special operations since they present a large scope, requires
more resources, and are considered complex in terms of difficult to solve. A famous

© Springer Nature Switzerland AG 2020
A. T. de Almeida and D. C. Morais (Eds.): INSID 2020, LNBIP 405, pp. 110–125, 2020.
https://doi.org/10.1007/978-3-030-64399-7_8

example is the Lava-Jato (Car Wash) special operation, which starts in 2014 and continues until now (The Economist 2015).

In Federal Police organization, a general protocol (Federal police 2014) is used to guide the prioritizing of the investigations. This protocol is necessary since human and material resources are scarce, and the whole group of investigations cannot be performed at the same time and/or using the same resources.

However, even using this protocol, the decision process to rank or select investigations do not use any formal methodology. In this context, given the multi-criteria scenario presented in this organization routine, since many investigations are presented and they have different characteristics, the Multi-Criteria Decision-Making/Aiding approach (MCDM/A) can be used to formally conduct the decision process based on the decision-maker (DM) preferences (Keeney and Raiffa 1976; Belton and Stewart 2002; de Almeida et al. 2016).

Therefore, in this study, the FITradeoff method for ranking problematic (Frej et al. 2019) is applied to rank special police operations of a particular Regional Superintendence of the Brazilian Federal Police. The chapter is divided as follows. Section 2 describes the FITradeoff method both for choice and rank problematic. Section 3 presents the prioritizing of the special police operations using the FITradeoff Method. Finally, Sect. 4 remarks the final comments and lines for future research.

2   Flexible and Interactive Tradeoff

The Flexible and Interactive Tradeoff (FITradeoff) method is a method for solving MCDM/A problems with partial information from the DMs (de Almeida et al. 2016). Partial information methods have the advantage of requiring less information during the preferences elicitation process, in such a way that the cognitive effort of DMs is reduced and therefore less inconsistency is expected during the process. FITradeoff was developed within the scope of the Multiattribute Value Theory (MAVT), in which each alternative a_j is scored straightforwardly according to Eq. (1).

$$v(a_j) = \sum_{i=1}^{n} k_i v_i(x_{ij}) \tag{1}$$

In (1), k_i is the scaling constant of criterion i (which are also called as weights in this chapter), and $v_i(x_{ij})$ is the value of consequence of alternative j in criterion i, normalized in an interval 0–1 scale, defined according to a marginal value function, in such a way that the value of the best consequence in criterion i is set to 1 ($v_i(b_i) = 1$) and the value of the worst consequence in criterion i is set to 0 ($v_i(w_i) = 0$). Criteria scaling constants are normalized according to Eq. (2).

$$\sum_{i=1}^{n} k_i = 1 \tag{2}$$

Partial information methods are useful when the DM does not have complete information about the parameters of the model, such as the criteria scaling constants k_i. The information required to elicit those paremets can be tedious, time consuming, and DMs may not be able to provide such information in a consistent way (Weber 1987; Kirkwood and Sarin 1985; Salo and Hamalainen 1992). The FITradeoff method was developed based on the classical tradeoff procedure and its strong axiomatic structure (Keeney and Raiffa 1976), but improves its applicability for DMs with an easier process for obtaining information from the DM. While the classical tradeoff procedure requires the DM to state the exact value of a certain criterion that makes him/her indifferent between two consequences, the FITradeoff method asks the DM about preference relations, which are easier to provide. The method supports both choice and ranking problematic, which are detailed in the following topics. FITradeoff is operated by means of a Decision Support System (DSS) which is available for free at www.fitradeoff.org.

2.1 Preferences Elicitation Process

The preferences elicitation process in FITradeoff is interactive, and it is conducted based on a question-and-answer process. The Decision Support System puts questions for the DM, which answers according to his/her preferences.

The first step is the intracriteria evaluation, in which the marginal value function $v_i(x)$ of each criterion is elicited. The FITradeoff method has the advantage of allowing both linear or non-linear value function for intracriteria evaluation, since it embraces the whole structure of the classical tradeoff procedure. The second step concerns the ranking of criteria scaling constants by the DM (3), which is conducted considering the ranges of consequences in each criterion.

$$k_1 > k_2 > \ldots > k_n \tag{3}$$

After defining the ranking of criteria weights, an interactive question and answer process for elicitation of criteria weights starts. The questions put for the DM concerns the comparison between two consequences, in which the DM has to perform tradeoffs between different levels of criteria. Figure 1 illustrates an example of a question put for the DM in FITradeoff DSS, in a problem with $n = 7$ criteria, in which all criteria are to be maximized. This question asks the DM to compare two consequences: Consequence A, with an intermediate outcome ($x_1 = 75$) in criterion 1, represented by the blue bar, and the worst outcome for all other criteria, represented by the red bars; and Consequence B, with the best outcome ($x_2 = 100$) for criterion 2, represented by the red bar, and the worst outcome for all other criteria.

When answering the question illustrated in Fig. 1, the DM declares preference for Consequence A or for Consequence B. If he/she prefers Consequence A, when the global value of this consequence, according to the aggregation function in Eq. (1), is greater that the global value of consequence B; otherwise, the global value of consequence B is greater that the value of consequence A. Let x_i' be a value for the outcome of criterion i for which the DM prefers consequence A; and let x_i'' be a value for criterion i so that the DM prefers consequence B. Therefore, according to the additive aggregation function in (1), the inequalities (4) and (5) can be obtained.

$$k_i v_i(x_i') > k_{i+1} \tag{4}$$

$$k_i v_i(x_i'') < k_{i+1} \tag{5}$$

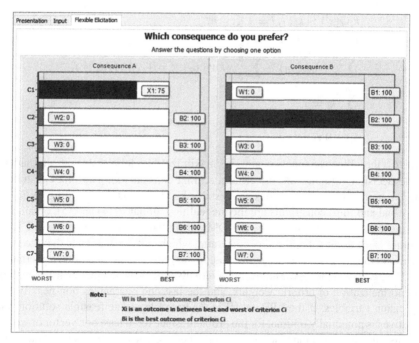

Fig. 1. Elicitation question for comparison of consequences in FITradeoff (Color figure online)

Inequalities of this type can be obtained for different pairs of adjacent criteria, in such a way that a space of weights is obtained. After each question answered by the DM, a new inequality of this type is obtained, in such a way that the space of weights gets tightened. The recommendation for the DM in FITradeoff is computed based on Linear Programming Problem (LPP) models, which vary according to the problematic being treated. The following subsections give more details on the mathematical model of FITradeoff for both choice and ranking problematic.

2.2 FITradeoff for Choice Problematic

In order to produce a recommendation for the DM when the goal is the choice of a unique alternative, the FITradeoff method works by verifying the potential optimality of each alternative, given the current space of weights (de Almeida et al. 2016). An alternative is considered to be potentially optimal if its global value (according to Eq. (1)) is greater that the global value of all other alternatives for at least one vector of weights within the weights space. The potential optimality of an alternative j in FITradeoff is tested according to the LPP below (6)

$$\max v\left(a_j\right) = \sum_{i=1}^{n} k_i v_i\left(x_{ij}\right) \qquad (6)$$

s.t.

$$k_1 > k_2 > \ldots > k_n$$

$$k_i v_i\left(x_i'\right) > k_{i+1}, i = 1, \ldots, n.$$

$$k_i v_i\left(x_i''\right) < k_{i+1}, i = 1, \ldots, n.$$

$$\sum_{i=1}^{n} k_i v_i\left(x_{ij}\right) \geq \sum_{i=1}^{n} k_i v_i(x_{iz}), z = 1, \ldots, m; z \neq j.$$

$$\sum_{i=1}^{n} k_i = 1$$

$$k_i \geq 0 \,\forall i.$$

In (6), the objective function aims to maximize the global value of alternative j, and the decision variables are the criteria scaling constants k_i. The first constraint is the ranking of criteria scaling constants established by the DM, according to Eq. (3). The second and third constraints are the inequalities similar to (4) and (5), obtained on the comparison of consequences by the DM during the elicitation process. The fourth constraint is the potential optimality constraint, which aims to guarantee that the global value of alternative j is greater than or equal to the global value of all other alternatives $z = 1, \ldots, m$, in which m is the number of alternatives of the problem. The fifth constraint is the normalization of criteria weights, and the last one guarantees non-negativity of the decision variables. If the LPP model in (6) has at least one feasible solution, then alternative j is potentially optimal for the problem, since for at least one vector of weights within its value is greater than the values of all other alternatives. Otherwise, if the LPP in (6) does not have a feasible solution for alternative j, then this alternative is not potentially optimal for the problem and therefore it is eliminated from the choice problem.

As previously mentioned, the FITradeoff process is interactive. At each interaction, the DM answers a new preference question, so the weights space is updated, and therefore the LPP model runs again for each alternative $j (j = 1, \ldots, m)$, in order to verify which alternatives are potentially optimal for the problem. Hence, at each interaction, the subset of potentially optimal alternatives is refined, and the elicitation process finishes when a unique alternative is found to be potentially optimal.

As a flexibility feature of the FITradeoff DSS, graphical visualization of the partial results are available for the DMs, as shown in Fig. 2.

Three types of graphical visualization are presented: bar graphic, bubble graphic and spider (or radar) graphic. In those graphics, each potentially optimal alternative is represented by a different color, and their performance in each criterion is shown in a ratio 0–1 scale. By analyzing these graphics, the DM can perform a holistic evaluation of the alternatives by comparing them. If the DM is able to choose his/her preferred alternative based on the graphical comparison, then the choice process finished here, and the elicitation process stops even before the end, which leads to saving of time and effort from DMs.

2.3 FITradeoff for Ranking Problematic

When the goal of the DM is to build a ranking of the alternatives, the preferences elicitation process in FITradeoff is similar to the one for the choice problematic, except for the mathematical model. The potential optimality concept is no longer sufficient to conduct the analysis for ranking problematic, and therefore the LP model is modified to

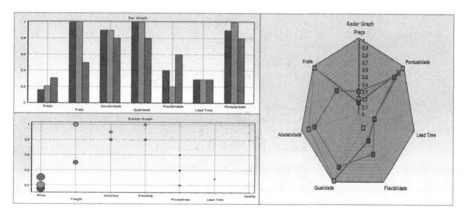

Fig. 2. Graphical visualization in FITradeoff DSS

deal with the ranking problematic. Now, dominance relations between alternatives are verified at each interaction through linear programming, and based on those relations, a ranking of the alternatives – which can be partial or complete – is constructed (Frej et al. 2019). At each interaction, the LPP model in (7) is run for every pair of alternatives (j, z), in order to verify pairwise dominance relations.

$$\max D_{j,z} = \sum_{i=1}^{n} k_i v_i(x_{ij}) - \sum_{i=1}^{n} k_i v_i(x_{iz}) \tag{7}$$

$s.t.$

$k_1 > k_2 > \ldots > k_n$

$k_i v_i(x_i') > k_{i+1}, i = 1, \ldots, n.$

$k_i v_i(x_i'') < k_{i+1}, i = 1, \ldots, n.$

$\sum_{i=1}^{n} k_i = 1$

$k_i \geq 0 \, \forall i.$

The objective function of the model in (7) is to maximize the difference between the global values of alternatives j and z. The constraints are similar to the LP model for the choice problematic (6), except for the potential optimality constraint, which is no longer presented. The LPP in (7) aims to find the maximum difference between two alternatives in terms of global values, for the current space of weights. If the maximum difference between j and z is lower than zero, this means that j cannot be better than z for any vectors of weights within the weights space, and therefore z dominates j (Frej et al. 2019). The process is interactive, and every time the DM answers a new elicitation question, the space of weights is updated and the dominance relations are refined.

Graphical visualization of partial results is also available for the DM here, in the form of a Hasse diagram of the alternatives, showing the dominance relations between them, as shown by Fig. 3.

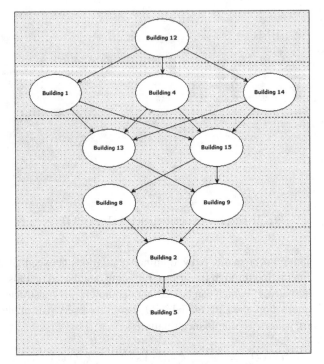

Fig. 3. Hasse diagram with dominance relations in FITradeoff DSS

Different ranking levels are separated by dashed lines. Dominance relations are represented by directed arrows. The Hasse diagram presents the transitivity reduction property, which avoid unnecessary arrows to be displayed. When there is no arrow between two alternatives in the same level of the ranking, this means that they are incomparable for the current level of information obtained from the DM; i.e., no dominance relation was found between them. As the DM provides more information, more dominance relations are found, so that the ranking is refined. The ranking problem finishes when a complete ranking of the alternatives can be derived from the dominance relations found by the LPP models. However, it is possible to stop the process even before the end of the elicitation process, if the DM thinks the partial ranking obtained is already sufficient for his/her purposes.

2.4 Applicability for Practical Cases

The FITradeoff method has been applied in a wide range of practical cases, in many different areas, such as: in the energy sector (Fossile et al. 2020; Kang et al. 2018; de Macedo et al. 2018); for selection of strategic information systems (Gusmão and Medeiros 2016); supplier selection (Frej et al. 2017); healthcare facilities location (Dell'Ovo et al. 2017); textil sector (Rodrigues et al. 2020); information technology decisions (Poleto et al. 2020); selection of agricultural technology packages (Carrillo et al. 2018); water resource planning (da Silva and Morais 2019); selection of scheduling rules (Pergher et al. 2020);

R&D projects portfolio selection (Frej et al. 2021) and health services (Camilo et al. 2020). Neuroscience experiments were also conducted with the aim of improving the design of the FITradeoff DSS (Roselli et al. 2019a).

In order to better analyze the performance of the FITradeoff method in practical problems considering different scenarios, Mendes et al. (2020) performed simulation studies with the FITradeoff method considering MCDM problems with different number of alternatives (5; 10; 15; 20; 30; 50; 70) and different number of criteria (3; 4; 5; 7; 10; 15). Different weight patterns were consider in the simulation scenarios. Simulation results show that, in 5% of the cases, a unique solution can be found after the ranking of criteria scaling constants in FITradeoff. Moreover, the results show that in 98% of the cases simulated, the subset of potentially optimal alternatives is reduced to up to 8 alternatives after the ranking of criteria scaling constants and, in 80%, only 5 potentially optimal alternatives are left after the ranking of criteria weights.

This results show that FITradeoff can be a useful tool for aiding the DM in decision-making processes without the need of spending much effort, which is an advance in the attempt of tighten the gap between theoretical methods in MCDM and practical real world problems. The next section shows how the FITradeoff method was applied for solving a problem of prioritization of special police operations in Brazilian Federal Police.

3 Prioritizing Special Operations Using the FITradeoff Method

3.1 Multi-criteria Problem Description

In this section, the FITradeoff method for ranking problematic (Frej et al. 2019) is applied in a real case of study to rank ten special police operations faced by a State Regional Superintendence of the Brazilian Federal Police. These special operations are the alternatives that should be ranked based on the DM preferences. It is worth mentioning that the DM is the chief of police or head of police (named *delegado*) of this State Regional Superintendence. Table 1 illustrates these ten special police operations

To evaluate the alternatives, some criteria or attributes are defined by the DM. These criteria are used to measure the achieving of the main objectives of the Regional Superintendence Federal Police (fundamental objectives) (Belton and Stewart 2002; de Almeida et al. 2016; Keeney 1993). In total, fourteen criteria are established by the DM. Also, five experts, who presented knowledge about these special operations, confirmed that the criteria are suitable for measuring the objectives in the problem.

The criteria are classified in four groups: Evaluation of damage, Standardization, Operationalization and Efficiency. The first group is composed for six criteria. The second group is composed for four criteria, the third and fourth group are both composed for two criteria. Also, most of them are constructed for this specific problem. Thus, thirteen criteria are assessed using the Likert scale. In other words, specific levels of magnitude, measured in a verbal scale, are used to evaluate the special operations. The criterion "Origin and amount of the misapplied resource" is the only measured in monetary terms. The criteria are illustrated in Table 2.

Therefore, from the evaluation of each special operation in each criterion, the decision matrix is obtained, as illustrated in Table 3.

Table 1. Special police operations

Operations	Description
O1	Misappropriation of education resources
O2	Misappropriation of health resources
O3	Misappropriation of infrastructure resources
O4	Drug trafficking operation
O5	Pedophilia on the internet
O6	Large-scale environmental offense
O7	International drug trafficking
O8	Social security crimes
O9	Alteration of therapeutic or medicinal product
O10	Armed robbery committed against a public servant

Table 2. Criteria description

Item	Groups of criteria	Levels of magnitude and consequences
G1	**Evaluation of damage**	–
C1	Damage to human	Nine levels (min: 0; max 8).
C2	Environmental damage	Five levels (min: 0, max 4)
C3	Over recurrence of the conduct (ranges of penalty in years)	Five levels (min: 0, max 4)
C4	Social repercussion of crime (aggravating type of the crime)	Binary level (yes, no)
C5	Origin and amount of the misapplied resource	Monetary value
C6	Extent of the crime	Four levels (min: 0, max: 3)
G2	**Standardization**	–
C7	Contemporaneousness of the crime (time elapsed from the fact)	Five levels (min: 0, max 4)
C8	Proximity to prescription (time limit on legal action)	Five levels (min: 0, max 4)
C9	Integration between the actors of the penal prosecution	Five levels (min: 0, max 4)
C10	Stage of the investigation	Four levels (min: 0, max: 3)
G3	**Operationalization**	–

(continued)

Table 2. (*continued*)

Item	Groups of criteria	Levels of magnitude and consequences
C11	Need for specialized human resources	Five levels (min: 0, max 4)
C12	Operational complexity	Five levels (min: 0, max 4)
G4	**Efficiency**	–
C13	Estimate of value of apprehended/sequestered assets	Four levels (min: 0, max: 3)
C14	Estimate of losses the union has avoided	Four levels (min: 0, max: 3)

Table 3. Decision-matrix

	C1	C2	C3	C4	C5	C6	C7	C8	C9	C10	C11	C12	C13	C14
1	2	0	4	2	10	2	0	1	4	1	0	4	2	2
2	8	4	3	2	5	1	0	1	3	3	4	3	0	1
3	0	0	4	2	42.5	3	1	2	2	2	0	4	3	3
4	6	2	4	3	0	1	3	1	3	2	0	2	2	0
5	4	0	4	2	0	3	0	1	3	3	0	2	0	0
6	0	3	1	0	0	0	4	1	4	0	3	4	0	0
7	4	2	4	4	0	3	0	1	3	2	2	3	3	0
8	0	0	3	1	1.3	1	1	4	3	2	0	1	1	1
9	4	4	4	1	0	3	0	1	4	1	1	2	0	0
10	5	0	4	2	0	0	4	1	4	3	0	1	0	0

3.2 FITradeoff Method for Ranking Problematic

In this context, using the DSS constructed to implement the FITradeoff method for ranking problematic the special police operations have been ranked based on the DM preferences. After the intra-criteria evaluation, the DM ranks the scaling constants. The scaling constant order is illustrated in Eq. (8).

$$K_{C1} > K_{C5} > K_{C4} > K_{C13} > K_{C14} > K_{C3} > K_{C2} > K_{C10} > K_{C12} > K_{C6}$$
$$> K_{C8} > K_{C9} > K_{C7} > w_{C11} \tag{8}$$

The inequalities presented in Eq. (8) are inserted in the LLP model. Thus, the LPP runs in order to ranks the special police operations. After this step, some dominance relations between the alternatives are constructed.

At this moment of the decision process, i.e. after ranking the scaling constants, the DM can continue the pairwise comparisons in order to provide more preference relations, that will be represented by inequalities and included in the LPP model, or the DM can use the Hasse diagram to evaluate the partial ranking obtained at this moment of the process.

In this application, the DM wishes to evaluate the partial ranking in the Hasse diagram, as illustrated in Fig. 4. Thus, based on the Hasse diagram the DM observes that the special operations O02; O03; O04, and O07 are incomparable in the top, and dominates the others.

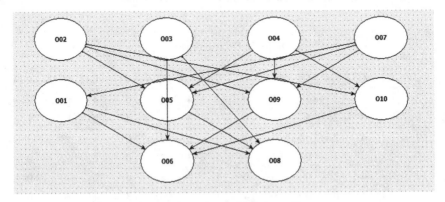

Fig. 4. Hasse diagram after ranking the scaling constants

In Fig. 4, the operations are presented in the same position in the Hasse diagram, even with dominance relations between them. Therefore, the DM wishes to return to the elicitation process in order to perform pairwise comparisons between the consequences presented in Table 3.

In this context, the first elicitation question answered by the DM concerns to the comparison between an intermediate consequence, named X1, in the criterion which presented the highest scaling constant (C1 – "Damage to human") and the best consequence, named B14, in the criterion which present the lowest scaling constant (C14 – equal to C11 in the Eq. 8 – "Need for specialized human resources"), as illustrated in Fig. 5.

In this elicitation question, illustrated in Fig. 5, the DM prefers the Consequence A than Consequence B. In other words, for the DM an operation which had medium damage to human in considered more critical than an operation which present extremely high requirements for specialized human resources.

This decision problem involves a ranking problematic, which requires more information for the DM than the choice problematic since dominance relations should be defined to obtain the complete ranking (de Almeida et al. 2016). Thus, the DM continues to answer elicitation questions in the form of the elicitation questions illustrated in Fig. 5.

Which consequence do you prefer?

Answer the questions by choosing one option

Consequence A			Consequence B		
C1	X1: 4		W1: 0		B1: 8
C2	W2: 0	B2: 42.5	W2: 0		B2: 42.5
C3	W3: 0	B3: 4	W3: 0		B3: 4
C4	W4: 0	B4: 3	W4: 0		B4: 3
C5	W5: 0	B5: 3	W5: 0		B5: 3
C6	W6: 1	B6: 4	W6: 1		B6: 4
C7	W7: 0	B7: 4	W7: 0		B7: 4
C8	W8: 0	B8: 3	W8: 0		B8: 3
C9	W9: 1	B9: 4	W9: 1		B9: 4
C10	W10: 0	B10: 3	W10: 0		B10: 3
C11	W11: 1	B11: 4	W11: 1		B11: 4
C12	W12: 2	B12: 4	W12: 2		B12: 4
C13	W13: 0	B13: 4	W13: 0		B13: 4
C14	W14: 0	B14: 4			B14: 4

Note :   Wi is the worst outcome of criterion Ci
Xi is an outcome in between best and worst of criterion Ci
Bi is the best outcome of criterion Ci

Fig. 5. Elicitation questions between consequences in the criteria C1 and C14.

After the DM answered twenty (20) elicitation questions, he/she desires to evaluate the Hasse diagram. At this point, the Hasse diagram presents five positions. Also, the operation O03 is defined as the first one in the ranking, as illustrated in Fig. 6. Therefore, at this point, the DM decide to stop the decision process, using this partial ranking to guide the prioritizing of the special operations of the Superintendence.

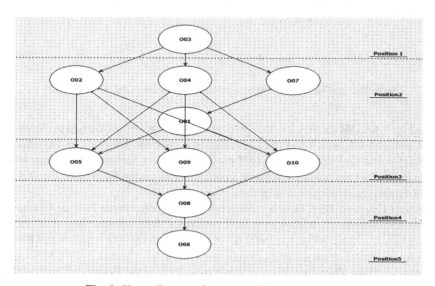

Fig. 6. Hasse diagram after twenty elicitation questions.

3.3 Discussion

In the case study decision process, many elicitation questions had to be answered in order to obtain the partial ranking with five positions. Assuming that the complete ranking could be required for the DM, the number of elicitation questions should be over twenty.

In this context, an important feature presented in the FITradeoff method is the possibility of use graphical and tabular visualizations to define preference relations between the alternatives.

Supposing that the DM wishes to evaluate the operations O02, O04, and O07 using a bar graphic visualization. Figure 7 illustrates the bar graphics constructed to compare these operations. Thus, based on this bar graphics, the DM can define dominance relations between these operations in order do identify the second alternative in the ranking. Also, these dominance relations can be represented by inequalities and included in the LPP model in order to shorten the obtaining of the complete ranking.

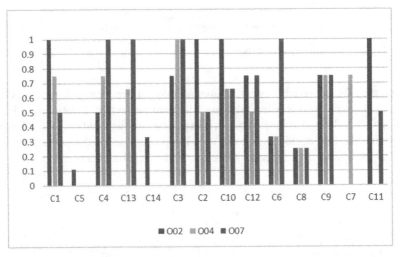

Fig. 7. Bar graphic constructed to represented operations O02, O04, and O07.

In Fig. 7, the DM can observe that the operation O02 presented the best performance in the criterion C1, which had the highest scaling constant. However, in the adjacent criteria, C4 and C13 the operation O07 presented highest performances. Thus, based on the trade-offs between the alternative's performances within the criteria, the DM can define dominance relations between these alternatives.

In the FITradeoff DSS, these visualizations are presented in the Holistic Evaluation step. Several behavioral studies have been performed to investigate the use of graphical and tabular visualizations to represent MCDM/A problems (de Almeida and Roselli 2020; Roselli and de Almeida 2020; Roselli et al. 2019a; Roselli et al. 2019b; de Almeida and Roselli 2017). Therefore, the preference modelling of the FITradeoff method is in continue improvement, combining the holistic evaluation and the elicitation by decomposition process in order to accomplish the DM preferences during the decision process (de Almeida et al. 2021).

4   Conclusion

In this study, the FITradeoff method is described in detail, and an application in the scope of Brazilian Federal Police is illustrated to rank ten special police operations based on the regional *delegado's* preferences. As result, after using the FITradeoff DSS, a partial ranking with five positions is considered by the DM to guide the prioritizing of the special operations in the Regional Superintendence.

It is worth mentioning that the partial ranking obtained is based on this DM preferences, if others *delegados* evaluates the same decision matrix (Table 3) the results can be difference since their preferences, expressed during the elicitation questions, can differ.

The FITradeoff method has shown to be a useful tool for aiding an important decision-making process of Brazilian Federal Police, within a structured elicitation procedure with appropriate methodological support. The actors involved in the process have truly appreciated using an organized structured protocol to aid such decision process, since those decision situations used to be conducted without any support methodological tool.

For future research, other applications can be performed considering improvements in the preference modelling of the FITradeoff method, which combines the elicitation by decomposition and holistic evaluations paradigms within an integrated manner during the decision-making/aiding process (de Almeida et al. 2021).

Acknowledgment. This work had partial support from the Brazilian Research Council (CNPq).

References

Brasil: Constituição da República Federativa do Brasil de 1988. Constitution of the Federative Republic of Brazil: text promulgated on October 5, 1988, with the changes determined by the Constitutional Revisions Amendments 1 to 6/94, by the Constitutional Amendments 1/92 to 99/2017. Brasília/DF: Senado Federal, Coordenação de Edições Técnicas (2017)

Belton, V., Stewart, T.: Multiple Criteria Decision Analysis: An Integrated Approach. Springer, Berlin (2002). https://doi.org/10.1007/978-1-4615-1495-4

Camilo, D.G.G., de Souza, R.P., Frazão, T.D.C., da Costa Junior, J.F.: Multi-criteria analysis in the health area: selection of the most appropriate triage system for the emergency care units in natal. BMC Med. Inform. Decis. Mak. **20**(1), 1–16 (2020)

Carrillo, P.A.A., Roselli, L.R.P., Frej, E.A., de Almeida, A.T.: Selecting an agricultural technology package based on the flexible and interactive tradeoff method. Ann. Oper. Res. (2018). https://doi.org/10.1007/s10479-018-3020-y

De Almeida, A.T., Frej, E.A., Roselli, L.R.P.: Combining holistic and decomposition paradigms in preference modeling with the flexibility of FITradeoff. Cent. Eur. J. Oper. Res. (2021). (forthcoming)

De Almeida, A.T., Roselli, L.R.P.: NeuroIS to improve the FITradeoff decision-making process and decision support system. In: Proceedings of the NeuroIS Retreat 2020 (2020)

de Almeida, A.T., Roselli, L.R.P.: Visualization for decision support in FITradeoff method: exploring its evaluation with cognitive neuroscience. In: Linden, I., Liu, S., Colot, C. (eds.) ICDSST 2017. LNBIP, vol. 282, pp. 61–73. Springer, Cham (2017). https://doi.org/10.1007/978-3-319-57487-5_5

De Almeida, A.T., Almeida, J.A., Costa, A.P.C.S., Almeida-Filho, A.T.: A new method for elicitation of criteria weights in additive models: flexible and interactive tradeoff. Eur. J. Oper. Res. **250**, 179–191 (2016)

da Silva Monte, M.B., Morais, D.C.: A decision model for identifying and solving problems in an urban water supply system. Water Resour. Manag. **33**(14), 4835–4848 (2019)

de Macedo, P.P., Mota, C.M.D.M., Sola, A.V.H.: Meeting the Brazilian Energy Efficiency Law: a flexible and interactive multicriteria proposal to replace non-efficient motors. Sustain. Cities Soc. **41**, 822–832 (2018)

Dell'Ovo, M., Frej, E.A., Oppio, A., Capolongo, S., Morais, D.C., de Almeida, A.T.: Multicriteria decision making for healthcare facilities location with visualization based on FITradeoff method. In: Linden, I., Liu, S., Colot, C. (eds.) ICDSST 2017. LNBIP, vol. 282, pp. 32–44. Springer, Cham (2017). https://doi.org/10.1007/978-3-319-57487-5_3

Federal Police: Portaria no. 4453/2014-DG/DPF, de 16 de Maio de 2014. Approves the update of the Strategic Plan 2012/2022, the Strategic Portfolio and the Federal Police's Sartorial Map and takes other measures. Brasília/DF (2014)

Fossile, D.K., Frej, E.A., da Costa, S.E.G., de Lima, E.P., de Almeida, A.T.: Selecting the most viable renewable energy source for Brazilian ports using the FITradeoff method. J. Clean. Prod. **260**, 121107 (2020)

Frej, E.A., de Almeida, A.T., Costa, A.P.C.S.: Using data visualization for ranking alternatives with partial information and interactive tradeoff elicitation. Oper. Res. **19**(4), 909–931 (2019)

Frej, E.A., Ekel, P., de Almeida, A.T.: A benefit-to-cost ratio based approach for portfolio selection under multiple criteria with incomplete preference information. Inf. Sci. **545**, 487–498 (2021)

Frej, E.A., Roselli, L.R.P., de Almeida, J.A., de Almeida, A.T.: A multicriteria decision model for supplier selection in a food industry based on FITradeoff method. Math. Probl. Eng. **2017**, 1–9 (2017)

Gusmão, A.P.H., Medeiros, C.P.: A model for selecting a strategic information system using the FITradeoff. Math. Probl. Eng. **2016**, 7 (2016). Article ID 7850960

Kang, T.H.A., Soares Júnior, A.M.C., de Almeida, A.T.: Evaluating electric power generation technologies: a multicriteria analysis based on the FITradeoff method. Energy **165**, 10–20 (2018)

Keeney, R.L., Raiffa, H.: Decision Analysis with Multiple Conflicting Objectives. Wiley, New York (1976)

Keeney, R.L.: Value-Focused Thinking: A Path to Creative Decision Making. Harvard University Press, London (1993)

Kirkwood, C.W., Sarin, R.K.: Ranking with partial information: a method and an application. Oper. Res. **33**(1), 38–48 (1985)

Mendes, J.A.J., Frej, E.A., Almeida, A.T.D., Almeida, J.A.D.: Evaluation of flexible and interactive Tradeoff method based on numerical simulation experiments. Pesquisa Operacional **40** (2020). https://doi.org/10.1590/0101-7438.2020.040.00231191

Pergher, I., Frej, E.A., Roselli, L.R.P., de Almeida, A.T.: Integrating simulation and FITradeoff method for scheduling rules selection in job-shop production systems. Int. J. Prod. Econ. **227**, 107669 (2020)

Poleto, T., Clemente, T.R.N., de Gusmão, A.P.H., Silva, M.M., Costa, A.P.C.S.: Integrating value-focused thinking and FITradeoff to support information technology outsourcing decisions. Manag. Decis. (2020). https://doi.org/10.1108/MD-09-2019-1293

Rodrigues, L.V.S., Casado, R.S.G.R., Carvalho, E.N.D., Silva, M.M.: Using FITradeoff in a ranking problem for supplier selection under TBL performance evaluation: an application in the textile sector. Production **30** (2020). https://doi.org/10.1590/0103-6513.20190032

Reis Peixoto Roselli, L., de Almeida, A.T.: Analysis of graphical visualizations for multi-criteria decision making in FITradeoff method using a decision neuroscience experiment. In: Moreno-Jiménez, J.M., Linden, I., Dargam, F., Jayawickrama, U. (eds.) ICDSST 2020. LNBIP, vol. 384, pp. 30–42. Springer, Cham (2020). https://doi.org/10.1007/978-3-030-46224-6_3

Roselli, L.R.P., de Almeida, A.T., Frej, E.A.: Decision neuroscience for improving data visualization of decision support in the FITradeoff method. Oper. Res. **19**, 933–953 (2019a)

Roselli, L.R.P., Pereira, L., da Silva, A., de Almeida, A.T., Morais, D.C., Costa, A.P.C.S.: Neuroscience experiment applied to investigate decision-maker behavior in the tradeoff elicitation procedure. Ann. Oper. Res. **289**(1), 67–84 (2019b)

Salo, A.A., Hämäläinen, R.P.: Preference assessment by imprecise ratio statements. Oper. Res. **40**(6), 1053–1061 (1992)

The Economist: Corruption in Brazil, Weird Justice, December 10, 2015 (2015)

Weber, M.: Decision making with incomplete information. Eur. J. Oper. Res. **28**(1), 44–57 (1987)

Author Index

Printed in the United States
By Bookmasters